JOHN KIRBY

Ships in the Making

Ships in the Making

A HISTORY OF SHIP MODEL TESTING AT
TEDDINGTON AND FELTHAM, 1910–1994

David Bailey
C.Eng., F.R.I.N.A.

FOREWORD BY

G.H. Fuller
Deputy Chairman, B.M.T. Ltd.

LONDON   NEW YORK   HAMBURG   HONG KONG
LLOYD'S OF LONDON PRESS LTD
1995

Lloyd's of London Press Ltd.
Legal & Business Publishing Division
27 Swinton Street
London WC1X 9NW
Great Britain

USA AND CANADA
Lloyd's of London Press Ltd.
Suite 308, 611 Broadway,
New York, NY 10012, USA

GERMANY
Lloyd's of London Press GmbH
59 Ehrenstrasse, 2000 Hamburg 50
Germany

SOUTH-EAST ASIA
Lloyd's of London Press (Far East) Ltd.
Room 1101, Hollywood Centre,
233 Hollywood Road
Hong Kong

British Library Cataloguing in Publication Data

A catalogue record
for this book is available
from the British Library

ISBN 1-85044-943-0

Text set in 10 on 12pt Sabon by
Mendip Communications Ltd.
Frome, Somerset
Printed in Great Britain by
WBC Print Ltd.
Bridgend, Mid Glamorgan.

PREFACE

When in 1987 major model testing facilities at Feltham near London were closed it seemed for a sudden moment that the end of an era had been reached. Large and expensive facilities used for testing models of ships and offshore engineering structures in simulated sea conditions had been under the control of British Maritime Technology Ltd. for two years. BMT, a company limited by guarantee, was formed in 1985 following a merger between NMI Ltd., a privatised Government research establishment and the British Ship Research Association (BSRA). BMT inherited from NMI a comprehensive collection of test facilities situated at Feltham, Hythe and Teddington that included four ship model towing tanks (the oldest, at Teddington, dating from 1910), two water basins, two cavitation tunnels, two circulating water channels and several wind tunnels.

In 1986, BMT's Board, under severe financial pressure and competition from overseas where similar facilities were being supported by Government finance, was forced to consider whether it needed, or could afford, so many of its facilities. Shipbuilding throughout the world was in serious recession and the price of oil had collapsed, the combined effects of which had seen the demand for model tests diminish to a fraction of the level experienced in earlier years. Theoretical methods of predicting full-scale ship performance, strengthened considerably by improved computer technology, were seen by some as viable and cheaper alternatives to physical measurement. After long consideration and in the face of diminishing support from Government there came the decision to discontinue model tests at Feltham and develop the redundant site there for other purposes. At the time it seemed that BMT might be forced to abandon all its test facilities. In fact the two towing tanks at Teddington survived uneasily for another seven years until in 1994 they too were closed, thus bringing to a sad end all model tests at Feltham and Teddington. However, an agreement with the Defence Research Agency was reached such that future tests for BMT would be done at Haslar where similar test facilities were still in operation.

The history of ship model testing at BMT since the early days has been of such distinction that it was thought appropriate to write a record of the achievements and progress made in 83 eventful years. Apart from conventional tests on models of new ships, programmes of research had been followed that contributed significantly to a better understanding of the fundamentals of ship resistance and propulsion and in two World Wars several of the special nautical problems posed were successfully solved in unique model tests. In later years test work had been extended to include the new and expanding field of offshore engineering.

The history of ship model testing at BMT really begins in 1901 when an experiment tank was proposed by a leading British shipbuilder of the time, Sir Alfred Yarrow. The tank was to be independent and unconnected with any private shipbuilding company or organisation. There were in 1901 two towing tanks in Britain, the Admiralty tank at Haslar and a private one run by the Denny shipbuilding company at Dumbarton. Yarrow's concept was for a "national" tank that could be largely devoted to research work for, as Yarrow put it, "the general advancement of British Shipbuilding and Shipowning". A suitable site for the tank had been found at the National Physical Laboratory (NPL) but seven years were to pass before building started. That it did was due to Yarrow's generous gift of £20,000 which with other smaller donations from industry allowed work to begin. The tank and associated offices and workshops were completed in 1910 and the long thin building became a conspicuous addition to the sober Georgian-style laboratory buildings that were scattered around the elegant Bushy House, the recently acquired home of the NPL and the residence of its Director.

From those early days when a staff of nine built and tested about 25 models a year, the demand from industry for such work grew to such an extent that in 1930 the Government saw the need for a second tank to be built alongside the first. At the same time Sir James Lithgow offered £5,000 for the construction of a water tunnel to study propeller cavitation. In 1932 at the opening of the second tank the national press had captured the public imagination by describing the laboratory as "an adult scientists' playground". Yet with both the new tank and the cavitation tunnel in operation demand for tests became even greater following the Second World War when the numbers of British merchant ships had been so severely depleted that a massive reconstruction programme was needed. Even with overtime hours being worked there was a long delay before new test work could be started and any time left over for research was almost nil. The overwhelming case for additional facilities was obvious and these were provided by the Government in 1959 when a very large towing tank, a basin for free-running models and a second cavitation tunnel were built five miles from Teddington at Feltham near Heathrow airport.

The new facilities offered enormous potential both for research and routine test work. The sheer size of the third tank meant that it need not be limited to work with ship models alone. For example, its extreme depth proved ideal for tests on offshore structures when these began in earnest in the 1970s. The site at Feltham included areas of relatively unoccupied space and soon other facilities, large and small, were added. A small circulating water channel built as a model prototype for a much larger channel proved so useful that it was kept for small studies after the larger version appeared in 1965. The needs of a particular task led to the construction, outdoors, of a large square pond and again this was retained for future use as a test area for free-running ship models.

Up to 1971 all of these facilities were in the hands of Ship Division, NPL (originally called the William Froude Laboratory as a tribute to Froude whose pioneering genius had shown how the resistance of a full size ship could be derived from a model test). The first 60 years were a period of great stability and enormous output and the name of Ship Division became famous as a centre of excellence where the shape of ship hulls (mainly merchant ships) could be optimised ahead of the final ship design. As the 1970s approached, Governments of the day became more and more concerned with rationalising the nation's scientific resources and began to examine its research establishments. A turbulent period followed during which successive organisational changes saw Ship Division and other parts of NPL emerge as a single separate Government research establishment, the National Maritime Institute, which in 1982 was privatised. Three years later came the merger with BSRA and the formation of BMT.

To place on record the name of every person who has worked at Teddington or Feltham or to have recalled everything that has taken place in these impressive and, possibly, unrivalled facilities would have been unrealistic. The account that follows is essentially one that covers ship model tests and offshore engineering projects as well as major items of associated research. It is written in chronological order both with respect to work done and the descriptions of various test facilities as they arrived. Some of the subjects of research (e.g. wave-making resistance) have been recurring themes taken up by different workers at different times. Thus a complete account of the progress made in a particular subject is not given at the time when it first appears in the narrative but the index and footnotes will enable the reader, if need be, to refer to associated work.

The improvements achieved worldwide in ship model test techniques are an inseparable part of the story. Full credit for the advances made is not claimed for workers at Teddington and Feltham but the importance of their contribution since 1911 cannot be denied.

CONTENTS

FOREWORD

As we end the first hundred years of the ordered and orderly use of the model of a ship in the prediction of ship resistance and so the expected full scale performance, it is timely to set down the history of this time of great scientific and engineering development and to link it with the evolution of the facilities at Teddington and Feltham in the United Kingdom.

Initially performance was essentially defined by a speed which could be specified in the contract and measured on completion of the ship in repeatable circumstances. It, therefore, concentrated on the contract or service speed in calm water with the hull reasonably clean and the power plant properly operated. Following W. Froude's realisation that the resistance could be split into two independent components, prediction from model tested by towing in a tank became feasible and credible. However the steps, at the time not being underpinned by strict scientific logic, had to be based on empirical methods and formulae.

Thus the model experiment became a critical feature of the ship design process, often involving hundreds of runs covering different operational conditions and small changes of hull shape. This called for bigger and bigger towing tanks in "experiment" works coupled with more and more "meticulous" methods of correlation, and the evolution of various, very precise, methodologies—each promoted by a "champion" usually the early, now legendary, Superintendents of these great "experiment" works of which Teddington was one.

Soon it became obvious that time could be saved if changes in the geometrical parameters were studied methodically in the towing tank. Thus the creation of "series" by many tanks for various well-used hull forms and their publication at the meetings of the Professional Institutions. In the more commercial and defence climates of today, it is remarkable how open the exchange of information was both between tanks and into the public domain. However, with hindsight, it can be seen that a number of facets of the prediction process were effectively ignored for many years but have always had a significant impact on total energy consumption of the ship in a real seaway.

It can only be surmised that the "accuracy" of the process of the model experiment towed in a straight line in a tank and the exhaustively discussed empirical correlation methodology captured the imagination of the ship hydrodynamicist for much of the period. The evidence is in the huge number of papers, articles and transactions, but why it was so has yet to be explained when the real ship had to operate in rough seas with a "fouled" hull and "power hungry" manoeuvrability coupled with "off tune" engines and poor total energy management. Only recently have these features been addressed with priority perhaps triggered by the fuel impact moving from "are the bunkers large enough to make the voyage safely" to "fuel being a major factor in operating cost". Particularly hydrodynamics must be seen as the "total" load on the ship, the seaway plus the wind, impact on structure, and a better understanding of the propulsor in its local environment—all considered probabilistically.

Also mentioned is the expectation that the mathematical modelling of the fluid flow would allow computational hydrodynamics to supersede the model experiment; with a better appreciation of the size of the computing task it is now realised that the model test can be cheaper and will have a place for a long time to come especially for complex shapes.

There is also the century-long anomaly in the UK that two sets of Government facilities developed side by side, also commercial and academic tanks proliferated. Indeed only at the end of 1994 have the two Government facilities come together at the DRA Haslar site which will form a strong national facility. A brief look at the other UK facilities and the major overseas tanks is included.

So as ship design moves into the next century, the task of the ship hydrodynamicist will move to a more complete assessment of the complete performance of the ship in the real, and very difficult, environment of sea. Mathematical modelling will have its place in the prediction process and will grow as computing power becomes both faster and cheaper, but I have no doubt the well designed and well conducted model test will remain economic and will be not only the bridge to the huge data base of past work but the simplest way of evaluating the novel. The "experiment" works will evolve to meet these new challenges, a different but still exciting future.

November 1994   G H F

ACKNOWLEDGEMENTS

It would not have been possible to embark with confidence on the writing of this history without the valuable help and recollections of past and present members of staff. The late Professor Conn who was a member of Ship Division, NPL for 17 years prior to the end of the Second World War provided answers to several uncertainties and W.J. Marwood's written account of his memories, left behind when he retired in 1972, covered 40 years and has been a continuous source of reference.

Dr I.W. Dand was closely concerned with the planning of this book and his help and encouragement is gratefully acknowledged. Discussions have also been held with Dr. J.W. English, Dr G.E. Gadd, D.J. Griffiths, D.I. Moor (lately Superintendent of the St. Albans towing tank establishment) and S.J. Rowe and all of these have helped to clarify certain aspects of some of the subjects covered. Mr K.G. Poulton went through some of the earliest records and provided a framework within which fuller research became possible.

Both the National Physical Laboratory at Teddington and the Royal Institution of Naval Architects in London have willingly given access to their respective archives and supplied illustrations for some of the plates.

Miss A. Church has shown infinite patience in converting sundry scripts and arranging the text in its final form.

Finally, all who have worked at Teddington or Feltham whether in Ship Division, NMI or today's BMT have in one way or another contributed to this history. Without them it could not have been written.

ABBREVIATIONS

Note: The names of government bodies that occur in the text were those in current use at the time referred to:

British Government departments:

BoT	Board of Trade
DoE	Department of Energy
DSIR	Department of Scientific and Industrial Research
DoT	Department of Transport
DTI	Department of Trade and Industry
Mintech	Ministry of Technology
MoA	Ministry of Aviation
MoD	Ministry of Defence
MoT	Ministry of Transport
SMTRB	Ship Marine Transport Requirements Board

British Government Research Laboratories:

BRS	Building Research Station
DMS	Department of Maritime Science (part of NPL)
HDL	Hovercraft Development Ltd.
HRS	Hydraulics Research Station
NIO	National Institute of Oceanography
NPL	National Physical Laboratory
RAE	Royal Aircraft Establishment
TRL	Transport and Road Laboratory
WFL	William Froude Laboratory (later Ship Division, NPL)

Miscellaneous:

ACA	Advisory Committee for Aeronautics
BHC	British Hovercraft Corporation
BHRA	British Hydromechanics Research Association
BS	British Shipbuilders
BSRA	British Ship (formerly Shipbuilding) Research Association

BTTP	British Towing Tank Panel
CEEMAID	Coast and Estuary Engineering Management for the Acquisition and Interpretation of Data
DRA	Defence Research Agency
IESS	Institution of Engineers and Shipbuilders in Scotland
IMCO	International Maritime Consultative Organisation (now IMO)
ISO	International Standards Organisation
ITTC	International Towing Tank Conference
MIT	Massachusetts Institute of Technology
NECIES	North East Coast Institution of Engineers and Shipbuilders
NERC	National Environmental Research Council
NRDC	National Research and Development Corporation
NRE	Naval Research Establishment, Canada
OSFLAG	Offshore Structures Fluid Loading Advisory Group
PHIVE	Propeller and Hull Interactive Vibration Estimation
PEV	Propeller Excited Vibration
RINA	Royal Institution of Naval Architects (formerly INA)
ROV	remotely operated vehicle
SERC	Science and Engineering Research Council
SMTRB	Ship and Marine Technology Requirements Board
SRC	Science Research Council
SRI	Stanford Research Institute
WFA	White Fish Authority

LIST OF PLATES

The following photographs and drawings are between pages 108 and 109 and pages 236 and 237. Except where stated they are taken from BMT archives. Otherwise they are reproduced by kind permission from the sources indicated.

1. William Froude [*Source*: RINA, London]
2. Number One tank
3. Number One tank and carriage
4. Small tank
5. Extract from R. E. Froude letter [*Source*: DRA, Haslav (Crown copyright)]
6. Resistance dynamometer
7. Number One tank and buildings
8. Opening of Number One tank
9. Opening of Number One tank
10. Detection of water flow over model hulls
11. Detection of water flow over model hulls
12. Model of submarine
13. Torpedo fitted to model
14. Seaplane awaiting trials
15. Seaplane model under test
16. Model fitted with rudder head torque apparatus
17. Calculated and measured wavemaking resistance
18. Experiments with Mauretania model
19. Ships tested in model form
20. Ships tested in model form [*Source*: IESS, Glasgow (Trans. Vol. 46)]
21. Ships tested in model form [*Source*: RINA, London]
22. Number Two tank
23. Number Two tank carriage
24. Opening of Number Two tank
25. Lithgow Water Tunnel
26. Lithgow Water Tunnel
27. Lithgow Water Tunnel with cavitating propeller
28. Ship Division staff, 1932
29. Memo from Prime Minister Churchill

CHAPTER 1

EARLY MODEL EXPERIMENTERS AND THE FIRST SHIP-MODEL EXPERIMENT TANKS

There must have been many attempts years ago to find the best shape of a floating object that would move easiest through water and it seems inconceivable that man did not try out a model of what he intended before building the real thing. We know that in the late 15th century Leonardo's interest in ships led him to carry out tests on three models[1] and long before Leonardo, Archimedes had established his principle of floating bodies. Leonardo's models were all of the same length, beam and draught with varying underwater cross sectional area such that the first model was the same fore and aft, its waterline narrowing down to give identical bow and stern endings whilst the other two had rounded terminations at bow or stern, the rounding being akin to today's bulbous stems. Nothing is known of how Leonardo went about his experiments but he observed:

Although the ships are made to move in each case by equal power they will however realise different speeds inasmuch as the ship which has the widest section nearer to the bow is the fastest ship ...

Early evidence of the benefit obtainable at certain speeds if a bulbous bow is chosen.

The first serious attempt to measure the behaviour of ship models was made by Samuel Fortree in the middle of the 17th century. He lived at the time of Isaac Newton who considered that least resistance to forward motion would be found in a solid of known mathematical form. Applying this to ship resistance Newton wrote in his *Principia* that such a solid may be of use in the building of ships. Newton's pre-eminent position in the world of science was naturally influential so it is not surprising to find that Fortree chose to experiment with solids, initially simple rectangles with tapered endings and then elliptically-shaped bodies all of which could be defined exactly by geometry. He carved his models in wood and towed them through water in a small tank timing their progress. No doubt in view of the earliness of Fortree's efforts, his data can only be regarded as qualitative but they did nevertheless consist of a well documented set of measurements which he reported in a 17th century manuscript[2] allowing him the opinion, somewhat contradictory to Leonardo's, that:

1

The best shape for a model to pass easiest through the water is a true and equal waterline. as distinct from a waterline which had hollowed endings.

Samuel Fortree died in 1681 and about 60 years passed before the next experimenters appeared. Prominent up to the end of the 18th century were Bouguer, Chapman, Franklin, d'Alembert, Romme and Beaufoy. The first of these was the colourful Pierre Bouguer. Born in France in 1698 he was appointed Professor of Hydrography at Croisic in Brittany when only 15 years old and 10 years later was appointed as Professor at Le Havre. His growing reputation helped him to be chosen with others drawn from the Académie des Sciences to answer questions on the shape of the earth. In an expedition to South America Bouguer conducted very accurate measurements of one degree of longitude near the equator. Whilst there he began his famous treatise *Traité du Navire*, a book which many regard as one of the finest ever written on naval architecture. His interest in experiments with ship models stemmed from the belief that the forward half of a ship was mainly responsible for its resistance through water. He thus designed apparatus in which the forebody only was balanced against a flat plate and then immersed in moving water. This unique approach and Bouguer's whole theory was, however, disputed by Euler in 1773 who argued that the whole of a ship's hull should be considered because the pressure acting on it as it moved through water would vary along its length.

Next on the scene in about 1760 was Frederick Chapman who was born in Sweden of English parents. Chapman became a ship designer of considerable skill and in attempting to verify his calculations of ship resistance from the plans of a ship form, he made models and tested them in a small pond. His method turned out to be very similar to Fortree's whereby a tow wire fixed to the model was led over a pulley to a weight which fell under gravity to provide the tractive force. Chapman used models which today seem wholly inadequate in size, just 70 cm long, yet he was able to publish a very extensive series of truly systematic tests.[3] At the same time as Chapman, a French triumvirate led by d'Alembert began experimenting in an ornamental lake in the grounds of the Ecole Militaire. d'Alembert was joined by the Abbé Bossut and the Marquis of Condorcet and their purpose was to improve the inland waterways of France. They were thus much concerned with the effect of restricted depth of water on ship resistance, a subject which a few years earlier had attracted Benjamin Franklin in America. Although Franklin was later to become famous as a politician, (he is widely credited with having played the principal part in drafting the Declaration of Independence), his scientific interests occupied much of his early life and included experiments with ship models.

The lake at the Ecole Militaire was 30 metres long, 2 metres deep and almost 20 metres wide and at one end Bossut erected a tall mast along which the tow rope to each model was led over a pulley and again a falling weight provided the motive power. To record the model speed, an army of observers was assembled and stationed at intervals, each observer recording the moments as the model passed to the accompaniment of time called every half second by a further assistant. To give conditions of shallow water Bossut built a horizontal floor which, laid on a frame, could be moved vertically and set to a selected height. d'Alembert abandoned solid geometric models and tested a variety of shapes showing that resistance increased, as expected, with speed but not exactly as the square of the speed. Nicholas Romme, also in France, used some of d'Alembert's results to illustrate his own theories and in agreeing with Euler tested replicas of actual ships to demonstrate that ship resistance was indeed influenced by its afterbody.

In England, at about the time of Chapman's experiments the Society of Arts offered prizes for scale models of ships, these models being required:

To ascertain by experiments the principles on which a good vessel is founded.

The vessels concerned were sailing warships (ships of the line and frigates) several models of which were submitted by rival designers and tested complete with their sailing rigs. Little is known as to who conducted these experiments but Anna Zinkeissen's painting depicts two models being towed in 1762 on a pool in the City of London and the apparatus appears similar to d'Alembert's. Towards the end of the century, the grandly named Society for the Improvement of Naval Architecture was formed in London. For want of funds it was destined to fold in 1796 after only a few years of existence but one of its last acts was to sponsor Colonel Mark Beaufoy to investigate the laws of ship resistance by means of model experiments. The Society had learnt of Beaufoy's work some years earlier in which he had experimented with small models fixed to a swinging pendulum. The young Mark Beaufoy, at the age of 15, had been baffled by a statement he overheard from an eminent mathematician who said that it was generally accepted that a cone drawn through water with its base foremost experienced less resistance than if its apex were foremost. Setting up a simple experiment in his father's brewhouse, he drew a cone over water using a large bunch of keys as a weight hung from a pulley and thus instinctively followed, albeit in rudimentary fashion, the method already used by others. He was delighted to disprove the mathematician's assertion as he demonstrated the difference in speed of the cone as it was towed in one direction or the other.

Beaufoy's interest grew and realising the inadequacies of his early experimental apparatus and without the resources to improve it, he decided on a different approach. Using a trough of water 2 metres long he attached small solid shapes to the end of a 2½ metres-long pendulum which he suspended above the water. He tried both Newtonian solids of least resistance and variations of these. Drawing the pendulum and its model to one side, Beaufoy released it and measured the ascending chord as each body swung through the water thereby determining that those of greatest resistance were those which described the smallest arc. His experiments were conducted with great care and amongst his conclusions were that the greatest width of a hull should be at 40 per cent of its length from the bow and that the bottoms of hull sections should be triangular

for least resistance to forward motion. His results evidently impressed the
Society for the Improvement of Naval Architecture leading them to support him
in an extensive investigation. In considering his approach, Beaufoy wanted to
experiment with large models of differing geometric configuration and was keen
to return to and improve on his very first experiments. With the Greenland Dock
near London being available in which it was possible to tow models over a
length of 120 metres, Beaufoy's course was set and with five helpers he designed
and built an ingenious falling weight system. The weights, placed in a large box,
were allowed to fall under gravity from the top of a tall tripod about 20 metres
high. Several ropes were led from the box to an array of pulleys arranged in two
blocks, the tow line to the model following the side of one of the legs of the
tripod to a lower pulley fixed at the dock wall just above the level of the water.
The passage of the model was translated to a carefully arranged measuring
system by unwinding a very thin wire on the axis of the lower pulley, over
another pulley and thence around the grooved surface of a cylinder. As the
model was towed through the water under the action of the falling weights the
wire pushed a thin batten over a pre-calibrated scale and a spring loaded pencil
was timed to mark the moving batten every second. At the end of the experiment
with the box of weights arrested, the batten was examined and the speed of the
model deduced from the length of discharged batten over which the spacing of
the pencil marks on it had become constant. Relative model resistance was thus
judged from the measured velocity against the known motive weight. The next
experiment could not begin until a horse had been persuaded to turn a capstan
which returned the box of weights to the top of the tripod. These weights
amounted to almost 250 kilograms for the higher model speeds. Difficulties
were experienced. It was found that the models all too easily veered away from a
straight course as they were towed. Also, modifications to the apparatus were
needed before satisfactory lengths of steady runs could be obtained. But once
refined, Beaufoy's experiments were impressive and in a five-year period
between 1793–98, some 10,000 tests were carried out on a huge variety of solid
forms. The degree of accuracy achieved was also impressive. In many repeat
experiments with the same model and motive weight, speed was found to deviate
by no more than one per cent. The experiments did not concentrate on solid
shapes only but included the measurement of frictional resistance on fully
immersed planks which were up to 6 metres long. These experiments presaged
Froude's investigations which were to become so famous some 80 years later. A
distinctive feature of Beaufoy's later work was the abandonment of measuring
the resistance of floating bodies. He, with others of his time, had not realised the
importance of wave-making resistance and finding that much water was thrown
up by a moving model such that at higher speeds it was impossible to determine
the resistance due to friction, opted to submerge his models two metres below
the surface attaching them to a slender body which itself was towed by his
apparatus. A small rudder was fitted to the towed body to reduce the disturbing
tendency to veer off. Beaufoy's fascinating work was completed in 1798 and his

several reports to the sponsoring Society were brought together with his earlier pendulum experiments and published by his son Henry in 1834.[4]

Beaufoy's work left a deep impression and his experimental techniques were later to be further developed by Wellenkamp in Germany. But soon it was to be the turn of William Froude the British engineer and mathematician. His interest in model testing began with a thorough trial and investigation of Beaufoy's method but he could not get it to work to his satisfaction. Froude eventually preferred to tow a model which was fixed to a moving carriage which spanned a long tank of water, an approach which was to have far-reaching consequences. Froude's appearance on the scene heralded a great advance and his work in the field of ship behaviour, resistance and propulsion was so distinguished and so full of fundamental discovery that he is rightly regarded as the father and founder of ship model testing as we know it today.

William Froude was born in Dartington in 1810 and came from a talented family. His father, Archdeacon Froude of Dartington, Totnes, sent him to Westminster School and then Oxford University. There he became a pupil of his elder (by seven years) brother, Hurrell who gave him his sound knowledge of mathematics. Hurrell went on to become one of the leaders, with Keble and Newman, of the Oxford movement. A younger brother, James, was an historian who ultimately became Regius Professor of Modern History at Oxford gaining eminence as an author of several historical works including, of maritime interest, "English seamen in the 16th Century". In 1837 William became assistant to Isambard Brunel under whom he worked on railway engineering. Although not directly concerned with Brunel's excursions into ship design, Froude did, nevertheless, quickly develop an interest and went on sea trials of the *Great Eastern* to observe roll behaviour. This led to an extensive study of ship rolling and his reputation grew. Leaving Brunel's service in 1846, he worked independently and appeared on a British Association committee set up to study stability, propulsion and sea-going qualities of ships. Soon he was to report his important findings on ship rolling and roll reduction methods. By about 1860 he began to turn his attention to model testing and experimented at home and on the river Dart. His practical skills enabled him to design and build all his own apparatus including the dynamometry needed for measuring resistance. At home using a large rainwater tank, he began by trying out Beaufoy's system of towing models but encountered Beaufoy's own problem, the difficulty in keeping the model to a straight line as it was being towed and also frequent sagging of the actual tow line. Unable to satisfy himself over accuracy, Froude became convinced that the only successful way to tow was from a driven carriage running over a long tank of water. It would be a simple enough matter to measure speed but model resistance would need to be measured on a specially designed balance or dynamometer and the system of towing needed careful consideration.

Meanwhile, on the river Dart, Froude towed a series of geometrically similar models from a steam launch to observe wave patterns and these tests led to his discovery of the importance of "corresponding speed" finding that the waves set up from similar forms of different scale were identical provided the speeds were in the ratio of the square roots of their lengths.

By 1868 Froude was so convinced of his methods and the need for a special indoor towing tank equipped for further experimentation that he wrote[5] to E.J. Reed, Chief Constructor of the Navy, giving his views and proposing a two year programme of model tests. He needed a tank with equipment and this he suggested could be built on leased land near his home for an estimated cost of £1,000. Reed was enthusiastic and with the support of the Controller of the Navy, advised the Admiralty. But the arguments were being placed at a time when others were critical of model experiments. Opponents that included Merrifield and Scott Russell favoured tests on full-scale ships as a means to understanding the laws governing ship resistance and power and a paper by Merrifield[6] indicated the majority opinion of a British Association committee to be in favour of the full-scale approach. In the debate which followed Merrifield's paper, Scott Russell, a prominent naval architect, supported the committee's view and went on to describe model tests that he himself had done. These had included tests on over 100 models in two groups, models up to 3·7 metres long and others ranging from 9–18 metres (very long by today's standards). Scott Russell had failed to reconcile results from the smaller models with those from the longer ones. In arguing against model tests, Scott Russell commented tartly:

You will have on the small scale a series of beautiful, interesting experiments, which I am sure will afford Mr. Froude infinite pleasure in the making of them as they did me . . . but which are quite remote from any practical results upon the large scale.

However, the Lords of the Admiralty decided differently and in 1870, Froude received official approval for a tank. Evidently Reed's recommendations were crucial and research by Brown[7] suggests that arguments given in Froude's later letters to Reed were influential. One of these observed that existing knowledge gave no guide lines for the determination of the proportions of ships whereas they could be found from model tests. Since Reed was currently being forced into designing bluffer warships, model tests, cheap compared to full-scale trials, were attractive.

Two years later in 1872 the world's first towing tank, 85 metres long, was built at Torquay and Froude, who by now was 62 years old employed his son Robert Edmund as his assistant. It was a happy choice since R.E. Froude was to contribute importantly in the application of his father's discoveries and in a much needed understanding of ship propeller efficiency. Also involved with the Froudes at Torquay was the son of the owner of the land on which the tank was built, Arnulph Mallock, who became a talented engineer and who designed instrumentation that was used in ship trials.

The last seven years of William Froude's life were marvellously productive. Fascinating work flowed from the tank fully justifying its existence. Classical experiments were carried out on flat plates to discover the resistance due to surface friction which Froude found to be dependent on the length of the plate and its surface finish. Combining these discoveries with his earlier work on wave patterns, he was at last able to postulate that ship resistance could be separated into two independent parts, friction and wave-making, which finally opened the way to an acceptable estimation of ship resistance from the results of model experiments. Before Froude's time, the idea that ship resistance was proportional simply to velocity squared had been put forward by Rankine. A much respected Regius Professor, Rankine produced a theory which argued that provided certain criteria for ship form as stated by Scott Russell were satisfied, then wave-making resistance could be ignored. His "proof" of this was little short of astonishing. Using his theory to estimate the speed of two existing ships Rankine fortuitously arrived at an exact agreement between his calculations and the actual recorded speeds at sea. However, his theory could not be universally applied and was refuted by J.I. Thornycroft in 1869 who in his turn proposed a cumbersome formula for ship power containing several empirical terms but, significantly, it recognised the importance of wave-making as a separate component. Froude, in developing his own approach, now went on to establish his famous law of comparison which he applied only to the wave-making (or residuary) part of the total resistance in scaling model resistance measurements to full-scale. Earlier Froude carried out experiments at sea using a ship (*HMS Active*) to tow the sloop, *HMS Greyhound*, measuring the tow force and speed. Fortunately they were conducted in excellent weather and the model tests which followed correlated beautifully providing Froude with the all important validation of his law. It became immutable and the bedrock on which accurate estimates of ship resistance from model measurements were founded. Froude's last major contribution was the design of dynamometry for the measurement of full-scale ship power and his many publications were deemed of such enduring value that at the instigation of the International Towing Tank Conference they were brought together in a single volume[8] and published by the Institution of Naval Architects in 1955.

Froude's success with models was not lost on others and he was soon to have followers although not all would copy his moving towing carriage system. From Froude's tank at Torquay in 1872 up to the turn of the 19th century, tanks were to appear at Dumbarton (1884), Haslar (1887), La Spezia (1890), St. Petersburg (1891), Dresden (1892), Bremerhaven (circa 1898) and Washington (1900). There were other smaller establishments, mostly ephemeral in nature, and some which were not purpose-built as tanks. For example, Tideman, Chief Constructor of the Dutch Navy, improvised quite brilliantly in Amsterdam in 1874.[9] For a tank he used an area of covered water between two sheds in the dockyard and suspended rails from the overhead roofing. On these rails Tideman mounted a towing carriage. Extraordinarily, it was driven manually by four men, one at each wheel who, working in unison, turned cranks geared to the wheels. Together they accelerated the carriage to a speed which kept pace with the model, the model itself being towed by a constant force exerted from the carriage. This "budget" tank remained in use for several years and some excellent work was produced including Tideman's own skin friction formulation.

R.E. Froude gave advice in the development of the Dumbarton tank which was more or less a copy of that at Torquay. The tank itself, the first in the world to be privately owned, was built by the Scottish shipbuilders, William Denny and Brothers when their shipyard at Leven on the Clyde was being enlarged. Initially, it was used exclusively for the purposes of the shipyard, large numbers of ship designs being tested and later the development of the Denny-Brown ship stabiliser resulted from many years of research. The tank remained in active use for 100 years before its closure and latterly much of the work undertaken was for outside clients not in possession of testing facilities. In 1988, under the auspices of the Scottish Maritime Museum, it was reopened for public viewing.

By 1885 the lease on the land at Torquay ran out and the Admiralty, now fully convinced of the value of test tanks, built a larger replacement. This was to William Froude's original specification and R.E. Froude was appointed as its first Superintendent although he retained his position as a private employee as distinct from the other members of staff who were civil servants. The new tank was built at Haslar, near Portsmouth, and completed in 1887. Its length, 122 metres, was increased to 168 metres in 1960. This tank became the model for many of those which followed and again R.E. Froude was to be prominent in offering advice to those concerned.

Of the tanks built and in operation by 1900, some were for government navy departments, others for private shipbuilding companies. The respective navies of Britain, Holland, Italy, Russia and the USA were served by the tanks at Haslar, Amsterdam, La Spezia, St. Petersburg and Washington whilst in the private sector Denny shipbuilders could boast theirs at Dumbarton and two German shipbuilding companies now had tanks at Dresden and Bremerhaven. Although these establishments followed very closely Froude's methods and had, apart from Washington, built tanks very similar to that at Torquay or Haslar, Beaufoy's system of measurement had not been forgotten; it was, after all, a system that could be set up with fewer resources without the need for large buildings or power-driven carriages. In about 1900 Wellenkamp in Germany tried again the falling weight system and was soon claiming a high degree of accuracy in the measurement of model resistance from apparatus that was obviously an advance on Beaufoy's. Using a waterway about 18 metres long (it was part of a dry dock in Kiel dockyard), he constructed two deep pits at either end. To the model under test he fitted thin piano wires fore and aft, leading them around a drum of known diameter and over pulleys into the pits, where weights were added and allowed to fall under gravity providing tractive force. With only a short length of water available it was essential to accelerate models rapidly to their desired test speeds and this was accomplished by giving an initial impulse to the model by means of an extra starting weight. This was temporarily connected to the model by a wire from the bow via a clutch which was released automatically at the end of the accelerating period. The model then continued under the influence of the towing weight only. To measure the speed of the model, Wellenkamp used a tuning fork of a calibrated frequency to scribe a sinusoidal trace on a blackened disc attached to the drum. The choice of a tuning fork was good since it maintained its frequency and guaranteed reliability. The whole apparatus was complicated and Wellenkamp stretched its delicacy still further by adding an additional array of pulleys, wires and weights connected to a propeller shaft fitted inside the model. Choosing a correct combination of weights, he was able to rotate the shaft and provide thrust from an installed propeller at the same time as towing the model through the water. Wellenkamp described his latest system in a paper[10] before the Institution of Naval Architects in 1908 and sparked a lively debate. As might be expected, R.E. Froude was unenthusiastic and recalled his father's difficulties, notably the problem of sagging wires (now perhaps exaggerated in this latest arrangement) and, in particular, the impossibility of achieving a sufficiently long run of settled speed in an experiment run. Richard Glazebrook, the Director of the National Physical Laboratory, questioned Wellenkamp closely and was evidently attracted to the apparatus likening it to a refined Attwood's machine (apparatus designed to study the motion of a falling body). Wellenkamp's strong argument was, of course, the relative cheapness of his tests compared to a large towing tank and moving carriage and this virtue remained in Glazebrook's mind when later he became involved in the birth of BMT's first tank. Elsewhere, Wellenkamp had supporters and in 1903 similar apparatus to his was built and used in the Charlottenburg tank near Berlin and in England, Thornycroft copied the system at Fort Stein on the Isle of Wight, this tank appearing in 1912.

Since these early days, a remarkable growth in towing tanks has been seen. Moor[11] has given an absorbing account of the history and derivation of towing tanks that have appeared throughout the world, which by 1985 had grown in numbers to about 200.

REFERENCES

1. Tursini L., lecture on "Leonardo da Vinci and the problems of navigation and naval design" (in Italian), RINA meeting in Genoa, 1952.
2. Of Navarchi, manuscript dated 1670, Pepysian Library, Cambridge.
3. Chapman F., Tractat om Skepps-Byggeriet, Stockholm, 1775.
4. Beaufoy M., Nautical and hydraulic experiments, published by H. Beaufoy, 1834.
5. Froude W., "Observations and suggestions on the subject of determining by experiment the resistance of ships", memorandum to E.J. Reed, December, 1868.
6. Merrifield C.W., "The experiments recently proposed on the resistance of ships", trans. INA, 1870.
7. Brown D.K., "William Froude and 'the way of a ship in the sea'", lecture to Devonshire Association for the Advancement of Science ..., June 1991.
8. The papers of William Froude, 1810–79, published by INA, 1955.
9. Dirkzwager J.M., Dr B.J. Tideman, 1834–83, published by Brill, Leiden, 1970.

10. Wellenkamp H., "A new method of research work on fluid resistance and ship propulsion", trans. INA, 1908.
11. Moor D.I., "Ship model experiment tanks. The first century—a British view", Sir Charles Parsons Memorial Lecture, 1984.

CHAPTER 2

A RESOURCE FOR THE NATION

In 1900 Britain had two towing tanks, the privately owned one at Dumbarton and the Admiralty tank at Haslar. Merchant shipbuilding was proceeding apace and it was noted by Francis Elgar, a former Director of Royal Dockyards, after a visit to the Washington tank that merchant ship as well as naval designs were being tested there. He thought British shipbuilders should be in a similar position and able to take their designs to a tank for model tests. In July 1901, the Institution of Naval Architects met in Glasgow[1] and the well-known shipbuilder Alfred Yarrow took the opportunity to present a formal proposal for a new experimental tank. He began by recalling Elgar's remarks and went on to say:

As you know, the British Admiralty have a tank of their own and ... Messrs Denny have their own private tank ... We also know that numerous tanks have been provided by various Admiralties in different parts of the world. Now, I would submit that, in view of the rapid increase in competition in our profession, it behoves us to advance with the times ... I would therefore submit to the consideration of the Institution of Naval Architects whether there could not be established under its auspices a tank which might be available, not only for the shipbuilders of this country, but for anyone willing to pay for the information obtained.

In the discussion which followed, no objection to the proposition was raised and there was considerable support for it. Sir Nathaniel Barnaby actually went so far as to say:

We shall make this meeting truly famous ... and if we can do what Mr Yarrow proposes today, we shall accomplish a great object.

Yarrow's proposal:

That this meeting, having regard to the desirability of establishing a tank in this country for testing the resistance of models, which might be available for all shipbuilders, requests the Council of the Institution to take the matter into serious consideration with the view of arriving at the best means of carrying out the suggestion.

was put to the meeting and carried unanimously.

Accordingly, a committee was appointed. Its first tentative steps were to take the easy approach and to inquire whether the Admiralty tank at Haslar might be available for tests for the shipbuilders of this country; that way a new and separate tank would not be needed.

The request to the Admiralty although sympathetically received, was turned down on the grounds that work at Haslar was already running at a high level with no room for extension. R.E. Froude was nevertheless given permission to help the committee in its consideration of the construction and equipment for a new tank. The committee now turned to the General Board of the National Physical Laboratory to enquire whether a tank might be established in its grounds provided that sufficient money was guaranteed and made available to the Board. The National Physical Laboratory itself had been founded in 1899 in accordance with recommendations made by a committee of enquiry[2] set up under the chairmanship of Lord Rayleigh and had settled in Bushy House at Bushy Park, Teddington. Funded partly by private philanthropy and partly by scientific and technical bodies it also enjoyed an annual grant from the Treasury. The original foundation vested the house and the responsibility for managing scientific and financial affairs in the Royal Society which appointed the Director and oversaw the operations of the laboratory through an Executive committee.

Bushy House had interesting associations. It was originally the home of the Ranger of Bushy Park, an important position when the Royal Court was at Hampton Court Palace. King William IV, when Duke of Clarence, was Ranger in 1797 and lived in Bushy House with Dorothy Jordan, a celebrated actress by whom he had 10 children (taking the name Fitzclarence), seven being born in the house. By an extraordinary quirk of history the Duke was the President of the Society for the Improvement of Naval Architecture in 1791. Later he married Princess Adelaide of Saxe-Meiningen before succeeding to the throne as William IV in 1830. He reigned for seven years only but the Princess—now Queen Adelaide—later assumed the position of Ranger until her death in 1849. Bushy House then became a gift of Queen Victoria and following the French revolution, with Napoleon III assuming control, the French royal family were expelled from France. Victoria offered the house to the Duc de Nemours, Louis Philippe's second son, as sanctuary, and he stayed there for seven years after which, following the result of the Franco-German War, he was allowed to return to France in 1872. A few years later the house was transferred to the Royal Society and today it serves as the residence of the current Director of NPL.

The NPL's purpose was to provide reliable physical standards, methods of testing scientific instruments and carry out original research in physics. In its first 10 years it rapidly gained international recognition as one of the leading Institutions in the world dealing with research in physics. In some eyes this was hardly good news, the *Deutsche Mechaniker Zeitung* writing in 1904:

Our German trade has every cause to watch carefully the development of the National Physical Laboratory and to take timely precautions before the advantages which it has already secured against English competition are too seriously reduced.

The quality of research at NPL naturally reflected the ability of its scientific staff. In addition to the influence of Lord Rayleigh, a physicist of monumental prestige, the Director and many of the Superintendents who led the various divisions of the laboratory were Fellows of the Royal Society. Their achievements were well known. For example, T.E. Stanton, the Superintendent of the Engineering Division, which later embraced an Aerodynamics section, had produced distinguished work in fluid mechanics which found immediate application to aerofoils and W.F. Rosenhain enjoyed a huge reputation concerning the mechanical and electrical properties of metallic alloys. Against this background the notion of siting a towing tank within a laboratory enjoying an academic atmosphere fostered by the Royal Society was attractive and in putting forward the idea the NPL were asked to assume the responsibility of maintenance, the council of INA wishing to retain a voice in the management of the tank. This proposal was accepted and NPL's Executive Committee gratefully acknowledged the proposed guaranteed funding and, if complete financial considerations allowed, were prepared to recommend the scheme for acceptance to the Royal Society.

Once the principle of the establishment of a tank had been agreed there followed a period of uncertainty as reservations began to be voiced. If this tank were to be available to private shipbuilding companies, how would it cope if at one and the same time, several requests for model tests were made? Had not the moment come when such a tank should be used for the specific purpose of systematic research into the general principles of ship resistance? The idea of a tank for research was persuasively argued by Sir William White in a paper[3] before the INA. On behalf of INA he proposed the establishment of a National Tank which would be chiefly devoted to research work. He went on to outline eight specific areas of research which should be addressed, including friction resistance, propeller efficiency and ship manoeuvring. Yarrow thought his arguments were convincing as did others, and he was particularly attracted to research since the findings from such work would benefit the whole of the shipbuilding industry. Nevertheless there remained a strong desire that tests for private firms should be accommodated in the programme of work undertaken by the tank. White's resolution was so phrased to allow representatives of ship owners and builders to be included in the working committee which was looking into the whole scheme and his proposal was carried unanimously.

After White's paper, little more was heard until 1908. The slump in shipbuilding did not help and in 1905 the shipbuilding fraternity both in England and France seemed to be more interested in celebrating the centenary of the Battle of Trafalgar. However, the Council of the INA had been doing its best to encourage the seemingly reluctant shipbuilders and owners to contribute towards the sum of money required. If this proved impossible there was likely to be no alternative to the dissolution of the working committee. Although assurances were given, they were insufficient and since 1901, when it had been estimated that £15,000 would be needed, this sum had by now been revised upwards. But in 1908, Yarrow in a letter to the INA made a magnificent offer to defray the costs of building the tank up to an amount of £20,000 with the proviso that the expenses of maintenance over the first 10 years would be guaranteed by other parties. Twenty shipbuilders, owners or associated organisations responded by promising to contribute annually for 10 years a total of £1,340. This fell short of the estimated £2,000 per year needed but nevertheless the General Board of NPL felt confident to proceed. It did so in the anticipation that the extra money would somehow materialise.

Alfred Yarrow was a remarkable man. From the humblest of beginnings he built a famous tradition in shipbuilding. He set up a small engineering works at Poplar on the Thames in 1870 where almost 400 steam launches were built. Torpedo boats followed and then destroyers, many for foreign navies. By the early 1900s when Thames-side shipbuilding was becoming uneconomic, Yarrow transferred to Scotstoun on the river Clyde to continue building ships in great numbers. Alfred Yarrow was a liberal philanthropist. His concern for the care of the sick led him to donate magnificent sums to the London Hospital (£25,000), the Nurses Home in Glasgow and in 1903 to the establishment of a convalescent home in Broadstairs. This latest gift in 1908 gave immediate impetus to the scheme for a National tank. A new committee was straight away formed by the INA which in turn set up a building sub-committee made up of Sir William White, R.E. Froude, W.J. Luke from the Clydebank tank (which had been built in 1904 for shipbuilders John Brown) and Glazebrook, the Director of NPL. The main committee drew up plans for the management of the tank whilst the sub-committee largely through Glazebrook looked closely at technical aspects and visited the tanks at Berlin and Dresden as well as a newly opened one in Paris. Glazebrook was initially much attracted by Wellenkamp's experimental method but despite his efforts he was not actually able to see a demonstration. Ultimately he rejected it on the grounds of unreliability and undoubtedly R.E. Froude's opinion was crucial. After discussions with Engels and Gebers at Dresden, who provided data on how resistance measurements can be affected by the finite boundaries of a tank's walls and bottom, Glazebrook was able to recommend dimensions for the new tank which would avoid these difficulties for the size of model that he expected at Teddington.

Although he was in favour of a towing tank as the main test facility, Glazebrook nevertheless made plans to include a separate smaller tank in the overall specification of the tank and its buildings. This smaller facility could be used to set up the Wellenkamp arrangement. Meanwhile, it had been decided that the National Tank should be managed by an Advisory committee under the chairmanship of Lord Rayleigh. Members of this committee would be drawn from the INA and NPL's executive committee. Alfred Yarrow was also invited. The committee would advise on the work to be followed and arrange for the publication of results and it was decided that the Tank would become a department of NPL under the general direction of its Director but with an appointed Superintendent.

Eight years had passed from the time Alfred Yarrow put forward his suggestion and now at last a National Tank was on the way. It was to become a valuable national resource and the first of others to be inherited by BMT. Work contracts were let and building was soon to begin.

REFERENCES

1. Trans. INA, 1901.
2. Report of the Committee appointed by the Treasury to consider the desirability of establishing a National Physical Laboratory, HMSO C-8976-7, 1898.
3. White Sir W.H., "On the establishment of an experimental tank for research work on fluid resistance and ship propulsion", trans. INA, 1904.

CHAPTER 3

THE NATIONAL TANK AND ITS EQUIPMENT

From the three tenders submitted, consultant engineers Mott and Hay were chosen to translate Glazebrook's requirements into practice and they in turn contracted Dick, Kerr and Co. of London to carry out the building works. The whole task, begun in July 1909, was expected to take nine months.

The tank was built on a north-south axis which meant the water in it would be exposed to direct sunlight through the windows of the tank building. It was undoubtedly appreciated that this would encourage the growth of algae but any other orientation of the tank would have meant its extreme length penetrating NPL's boundary into Bushy Park which was Crown land. The rails which were to run along the top of the tank walls and bear the weight and traction of a moving carriage were fitted once the tank was built. Whilst the long business of laying the rails was underway the design and construction of the carriage and its drive system were proceeding. The carriage spanned the whole width of the tank and was borne on four 900 mm diameter wheels. It was built in steel to overall dimensions of 10·5 metres × 9·9 metres and made up of a number of lattice girders 80 mm deep. The carriage arrangement included a central open space for the installation of dynamometry and apparatus. Drive to the carriage was provided by four 35 h.p. motors, one per wheel with their axes vertical. The electrical power needed was considerable and as the demand would be intermittent it was feared that to supply the tank direct from NPL's generating station would interfere with experiments in other NPL departments. To avoid this an independent motor generator set of 52 kW output driven by a 1,000 ampere hour battery of 55 cells was installed and located on one side of the tank at about one third of its length from one end.

A carriage driver was stationed next to the generator and sat at a desk from which he set and controlled the required voltage for the requested carriage speed.

Glazebrook's overall conception of the tank and its buildings included a separate but much smaller tank. This was primarily intended as a facility where experiments of a general exploratory nature could be conducted but Glazebrook introduced a two-fold capability. It could be used to set up and test Wellenkamp's latest towing method and also, by installing a pump, water could be moved at a known speed past a fixed model whose resistance could be

17

measured on a dynamometer arm to which the model was connected. The idea of moving water was not new, it had been proposed and tried in rudimentary fashion some 100 years earlier, but Glazebrook produced what must have been the first serious flume or circulating water channel in this country.

The smaller tank was built in reinforced concrete alongside the east wall of the main building and just south of the electricity generating set. The need for flowing water influenced its layout and dimensions and within the overall length of 20 metres a stretch of 6 metres was chosen ahead of the pump (which was to be installed at one end) over which the water from the pump could travel and settle to a reasonably uniform flow before it reached the model. Having passed the model it then fell abruptly into a 3¼ metre deep pit from which a culvert 1½ metres in diameter extended back to the pump through which the water returned. A sluice with a vertically sliding gate, operated by a handwheel, was arranged at the bottom of the pit. The section of the tank in the vicinity of the model was uniform, 1½ metres wide × 1 metre deep. To control the flow of water and encourage uniformity extraordinary large undulations were built into the bottom of the 6 metres settling length together with side and surface deflectors at the tank sides. Because water would build up at the pump end of the tank with the pump in action the walls were built up to a higher level at this point. The pump, driven by an 80 h.p. motor had a capacity of 2 cubic metres of water per second and circulated the water at a maximum speed of 3 knots. For still water experiments 45 cm diameter shafts were sunk at each end of the tank and on its centreline. These gave the necessary drop for the falling weights in Wellenkamp's arrangement. The photograph in plate 4 taken shortly after the construction of the small tank shows a view from its southern end, the main tank being visible through the arches. A slot through which the model towing cord passed when experimenting in still water can also be seen.

It will be remembered that Glazebrook was sceptical of Wellenkamp's method and claims. In an attempt to overcome one of the weaknesses, that of the difficulty in achieving a steady towing speed, he designed drums with spirals which were set up above the pits into which the falling weights fell. Thornycroft was later to copy and perhaps improve on the spiral arrangement (or snail as he called it) in his tank at Fort Stein. The drums were threaded to take two wires, one passing over a pulley in the roof of the building and attached to a weight pan and the other fixed to one end of the model. The thread on each drum had a few turns of maximum diameter and then by means of the spiral the next few turns reduced to the diameter needed for a steady run. By this means a length of about 5 metres was taken up in accelerating and retarding the model with a steady run of about 7½ metres. The model's resistance was obtained simply by taking the difference between the weights needed at the bow and the stern after correction for the friction in the apparatus. To obtain model speed a circuit breaker was fitted to record the revolutions of the towing drum.

With building work well advanced by Christmas 1909 it soon became necessary to appoint a Superintendent to work with the Contractors and to manage the tank. At the first Tank Advisory Committee nominations were considered and following strong recommendations from Sir Philip Watts, the Admiralty's Director of Naval Construction, G.S. Baker was proposed. In due course Baker was appointed by NPL's Executive Committee, beginning his duties at Teddington on 1 March 1910. Baker's association was to last 31 years during which he became a dominant even dictatorial figure whose influence on ship hull form designers was immense. He was born in 1877 and at 15 became a Shipwright apprentice in Portsmouth dockyard achieving the highest distinction in the final school examinations. He went on to the Royal Naval College at Greenwich where he gained a first class professional certificate and membership of the Royal Corps of Naval Constructors. After serving at the Admiralty under the Director of Naval Construction he was sent to the Haslar tank to work under R.E. Froude, staying there almost four years. In 1906 he returned to the Admiralty to become Professional Secretary to the DNC.

On arrival at Teddington Baker became involved at once with matters not only concerning the tank itself but model manufacture methods and the design of measuring apparatus. He needed help and by the early summer of 1910 two assistants had been appointed, G.H. Millar and J.L. Kent. Millar was a Cambridge graduate and Kent, later to succeed Baker as the tank's second Superintendent, began as an apprentice at Portsmouth going on as a private student to complete the advanced course at Greenwich. Before coming to NPL Kent spent a year at the Haslar tank so that like Baker he was able to draw on useful experience and knowledge. These three worked together devising and developing the various requirements, R.E. Froude being frequently available to give advice and assistance.

The method of manufacturing models not surprisingly followed Froude's practice at Haslar. The rough shape of the hull was moulded in clay and the model cast in wax to this shape before being profiled in a shaping machine. The clay for the moulds was put in a large steel bin 13 metres long. Its top edges formed a level track along which travelled a cutter which levelled off the top of the casting. The rough shape of the mould was fashioned by hand, the moulders following a series of wooden templates spaced at intervals along the length of the model. This was a back-aching job for the four men who usually made up the moulding party. Models were usually 5½ metres long and about 8 cm thick and a wooden core covered by a canvas sheet was made at the same time as the mould and lowered into it leaving an 8 cm gap all round into which melted wax was poured. Hundreds of wax models were cast over the years and when demand was great the process took about three days and involved four moulders, a carpenter and a draughtsman. The casting was of course only the rough shape required. The next stage was to cut successive waterlines into the surface of the model following a faired lines plan of the vessel in a shaping machine. The final shape was then obtained by hand using the cut lines and templates as guidance. The shaping machine was vital to the whole process and its design was largely based on William Froude's original at Haslar, a machine similar to that on display at the Dumbarton museum.

It was designed to take models up to 7½ metres long and just over a metre wide and consisted of a bin for the model which could be driven longitudinally forwards or backwards at any speed up to 2 metres per second. The model was placed keel up in the bin and held firmly in place by centreline plugs located in holes in cross-beams fitted to the top of the model. A half-breadth plan of the ship to be modelled was placed on a table which could also be driven longitudinally. Both bin and table were geared to the same motor and by adjusting the gearing on the table drive, the table and drawing could be made to imitate, in the appropriate ratio between model and drawing size, the longitudinal motion of the model and bin. Spanning the bin a fixed frame carried two revolving cutters which operated on both sides of the model. The height of the cutters could be set by a handwheel and transverse motion provided by a right- and left-handed screw operated through a level gear by a handwheel. The transverse motion of the cutters was transmitted by a copying lever to a circular tracer whose diameter represented, to scale, the diameter of the cutters. Thus, as the model moved longitudinally the machine operator using the handwheel kept the tracer in contact with the line on the plan being cut. Some 20 or 30 waterlines were cut depending on the size or complexity of the hull surface before the model was removed from the bin to be finished by hand. Over the course of many years when it was the norm to make two models a week, castings were usually poured on Tuesdays and Thursdays. A new model was then cut in a morning on the machine and finished in the afternoon by a team of five people who were joined by the machine operator who was the draughtsman who had prepared the lines plan. After test the model was broken up and the wax melted down for use again. The whole business of making a model was cheap and quick. The shaping machine worked very well for almost 40 years until it was replaced by a modernised version that retained the same principle as the original. Finally in 1990 a numerically-controlled machine was purchased and this undoubtedly provided a higher standard of accuracy. It could also machine material other than wax. Wax was abandoned in the 1960s for polyurethane to overcome the several problems that arose at the time.

INSTRUMENTATION AND EQUIPMENT

Running in parallel with these developments was the design of a resistance dynamometer. William Froude at Torquay and Haslar had spent much time in developing a suitable balance with which a model's resistance to forward motion through water could be measured accurately and naturally R.E. Froude in advising Baker suggested that Teddington's dynamometer should follow the same Froude pattern such that the model under test should be allowed a certain amount of freedom in the fore and aft direction balancing the pull against counter weights and a spring. Some thought was given to towing a fixed model as adopted in the Dresden tank but after some experiments at Teddington by Baker and similar efforts by R.E. Froude at Haslar the two evidently agreed that a degree of freedom in the model was preferable so that the design proceeded along the lines of Froude's principle. In suggesting improvements R.E. Froude wrote long letters to Baker which dealt mainly with the preferred ratio of lever arm and knife edge arrangement.

The dynamometer as finally evolved is shown in plate 6. A tubular diamond-shaped frame was supported on two knife edges, its lower end linking with the model by a towing rod. The upper end was connected via a short rod to a lever carrying a balanced pen which recorded the fore and aft movement of the model as it was being towed through the water, the trace appearing on a sheet of paper mounted on a revolving wooden drum. The ratio of movement of model to movement of pen was chosen to be five to one in line with R.E. Froude's suggestion. Part of the resistance of the model was taken by dead weights added to a pan, the remainder by the spring riding on another knife edge at the end of an arm. A simple calibration of the movement of the spring against that of the pen for a known weight enabled the total resistance of the model to be determined. The complete dynamometer was carried on a rectangular frame which was held down by screws such that when working it always took up the same position. The frame included the gear necessary to grip the model to avoid strain on the dynamometer as the carriage accelerated from rest or slowed down. The grip consisted of a cam worked by a hand operated worm wheel and swung two arms outwards to press against beams fixed to the model. The grip was gradually released by the experimenter as the carriage accelerated so that the model during the steady run "floated" free, its fore and aft movement being translated to and recorded by the dynamometer pen on the revolving drum. Records of time and distance were also taken on the drum, time from an electric clock which had a make and break contact every half second and distance by a trigger fitted to the fore girder of the carriage striking against points fixed to the rails at 6 metre intervals. The trigger as it swung completed an electro-magnetic circuit.

The change of trim experienced by the model as it moved ahead was recorded on two further drums placed fore and aft. A light vertical rod with its lower end resting on a fork in the model was attached at its upper end to the arm of a balanced rocking lever. The arm carried a pen which traced a record on to the revolving drum.

By the autumn of 1910 the main tank and most of its equipment was ready for use. Great credit was due to the contractors whose painstaking efforts produced a facility of high quality which fully satisfied Glazebrook's specification. The precision achieved in laying the rails was outstanding and this together with the excellence of the carriage speed control meant that no damping device was needed for the resistance dynamometer allowing Kent to boast in later years that the NPL tank was the only one in the world where a damping device was not needed to achieve satisfactory recordings of resistance.

Time has shown the extent of the contractors' achievement. Little has gone wrong with the tank in 83 years and at the time of its closure it was virtually the same as in 1910. The carriage of course received regular maintenance over the years but few replacement parts or improvements were needed. Credit is also due to the workshop mechanics whose skill enabled the realisation of a resistance dynamometer of considerable delicacy. It remained in continuous use for over 40 years until in 1954 a more robust replacement was designed to give greater range and flexibility using the same principle of dead weight and spring.

Baker immediately launched into an initial programme of work, his intent to monitor experimental readings against known standards. Three models were soon tested and compared with R.E. Froude's measurements at Haslar and also a standard model was made which could be tested regularly to note any changes in resistance that might occur due to dynamometry or even tank water variability. So far as the water was concerned Baker worried that gnats and mosquitoes would breed and to allay this he obtained several eels and put them in the tank. They survived for many years to provide a source of amusement to staff and visitors alike as they rose to feed from the hand. Baker also, at a later date, added a trace of copper sulphate to the water to assist clarification. The heating, provided to the tank from a boiler to two overhead pipes under the roof girders which returned along the side walls lower down, proved very satisfactory. Used continuously in winter months water temperature throughout the year varied over an acceptable range of 50–62°F.

At the start of 1911 the Tank staff had risen to nine. They can be regarded as the original members at the time of the beginning of the National Tank's work. They were:

G.S. Baker   Superintendent
G.H. Millar   Assistant
J.L. Kent   Junior Assistant
E.H. Dawes   Workshop mechanic
J.T. Woollett   Workshop mechanic
G.E. Unsted   Carpenter
S. Bunday   Moulder
F.J. Chaplin   Office
H. Hitchman   Office

Remuneration of the staff was not high by the standards of the time. The salaries of Baker and his assistants as stipulated by the Treasury were £500 and £250 per annum respectively and a note of Baker's to NPL indicates that the two mechanics each received £126 per annum, the carpenter £108 and the moulder £88.

The time had come for a formal opening of the National Tank. 1911 was the year of the INA's jubilee and it was convenient to include the formal opening as part of the celebrations. An International Congress on Shipping had also been planned for July in London so that the date chosen for the opening of the Tank was 5 July. About 200 people attended, many from overseas. Alfred Yarrow whose generosity allowed the Tank to become a reality addressed the gathering and Lord Rayleigh duly proclaimed it open. Yarrow had been unwilling to have his name formally linked with the Tank and so, in honour of William Froude, it was named by Lord Rayleigh as the William Froude National Tank. The Marchioness of Bristol, wife of the President of the INA, was invited to operate the carriage speed control whereby the carriage set off on its inaugural run. Visitors were shown around the Tank and the occasion, luckily blessed with good weather, ended with an open air luncheon in the garden of Bushy House. Remarkably, no record has survived of the speeches made, but it is certain that Alfred Yarrow's magnificent gift was acknowledged as well as Glazebrook's design, R.E. Froude's contribution and the excellent realisation of the plans by the Contractors. Baker of course had already led the Tank through a thorough testing period and it was now ready to carry out both research into ship hull performance and to carry out test work on designs submitted by many of the shipbuilding representatives present.

CHAPTER 4

EARLY YEARS: 1911–1914

Leading up to the official opening of the Tank in 1911, Baker and his staff were engaged in satisfying themselves that everything worked and that reliable measurements could be obtained from the new tank and its equipment. It was an obvious step to carry out resistance measurements on model forms that had been tested elsewhere and to make comparisons. R.E. Froude, W.J. Luke and D.W. Taylor at Haslar, Clydebank and Washington all co-operated by sending hull lines of models that they had already tested. Froude sent three sets of lines of different character, Luke and Taylor one each and 4·8 metre models were made of the five forms. The NPL annual report[1] for 1911 described the results as excellent saying:

... the results of these tests agree very well with those at Haslar, at Clydebank and at Washington, and it is considered, in view of these tests, that the National Tank is ready to go forward with general experimental investigations of ship resistance.

An examination of the records broadly confirms this (the Teddington result was slightly lower than Haslar and Clydebank) which today is a little surprising in view of similar exercises conducted in recent years on a common model in different towing tanks where such good correspondence has not always been found.

Baker was now convinced that he had a tank and equipment which was fully up to the standards elsewhere and that he could proceed with confidence. Nevertheless he thought it prudent to monitor resistance measurements by conducting experiments at regular intervals on a standard model. This followed the practice at Haslar where since 1887 R.E. Froude had tested the same model and used the results established in that year as a standard against which subsequent results from any future model could be corrected. Froude's model was a 4 metre version of *HMS Iris*, a 91 metre despatch vessel of fine form (block coefficient about 0·5). Baker, aware of the possibility of even further tank to tank comparisons, copied the *Iris* but made it slightly longer (4¼ metres) to take account of the larger models to be tested at Teddington compared with those at Haslar. Teddington's first *Iris* was made in wax, it was NPL model number 1, and was first run in July 1911. As with the earlier comparative tests the results were well in line with Haslar's. A year later a "permanent" *Iris* was made, this

25

time in brass and run once a month on Saturday mornings until the end of 1914, the only difference noted during this period with the Haslar results being a more marked secondary hump in the resistance curve. Over the whole set of measurements during this 30 month period NPL results remained consistent the total scatter never exceeding 2 per cent and Baker thought continuous regular measurements no longer necessary and did not run *Iris* again until 1919 when a similar consistency was found. Baker's evidence led him to decide that no correction to current model test results would be necessary at Teddington and this practice was maintained. He accordingly abandoned regular tests with *Iris*. But Haslar continued, it was after all their habit to apply a correction, until suddenly in 1925 alarming differences in their standard correction appeared.[2] They amounted to 14 per cent, were happily short-lived, yet reappeared at a slightly lower level in 1926 and again during periods between 1930–36. Never satisfactorily explained, biological changes in the tank water during hot spells of weather being the most popular theory, these tank "storms" gave some weight to the argument that regular standard model measurements should be made to alert the experimenter to any unexpected circumstance that may occur. So far as NPL's *Iris* was concerned it was last run in 1943, again with the same results as earlier and it was eventually destroyed in 1955. Since then G.E. Gadd has devised a simple piece of equipment which will measure the viscosity of a sample of water taken from any towing tank so that in the event of an unexplainable result from a model test a quick test can be made, and a comparison made with the expected viscosity. One of the advantages of continuous measurements with the same model was that it allowed the effect of changes in water temperature on resistance to be assessed. Baker plotted *Iris* results to a temperature base and added the results of other workers which gave the effect of temperature on fluid resistance and found good agreement between the various results, although some had been obtained in different ways such as tests on water flow in pipes or on revolving discs in water. Baker deduced that a 10° rise in temperature caused a 3 per cent reduction in frictional resistance and he was later able to use this to apply a correction to the total model resistance on a given day to make it equivalent to a standard temperature of 59°F, since it became Tank practice to extrapolate model results to ships which were with respect to a sea water temperature of 59°F.

Although most attention was paid to the main tank, time was found to explore the possibilities of the small tank. It was important to establish to what accuracy tests could be conducted in view of the fact that small models were involved. A hull form already tested as a 4½ metre model in the main tank was taken and two small models of this, ¾ and 1⅓ metres long were made and towed in calm water in the small tank using the falling weight system. Comparing the results obtained on the three geosim models Baker was disappointed,[3] particularly in the lower range of speed tested. Worse, the resistance of the ¾ metre model at low speeds varied considerably in different experiments on the same day. At higher speeds the two smaller models gave results reasonably close to the larger model, a maximum variation of resistance of 6 per cent being noted. Baker could not offer a satisfactory explanation but suggested that unsteady speed and variable friction in the towing system were the main reasons for the lack of repeatability or disagreement with the large model results. Discussing Baker's paper Professors Abell and Henderson both agreed low speed measurements on such small models could not be relied upon and Henderson, who had been attempting similar experiments in a small tank at the Naval College Laboratory, admitted to similar problems over unsteady towing speeds. With the benefit of today's knowledge it is clear that the experiments at low speed were more likely to have suffered from the effects of laminar flow which must have been present on such small models, Reynolds numbers in the tests being less than a million. At such speeds the effects of laminar flow would have affected the resistance measurements crucially which explains the lack of repeatability in the results. In later years, even when working with large models, the importance of ensuring a turbulent boundary layer over model surfaces was to lead experimenters to deliberately force the flow into turbulence by adding at the bow a "tripping" device. Baker promised to seek solutions but left the impression that he was pessimistic of success at lower test speeds. The small tank lay idle for a while due to the pressure of work in the main tank but at the outbreak of the First World War it proved useful for *ad hoc* investigations.

With the Tank now available for regular use the Advisory Committee, conscious of the fact that the work at Haslar and Washington was concentrated on warship forms and work at Clydebank and Dumbarton on specific ship designs about to be built, drew up recommendations for a programme of research for the new William Froude National Tank. This included methodical tests on merchant ship forms and, following Lord Rayleigh's suggestion,[4] an investigation into changes in bow shape to see whether the diverging wave system of a moving ship could be influenced to advantage, early efforts to understand and develop the reduction in wave-making resistance through the use of todays modern bulbous bow shapes. An extension of William Froude's friction experiments was also proposed.

With requests for tests coming in from private shipbuilding companies and others, conditions for the execution of such tests for a fee needed to be made clear and the Tank Advisory Committee drew up guidelines. These stated that confidentiality had to be assured to prospective customers. For a fee of £60 a wax model would be made and tested at one draught to give resistance data. Predicted values of ship speed and effective power would also be provided. For a further £21 the model could be modified and retested. The model used in experiments was to be identified by its Tank number only and the lines of the hull form were to be held in the custody of the Tank Superintendent. Such strictures were of course necessary but from the first Baker was not content merely to test a submitted form, present the results and leave it at that. Instead wherever he saw the chance he pressed for changes in hull shape in seeking reduced resistance and was soon to gain a reputation many envied.

INSTRUMENTATION AND EQUIPMENT

By the end of 1913, requests for tests from private companies were growing and the desire to know more of the propulsive qualities of a ship became stronger (effective power from the model resistance experiment was known but so far propulsive efficiency could be deduced only from full-scale ship trial results). Baker was aware of the need to make and test model propellers both in isolation and when installed at a model to provide propulsive power. Work to develop suitable apparatus had begun a year earlier and included the design of four separate gears which could cater for hulls driven by more than one propeller. Each gear would be separately driven by independent electric motors, propeller thrust to be recorded on dynamometers. Much thought had also been given to propeller manufacture. With the emphasis of the Tank's work on resistance and with so few staff available for additional tasks, numerically the staff was the same as in 1911, progress was slow but in March 1914 Baker was able to report that all should be complete and ready for test within two months and that it was hoped that wake and hull efficiency experiments with twin or single propellers could soon begin.

A simple piece of apparatus that was developed at this time and which remained in use for many years was the "flag", a name given to a thin blade of wood 10 cm long that when fitted to and projecting from the surface of a model indicated, locally, the direction of the water flow over the model as it was towed through the water. The technique was developed to determine the best alignment of hull appendages, principally bilge keels. A number of flags were fitted to one side of the model in the region of interest and were carried on spindles which could swivel in a gland bedded into the wax model. To achieve neutral buoyancy the flags were weighted so as to exert no moment on the spindle. The spindles extended to within the model and indicators fixed to them. With the model towed at a steady speed the position of the indicators were noted and then with the model out of the water the flags were reset to the indicated positions allowing a line of flow to be deduced. In the 1950s a quicker and more accurate method was used instead, lines of an oil-based paint being applied to the model surface, the paint running and setting in fine streaks as the model passed through the water.

Novel instrumentation was needed when tests on seaplane floats were requested. This entailed a complete departure from that used in conventional resistance experiments. A resistance dynamometer was used to tow the floats but the tow point had to be at the centre of gravity of the whole seaplane so that the float would trim correctly as it moved through the water. It had also to be arranged at some distance aft of the resistance dynamometer to facilitate the application of an upward force on the model, this force being equivalent to that part of the weight of the seaplane taken by the wings in forward motion. The upward force, achieved by adding a small weight to a wire led over a pulley, naturally increased with speed. The whole apparatus was complex and delicate and allowed the model freedom in the vertical plane only whilst being able to take up a running trim angle and change of vertical height under the action of the forces due to motion.

TESTS FOR FIRMS

With rules for fee-paying customers approved such work could begin and the first recorded series of such tests was carried out for the Irish Lights Office, Dublin in August 1911. The office deployed lightships which on their stations rolled to an unsatisfactory extent and the purpose of the experiments was to determine the best position and depth of the vessel's bilge keels. The experiments showed that the extinctive effect of bilge keels changed little with large changes in metacentric height which seemed to confirm experience with existing lightships although many of these were wooden with noticeably different centres of gravity than the latest steel vessels. The effectiveness of the keels was found to improve when they were placed above the turn of the bilge rather than below but changes could not be carried too far since the keels would soon project beyond the ship's beam. The data produced were presented by G. Idle of the Irish Lights Office to the INA in 1912[5] and his paper described as Part I was followed by another (Part II), this time written by Baker.[6]

During 1913 and the early months of 1914 numerous tests for shipbuilders were done. The number of models tested for private companies grew steadily from four in 1912, nine in 1913 to a startling 47 between April 1914 and the outbreak of the First World War in August 1914. Many of these were tested several times as modifications to the original forms were tried, these changes being inspired by Baker and in most cases resulting in useful reductions in model resistance and hence ship power. To give two examples. Clyde Shipbuilders submitted two alternative forms for a new ship; they were uncertain which was better. Following the tests, which showed little difference between the two, Baker immediately recommended shifting forward the centre of buoyancy by a change in the curve of areas and achieved an improvement of 9 per cent at the service speed. Esplon, Son and Swainston were unhappy about the speed of SS La Rosarina on trial and, anxious for better results from their next ship, sought the Tank's advice. Using La Rosarina's trial data, Baker deduced a propulsive coefficient after resistance tests on the La Rosarina model (NPL number 105) and applied the coefficient to further models modified from La Rosarina's form. Baker's best form reduced resistance by some 13 per cent and if his assumption that under propulsive conditions his derived coefficient applied then this large improvement would have been reflected in a similar reduction in the power for the next ship. Certainly Esplon and Swainston departed happily.

By now most of the leading shipbuilders in this country were seeking tests at NPL. The Fairfield Company commissioned its first tests in 1911, Clyde Shipbuilders, Yarrow and Samuel White in 1912 (the White test was the first high speed ship form tested at the Tank requiring resistance tests up to 40 knots, a Froude number of 0·75) and Swan Hunter in 1913. Blyth, Scott and Sunderland shipbuilders appeared in 1914 with many others following soon after. During this period the Tank report included the area curve for the hull tested and values of effective power against ship speed for each ship condition tested. As yet no propulsion tests were possible. By April 1914 the Tank staff had increased by four, two draughtsmen and two workshop mechanics— Bottomley, a draughtsman and Wise, a mechanic both destined to make major contributions. The increase in numbers was entirely justified and overdue in view of the growth of commissioned work. The overall response of the staff to repayment work was such that hull forms were tested and the report on the result in the hands of the private firms in less than a fortnight. Such efficiency was applauded by Sir Archibald Denny of the Dumbarton tank when discussing a paper by Baker,[7] but he feared that little time would be found for research work at the National Tank.

RESEARCH

Interaction

In September 1911, HMS Hawke left Portsmouth and in the open, but relatively shallow sea, collided with the White Star Line's SS Olympic. The subsequent litigation sought to prove or disprove the contention that the accident had been due to the suction of Olympic, the larger ship and the Treasury Solicitor asked the Tank to ascertain by way of experimentation the likelihood of collision when two ships made way close to one another. Thus was the Tank's first work on interaction born and experiments began in October 1911. Olympic, sister of the ill-fated Titanic, was a twin screw vessel 265 metres long, Hawke being some 150 metres shorter than this. Both had similar draught beam ratios of about 0·39. The experiments simulated deep and shallow water since the latter were considered more representative of the conditions which prevailed. Models of each ship were made to a 1/44-scale and tests conducted at a corresponding full-scale speed of 18 knots. The question posed was would Hawke be drawn into Olympic at 18 knots if Olympic were to take up successive positions more and more ahead of Hawke and whether if any interaction force asserted itself, the operation of Hawke's steering gear could resist it and so avoid collision. For experiments in shallow water a depth of $2\frac{3}{4}$ metres was required in the tank and a false bottom had to be made and fitted to span the tank over a suitable length. This in itself was a large undertaking. The challenging experiments were led largely by Kent who with the Tank staff had first to produce a suitable towing system which would allow both models to be towed simultaneously at the same speed on parallel courses 2 metres (91 metres full scale) apart. Olympic was kept straight by two rods fitted one at the bow and one at the stern which allowed the model freedom in surge and trim and the whole towing system could for any given experiment be moved laterally or fore and aft relative to *Hawke*'s position. *Hawke* was towed on a triangular frame, its apex 60 cm ahead of the bow, the base fitted to a pivot fixed to the centreline of the model. This allowed *Hawke* to sheer sideways or swing under any interacting force that might develop.

To measure the forces of interaction athwartships special dynamometers were designed made up of springs and rotating drums producing a creation of the utmost delicacy, a tribute to the skill of the workshop mechanic Dawes. Unfortunately the dynamometers did not give the greatest reliability but they were capable of detecting and recording the very obvious interaction forces that occurred in the experiments. Questions were asked as to whether the action of the ship propellers would affect behaviour and so model screws were made and fitted to *Olympic* driven by a small motor installed in the model. The screws were the first made in the Tank before a proven manufacturing method was established and almost certainly they were crude. Their purpose, however, was no more than to simulate propeller action. The speed of each propeller was adjusted under way such that *Olympic* was always kept loose of its towing rods.

The results of the experiments were most convincing and provided the Court with valuable guidance as to what would have happened at sea. In shallow water very large interaction forces were experienced and with *Hawke*'s bow 200 metres abaft *Olympic*'s (or *Hawke*'s bow 60 metres ahead of *Olympic*'s stern) *Hawke* veered off and a collision would have occurred had not the experimenters intervened. In deep water the effect was not so great. Repeat experiments with driving screws fitted to *Olympic* showed little detectable difference in *Hawke*'s behaviour. To see whether the action of *Hawke*'s rudder could resist the force an ingenious steering arrangement was devised. The rudder was operated by a 20 cm radius yoke fitted to the rudder head. Connecting rods from the yoke were taken to a similar yoke which pivoted at a position near amidships. This second yoke could be worked by strings and a rudder angle to port or starboard set. In shallow water a collision could not be avoided even with 20° of rudder applied and it was plain that unless early avoiding action by way of a reduction in power of either ship together with rudder action had been possible, collision must have been inevitable. Those who witnessed the experiments were greatly impressed and any doubts in people's mind of the value of a towing tank would have been quickly dispersed for here was an example of how other kinds of maritime problems could be tackled. The work was of course highly confidential but the fascinating problems which emerged from the collision stimulated work by others and Professor Gibson carried out and published some interaction experiments which were designed to reproduce conditions similar to those obtaining in *Hawke* and *Olympic*, albeit on very different types of hull.[8]

Methodical Series Tests on Hulls

The first programme of research for the Advisory Committee consisted of methodical tests on five sets of ship models of mercantile form and an investigation into Rayleigh's ideas on bow endings. The sets of models consisted of 23 variants and were drawn up and tested for resistance, the large quantity of results together with the findings of the Rayleigh bow shapes being presented by Baker in 1913.[9] They are the first published account in this country of systematic ship model tests.

In preparing the model variants Baker felt sure in his mind that, provided the general form of a hull and its principal dimensions remained constant, changes in the ratio of entrance to run (entrance and run being those portions of the hull forward or aft which are clear of a perfectly parallel middle body) would influence ship resistance. Now these ideas on parallel middle body were not new; William Froude had published results in 1877 which showed that economic lengths of parallel body could be found, at least in finer warship forms. However, Baker established five sets of models which he labelled A–E of varying fullness and by changing the distribution of displacement in the longitudinal direction parallel middle body was varied over a range of 10–50 per cent of the hull length. The matrix of models produced naturally threw up variations in prismatic coefficient between 0·59 and 0·83. The results were presented using constants of resistance, $\textcircled{C}$ and speed, $\textcircled{K}$ that Froude had introduced earlier. Diagrams plotted to a base of entrance run ratio showed very clearly the best ratios to adopt for given values of $\textcircled{K}$. Other plottings showed the incidence of the humps in the resistance curve, the humps representing growth in wave-making resistance and limiting speeds for individual hull forms. The main wave-making hump was common for all forms tested, occurring at $\textcircled{K}$ about 2·7 but the first hump at lower speeds varied with entrance run ratio and allowed an assessment of the highest speed capable in a given design. So far as Rayleigh's idea was concerned results were less satisfactory. None of the waterline endings tried, and they included modifications to both fore and aft endings, achieved very much. Rayleigh had suggested that hollowing and filling bow waterlines would promote the growth of a neutralising wave in phase with that formed naturally by the original bow shape. The original bows produced a wave crest about 50–75 mm aft of the stem and the hollow in the Rayleigh bow was chosen to coincide with the crest but unhappily no real reductions in resistance were seen. Seeds had nevertheless been sown. To complete a memorable and classic paper, Baker included complementary tests carried out by one of his colleagues at NPL, T.E. Stanton. This collaborative work was a good example of how the resources of NPL could be brought together. Digressing, as a point of historical interest, Lord Haldane, Secretary of State for War, suggested in 1909 that aeronautical work was needed and as a result an Advisory Committee for Aeronautics was set up, its inception being announced in Parliament by Prime Minister Asquith on 5 May. Asquith said that NPL had been asked to organise a special department to study experimental and theoretical work. In fact a small group of aerodynamicists had existed under L. Bairstow in NPL's Engineering Department since 1903. Bairstow was to leave in 1917 and Stanton, then Superintendent of Engineering Division, assumed control until 1920 when an Aerodynamics Division was formally set up in its own right, R.V. Southwell being appointed as its first Superintendent. Stanton's work, which Baker described, dealt with models tested in a wind tunnel that were equivalent to fully submerged hulls which in the absence of a free surface produced no wave-making. A series of photographs taken from beneath each model recorded the characteristics of the flow allowing the onset and degree of eddy making to be seen. From this, Baker judged the best length of run in the after body to avoid eddies and concluded that the best angle of the run should be 18°.

Baker's paper was enthusiastically received, he was later to be awarded the INA's gold medal for it, and encouraged him to follow up with another outstanding offering,[10] this time jointly with Kent. The paper included an original idea. A new law was proposed which indicated the manner in which the resistance due to transverse wave-making varied with hull length, L, speed and, in particular, hull fineness. Wave systems had been closely scrutinised on several models as part of the Rayleigh study and it was concluded that the speeds at which the familiar humps in the resistance curve occurred depended on $\sqrt{PL}$, P being the measure of fineness of the hull, the prismatic coefficient. Baker and Kent introduced a new speed constant to go with the established ones of Froude. The new constant which they called $\circledP$, connected ship speed, V, with its wave-making length and the prismatic coefficient. It was shown that the humps and hollows in a resistance curve for any form occurred at the same numerical value of $\circledP$. The designer aims to work in a hollow where economic speeds should occur. These hollows were stated by the authors to appear when $V/\sqrt{PL}$ equalled 1·5, 1·05 and 0·85 or below and that the position of humps and hollows could be controlled by introducing to the hull shape more hollowness forward at the same time as preserving the value of the prismatic coefficient. These findings were of great importance and applied to all mercantile vessels of ordinary form and moderate speed.

The resistance results from five models of varying form which were presented in 1913,[9] plotted to a base of $\circledP$, show up very clearly the incidence of critical hump speeds which occur successively at $\circledP$= 1, $^1/\sqrt{2}$, $^1/\sqrt{3}$ etc. To complete the diagram barge data from a Dumbarton tank test were included. Although Kent in later papers,[11] for example, forcefully advocated the use of $\circledP$ as a powerful instrument in design it never became popular. Pragmatic naval architects preferred a more direct way of recognising a superior form. This could simply be done by comparing resistance curves from similar hull forms at the same speed length ratio.

Following its introduction by Baker and Kent, $\circledP$ was used regularly by the William Froude National Tank and records of the period show model results plotted to a base of the new speed constant. The aim was to use accumulated data from models as an aid to future design where movements in the humps and hollows of the resistance curve might profitably be exploited following Baker's suggestions. Ultimately with (P) failing to become generally accepted the practice lapsed and data presentation based on (C) and speed length ratio reverted to. Soon, model results were scaled or extrapolated to two ship lengths following Froude's law of comparison, the actual ship length and a standard length (400 feet) at which all earlier and future tests could be compared. The practice is still in use today.

Seaplane Tests

Millar, Baker's other assistant, had helped considerably in the work leading up to Baker's first paper[9] but his talents were shown to the full when a request came to the Tank from the Advisory Committee for Aeronautics who wanted to design and test new hydro-aeroplane floats, devices which took the place of an aircraft's undercarriage to allow landing and take off on water. Seaplanes were to evolve as two types, land aircraft mounted on floats or flying boats where the fuselage was turned into a hull. Flying boats were generally used for larger sizes and float planes for smaller and faster types. The first work for the tank dealt with floats and existing ones in 1912 had toboggan-like bottoms that were found to be of high resistance. The National Tank's experiments were aimed at producing a float that would run dry and hopefully reduce the level of resistance. The special apparatus already described was needed to measure vertical and horizontal forces on the floats and also the all-important trimming moment. Initially, Baker worked with Millar, Baker's instinct for ship form leading him to recommend floats more ship-like in shape but with predominantly flat bottoms. The first experiments were promising and three reports were published by the ACA,[12, 13] written jointly by Baker and Millar. Thereafter the work was led and controlled by Millar who embarked on a large series of tests in which both float shape and its attitude to ahead motion were varied. Millar's appreciation of the mechanics of planing at high speed was impressive and he saw the advantage of stepped hulls whereby the planing surface of the float was separated in two parts which encouraged a reduction in the total trimming moment. Eventually Millar was able to recommend the most efficient form for the floats that were subsequently used in later aircraft. A mudguard added to a float was similar to the spray rail used in high speed craft today and was fitted to throw water clear of the float's side at high speeds. Millar presented a major paper,[14] in which he described both the design of the apparatus required for the tests and the best float shapes he had found.

He went to great lengths to explain the method of running which obviously required a painstaking balancing technique and a patient experimenter. It is interesting to note that the complicated apparatus which entailed much workshop time and the extensive series of tests devoted to each float were charged to the ACA at the rate of £25 per float. Similar work was being done at

Washington by Richardson,[15] and Millar was pleased to report good general agreement with his own work. Lest it be thought that the very small float models that Millar tested would have suffered a similar fate in terms of unreliable results as Baker's ¾ and 1⅓ metre models tested earlier in the small tank, the high speeds at which Millar's were tested produced Reynolds numbers well above two million and were thus conducted in a region of fully developed turbulent flow. This was the first genuine high speed work to be done in the Tank and preceded the work on flying boats which followed in later years.

Effect of Hull Surface Finish

With more and more models being tested, the problems which some of these highlighted acted as a stimulus for future research work, a perfectly natural and satisfactory state of affairs. One such problem concerned the treatment of hull appendages. Most earlier models had been tested without appendages such as bilge keels or shaft bossings, the tests becoming known as naked resistance experiments. When appendages were fitted, Baker was unwilling to apply the model measurement of appendage resistance in full to the ship and recommended a programme of work to the Tank Advisory Committee to investigate the matter. This was accepted and from the early work there also developed a substantial body of research which looked at the effect of hull surface finish on ship resistance. Initially this took the form of investigating the effect of ship plate terminations, in particular butts, on resistance and running in parallel was Baker's interest in model surface finish which led him to another comparative exercise this time with Taylor at Washington. Models at the Washington tank were made in wood and finished with a varnished surface. A similar model form was tested at Teddington when experiments were conducted on the wax model with its surface finished successively as that naturally occurring after manufacture, freshly coated with a shellac varnish, the same with blacklead rubbed in and finally with a red lead paint finish. The results from all four surfaces were indistinguishable and led Baker to conclude that provided the surface was smooth and free from grit, the same results would be obtained. This was useful to know for it was conceivable that some future models might be made in materials other than wax. Yet, as these researches began to make progress they were soon to be disturbed and delayed by the impending war with Germany.

REFERENCES

1. Report of the National Physical Laboratory for the year ending 1911.
2. Newton R.N., "Standard model technique at AEW, Haslar", trans. RINA 1960.
3. Baker G.S., "The William Froude National Tank"—Part II, trans. INA, 1912.
4. Rayleigh Lord, "Philosophical Magazine", September 1909.
5. Idle G., "The effect of bilge keels upon the rolling of Lightships"—Part I, trans. INA, 1912.

6. Baker G.S., *Ibid*—Part II.
7. Baker G.S., "Model experiments on the resistance of mercantile ship forms", trans. INA, 1914.
8. Gibson A.H. and Thompson J.J., "Experiments on 'suction' or interaction between passing vessels", trans. INA, 1913.
9. Baker G.S., "Methodical experiments with mercantile ship forms", trans. INA, 1913.
10. Baker G.S. and Kent J.L., "Effect of form and size on the resistance of ships", trans. INA, 1913.
11. Kent J.L., "Influence of prismatic coefficient and length on resistance of ships, and further model experiments with mercantile ship forms", trans. INA, 1915.
12. Baker G.S. and Millar G.H., "Some experiments in connection with the design of floats for hydro-aeroplanes", Report of ACA, No. 70, 1912–1913.
13. Baker G.S. and Millar G.H., "Experiments with models of hydro-aeroplane floats", Reports of ACA, Nos. 98 and 99, 1913–1914.
14. Millar G.H., "Some notes on the design of floats for hydro-aeroplanes", trans. INA, 1914.
15. Richardson H.C., "Hydrodynamic experiments with flying boat hulls", Smithsonian Miscellaneous Collections, Vol. 62, April 1914.

CHAPTER 5

THE FIRST WORLD WAR

The major threats to shipping at the outbreak of the war, apart from actual surface conflict, were submarines, torpedoes and mines, and the Tank was to become involved with tests on defence systems, new types of mine and the firing of torpedoes. This was not all, for apart from conventional tests on ships which included destroyers and fast small naval craft, there was a rapid growth in flying boat tests.

Just after the outbreak of the war, but not as a direct result of it, changes were made to the Advisory Committee to broaden the interest taken in the work of the William Froude National Tank. The original membership of 10 was increased by adding Sir Kenneth Anderson of the UK Chamber of Shipping, representatives of the engineering and shipbuilding institutions in the north-east and Scotland (Sir Charles Parsons and P.D. Ewing, respectively) and finally C. Livingston who represented the Liverpool Steam Ship Owners' Association.

The immediate effect of the war on the Tank was the loss of certain staff to one or other of the armed forces. The departure of Millar, Studd and Unsted may not today seem many but it cut the staff by one third, a deficit that was not immediately replaced. Overall, in NPL, 50 out of the 210 men joined up. As a short-term measure Baker tried to recruit suitably skilled people but found them difficult to find and secure on a temporary basis. Those who left met with a variety of experiences. Millar joined the Marine Brigade which under Churchill was sent to defend Antwerp but was captured and with other prisoners sent to Doberan near Rostock. Undeterred he plotted an escape and succeeded, taking with him a compass stolen from a Russian, a map from a Frenchman and enough food for a few days. Thus equipped he broke through the wire defences of the camp and somehow reached the Baltic where finding a rowing boat he pushed out to sea in an attempt to cross the 40 miles to Denmark. This apparent act of madness was fortunately cut short by a ferry which spotted him, picked him up and once ashore at Gedser he made his way back to England to relate his tale to the delight of his colleagues at the Tank. In a few weeks he had returned to duty with the Royal Naval Air Service. His experience of flying boat technology did not perhaps go unnoticed and he joined *HMS Furious*, the naval ship soon to be involved in early attempts at landing aircraft on ships (in 1917 a Sopwith Pup was landed successfully on *Furious* under way and led to the ship being fitted with a rear landing deck). Millar became a pilot but tragically met his death in April 1918 when his seaplane crashed shortly after take off. Studd became an Army captain commanding a heavy battery but during prolonged action suffered severe shock. After a period of convalescence in England he returned to active service. Unsted also joined the Army, served in France, and was decorated. With these three absent the staff numbered just nine until the end of 1914 and it was not until the early summer of the following year that more were secured on a permanent basis. Baker was acutely aware of the importance to the national effort of the entirely new kind of work which came to the Tank and rose to its challenge. His appetite for work was immense and he drove his staff unceasingly to greater efforts. The response was magnificent and many hours of overtime were worked. In 1913 the number of experimental runs conducted on the tank carriage was almost 2,000. In the first year of the war this increased to 3,000, continuing at this level and at times exceeding it for the next three years, roughly equivalent to a 60-hour working week. As a result the research programme, so valued by the Advisory Committee and Baker himself, suffered and less and less of this work became possible as the war proceeded. The long-term effect so far as the main purpose of the National Tank was concerned worried Baker yet there was no option but follow the urgent needs of the moment and the Tank responded with enthusiasm to the unique and interesting problems set, the solutions to which must have excited and given the staff much satisfaction and no doubt amusement too. In June 1915 Baker was at last able to increase his staff to 14 and in doing so recruited the first woman member, Miss E.M. Keary from Newnham College, Cambridge. Three other newcomers were mechanics who brought the workshop numbers up to eight. The need for a replacement for Millar was urgent because requests for further work on seaplane floats were coming from the ACA and Miss Keary was employed for this purpose.

WAR PROJECTS

Protection of Ships

The first direct approach to the Tank for tests pertaining to the War came from Alfred Yarrow who was interested in trying out an arrangement of nets and wires slung from a ship so that under way it would be reasonably protected from torpedoes and mines. A suitable model was made and equipped with rigidly set side screens covering two thirds of the length of the hull equally disposed about amidships and supported port and starboard by two rows of booms, the lower edges of the screens being about 1½ metres below the water. The screens overhung the ship's side by about six metres. At the bow, as a protection from mines, horizontal wires stretched from the forward edge of the torpedo screens to projecting struts from the ship's stem. In the tank spherical balls of wax were moored to represent mines. Not surprisingly the added resistance due to screens, booms and wires was very high suggesting large penalties in propulsive power and a consequent reduction in ship speed. The Tank was not at all happy when scaling the results to ship size in view of the problems already experienced in model tests with ship hull appendages. The whole idea seemed unpromising particularly when it was seen that the mines entangled themselves in the wires and were dragged along with the ship. A closer spacing of the wires improved matters but increased resistance and although a workable arrangement was eventually found, overall the scheme appeared unlikely to gain acceptance. An alternative was to fit large external side swellings in the region of a ship's magazine spaces. The bulges could not extend beyond the beam of the ship but widths of almost 3 metres were possible. Of course with the swellings filled with water a large increase in displacement was inevitable and again the increment of resistance was high (this time the Tank was very confident of its prediction) and for a 120 metre cruiser, speed dropped from 22 to $18\frac{3}{4}$ knots at a given power. It was too much perhaps to expect that such a crude arrangement of screens and wires would work although by about 1916 side nets were in fact developed successfully. Also a solution was later found to allow side bulges to be adopted. *HMS Hood*, the battle cruiser launched in 1918, was fitted with bulges the resistance of which diminished speed by less than a knot.

Mines and Minesweeping

The mines in use in 1914 were spherical and about a metre in diameter. When moored on the sea bed they would not keep to the desired depth when tidal flows exceeded 2 knots. They were swept under by the force of the tide sometimes to the sea bottom. Following a request from *HMS Vernon*, the Royal Navy's shore establishment at Portsmouth where there was a mining school, tests were made on 1/5-scale models to try to correct the defect. It was soon found that real improvements were possible if a mine was given more reserve buoyancy and *Vernon* redesigned a standard mine to give it 20 per cent reserve buoyancy and a model was tested in the tank. It was attached to the carriage on a gantry and immersed at different depths and towed through the water at corresponding tidal speeds up to 7 knots. Although the new design held very satisfactorily to its required depth at all speeds, an oscillatory instability and sideways drift began at about 5 knots. The Tank suggested changing the shape of the mine and tests on a cylindrical body with a cone shaped nose and on a body of more streamlined shape (Tank models 160 and 169) gave good results on both, particularly the latter when an angled fin was added aft to eliminate a sideways drift. *Vernon* were reluctant to accept this more complicated shape so a return was made to the spherical mine but with a greater amount of reserve buoyancy (50 per cent) provided. Behaviour then came up to requirements.

Enemy mines had to be destroyed by first cutting them from their moorings. This led to the development of the paravane. Shaped like a cigar, a paravane was towed on each side of a ship by wires attached to the bow and adjusted to run slightly below the level of the keel. The towing wires, coming into contact with the mooring line of a mine deflected it away from the ship and led the mooring line to a powerful wire cutter at the nose of the paravane where it was severed. Once cut and released the mine could then be destroyed by gunfire. The problem with the paravane which was brought to the Tank by the Admiralty and the Board of Invention and Research, was to ensure its ability to act like a fisherman's otter board and force the towing wire outwards away from the ship's side as well as keeping it to a specified depth below the water. This was not easy with the models sent to the Tank. Initial experiments examined the towing behaviour of different types, an Admiralty pattern and one each from Commander Usborne and Dennistoun (later Sir Dennistoun) Burney. None of these proved entirely satisfactory and needed modifications to the shape of fin fitted on each which was intended to provide the necessary bias to allow the paravane to swing out to one side as it was towed through the water. Erratic diving characteristics had to be eliminated and after many experiments covering changes to the weight distribution, fin geometry and its position, a combination of the Usborne and Burney designs appeared best. To hold the paravane to a fixed depth in the water, two rudders were fitted at the tail-end and the right combination of rudder angle and depth as well as length of wire was eventually found. The development of the paravane as used during the war on deep draught warships allowing them to cross minefields was attributed to Usborne and Burney but the data and guidance from the tank tests were indispensable to them and Baker was gratified to receive in 1915 a letter of appreciation from the Lords of the Admiralty.

Concurrent with the various tests on mines and paravanes a large programme had begun at the request of the Admiralty on the design and behaviour of naval kites and floats. These were part of the development of the new *Oropesa* minesweeping system, a system whereby a single minesweeper towed a long wire which carried a kite, wire cutters, otter and float. The kite, positioned about 10 metres from the stern of the minesweeper from which the wire was towed, dived under the surface as the ship accelerated from rest and stayed under the water to a desired depth. The wire stretched beyond the kite for about 170 metres to an otter which, like the paravane, swept the wire sideways keeping it at a distance from the ship and a float a little aft of the otter brought the free end of the wire to the surface. The cutters were spaced at intervals along the wire. The kite had to act in a similar way to a fisherman's otter but in a vertical rather than horizontal plane.

The tests at the Tank were concerned with each of the items that made up the total assembly, the solution to the best type of kite proving most difficult. Those originally tried would either dive and behave unpredictably or, having dived, would soon develop a jerking action. Three kinds of kites led to exhaustive tests and the choice rested between a standard service type, a monoplane arrangement or a kite shaped like a flatfish. The service type had already been tried at sea and attempts to stabilise it had led to the attachment of side boards. A full-size kite was brought to the tank and the boards adjusted to allow a large number of different settings to be tried and also a range of different angles of the towing wire. Improvements were seen but the familiar jerking tendency could not be wholly eradicated. The monoplane kite had two flat surfaces, rectangular in plan, with aerofoil sections. The surface at the front end was much larger than at the rear and the two were connected together by three longitudinal fins. This type almost succeeded and at 9 knots gave a good steady pull of 224 pounds with the towing wire at 22° to the vertical but slight intermittent instability still persisted. After several modifications the preferred behaviour came from the flatfish type, a kite which also had two flat surfaces of similar area and proportion to the monoplane. In elevation the underside of the forward surface was aerofoil in shape whereas the after and smaller surface was flat and inclined downwards. Pull was less but the kite remained stable. Experiments were next carried out which simulated the process leading up to the cutting of the swept mine. The angle of the wire swept out by the otter (not present in the experiment) was reproduced by fixing one end of the wire to a supporting boom fixed to the moving carriage and with a mine moored in the tank a metre below the water runs were made with a cutter positioned at various distances from the kite. The pull of the mine's mooring line was important and the tautness in the wire from the kite had to be sufficient to allow the mine to be led smoothly to the cutter. At 10 knots a large gap between kite and cutter was not good and the angle of the wire proved to be quite critical.

The choice and design of float to join to the otter was not so difficult although since the model tests were conducted in calm water, full-scale tests in rough water were later to become necessary. Several configurations of float were tried in the tank—hydroplane, toboggan and pram shaped types. There was little to choose between the three but in tests at sea off Dover when the full-size floats were towed from a destroyer with a kite providing the downward inclination of the wire, the pram type, after a slight change in its buoyancy and with its rear end open to the water, was best.

The whole arrangement was now ready for full-scale trials with the minesweeper *Oropesa* and the new system eventually came into use just before the end of the war to clear the northern mine barrage laid across the North Sea from the Orkneys to the Norwegian coast. Between the two world wars it was to be improved by the substitution of multi-plane otters for a single otter and better cutters were also introduced.

Defence Against Submarines

Submarines were established in the 19th century, Britain's first vessels being largely based on J.P. Holland's petrol driven designs which were used mainly in coastal waters. Germany on the other hand waited until diesel engines became reliable before building in very large numbers the *unterseeboot* or U boat which with its operational ability in oceans made it such a potent threat. Although both British and German submarines could remain submerged for limited periods only before needing to surface and recharge batteries, they could nevertheless penetrate defence systems.

The Submarine Attack Committee wanted to find the best method of supporting defence nets, and the Booms Trial Committee asked for a study on the behaviour of certain net configurations when attacked by a submarine. The required strength of the nets was not known and it was hoped that they could stop a submarine from piercing them at top speed. The staff at the Tank were faced with several problems; the manufacture and fitting of a free-running model—a task that had never been attempted, the rigging of nets and devices to measure their movement and tension, and a means of recording on film the behaviour of the submarine as it approached and struck a net. Commander Bircham and Lt. Powell of the Cameronians helped at the Tank, Bircham bringing with him valuable expertise on underwater filming.

A 1/18th scale model of an E class submarine was built in wood and fitted with representative horizontal and vertical fins aft and a bow plane forward. The fins were movable and the vertical one could be adjusted so that when the model was submerged and propelling itself it would follow a straight course to the net. To bias it allowing an oblique approach a small fin fitted to the superstructure aft could be pre-set to a suitable angle. Two propellers positioned port and starboard at the horizontal fin were driven by two electric motors installed in the model, powered by 28 accumulators placed near amidships. With all 28 accumulators in use at the same time a top speed of 11·7 knots was possible. By distributing ballast inside the model, correct transverse metacentric height and rolling period when submerged were set and the full-scale longitudinal radius of gyration, assumed as 20 per cent of hull length, represented, or nearly so, after timing oscillations of the model in air and rearranging the ballast where possible.

The nets which spanned the full width of the Tank were supported on floats in the water connected together by jackstays loaded at their ends. Drawing on experience from earlier tests the Tank drew up the design of the floats which had to be capable of resisting tidal flows, arranging their buoyancy to be well forward and giving them spoon-shaped bows and open V shaped ends. The material of the nets needed to be hard and capable of maintaining shape and size in the water. Trials with various materials led to a suitable gauge and the assembled netting was brought to its correct scale weight by suspending sinkers at its bottom edge. The mechanism to record the movement of the net on impact with the submarine model consisted of a weight attached to a string from the jackstay led over pulleys to a light carriage which ran over levelled rails. The tension in the jackstay varied with the movement of the string. On impact as the jackstay moved it lifted the weight and the distance travelled was recorded by a dotter which was activated every 1/50 of a second by an electrical circuit synchronised with a tuning fork. This clever arrangement owed its success to the great skill of Wise, the workshop mechanic who had shown himself to be an engineer capable of precision and ingenuity.

The experimental technique had to be worked out carefully and it was found best to lock the submarine model to the carriage, accelerate the carriage at the same time as running the propellers up to their required speed. The carriage was then stopped about 6 metres from the net and the model released. Tests were conducted at different submarine speeds, approach directions and immersion and produced a fascinating array of data and film record. At slow approach speeds the overall strength of the net and its resistance to movement through water prevented the submarine's progress but at higher speeds the net bulged on impact to ensnare the bow. When the forward movement of the submarine had been arrested the backward pull of the jackstay was often sufficient to overcome the propeller thrust and push the model backwards, upending it. On the other hand depending on the speed and make up of the net's mesh impact was such that some of the wires broke before a bulge could form.

The stresses in the net wires were complicated by several factors dependent on the nature of impact. The bow of the submarine might enter a mesh or catch on a horizontal wire. Either way, the push was resisted by the water resistance of the net and the pull in the vertical wires locally and as the net bulged, the jackstay and floats moved under the influence of the impact. The net was seen at its most vulnerable when the submarine attacked it near the surface of the water when the combined effects of the resisting forces in jackstay and floats were at their greatest. The breaking load of the net wires had to exceed the highest force measured and the experiments showed that the speed of the submarine that could be stopped by a given net varied approximately as the breaking load of the wires and for best results jackstay strain should be about a third of the breaking load.

The experiments must have posed many problems and one can imagine the frustration of the experimenters as they struggled to get things to work. Even today with modern sophisticated equipment, free-running models cause innumerable problems and often break down so that in 1916 experiments of this kind carried out for the first time, and moreover with an underwater model, must have been plagued with difficulty. Baker, never a man of inexhaustible patience, would have supervised rigorously and driven the work to a successful outcome. At any rate some of the experiments were witnessed by several Admiralty Lords who evidently departed well satisfied and later sent a letter of appreciation to the Tank. The submarine model, unique in its day, lived to serve another purpose when the Board of Invention and Research asked the Tank to measure the change in pressure on the sea bottom due to a submarine travelling at speed. The false bottom to the tank which had been used in the earlier, Hawke-Olympic interaction tests was installed again and a mercury manometer was connected to a point on the false bottom which recorded pressure changes for a range of model speed and immersion.

Torpedoes

In late 1915 a conference was held in Portsmouth at *HMS Vernon* to which both Glazebrook, R.E. Froude and Baker were invited. The subject discussed was the firing of torpedoes from ships through submerged tubes. By 1913 the Royal Navy was using 21 inch diameter torpedoes developed from Whitehead's original 1867 design. The 21 inch torpedo was 22 feet long and carried a 330 pound charge at its head. Capable of 27 or 41 knots according to type its range was either 3,000 or 8,000 yards. An engine room positioned aft contained a Brotherhood reciprocating engine which drove two contra-rotating propellers and actuated the horizontal rudders that controlled the torpedoes' depth. A gyroscope housed in a buoyancy chamber at the tail of the torpedo connected to vertical rudders and provided constant course keeping. The conference at *Vernon* was called to discuss and seek ways of overcoming the problems currently experienced. Uncertainties needed clarification and amongst these were the significance of the proximity of the water surface on firing and knowledge of the loads and moments exerted on a torpedo as it left the tube and also its behaviour thereafter. The Tank was asked to arrange some experiments although it was realised that model conditions would be materially different to those at the ship.

Four wax models of ships were made representing *Calliope*, *Tiger*, *Renown* and *Hood*. For the torpedo to be of reasonable size very large models were required, *Hood*, 12 metres long, proving to be the largest ever to be made at the Tank. Each was fitted with a tube and torpedo and arrangements were made using compressed air to fire and eject from any of several tube positions, although the model torpedoes themselves were not fitted with propulsion apparatus. The experiments could only be of an observational kind and with the huge models fitted under the carriage a large number of firings were made from the model underway. In initial experiments the torpedo was positioned at the end of its bar, an equivalent 21 feet beyond the ship's side. Violent vibration was set up by the flow of water past the torpedo as the ship model made way at the test speeds of 22–33 knots. To eliminate this, local flow directions were obtained at different positions along the hull using an assembly of vanes and the best position for the tube (60 feet forward of *Hood* and *Tiger*'s after perpendicular) was found where no vibration at all occurred. Attention next turned to the forces acting on a torpedo once released and its subsequent motion. The Navy complained of deviations in path and a tendency for the torpedo to roll. This was confirmed in the experiments and it was decided to measure the forces on a released torpedo and, since the model torpedo had no motive force, to use a mathematical approach to estimate subsequent behaviour. A special rig was set up in the tank dock and large ¼-scale torpedoes were fired at different angles of yaw. $^{Force}/V^2$ ratios were obtained but Baker was not entirely happy with the method of scaling and did not place great reliance on the full-scale figures obtained. He believed the characteristic shape of the $^F/V^2$ curves and their relatively high level to be valid and argued that reasonable conclusions could be drawn. Lateral forces on the torpedo were also obtained and the mathematical approach, following long correspondence with R.E. Froude, used the measured data as a basis and indicated how the metacentric height of the torpedo could be selected to reduce roll. Shortly after the war *Vernon* asked for resistance tests on eight different types of "barless" beam torpedoes. Wooden models were made (numbers 515A–J) to a ¾-scale and towed from a strut. At an immersion of 2 metres, resistance was entirely skin friction and W. Froude's speed index of 1·85 was used in scaling the results to a full-scale speed of 45 knots.

TESTS FOR FIRMS

The exciting and dramatic experiments that were going on as a consequence of the war should not be allowed to overshadow the more conventional work that had still to be fitted in. This naturally concerned resistance tests on new ships both of commercial and naval kind. New ocean-going liners were held in abeyance but the demand for large numbers of cargo vessels led to the desire for standard vessels that could be built quickly. These were straight line forms of fabricated construction and the designs tested at the Tank showed length of run and the number of chines introduced to the hull shape to be important and after several modifications to different designs resistance was brought to within a few per cent of the more conventional curved frame ship.

Altogether during the war years 120 models were tested for private firms, an average of about 30 per year. The tests were almost all concerned with hull resistance but an unusual series of experiments were conducted on a model of the *City of Lucknow* for the Board of Trade and the Ellerman line. It was required to know the effect of bilging certain holds in the ship to see whether by making them airtight stability could be improved. The model, complete with all its compartments, double bottoms, holds, etc. was built and simulated cargo put inside to give the correct permeabilities. The model was then floated in the tank and flooding experiments conducted as various cargo spaces were opened to the sea.

Resistance tests included experiments on destroyers and smaller higher speed craft intended for submarine chasing. The design technology of the latter was by now well advanced stimulated largely by the interest in flying boats and any way of increasing the speed of surface craft became important. One such idea was to feed air to a moving hull so that air rather than water became the resisting medium. In 1915 the Admiralty commissioned tests on three separate forms. The first of these, known as a Craig design, was a two step form with an odd ram bow, the second, a Pratt design, a hydroplane type without ram and the third, attributed to Byles, looked more like an attenuated destroyer form. The models were towed at corresponding speeds up to 40 knots which for the shorter Pratt design was equivalent to a maximum Froude number of 1·5, a genuine planing speed. Ventilators were fitted in the after body of each model and pipes were brought up to the top of the model and bent forward. The ram bow form was disastrous. With pipes open or closed to the air all seemed well at speeds up to 15 knots although ventilation had no effect on resistance but with pipes open at 28 knots the model suddenly went out of control, nose dived and finished at the bottom of the tank. After repair the experiments were repeated, this time with pipes closed, only for the model to nose dive again at 25 knots. The ram was blamed—even at low speeds water flowed awkwardly at its lower surface and up to deck height level. The shorter hydroplane fared better, lifting and planing at 40 knots but at a second lighter displacement a dangerous transverse instability appeared which persisted whether the pipes were open or not. The third form ran with good stability but was very wet and gave higher levels of resistance. But the purpose of the experiments was to see whether air lubrication worked. It did not. Subsequent attempts in later years on different types of ships were similarly frustrated. Maybe, had it been possible to pump air to the underside of the hull at higher velocities, some success might have been experienced, but it was not until much later when the hovercraft principle was invented that the frictional resistance due to a hull's contact with water was eliminated and only then by dint of lifting the complete hull from the water, turning it into a hybrid ship–aircraft vehicle.

Alfred Yarrow who became a baronet in 1916 was aiming for faster destroyer forms. He commissioned tests on a 1916 Yarrow design, a destroyer 82 metres long of block coefficient 0·524. It seems that Yarrow thought this to be an excellent form which might however be improved a little by reducing the stern overhang. The results from different lengths of overhang in the Tank's resistance tests were more or less the same, but Baker remembered earlier experiments on the destroyer *HMS Firedrake* (Tank model 39) tested in 1912, in which by changing parallel middle body, a favourite hobbyhorse, improvements had been made at higher speeds than Baker had at that time experienced. He thus proposed to Yarrow a redistribution of displacement and keeping the same hull midship section but reducing parallel middle body he easily achieved a finer entrance forward for the same displacement, at the expense of a fuller afterbody. Baker's idea (model 226) worked and for the same power and displacement the revised hull was ¾ knot faster than the Yarrow form. Sir Alfred was later to give eloquent praise to the Tank when he publicly credited the Tank with drawing out the lines of the world's fastest destroyer.[1]

RESEARCH

Skin Friction

Before the full effects of the war were felt, Baker was able to complete by the end of 1914 an important item of research which had in fact begun as early as 1911 following initiatives put forward by the Advisory Committee at that time. This was an appraisal of W. Froude's, Gebers' and Zahm's work on skin friction resistance and for good measure included Baker's own latest work where several model planks had been made and towed in the tank. Froude's empirical formula for frictional resistance, $R = fSV^n$, which derived from his early experiments with thin planks, was serving the purpose of model experimenters well but it did not explain the mechanism of skin friction. Following Lord Rayleigh's demonstration of the connection between Froude number and that defined by Osborne Reynolds, who in his classic pipe experiments had shown the significance of laminar and turbulent flow, the feeling grew that Reynolds rather than Froude number should be used as a basis for the estimation of skin friction. Baker's latest research[2] published before the North East Coast Institution in 1915 included plottings of frictional resistance against Reynolds number, one of the earliest examples of this form of presentation. Baker really began a huge debate which was to continue for many years and involve several different friction formulations from such eminent workers as Prandtl, Schlicting, Schoenherr and, in later years, the Tank's own Hughes. Taking the work of Froude, Gebers and Zahm which stemmed from experiments with smooth planks, of which Zahm's were in air, and his own latest data, Baker was able to collapse the results on to a single curve which in logarithmic form became practically straight over the higher ranges of speed and enabled an extrapolation to ship speeds. Gebers' and Baker's results fell below Froude's but this was expected since Gebers of the Vienna tank and Baker had both gone to great lengths to ensure that the planks they towed had very smooth surfaces with carefully faired endings whereas it is almost certain that Froude's results contained a degree of residual resistance. Despite the linearity found, Baker was unwilling to suggest an extrapolation formula but instead advocated further experiments on large-scale planks to determine the correct extension of the curve he had found. In introducing the all important effects of surface roughness, since ships of the day had irregular surfaces arising from overlapping plates and butts, Baker included model results obtained on *Iris* fitted in turn with raised and sunken strakes of plates and butts. The measurements showed frictional resistance to increase by almost 4 per cent for plate edges and 10 per cent for plate edges and butts and allowed Baker to arrive at additional lines that ran parallel to but above his line for smooth planks. The paper attracted enormous interest, no fewer than 26 speakers contributing to the discussion and the award of the North East Coast Institution's "Shipbuilding" gold medal came as no surprise.

Seaplanes

The war saw a great advance in the development of seaplanes and it was realised that they could be used in several capacities two of which were minelaying and submarine detection. Much of the development was due to Curtiss in America and his "America" design was an attempt at transatlantic flight before the war. British designers extended Curtiss's ideas, the F boats which were developed at Felixstowe being the result. They were eventually used to fly over strictly controlled courses in the shape of large spiders' webs. The North Sea was scoured in this way and in 1917 a Curtiss large "America" did in fact locate, bomb and sink a German U boat. The involvement of the Tank in the early years of the war was largely concerned with the development of the CE1 flying boat, a machine which preceded the F type. In the CE1, the tail abaft the second step of the hull was removed and in the tank tests the model ran successfully without porpoising, a defect which had often plagued previous designs when they were pressed to higher speeds. The wing floats of the CE1 were also tested up to take off speeds. The testing rig and measuring system devised by Millar was refined to provide a technique better suited to the actual machines and to allow the use of larger models.[3] Later, as the whole field of seaplane work expanded and continued into post-war years, Bottomley became involved and eventually the ACA agreed to bear the salaries of Miss Keary, Bottomley and a carpenter until most of the investigations were complete. These were soon to include tests on larger flying boat hulls comprising a main fuselage body with side floats fitted to the wings, the question of transverse stability receiving special attention in tests which were done to find the best position of the wing floats.

The rapid growth in seaplane technology had made it increasingly necessary that predictions of power based on model results should be seen to be accurate. The Tank in scaling its measurements to full size had followed, in general, Froude's law but had made certain assumptions concerning the skin friction correction. With the building of the CE1 machine both its Authorities and Baker combined to carry out a series of towing tests at sea off the Isle of Grain.[4] The Royal Navy provided a destroyer which towed number 97 machine at a series of speeds up to 20 knots. A towrope 90 metres long connected the two. Resistance was measured simply, but apparently quite satisfactorily, from weights hung on a pan set up in the seaplane and speed through the water was taken from a Dutch log. Ten runs were made in short seas with wave height about ½ metre. For the seaplane weight of 4,000 pounds the maximum pull at 20·2 knots came out as 870 pounds. To complete the picture the Royal Aircraft Establishment at Farnborough tested a complete model of the seaplane in their wind tunnel and arrived at estimated figures for air resistance. At the same time the staff at the Tank made their own estimate of this. A comparison between model and full-scale resistance could now be made. At the top towing speed of 20·2 knots the predicted water resistance from the tank test was 679 pounds and when adding to this the RAE estimated air resistance of 201 pounds (which was within a few pounds of the Tank figure) the sum at 880 pounds compared very favourably with the pull at sea of 870 pounds, a heartening result for the Tank. Such good agreement was seen at all speeds between 15 and 20 knots; at low speeds (9–11½ knots) the Tank's figure for water resistance fell off leading to a lower estimated total than the full scale pull by about 10 per cent.

In addition to the work which led to the CE1 machine, comparisons of larger P, F and N types of flying boat were made[5] with the aim of reducing the resistance of a 32,000 pounds machine currently under construction. At such a late stage the alterations possible were necessarily limited but model experiments did show that a considerable reduction in resistance could be obtained from a more efficient lifting surface at the step. Before the end of the War a request came from the Aircraft Production Department of the Ministry of Munitions for an investigation into the impact of flying boat hulls when alighting or running on water. Bottomley took charge of this work[6] and with Wise designed apparatus capable of dropping a model into the water as it moved over it at speeds up to 6 metres per second, equivalent to a full-scale air speed of 60 m.p.h.

A model was made of the hull of a CE1 type machine but with alternative transverse sections in the after half of its body to give three different forms. The section of the first (model 377A) was perfectly flat and horizontal, 377B introduced a pronounced V section and 377C softened this by having a hollowed shape. Each of these models were tested in turn and fixed to a vertical rod at any desired fore and aft angle. The rod was free to move against rollers, its vertical movement being transmitted to a paper strip which could move horizontally over a platform by means of an enlarging lever. The record of movement as the model was dropped was drawn by a vibrating pen synchronised with a tuning fork which beat 155 times per second. To deduce impact or slamming force a space diagram against time was prepared after analysing the results from each experiment which showed constant acceleration as the model fell in air followed by varying retardation after it struck the water and the maximum force of impact was the product of the falling mass and maximum retardation.

The experiments did not produce surprising results. As would be expected impact forces reduced with speed of flight and low landing, but it was seen very clearly that model 377B with its V sections forward gave the lowest impact at all speeds above 25 m.p.h. Of particular value was the formula for the force of impact that Bottomley was able to deduce. This included the seaplane's air speed, its weight and angle of approach and a constant deduced from the experiments.

Transverse Stability of Ships

A small but unique piece of research conducted by Baker and Miss Keary looked into the loss of transverse stability of ships under way, a phenomenon first seen at the Tank during some of the fast seaplane tests. Because of the war and the shortage of time for a systematic research programme Baker and Miss Keary worked with fewer models than they would have preferred but with data from six, one a destroyer form, they measured the change in transverse metacentric height GM from its value at rest for a range of speed allowing the models as they were towed freedom in roll. For low speed mercantile forms they detected a slight reduction but in the destroyer, GM fell away rapidly at speeds above the main resistance hump. At the maximum design speed GM had reduced from its value at rest by 20 per cent. Their paper[7] was the first of its kind on the subject and anticipated the dangerous condition that can arise in high-speed craft when a loll develops due to loss in transverse stability.

Hull Appendages

The research recommended by the Advisory Committee just before the war included an attempt to resolve the uncertainty concerning the scaling of ship hull appendage resistance from measured model values. Baker had measured the resistance of struts of different scale just before the outbreak of war and now Stanton had tested some of these at high Reynolds number in a wind tunnel. Baker was able to show, as an example, that the estimated resistance of a full size strut from a 1/24-scale model was approximately twice the actual result. This was the genesis of Baker's scale effect correction factor for small hull appendages and the practice of halving the model resistance increments due to appendages such as shaft support brackets is still followed at BMT.

In the midst of all the activity connected with projects for the war the NPL was pleased to welcome King George V who visited the laboratory in November 1917. Like the Tank, NPL's other departments had been actively concerned with the war effort, the Gauge Department for instance undertaking a large number of tests on gauges for gun ammunition and the Engineering Department with its Aerodynamic section were testing aeroplanes, airships and kite balloons. Glazebrook (now Sir Richard) brought the King to the Tank where he was shown round by Baker, Kent and Wise. Models of the submarine, a standard ship and the large wax *Hood* used in the torpedo firing tests were on display and an experiment on the carriage demonstrated the action of an otter, part of the *Oropesa* system, as it was towed through the water.

The demands of the war had shown once and for all the value of a model testing facility. Sir Richard Glazebrook in a lecture before the Royal Institution[8] reviewed the work of the NPL and was able to say with confidence that the Tank had repaid its cost many times in the services rendered to naval warfare. A tangible tribute was the award in 1919 of the OBE to Baker yet many thought the recognition insufficient.

The war had greatly increased the workload of both the Tank and other NPL divisions and the essential research work undertaken for Government led to it being carried out under formal contract conditions which imposed financial management unfamiliar to NPL's Executive Committee. It soon became clear that should NPL's involvement with Government continue after the war a radical change in management policies would become necessary. It was equally clear, in those more enlightened days, that the Government itself would need to be involved with scientific and industrial research for fear of jeopardising the nation's future competitiveness. By 1918 the Government was determined to bring together its resources and formed an Imperial Trust for the encouragement of Scientific and Industrial Research into which the William Froude National Tank was absorbed. The income of the Tank, which included money received from the original guarantors whom it will be remembered agreed in 1908 to contribute annually for a period of 10 years to the new tank, was in future to be controlled by the Committee of the Privy Council for Scientific and Industrial Research with the responsibility for the management of the Tank remaining with NPL's Executive Committee. The Tank Advisory Committee was preserved and continued as a recommending body. The ordinary working expenses of the Tank were to be met out of the funds voted by Parliament and fees received from private firms would go to the Tank. It was agreed that the balance of money received from the guarantors would be held by the Trustees of the Imperial Trust as an endowment fund for research or an enlargement to Tank buildings or equipment as became necessary. A year later the Trust itself was absorbed into a new Government department, the Department of Scientific and Industrial Research (DSIR). By coincidence, this new department grew out of the Naval Board of Invention, set up in 1915, which had sent to the Tank so many requests for model tests on paravanes and floats.

The DSIR at once took the whole of NPL under its wing and had it not been for the Royal Society's active interest in NPL this would have occurred naturally. As it was a compromise was needed and the arrangement reached was that NPL, including of course the Tank, would become a sub-division or out-station of DSIR, the department being in control of financial and administrative matters whilst the responsibility for scientific policy rested with the Royal Society. Unfortunately the process of absorption led to disagreement and acrimonious exchanges between Sir Richard Glazebrook and the DSIR senior official, Sir Frank Heath over proper staff numbers and salaries. Heath was not a scientist and it is hardly surprising that their views were irreconcilable. Glazebrook reacted sharply to what he saw as the department's overbearing attitude towards scientists and the implication that they should be regarded at a lower level to their administrative equivalents. Glazebrook won in the end, certainly over the numbers and calibre of staff required, but the impasse over salaries dragged on, being satisfactorily resolved only in recent years. Nevertheless, despite these difficult beginnings DSIR flourished to become an outstanding department and an excellent rapport and understanding between administrators and scientists was built up, so much so that many of today's older scientists remember with nostalgia the "good old days" of the DSIR.

The changes in a sense came as a relief to the Tank since guarantor funding was expected to stop in a year or two and the future financial position of the Tank needed consideration. Now its finances were in the hands of a Government department which needed to submit to the Treasury estimates of expenditure supplied by its various out-stations such as NPL. This did not affect the Tank greatly since its Superintendent was now called upon to submit to NPL's Executive Committee his own proposals for research which of course rested with the recommendations of the Advisory Committee. In practice these recommendations were rarely seriously reduced. However, the whole financial cost of maintaining the Tank and its work was not expected to come from Government alone and naturally the Tank hoped that contributions would continue to come in from guarantors and others, not only for the prosperity of the Tank but as a means of maintaining a lively interest in its work amongst shipowners and builders. In making this known, subscribers were invited to suggest areas of work which they would like to see followed. Baker too was never slow to avail himself of the opportunity of extolling the value of model experiments and his lecture to the Liverpool Engineering Society[9] is a typical early example. It was at this time too that Baker spoke to a wider audience in his first book.[10] It described the work of several experimenters including those at the National Tank and used the results to give guidance in ship design, much of which remains valid today.

At the end of the war in November 1918 the Tank and its staff took stock. Unsted returned from active service to take up his earlier position but Studd decided on a career in teaching. A few newcomers had in the last few months of the war joined the Tank and included A.W. Riddle on the experimental side (in those days such members of staff were graded as Observers). The total staff was now 18, nine in the workshop and nine on the scientific side. The loss of Millar was a blow and his senior position was taken by Kent who now became an Assistant and effectively the deputy Superintendent. Miss Keary was made a junior assistant and Bottomley a senior observer. As to the work of the Tank it had now become clear that tests for private firms had advanced considerably beyond that originally anticipated. This had led to a comfortable financial position, a balance of £4,680 having accumulated. It was hoped that the natural growth of test work would continue side by side with research in which case further increases in staff would become necessary. So far as research was concerned a programme had been approved. Kent was to take charge of a research into the effect of rough water on resistance with particular reference to how reduction of speed in waves varied with ship form and Bottomley was asked to begin a long overdue investigation into the manoeuvring power of rudders. Work on the latter, started by the Admiralty 40 years earlier, had been curtailed and now the Chief Surveyor of Lloyd's had drawn forcible attention to its importance. The work would need special apparatus since rudder head torque was to be measured and it was hoped that additional staff would become available. Finally the work on seaplanes was to be advanced since it was thought that these machines would have application to both commercial and defence requirements and it was decided to continue with the investigation of pressures on the hull of a flying boat using models and, where possible, full size seaplanes.

For the proposed work in rough water a means of creating artificial waves in the main tank was required. Towards the end of the war a start had been made on the installation of a wavemaker at the south end of the tank. Intended to produce regular waves it was designed as a flap device capable of creating waves over a large range of amplitude and period. The cost was largely defrayed by the Admiralty whose desire for rough water data from ship models grew. The conditions put on the money provided was that tests for the Admiralty could be done at any time but in the event such requests were never made.

So far as other tank apparatus and equipment was concerned, dynamometry for testing model propellers had been made and by the end of the war the gear was ready for trials. However, the problems over the small tank had not been resolved largely because of insufficient time. But uses had been found for it, notably the provision of buoyancy information on life saving appliances. Several types of these were immersed for periods of time and their ability to maintain weight support observed. At the end of 1917 the tank was emptied and its metal work repainted. Efforts would soon follow to attempt once and for all the conversion of this facility into one where ship model measurements or flow observations could be carried out successfully.

Sir Richard Glazebrook, the Director of NPL, who had done so much towards the design and successful promotion of the Tank was soon to retire. He was succeeded in 1919 by Professor (later Sir Joseph) Petavel. In the same year Lord Rayleigh died and his inspirational leadership was greatly missed but the work of the Advisory Committee continued under the chairmanship of Sir William Smith who had been Rayleigh's deputy.

REFERENCES

1. Holmes W.M., "National Physical Laboratory—how British industry has been helped", Journal of Institute of Science and Industry, April 1920.
2. Baker G.S., "Notes on model experiments", trans. NECIES, Vol. 32, 1915.
3. Baker G.S. and Keary E.M., "Experiments with models of seaplane floats", R & M, No. 412, April 1918.
4. Baker G.S. and Keary E.M. in conjunction with Capt. Gundry, RAF and Lieut. Hackforth, RAF, "Experiments with full-sized machines", R & M, No. 473, September 1918.
5. Baker G.S. and Keary E.M., "Experiments with models of flying boat hulls", R & M, Nos. 472 and 483, September and December 1918.
6. Bottomley G.H., "The impact of a model seaplane float on water", R & M, No. 583, March 1919.
7. Baker G.S. and Keary E.M., "The effect of the longitudinal motion of a ship on its statical transverse instability", trans. INA, 1918.
8. Glazebrook, Sir R.T., Royal Institution Lecture, 1918.
9. Baker G.S., "The immediate commercial advantages of experiment tank tests", trans., Liverpool Engineering Society, 1916.
10. Baker G.S., Ship Form, Resistance and Screw Propulsion, published by Constable, 1915.

CHAPTER 6

THE TANK FULLY ESTABLISHED

The needs of the war had demonstrated only too clearly the value of maritime test facilities and the sure foundations laid by Yarrow, Rayleigh and Glazebrook were ready to be consolidated. Under Baker's forceful and determined leadership the National Tank moved forward into one of its more rewarding periods. In 1919 the Tank could, for ship or seaplane hulls provide resistance data and soon there was to be a pressing need to understand ship propulsion and propulsive efficiency. With a staff of just 19 the next seven years saw the Tank progress from resistance tests to tests on propellers in isolation and finally to the complete realisation of the ship in its environment with propellers fitted allowing models to be propelled through calm or rough water (the effects of wind on the ship superstructure became a separate investigation). Time was also found to attend trials on completed ships to collect the all important full-scale data for comparison with corresponding model measurements and as though this were not enough the same period of time saw the development of additional apparatus needed for the measurement of rudder forces and the associated effects on a ship's hull when its rudder was brought into operation. Also, in 1920, with the arrival at the Tank of the mathematician W.C.S. Wigley from Cambridge, theoretical studies on ship wave-making began. Running in parallel with these were experimental tests on mathematically defined hull forms which tested the assumptions made in the mathematical approach to wave-making resistance.

That such progress was possible with so few staff and at a time when the demand for model tests from private firms was great is remarkable. It was due to two things, overtime and the successful development of new instrumentation. The output of models for both research and private purposes averaged 60 a year and the demand could be satisfied only by increasing the length of the working day. A shift system was introduced which enabled the tank to be in use from early morning to 9 o'clock at night on most weekdays. The instrumentation required comprised a wavemaker for the main tank, an accurate means of making model propellers, dynamometry for measuring propeller and rudder forces and apparatus to determine the effect of rudder action on the immediate behaviour of a ship. The skill of the workshop mechanics Dawes, Wise and Woollett was crucial.

Before looking at the new instrumentation we should return to the small tank and its progress. Fallow since the last years of the war, an attempt was soon made to improve the flow of water as it was pumped through the test section. The Advisory Committee was keen to pursue a programme of streamline flow and the small tank with steady flowing water would be ideal for an experimental determination of stream pressures around a hull form. As things stood the variation of flow across the test section was too irregular so the cross-section of the tank between the pump and the test section was changed and also the shape close to the pump inlet. This improved matters and reduced the variation of flow across the tank to 10 per cent, but this was still not good enough. A new motor capable of giving a water speed of 1½ metres per second was ordered but when it arrived in 1922 the Tank staff were so busy that time could not be found to install it. Hopes for the success of the tank seemed to be fading and despite later efforts, involving a few more changes to the tank section and with the new pump fitted, no significant improvements could be made. In 1925, although it was not realised at the time, the last test work in this small tank was carried out. The Royal National Lifeboat Institution wanted to determine the path followed by a lifeboat's keel during and after launch from a slipway. A model and a slipway were made and records taken of the position of the model at a given instant during launch. Different slipway declivities were tried and a small wavemaker simulated disturbed water conditions at the time of launch. After this, with confidence in the main tank very high, as was the demand for its use, Baker saw little point in persevering with the small tank even for use in *ad hoc* investigations and it was ultimately abandoned and dismantled in 1932 to make room for the first cavitation tunnel. Traces of the outline of the small tank can still be seen today.

INSTRUMENTATION AND EQUIPMENT

Before Kent could begin work on ship models in rough water a wavemaker was needed. As already mentioned work had begun on a design during the war and by 1920 a device had been installed and successfully calibrated. It consisted of a simple flat plate or flap braced along its length which spanned the width of the tank. It was hinged 10 cm below the water surface along its lower edge to a steel framework secured across the tank and fastened to its walls. A connecting rod was linked to an adjustable crank arm to give crank lengths of 2½–30 cm.The arm was rotated by a belt drive from a 5 h.p. DC motor and during operation the flap oscillated backwards and forwards on its hinges to create waves which on the wavemaker side were broken down by a beach just behind the flap. Those on the other side travelled down the tank to reflect at the far end. The height and length of the waves were governed by the length of the crank and speed of rotation of the arm. Regular waves were produced but remained so for only about three minutes when they collapsed to become thoroughly confused and

Kent had to time his experiments carefully to make sure the model under test met waves of consistent regularity. For a 1/25-scale calibrations showed that it was possible to produce waves from $\frac{2}{3}$–$1\frac{3}{4}$ metres high for a 180 metres wave length or $\frac{2}{3}$–$3\frac{1}{2}$ metres high for a 35 metres length. In 1948 when a second wavemaker was installed, this time of plunger type, the same degradation of regular waves was experienced and it became clear that the sloping walls of the tank were mainly responsible. Accordingly when BMT's third tank was designed its walls were built vertically and as a result waves remained consistent for a long period of time. However, Kent exploited the "natural" ability of the tank to provide irregular waves and attempted model experiments in them but he was working before the day when an irregular wave system could be defined by its spectral properties and his results can be regarded only as qualitative.

The first, albeit rudimentary, model propellers were made at the Tank in 1911 at the time of the *Hawke-Olympic* interaction tests. At Haslar, the staff there had developed a method of casting rough propeller blades, their final shape being finished by hand. Riddle who had joined the Tank in 1918 from Haslar knew the process and his strong grasp of solid geometry and supreme talents as a draughtsman (his drawings in the Tank archives are classic) were just what Baker needed. With R.E. Froude's acquiescence Riddle set about establishing a system at the Tank which was based on what he had seen at Haslar. Riddle was an individualist, eccentric and had great strength of character. Born in Portsmouth in 1892 he refused a Martell scholarship at the age of 16 working instead under R.E. Froude for five years before coming to Teddington. He hated noise and worked quietly with three others who themselves were expected to respect the peace that reigned. During the hunger marches on London in the 1930s Riddle saw in a National newspaper a photograph of a woman carrying a banner. In one of his rare utterances he announced he would marry the girl, tracked her down, and within months had carried out his prediction.

In the propeller manufacturing system that transpired, the helical surface on which the blades of a propeller lie was first formed from clay using a pitch strickling apparatus. This consisted of a vertical plate cut to the required blade rake angle held by a sleeve which slid on a vertical shaft. At the outer end of the vertical plate a pivoting shoe slid along the edge of a guide plate which itself could be set to any desired pitch angle. As the vertical plate swept over a block of soft clay its edge strickled or struck out the required helical surface. From the mould produced a plaster of Paris cast was made. Meanwhile from the propeller drawing the rough outline and thickness of the blade were carved into a block of wood from which separate clay moulds or leaves, one for each blade, were made and placed on the clay helical surface at their correct positions. A second plaster cast was then made and when both were brought together molten soft metal was poured into the gap between them to produce the cast propeller. The propeller was finished by hand filing, the thickness of different points on each blade being checked by caliper.

This system proved satisfactory for early propellers whose sections were based on flat pitch faces but in later years when aerofoil shaped sections were introduced the finish of these to an acceptable accuracy proved difficult. Final accuracy largely rested with the skill of the individual workshop mechanics and in particular their interpretive skills of the drawings supplied. To overcome the difficulty additional information was supplied which gave drawings showing contours of constant blade thickness and also edge thickness profiles. By point drilling the contour lines could be transferred to each blade and assisted greatly in the finishing process. A description of propeller geometry and the manufacturing method was given by Riddle[1] in 1942 and remains a definitive work.

The improved system continued in use until after the Second World War. Thereafter as propeller shapes became even more complicated to include hollowed pitch faces, extreme skew, variable rake, etc, an entirely new procedure was developed at the Tank, coming into operation in 1957.

The apparatus to measure propeller forces was a form of dynamometry that could drive a propeller and measure the forces it generated. As with the wavemaker, development had begun during the war. A propeller dynamometer was already in existence at Haslar and again R.E. Froude helped the Tank to produce its own version. At Haslar, Froude was using his gear in two ways, to measure the performance of a propeller operating by itself in unrestricted "open water" or, by positioning it behind and separate from a model hull he drove the propeller as the model was towed by the carriage thus simulating ship propulsion conditions. This system of propulsion testing became known as Froude's method and was adopted at the Tank just after the war when at that stage the gear could measure propeller thrust and rotational speed. Later the ability to measure torque was added so that then a full assessment of propeller and propulsive efficiency was possible. Four of these gears were made at the Tank to cater for the need of single, twin, triple or quadruple modes of ship propulsion. For open water experiments or when behind a single screw hull it was fixed to the centre line of the tank carriage but in multi-screw designs separate gears had to be rigged on either side of the carriage centreline at the position of each propeller.

The propeller was suspended at the forward end of a horizontal shaft which formed part of a parallel motion frame the rear vertical leg of which acted as a shroud for the vertical driving shaft. Thrust was measured in a similar way to the existing resistance dynamometer but its recorded value included the resistance of the carrying frame. Additional experiments were therefore necessary to obtain the correction to the thrust measurement. Torque was measured from the deflection of a spiral spring which was coupled to an intermediate horizontal shaft geared to the propeller and the record taken on a paper strip fixed to a hollow brass cylindrical drum which shrouded the spring. Torsional losses due to friction in the toothed gearing were accounted for and measured from brake tests. The accuracy of the torque reading was not great, readings varying from day to day by as much as 10 per cent. Under torsional deflection the spring in all probability fouled the collar at the right hand side of the small assembly. In an attempt to overcome the difficulty an alternative design conceived by Baker and drawn up by F.H. Sargeant, a draughtsman who had been recruited in 1922, was tried but it was not until 1925 that improvement was sufficient to allow a new propulsion dynamometer to be considered.

Froude's method of propulsion in which the propeller was carried on a shaft separate from the hull was not without its detractors notably E.V. Telfer, the fast-emerging talent who in later years was to become the scourge of many model experimenters. On the practical side the complexities of setting up the apparatus, particularly in multi-screw cases, was complicated and time consuming. More importantly, Telfer, and Taylor at Washington, argued that there would always be a certain amount of fore and aft play between model and propeller. This was undeniable and the clearance between hull and propeller, which could be so crucial to performance, varied from one experiment to another leading to inconsistent results. Surely, argued Telfer, the ship condition must be reproduced with the propeller or propellers at their precise location and working at all times in the true wake of the hull they were driving. This was all very well but the current technology had not yet advanced to allow a model to be set up as a ship with mechanism to drive the propeller within the hull. Also Baker, who accepted the criticism, valued the opportunity of being able, in multi-screw designs, to conduct propulsion tests with and without hull appendages such as shaft bossings which of course were easily achieved using external Froude gears. It will be remembered that Baker was uncertain as how best to deal with the model measurement of hull appendage resistance and his doubts were not reduced when he compared good full-scale trial results from a twin screw ship with corresponding model tests and found the comparison good when he used the model propulsion data obtained *without* the twin bossings fitted. However, this was one case in a very limited amount of model ship comparison data that were then available and on further consideration Baker eventually preferred to rely on the results he and Stanton had found in 1916 and accordingly corrected the model measurement of appendage resistance when scaling to the equivalent ship value.

The stage had apparently been reached when the external method of propulsion could be replaced. Much of course needed to be achieved at the Tank before an internal method was possible and by 1926 a workable arrangement was at last found. It included the new Baker/Sargeant dynamometer which by 1925 had given encouraging results in open water tests with consistent and repeatable torque readings. The frame of the Froude gear had been replaced by a long slender streamlined body (to become known as an "opens boat") and the new dynamometer with a drive motor placed inside the opens boat. A long shaft housing projected from the boat at the end of which was fitted the propeller to be tested. The opens boat was lowered into the water and fixed at the required depth of propeller immersion. When using the new dynamometer for propulsion tests on model hulls an assembly comprising a motor, dynamometer and propeller shaft was set up inside the model, the shaft extending from the gear some 100 cm to pass through a stern tube which was cast into a hole drilled into the stern aperture.

This new dynamometer became the basis of many successful future gears and was purely mechanical. It was similar in conception to one under development at the Vienna Tank at about the same time. Planned initially for use with a single screw hull form it included a ½ h.p. DC motor to provide the power to rotate a transmission dynamometer through gear wheels. The driven shaft of the dynamometer was connected through a roller clutch to a thrust meter which was in turn connected to the propeller. When torque was applied to the rotating shaft the movement of the free mitre wheels of the dynamometer was communicated through levers to a compression spring whose movement was magnified and recorded by a pen on a strip of paper fixed to a revolving drum. To measure thrust the shaft was allowed a slight longitudinal movement, its maximum travel limited to 3 mm either way. By means of a double thrust bearing this movement was communicated to another compression spring and its movement magnified and recorded in a similar way to the torque. To obtain constancy in friction the usual system adopted at a ship wherein a stuffing box was fitted to stern tubes was replaced by an oil seal. The propeller shaft was carried on plain journal bearings. To record shaft speed a "make and break" counter operated a pen electrically and this pen with others, recording ½ second intervals and 6 metre distances travelled down the tank, operated on the same paper strip.

The internal method of propulsion testing, once established, became accepted universally and it was perfectly possible to complete a comprehensive programme of resistance and propulsion experiments at one ship condition in one day. Gradual improvements were made to the dynamometry following experience gained and as better materials and motors became available. Similar smaller gears were built for use in multi-screw designs. The London based firm Munro's, who by the early 1920s were specialising to provide instrumentation to towing tanks worldwide, were asked to make these gears. They were driven by a single motor through transmission gearing which rotated all the shafts at a common speed. For many years the Tank's dynamometers gave very reliable and repeatable results, so much so that there was a great reluctance to abandon them for alternative methods of measurement (principally the electric strain gauge) when these became available in later years.

From 1920 the Tank, in common with others, was able to measure all the quantities needed to assess and predict from model data the power required at the ship's engines to achieve a specified speed in calm water, provided certain assumptions were made when analysing and extrapolating the model measurements. At that time the accuracy of the torque measurement was not good. It became reliable only when the new internal gears were introduced in 1925. The model measurements came from three separate sources—hull resistance, hull propulsion and propeller open water tests. Resistance data were collected from the model in its basic or naked state with no hull appendages of any kind fitted to it and also, just prior to propulsion tests, in its "associated" state when such appendages associated with its stern propulsion gear were added. In the propulsion experiments the model was towed with its propeller operating, measurements of the propeller forces being taken for a range of steady propeller revolutions at a given corresponding ship speed. The tow force necessary to keep the model at the same speed as the towing carriage was measured at the resistance dynamometer. In the open water experiments the propeller was mounted on the propeller dynamometer already described and tested over a range of speed through the water and revolutions. The experimental method employed is the same today although the actual techniques differ in some Tanks. The analysis of the results and the extrapolation method used to arrive at estimated ship values is also the same today, an engineering solution first proposed by Froude to the very difficult problem of dynamic dissimilarity that exists between model and ship. This problem which poses so many difficulties, including uncertainties over the effect of model scale, continues to occupy the thoughts of experimenters everywhere, but so far a better alternative to Froude's approach remains elusive.

The impending research into rudder performance and its effect on a ship's manoeuvrability required different instrumentation altogether. It was designed by Bottomley, Dawes and Wise but largely built in the Engineering Division of NPL at a time when the Tank's own workshop was busy. Three different measurements were needed, torque on the rudder when it was swung to a predetermined angle port or starboard, the ensuing moment exerted on the model hull and the angle to which the model would yaw under the forces brought into play.

For rudder torque a rotatable assembly of levers and springs was mounted on a horizontal board at the stern of the model. The force required at the end of a short tiller to balance the rudder when swung over was measured by the extension of a vertical spring through a bell crank lever and this force multiplied by the leverage gave the torque at the rudder stock. Care was needed in the experiments before taking measurements to ensure a true "floating" zero position of the rudder and with the towed model running steadily the whole apparatus was rotated to a fore and aft position at which the rudder balanced itself freely. The desired rudder angle was then set and locked and the water pressure on the rudder balanced the torque transmitted at the vertical spring. By changing the axis (from the rudder stock to a parallel axis further forward) further measurements of torque could be made about this second axis and it was then possible to derive the pressure on the rudder and its centre of action. For measurements in the opposite (i.e. port) direction a second vertical spring was needed in the apparatus as originally designed and a later version of the gear was built to include this.

The method chosen to measure the forces acting on the model as it moved forward under rudder action involved the design of two dynamometers positioned fore and aft in the model. Each measured the transverse force exerted for a given rudder angle. The sum of the forces gave the lateral force on the model and their moment about the centre of gravity of the hull the moment which produced yaw. To achieve reasonable accuracy in the determination of yaw, lateral movement of the model was restricted to 10 cm. With steady conditions reached, the rods which towed the model were released and the lateral movement of two points, one forward and one aft, measured with time. The difference between the two gave yaw, which was expressed in degrees.

RESEARCH

Cargo Ships

The first results of post-war research from the Tank were published by Baker and Kent in 1919. This was really a hull design manual for slow speed cargo ships and drew on some of the Tank's earlier model data to provide guidelines to the design of such ships operating at Froude numbers close to 0·2. This invaluable work[2] included data for both curved and straight-framed ships with guidance and formulae for preferred values of prismatic coefficient, midship area, entrance run ratio, position of centre of buoyancy and so on. A typical design was worked through and a lines plan produced. Using their preferred Ⓟ approach, Baker and Kent presented plottings which enabled practitioners to choose the right combination of Froude number and Ⓟ to avoid high wave-making. The paper was a classic example of how a large body of tank data for a single ship type could be brought together to provide positive and practical guidance to the designer and was the forerunner of similar offerings that were to emanate from the Tank's workers.

Skin Friction

At about this time most model experimenters would have agreed that what was wanted more than anything else was an answer to the skin friction problem. There was no difficulty in accepting William Froude's original hypothesis, which laid down for posterity the principle of extrapolation, but the burning question was how to calculate skin friction resistance. A huge gap existed between model and corresponding ship Reynolds numbers and there was a diversity of opinion as to how the results from short planks should be used for extended application to longer ship lengths. Originally W. Froude formulated a set of constants for use in calculating the frictional resistance defined as fSv^n which extended to lengths beyond the range of his plank tests and in 1888 R.E. Froude, taking n as 1·825, made further length extensions and listed values of f against length. The "O" constants he listed are still in use today in the Froude analysis. But other workers had proposed alternative formulations, all derived from tests on flat surfaces in water; Beaufoy and Baker in England, Gebers in Vienna, Taylor in Washington (who later advocated a standard extension which could be adopted universally) and Tideman in Holland, who had re-analysed Froude's earlier work. Added to these, Zahm and Stanton had provided skin friction data obtained from tests on flat surfaces in air whilst Kempf in Hamburg had published data for rounded surfaces. Of all these, Gebers had reached the highest Reynolds number in his tests, 54 million, but even this was a mere $\frac{1}{10}$ of the average ship value. Moreover the extrapolation method as it stood included one of William Froude's major assumptions. He applied his data to ships as if hull surface was a uniform plank of the same wetted surface and length, which meant that no account of form or hull roughness was taken into consideration.

In 1924 Baker sought to bring matters to a head and proposed to the Advisory Committee that a programme of research into the problem should be launched. Since data at very high Reynolds numbers were required and also information on the effect of form, there appeared to be no alternative to tests on an actual ship, in effect an extension of Froude's original work on *Greyhound*. Such an expensive undertaking would need strong support and the Committee approached the Council of the INA to request the Admiralty to make a destroyer available for tests at sea. The Council's response was to appoint a Skin Friction Committee to review the current position and make proposals for action. Sir Richard Glazebrook chaired the Committee and other members included representatives from the Admiralty, each British tank and a representative from Parsons Turbine Company. Its work,[3] reported in 1925, began by taking the results of a model resistance test to calculate the estimated values for an imaginary ship using three alternative skin friction methods, R.E. Froude, Baker and Gebers. Differences of 15 per cent were found, which only emphasised the severity of the problem and encouraged the recommendation that work at higher Reynolds numbers was indeed needed. Tests at sea on a 100 metres destroyer were suggested but nothing came of this despite the Tank's offer of staff and equipment. It was made at a time of a depression in trade and no doubt the need for a large outlay of money was decisive. Nine years later the Japanese carried out full-scale trials on the destroyer *Yudachi*[4] with controversial results and it was not until the end of the Second World War that the idea was resurrected in Britain, when the famous *Lucy Ashton* trials were carried out by the British Ship Research Association.

Manoeuvring

In 1922 the first of a series of papers on ship manoeuvring was published, a joint offering from Baker and Bottomley. Since the work planned was to rely so much on the measurement of rudder forces and the size of model rudders compared to the hull to which they were fitted was small, the old problem of scale arose. To determine what the scale effect might be, some remarkable experiments were done. Taking the design of a typical unbalanced rudder commonly seen in single screw ships, three separate rudder models were made at different scales, the largest, as tall as a man, being to a ¼-scale and 1¼ metres long. They were tested in open water on a special rig with a flat plate fixed ahead of them, the plate being needed later to examine the effect of stern aperture and hull wake on rudder performance. Measurements of rudder head torque and pressure were made over a range of rudder angle and ahead speed. Happily the results revealed no scale effect, the scatter in the results being ascribed to normal experimental error. Baker and Bottomley could thus proceed with confidence and the first publication[5] in 1922 dealt with a 1/25-scale model of a single screw hull of 0·78 block coefficient fitted with and without a driven propeller. The wealth of data included numerical values for the constant K in the formula for rudder pressure for different angles of rudder. Also four different shapes and sizes of unbalanced rudder were tried and the changes in rudder head torque and ship turning moment shown. The work enabled the separate effects of propeller race and hull wake to be isolated and these data were unique because, although it was appreciated that the impingement of a screw race on the rudder enhanced steering, the degree of improvement was not known. These separate effects required systematic experiments. For example, to see how the wake of the hull affected rudder pressure and torque, tests were first performed in open water on a given rudder, with the flat plate mentioned earlier substituted for the normal stern aperture. The experiments were then repeated behind the ship model with its stern aperture replaced by the flat plate, the whole being towed by the normal resistance dynamometer and by subtraction, the effect of wake deduced. Similarly, to determine race effect, tests were done on the ship model fitted with its rudder and with a propeller either driving or removed. The results obtained from the latter set of experiments were revealing and the strong effect of propeller race on the ship turning moment was very clearly seen. Also the presence of the hull or wake was shown to have a significant effect on rudder performance, the values of pressure and torque in open water being almost twice those found when the rudder was fitted behind the hull. The work was done most thoroughly. An instance of this was the desire to test the validity of the square power in the accepted formula for rudder pressure, $P = k A V^2$, the power of 2 having been deduced in earlier years from experiments on deeply immersed plates. Ship rudders were not deeply immersed but Baker and Bottomley's experiments confirmed that for all practical purposes 2 could nevertheless be used. In examining the effects of varying rudder immersion and rudder aspect ratio some very useful data were provided, some of which linked up with work done much earlier by Mallock, William Froude's assistant at Torquay.

The results produced by Baker and Bottomley were warmly welcomed and encouraged the Tank to press on with further studies, for this type of work was breaking new ground. Baker moved over to other matters and left Bottomley in charge. Four further papers of utmost importance transpired and the achievements Bottomley made were remarkable considering his background. A nephew of Lord Kelvin would be considered a fine start but he was born totally deaf and was sent to a special school where, after long and laborious efforts, he managed to speak in strange guttural-like sounds. He could lip read and so was able to conduct intelligent conversation but there is no record as to how he presented his papers for these, apart from "Manoeuvring of Ships. Part I—unbalanced rudders of single screw ships", 1922,[5] were written by himself. His unfortunate beginning matched his untimely death. In 1934, seeing a friend on to a train at Kingston, he returned to his car to discover a bag had been left behind. He drove rapidly to a station further up the line and ran on to the platform to await the train. Unaware of its imminence and in a state of confusion, he lost balance and fell off the platform into the path of the incoming train, which killed him instantly. The inquest appeared ready to return a verdict of suicide but Baker in giving evidence of Bottomley's character and behaviour was quick to squash this.

Bottomley's second paper in 1924[6] was complementary to the 1922 paper, above,[5] a twin screw installation replacing the single screw on the same ship form, the stern aperture being filled in and a centreline rudder fitted. The experiments covered much the same ground as before, except that yaw measurements were omitted, following experience in the 1922 paper, where difficulties had been met, with the gear necessitating modifications to it. Experiments with the model moving astern were added and, since this was now a twin screw vessel, some of the tests were repeated with screws driven in the opposite direction. The effect of the propeller races became noticeable at high rudder angles only and inward rotation of the screws gave 20 per cent greater force on the rudder, which amounted to a 5 per cent increase in the ship turning moment.

Since the presence of the hull ahead of the rudder had been shown to be influential, Bottomley's next two papers in 1927[7] and 1930[8] looked at the effect on manoeuvring of changes in after body shape. In 1927[7] he took the same hull as in 1922,[5] equipping it as a single screw form and used the same four unbalanced rudder shapes as before. He then filled out the stern, increasing the after body prismatic coefficient to 0·8 from the original 0·75, leaving the fore body unaltered. The new apparatus for the measurement of rudder head torque was used in the experiments, which showed that under propulsive conditions, the extra stern fullness had little effect on rudder forces or ship turning moment. Tests astern produced some interesting information on relative ahead and astern speeds for the same rudder head torque. It was found that the ratio of astern to ahead speed should not exceed ¾ if the rudder head torque was to equal that ahead for a rudder angle of 30°. Bottomley then reduced the stern fullness of the hull to give an after body prismatic coefficient of 0·7 and repeated the experiments. Similar results were found indicating overall, for this hull at least, that hull shape aft was of little significance to manoeuvring, by far the most important factors being rudder design and propeller race. The 1930 paper[8] went over the same ground except that the original model was fitted as a twin screw with centreline rudder. This time stern fullness was influential, measurable reductions in rudder forces and turning moment being seen as after body prismatic coefficient reduced.

Bottomley's last major paper in 1932[9]—there were other offerings which summarised his work as it proceeded, given to bodies such as the Liverpool Engineering Society—looked at semi-balanced, as opposed to unbalanced rudders. Two alternative twin screw models were taken both having a prismatic coefficient of 0.7, one with a so-called mercantile (raised) stern, the other a cruiser stern. Six different centreline rudders were tried with outward turning propellers. The work, again most thoroughly done, determined values for k in the formula for pressure for a range of rudder angle and also showed the effect of screw race and hull wake. Comparing results from unbalanced and semi-balanced rudders showed rudder head torque to be higher in the unbalanced type.

A comparison between model prediction and ship performance was just as desirable for manoeuvring as it was for speed and power and in presenting his work Bottomley appealed to shipowners to make their ships available for trials. Both the Ellerman and White Star lines responded and *Dolius*, a twin screw ship from which Baker had collected measured mile data, became available for manoeuvring trials as, later, did the single screw *City of Lyons*. Both ships were fitted by Tank staff, with instrumentation for the measurement of rudder head torque and the pressure in the steering rams. As things turned out, data of sufficient reliability were not numerous, but solid evidence emerged from later model experiments that good correlation existed for rudder head torque in both ships up to a rudder angle of about 20°. At higher angles model predictions were higher than those measured full-scale.

Bottomley had laid the most secure foundations for future model work on ship manoeuvrability. Already, at the time of his death, his work had given great assistance to designers and the gears he developed proved wonderfully reliable. They are still used today, a tribute also to Wise who did so much in their realisation.

Seakeeping and Ship Trials

The research into ship behaviour in waves began at the Tank at about the same time as that on manoeuvring and was to become the province of J.L. Kent for many years. In fact, history will remember Kent for his work in this field more than any other. His enthusiasm for it never waned and he revelled in every opportunity of going to sea in ships, measuring and observing their behaviour. His activities even excited the popular national press. The *Sunday Express* in 1932:

There is a man living near London who never goes to sea unless it is rough ... Part of his job is to go to sea in all kinds of ships, in the nastiest of weather expert prophecy can forecast and make observations. And as Mr. King (sic) is invariably ill the first day out, his earliest observations are not official. Later he becomes highly technical. All over the rolling ship he goes with little instruments that record the height of the waves, the roll of the ship, the action of the propeller, the slight variations in action of the different steersmen and many other things ...

Kent brought back all kinds of tales from his trips; the reassurance he gave to passengers who thought his presence meant there was something wrong with the ship, how he was slung over the side in a rope chair to observe the waves over the bow and so on. But it was not until he aroused the interest of ship owners by publishing his first paper in 1922 on model tests in waves that opportunities came for him to go to sea. Owners were keen to know what margin of power was needed to maintain a ship's speed in heavy seas.

Kent's 1922 paper,[10] which was to prove so influential—it also received the INA's gold medal—describes experiments on three models. The main purpose of the work was to see how much the resistance of a low speed cargo ship increased when running into head seas and to see how this might be minimised by changes in bow shape. Measurements of pitch and heave in waves were taken on specially constructed apparatus. Two light vertical rods, supported at their upper ends by balanced hinged frames, were connected to each model and the difference between rise and fall of the rods gave a direct measure of the longitudinal angle of the model at any instant. A continuous written record was taken from a pen moving against a revolving drum, the pen being carried on a bell crank lever connected to the two rods. The aftermost of the two rods was placed at the centre of gravity of the hull and the maximum movement of this rod indicated the heave at that point. Resistance through waves was recorded on the normal dynamometer, which seems incredible today, even though the tests were done in regular waves, but evidently a dash pot was added and presumably a very stiff spring to keep fluctuations of resistance within the span of the recording drum.

The models were all of common length, beam and draught. Model 484 had V shaped bow sections, 487A U shaped sections with considerable flare and 487B was the same as 487A except that flare was removed, the sections above the waterline being carried up vertically. Before tests the natural pitching period was measured by timing horizontal oscillations of each model when suspended in air. The tests in waves confirmed the expectation that heavy pitching, accompanied by wildly fluctuating resistance, occurred when the natural period of the model coincided with the period of encounter (the time which elapsed between the model's bow meeting successive wave crests). Clearly this demonstrated that the natural period of a ship should be as different as possible to period of encounter and Kent observed that it would be better to dispose hull weight and cargo such that weight was concentrated near amidships. Then heavy pitching in long waves would be avoided. Kent averaged the resistance records and deduced that for the same height of wave each model experienced a similar percentage increase in resistance over its calm water value. The percentage increased in proportion to the wave height or in other words for the same effective power, loss of ship speed was proportional to wave height. With regard to hull shape, observations of deck wetness showed little difference in the three models and it was concluded that whereas freeboard was important, flare was not. This surprised Payne from Haslar whose experience with finer naval forms had shown flare to be very important. His forms were of course considerably faster than the slow cargo vessels that Kent had dealt with.

In applying his results to ships Kent was conscious of obvious differences. Regular waves were rarely met at sea, his models had been towed and not propelled and air resistance had been neglected. To tackle the first of these, tests in irregular waves were attempted. These must have been extremely difficult given the apparatus, not least the wavemaker, available, yet Kent reckoned his results to be sufficiently reliable to allow him the conclusion that the resistance increment found was much the same as in regular waves.

The first opportunity for Kent to go to sea came in 1922 when the Canadian Pacific Company offered him a return trip from St John's in Canada to Liverpool in their twin screw steamship *Montcalm*. This was followed by later voyages on the single screw *London Mariner* (London–Queenstown), *San Gerardo* (Tilbury–Mexico) and *San Tirso* (Mexico–Rotterdam). All four ships were much the same length, 150 metres. To obtain wind speed and direction, the workshop built a special pitot tube with wind vanes which was connected to a pressure gauge. The measurement of wave height was virtually impossible and Kent admitted to much guess work. All that could be done was to observe waves close to the ship, comparing their heights with known heights on the ship. Various ship's officers were enlisted and independent observations were collected and means taken. The direction of the waves was obtained by sighting along wave crests using a light rod pivoted to move over a quadrant fixed to the ship. As to the behaviour of the ship, its speed was obtained from the Walker log fitted, course from the magnetic compass and power from the ship's Hopkinson-Thring torsion meter. Ship pitching was taken from the movement of a long period pendulum, time being recorded simultaneously to allow pitch period to be calculated, and roll was obtained from a simply constructed "horizontal" apparatus.

This was an ambitious series of observations, but with much time available during a voyage to improve apparatus and the technique of measurement, many records were obtained. As a result, Kent's paper[11] is packed with information, only the measurements on *London Mariner* failing to provide extensive and reliable data. The most valuable conclusion reached from the shipowners' point of view was the increase in power required if a given speed in calm water was to be maintained in rough seas. The increase was dependent on ship's fullness since *Montcalm* ($C_B = 0.735$) needed, on average, a 21 per cent increase in power, *San Tirso* ($C_B = 0.79$), 47 per cent and *San Gerardo* ($C_B = 0.86$), 100 per cent. Analysing his results in great detail, Kent produced a power constant, based on shaft power, ship displacement and speed and by estimating effective power and propeller thrust from corresponding model tests in calm water, he isolated the effects of hull form, propeller power and power due to wind and waves.

Further opportunities for observations at sea came a few years later when Kent went aboard two finer-form ships, on passage between Liverpool and Havana. One of these, the 160 metres twin screw passenger ship *Oroya* (C_B = 0·67) encountered horrendous weather, wind speeds of over 80 knots being met with 10 metres high waves. This so upset a group of Spanish passengers that on hearing of Kent's purpose they held him responsible and complained to the Shipping Company, writing:

We should have been warned of Mr Kent's presence on board because your Company must have known that this was going to be a very bad voyage.

Another story to add to Kent's fund.

The weather was such that at its severest, *Oroya's* speed fell by over 5 knots from 13·5 but the conditions were just what Kent wanted and enabled very useful tables to be presented in his 1927 paper[12] which listed the incidence of wave height and Beaufort numbers as percentage of occurrence during the voyage. It was then possible to derive the margin of power needed to maintain the ship's speed through rough seas, very valuable data and an advance on the findings from *Montcalm*, etc. which were averaged figures. Baker was so pleased with the results obtained that in discussing Kent's 1927 paper[12] he was able to say that the National Tank could now use Kent's data to select a power margin for a given ship and then design its propeller for average sea conditions.

Kent's hard and demanding work was truly pioneering and gave the industry much needed information. As a respite he returned to model tests and using the newly developed internal propulsion gears, propelled two models through waves. He wanted to investigate propeller efficiency in waves since the loss of ship speed could not be wholly accounted for by increased resistance alone. Two typical forms of differing fullness were used and tests in regular waves conducted. Kent was able to show, for the fuller form in particular, that the loss of performance in waves was due more to a reduction in propeller efficiency than increase in resistance.[13] E.G. Barillon from the Paris tank asked how thrust and torque had been measured in waves, emphasising the problems of inertia that must have existed, doubting that the difficulties in using the gears in waves had been overcome. This was surely true since the records obtained from the mechanical gears must have been subject to inspired interpretation. Kent deflected the criticism by saying the gears had taken a long time to develop, but divulged nothing more.

The full-scale measurements that had been going on were examples of the growing need of shipbuilders and owners to know more about the actual performance of newly completed ships. Baker was keen to gather as much full-scale measured-mile data as he could to compare with his own model figures. He persuaded one or two owners to allow his staff access to new ships to measure propeller thrust and, later, torque, whilst the normal trial speed runs were under way. 10 ships had been fitted with thrust meters by 1923, yielding data of variable quality and Baker was shocked to note that in several trials, single rather than double runs over the mile had been accepted. He published such results as he had in 1923[14] really with the intent of adding fuel to the unease being shown by other interested parties, a state of affairs that a year earlier had led the INA, in conjunction with the Institution of Mechanical Engineers, to appoint a Committee under the chairmanship of Vice Admiral, Sir George Goodwin, to carry out tests on oil engines and oil-engined ships. This Marine Oil-Engines Trials Committee arranged trials on several ships and issued several reports, typical of which is that of 1931.[15] The report dealt with the twin screw ship *Polyphemus*, describing in detail its engine room arrangement, the engine test ashore and finally an analysis of the results of the measured-mile trials at sea and corresponding model experiments conducted by Baker. These trials, together with earlier ones conducted under the control of the Trials Committee and also other trials arranged by Baker through the co-operation of shipowners, can really be regarded as the beginnings of serious ship-model correlation studies that were to reach a climax of intense activity 30 years later under the direction of the British Ship Research Association. Before the publication of 1931[15] Baker presented data dealing with speed and power correlation aspects only, including trials data from a variety of ships.[16] In attempting to find reasons for the discrepancies found in ship-model comparisons he did not produce one of his better papers. To be fair, he no doubt felt it necessary to present such data that he had in order to ventilate the pressing problems that existed, but unfortunately the quality of the full-scale data was poor. Of the 10 ships Baker examined only two had produced reasonable sets of data. Two had not been run on measured distances, data being collected on passages between Newcastle and Holland, several had yielded indicated horse power only and one had been afloat for two months before being taken on trial. It seemed, despite the poor data, that ship thrust came out consistently higher than the model prediction and led Baker to wonder whether this was due to thrust deduction differences or errors in the estimates of effective power from the model test. The discussion which his paper stimulated might profitably have been left to a later date when more reliable evidence was available. As it was it led to much heart-searching over the validity of Froude scaling for both residuary resistance and propeller data but Taylor from Washington calmed down things by seeing no reason to doubt the general application of Froude's law, pointing out that it was obvious that flow conditions at ship and model could not possibly be expected to be the same. In analysing the results, Baker had introduced an arbitrary allowance for wind resistance which Liddell objected to describing it as a blanket correction. Baker was pleased to agree since it supported his own argument for research into this aspect of ship resistance. The subject was currently under consideration by the Advisory Committee and, when Hughes arrived at the Tank in 1926, studies were soon to begin. The final unsurprising conclusion Baker made most forcefully was the need for greater accuracy in the measurement of ship power. He pressed the case for all new ships to be fitted with both thrust and torsion meters and recommended that continuous measurements be taken as a matter of course.

The thrust comparisons that Baker had made had been obtained from relatively full ships and when in 1926 the destroyer *Ambuscade* of fine form became available Baker expected its low wake to produce a small interaction between ship and propeller, which after correction for the augment would lead to a propeller thrust very close to the ship resistance. Thrust measurements were duly obtained on *Ambuscade* and ship resistance deduced using the thrust deduction fraction obtained from the corresponding model propulsion experiment (the Froude propulsion gear was used, thrust only being measured). A comparison of this deduced resistance with that estimated from the model resistance test gave disappointing discrepancies over the speed range of between 8 and 20 per cent, the model prediction being lower. Two more ships, the twin screw vessels *Empress of Australia* and *Pacific Reliance*, were taken on trial in the same year and gave similar differences. All three ships led to the same conclusion; the ship resistance estimated from ship thrust measurements exceeded that estimated from model resistance experiments; but matters were to improve, particularly when torsion meters began to be fitted more frequently. Then better comparisons were seen. In 1928 trials on the *Viceroy of India* showed model predictions for power and propeller r.p.m. to be within 1 per cent of the ship and other ships tested during this period gave differences that never exceeded 5 per cent, allowing Baker to venture the opinion in his annual report to the Advisory Committee that:

results to date now show Tank powers to be 2–4 per cent lower than the ship.

In the years which followed, ship-model correlation studies were done whenever opportunities arose. The approach changed as knowledge and experience of ship performance increased. For example, the importance of hull surface roughness on completed ships was soon appreciated and when ultimately BSRA began their huge programme of work it became regular practice to measure hull roughness on all ships before their trials.

The full-scale work at sea going on at this time cannot be left without reference to Baker's study on ship wake and its frictional belt. He had long felt the need to learn more of ship conditions to strengthen the assumptions R.E. Froude had made in estimating ship propeller efficiency from model results. Baker had done some preliminary experiments on a flat plate towed in the tank, measuring velocities in its wake by pitot tubes and in discussing his results with R.E. Froude, the latter provided some full-scale data obtained by the Admiralty at sea on a destroyer. A model of this was run at Teddington only to give a poor correlation between the two sets of results, leaving Baker with the desire to obtain more full-scale data, ideally from ships of different type. Messrs Dalgleish offered two ships, *Snaefell* and *Ashworth* and Dawes in the workshop was given the job of constructing the robust instrumentation needed which was based, essentially, on R.E. Froude's earlier experience. R.S. Cutland, who had arrived at the Tank in 1920 and who was subsequently to serve with distinction for many years, worked with Dawes designing the whole assembly, which with the co-operation and assistance of the Dalgleish company was fitted to both ships in turn. The pitot tube arrangement devised projected through the ship's shell plating through special cocks, one near amidships at the ship's side, not far below the waterline, and the other just aft of the termination of the parallel middle body on the ship's bottom and near its centreline. Through each cock a telescopic tube enclosing the pitot tube projected and selected distances from the ship's surface could be reached. The pitot tube was made up of three small bore pipes, one transmitting head and the other two, pressure readings. The pipes were led back to a mercury manometer set up inside the ship. Baker, Cutland and Dawes went aboard both ships on passages from Holland to Sunderland and experienced variable weather conditions. A great number of measurements were taken but unfortunately in the poorer weather the pitot head at the amidships position came out of the water and with air entering the pipes many readings were spoilt. Nevertheless, enough data were collected on *Snaefell* to allow a comparative model test to be run. Baker presented the findings in his 1929 paper[17] and included for good measure the results from his earlier plank tests. He was able to improve the accuracy of von Karman's formula for the width of the boundary layer, expressing it in terms of ship length and also showed that wake velocity was dependent on the distance from the hull and the width of the wake. Baker's formula for wake velocity included a term for distance from the hull. Its power, n, could be deduced from the pitot tube measurements allowing a direct comparison between ship and model. For *Snaefell* and *Ashworth* n appeared to vary between 0·115 and 0·21 depending on length and hull surface roughness. At the model, results showed very clearly that the width of the boundary layer was greater than found on *Snaefell* and considerably fuller in character. Comparative values for n were 0·115 (*Snaefell*) and 0·208 for the model, which served to demonstrate the influence of scale. The results left several unanswered questions and stimulated the need for further work, which later in 1935 became possible when Furness Withy made available for similar trials the *Pacific Trader*.

Wave-making Resistance

In 1920 the National Tank was fortunate to recruit W.C.S. Wigley, a scholar of Emmanuel College, Cambridge, who after completing the mathematical tripos with considerable distinction in 1912 went on to do war service and then worked for a short time at RAE. He became interested in the theory of ship wave-making resistance and was convinced that if the theoretical approach as it stood was to progress then it needed validation. He was thus attracted to the Tank's testing facilities and on arrival was encouraged to pursue a programme of measurement.

Attempts at establishing a mathematical theory of wave-making resistance were being made by Michell at the end of the 19th century and in 1898 he produced his classic paper[18] which described an approximate method for calculating the resistance of a ship in deep water. This involved the use of a Fourier expansion and the summation of triple and quadruple integrals, enabling Michell to calculate three things, wave resistance, the wave form produced by the ship and the conditions of motion which influence ship sinkage and trim. Hogner and Havelock followed Michell in this very difficult field and Havelock produced his own theoretical method based on the resistance of immersed spheroids. It used doublets to satisfy boundary conditions but both the Michell and Havelock methods, like so many theoretical approaches, relied heavily on certain assumptions, chief of which was the neglect of turbulence and viscosity effects in the fluid which was regarded as ideal, that is, a frictionless medium. Wigley wanted to test the accuracy of the assumptions and did so by testing model hulls. Measuring their total resistance and subtracting resistance due to skin friction obtained from R.E. Froude's O constants for model length he arrived at a remainder C_R. If, as Wigley argued, eddy making resistance could be neglected then C_R should equal the calculated wave resistance, C_W, according to Michell or Havelock. However, C_W could be calculated only for hull shapes of known mathematical definition and so Wigley began by using hulls of sine curve form which were symmetrical fore and aft and in so doing simplified the extremely complicated calculations necessary in Michell's method. The quadruple integral was eliminated leaving a single triple integral but even so an enormous amount of calculation was necessary, which without the assistance of today's powerful computers took Wigley four days of solid calculation work to arrive at C_W for just one speed. Since a reasonable measurement curve included at least 15 speeds the extent of Wigley's determination and labour speaks for itself.

Three models were made and run in the tank. Model 713 reproduced a form suggested by Michell in 1898,[18] 714 had a flat bottom and allowed any discrepancies between theoretical and actual wave resistance to be determined more easily and model 755 was finer and allowed higher test speeds to be reached. From the calculations described Wigley arrived at C_W and plotted values against Ⓟ comparing C_W with C_R derived from the model measurements.[19] Results from model 714 were discarded when it was realised that the sharp bilge radius which it included would have led to undue eddy resistance, confusing the comparison. For the other two models the curves of C_W tended to be less than C_R, particularly at mid and high speeds and the theoretical humps were exaggerated and occurred earlier. It was thought that the discrepancies in the level of resistance were due mainly to two things, the neglect of eddy making and the neglect of a form factor allowance when calculating the skin friction resistance from Froude's flat plate data. The disagreement in the position of the resistance humps was put down to the neglect of viscosity. To throw light on the effect of form, two further models, numbers 825 and 829 were made, both derivatives of 755 and representing a progressive reduction in beam. The results[20] confirmed that the differences in C_W and C_R decreased with model beam and were least in model 825, this model being the slenderest of the three models 755, 829 and 825. However, Wigley still thought the differences too great and he turned his thoughts to modifications of the mathematical treatment. He continued to experiment because he was keen to see what happened when model shapes more akin to actual ship forms were tried. He introduced asymmetry in two further models, the results from these[21] together with measured wave profiles being presented in 1930. The new models, 1008 and 1009 each had the same forebody as 829 but after bodies were filled out to give two different shapes (elliptical and mathematically defined). Wigley then ran each model twice, first with the fore body leading and next by turning the model round with its after body leading. The two curves of C_R from the two sets of measurements were naturally different, but in calculating the respective C_W values from Michell, Wigley found to his chagrin that they were the same whether the bow or stern was leading. Considering this, he argued that it would indeed be the case in an ideal fluid without viscosity. Overall, Wigley in his concluding thoughts to his 1930 paper[21] was pessimistic of the success of calculating wave resistance for an actual ship form but G. Weinblum from the Berlin tank was more sanguine and in complimenting Wigley said:

no research work on residuary resistance can be carried out without reference to Mr. Wigley's tests ... the present paper is of the highest value and fixes an upper limit to the application of Michell's theory.

Wigley's experimental work was in fact the first of its kind; his earlier 1927 paper had earned an INA premium and now his latest one received the award of the Institution's Gold medal.

For the next few years Wigley pondered over the mathematics, expanding Michell's theory to include the calculation of wave profiles. Using Ⓟ theory he found that it predicted the humps and hollows in a resistance curve fairly well except for the largest hump which was known from practice to occur at Ⓟ = 1·6. Theory persisted in predicting this at Ⓟ = 1·5. Wigley's thoughts led to another paper[22] in 1932 which again drew forth praise from Weinblum who paid tribute to Wigley's dual gifts as theoretician and experimenter. Weinblum though favoured abandoning the Ⓟ theory preferring to believe that humps and hollows depended more on the combined influence of prismatic coefficient and the tangent of the hull section area curve. Ⓟ theory included prismatic only.

Propellers and their Interaction with a Hull

On the subject of propellers Baker had long favoured the use of aerofoil type blade section shapes instead of the conventional circular back type. He also believed that both the geometry of the propeller and its proximity to the ship's hull were important to ultimate efficiency. The Advisory Committee was conscious of the growing demand for improved ship efficiency and approved a programme of research to look into these things. This began a very extensive study which spread over several years and included the drawing up and testing of a series of 30 cm diameter propellers, many of which were used to propel a 7⅓ metres single screw wax model, a larger than usual model which became a familiar sight at the Tank earning the nickname "Big Ben".

The idea of introducing aerofoil sections was not new, the first propeller of this kind having been fitted to *Northwestern Miller* in 1914. She was followed 11 years later by the twin screw *Empress of Australia*. But before looking into the possible benefits of alternative blade section shape the Tank felt it necessary to learn more of hull propeller interaction. Little was known of how propulsive efficiency might be improved by changes in clearance between the propeller and the stern aperture. Baker and Kent took a typical 0·76 block coefficient form and by fitting detachable plates at the stern frame a variety of propeller, rudder and hull clearances were artificially created. In the extreme case, an almost completely closed aperture was produced. A series of propulsion experiments were conducted using a conventional propeller ringing changes in the aperture configuration. An alternative propeller with aerofoil sections was also used. Some interesting results were obtained.[23] So far as hull propeller clearance was concerned highest efficiencies occurred when the aperture aft of the propeller was filled in or, in other words, when a fin forward of the forward side of the rudder was fitted. This improved efficiency by 10 per cent. When the propellers were changed it was clear in every case that the aerofoil type gave an improvement, about 6 per cent being noted. The importance of the relative position of propeller, rudder and hull had been shown for the first time and the whole question of improved efficiency obtained by adding fins, nozzles, plates to the ship at its stern has become the subject of intermittent study over the years, such devices having been adopted on several occasions to certain types of ship.

Air Resistance

There was one other major research undertaken during the 13-year period we have been following. This was led by Hughes who came to the Tank from the Royal Naval College at Greenwich in 1926. Recruited as a junior assistant, Hughes was to become one of the leading figures at the Tank, gaining a huge reputation as a meticulous experimenter and indefatigable worker in the field of skin friction. His greatest achievements came in later years but he got off to a splendid start in 1927 when he examined the important problem of the air resistance of ship superstructures. Some extraordinary experiments were done in the tank on models towed upside down. Today air resistance tests are normally carried out in a wind tunnel but the tunnels available to Hughes in 1927 could accept only short 2 metre models and although tunnel speeds were greater than the tank carriage, tank models were three times longer and with the kinematic viscosity of air 13 times that of water, higher Reynolds number could be reached by tests in water. High numbers were very desirable but it was also important in water tests to be sure that no wave-making should be present at the model otherwise spurious results would emerge. Since the laws of motion were the same for air and water, the resistance of any body in air could be deduced from its resistance in water provided wave resistance was eliminated, the value of the resistance coefficient being the same in both fluids at the same Reynolds number. Test speeds were limited to ¾ m per second and at this a Reynolds number of 4 million was achieved.

At the time only visual observations and measurements of wind strength had been made by Kent in his rough water trials at sea and two of the ships he used, the tanker *San Gerardo* and the fast cargo vessel *London Mariner*, were chosen by Hughes for the new study. A third, Cunard's passenger liner *Mauretania* was added and three models, 970, 1057 and 1086 were made. Beautifully crafted, their hulls in wax and superstructures in varnished wood with enamelled tin plate, the models included in all but the smallest detail the various superstructures. Each model was divided into two detachable parts, the main wax hull which extended from the uppermost continuous deck to a few centimetres below the waterline and the superstructure with its deck erections. This division was provided so that tests could be done on the main hull only to determine its relative resistance. In the experiments each model was ballasted so as to float upside down at the correct waterline. Thus the original few centimetres of draught were reversed to become freeboard. By rotating the model it was possible to carry out tests at any angle to the flow.

These were unique tests and provided data of permanent value.[24] According to theory, air resistance depended on Reynolds number but Hughes found, at least for the range of Reynolds numbers tested, that it did not. Of greater significance, air resistance reached a maximum when the flow direction was 30° off bow or stern. Hitherto it had been assumed that a dead ahead direction would be the worst case. Hughes produced important diagrams giving values of the resistance coefficient for all directions of wind for the three ship types.

Although Hughes' results were of great importance doubts were nevertheless cast on the applicability of such low speed tests in water to the estimation of high speed wind forces. So, some remarkable tests were done in the open air, a new model of *Mauretania* being made (model 1124) which replicated 1086 in all except the slender masts. It was built on a base board the top of which represented the load waterline and floated in four cylindrical tanks of water. The tanks were rigidly secured to a rotatable platform on a 20 metres high open work tower situated in an open space in the grounds of NPL. A pitot tube which gave wind speed and direction was set up 2 metres clear of the model. The wind force acting on the model was balanced by two component forces acting along the model centreline, the forces being measured by a strong spring balance which also kept the model floating free. The photograph in plate 18 shows the model at the top of the tower, a sight which must have fascinated passers by. Apart from the required verification of earlier measurements in water, Hughes also looked into ways of reducing air resistance by changing the shape and distribution of the superstructure. Some work by Stanton[25] was helpful. He had shown how the resistance of a constant diameter cylinder varied with length when placed along the direction of flow and for a given cross-section area of the cylinder resistance could be reduced by selecting a certain length. Where possible the preferred lengths of deck erections were chosen accordingly. Hughes presented his latest results to the Scottish Institution[26] and it is evident when reading his paper that difficulties were experienced when carrying out these unique tests. Measurements were taken whenever wind conditions became reasonably steady, which in a natural wind rarely lasted for more than a second or two. It was also hard to obtain reliable readings unless the wind was directly ahead, astern or on the beam and reluctantly the experiments had to be restricted to these three directions only. Nevertheless some useful results were possible at wind speed up to 30 m.p.h. and, so far as a comparison with the earlier measurements in water were concerned a satisfactory verification was found, mean ratios of air and water resistance being fairly close to unity at all Reynolds numbers. The results showed that wind resistance could be reduced by up to 30 per cent if certain changes were made to superstructure shapes. This was of no real significance in calm air conditions but it did mean that considerable differences in speed and power would be seen when steering into a high wind. For example, a 16,000 tonnes tanker steaming at 10 knots into a head wind of 20 knots would save ⅓ knot in speed if its resistance in air were reduced by 30 per cent. But Hughes had forgotten a vital factor. Frodsham Holt in discussing,[26] pointed out that a wind gradient existed in real life, wind velocity over a ship's superstructure varying depending on its height above water and that Hughes ought to have found a means of taking such a gradient into account. Its presence was certainly important to overall resistance and Frodsham Holt's astute observation was not forgotten in later experiments; it is now common practice to make due allowance in modern wind tunnel tests.

Airships

The affinity between aero and hydrodynamic flow problems occasionally led to co-operative research between workers in the Tank and NPL's Aerodynamic Division, Baker and Stanton's work on strut resistance being an example. A long-running research had begun at the end of the First World War when there was much interest in kite balloons and airships.

It was decided to test an egg-shaped form in both air and water over a range of Reynolds number. The wind tunnel and tank were used and the same model was tested in each using common measuring apparatus. The egg-shaped airship model tested in 1922 proved to be too small, the required speed in the tank to overlap the results from the wind tunnel being too low, failing to produce turbulent flow over the model surface. A larger model almost twice the size of the first gave a stable set of water results but the corresponding tests in air which did not materialise until 1928 gave results (after correction for pressure drop in the tunnel) 8 per cent higher than the tank figures. The discrepancy was never resolved and Baker doubted the accuracy of the wind tunnel results pointing to recent work in America and elsewhere which had shown that in addition to the known error due to pressure drop there was in all probability an unknown amount of laminar flow on such forms when tested in a wind tunnel. Although the results were discussed and referred to the Aeronautical Research Council nothing more was done and the work left in abeyance until such times as an open-jet wind tunnel became available.

Cruiser Sterns

The idea of the cruiser stern instead of elliptically shaped raised sterns came, as is often the case, from delightfully simple observation and experimentation. Kent in one of his trial trips at sea in the late 1920s watched the flow around the ship's stern and reckoned that an area of dead water with eddies built up and was carried along by the ship. Dropping a piece of wood into the wake he saw the wood twist and turn but accompany the ship for many miles. Back at the Tank he took a similar hull form with an elliptic stern and raised counter and dangled a piece of wood from a string over the stern. As at sea and with the string slack the wood came along with the model as it moved through the water. Baker saw this and suggested that Kent should pour condensed milk around the hull just ahead of its stern. The milk showed a very clear pattern formed by the boundaries of the dead water and Kent took photographs from which he drew up a faired shape which could be added to the stern. Wax was cast on the model to give the new shape and experiments showed a very satisfactory reduction in resistance. The cruiser stern was born and thereafter gradually came to be adopted in merchant ship design.

   With research now a regular feature, opportunities were given to students to follow chosen topics for postgraduate research. The first to arrive at the Tank was W.G.A. Perring who in 1923 took up an Exhibition Scholarship awarded by the 1851 Royal Commissioners. He chose to look into streamline flow, work earlier earmarked for the small tank, but with the problems with this facility unresolved Perring used the main tank instead. He tested three models of mathematical shape and varying fullness and by measuring pressure variations around each he was able to make comparisons with streamline theory. Test speeds were low and avoided wave-making and the results enabled Perring to ascertain a form effect which he concluded to be 10–15 per cent of the flat plate friction resistance.[27] Perring enjoyed his study so much that he stayed on at the Tank contributing usefully for another two years, by which time he had published a second paper which dealt with skin friction experiments on smooth surfaces.
   Postgraduate students were welcome, though temporary additions to the

Tank staff and in later years the Tank was to host many others both from home and abroad. So far as staff numbers at the Tank were concerned a gradual increase was seen from 19 in 1919 to 36 10 years later. In 1920 when the demand for model tests was recovering rapidly from war conditions NPL's Executive Committee agreed to increase the staff to speed up the work, the expense to be borne by the Special Reserve Fund and DSIR. Even though several newcomers, including G.S. Selman, an observer, arrived within a year, the only way to maintain output to meet the demand was to lengthen the daily working hours and, as has been mentioned, a shift system was introduced that continued for several years. In 1930, with the Tank fully established, staff numbers had grown to 37. Prominent amongst newcomers since the early 1920s were, in order of arrival, L.W. Berry, F. Gridley, G. Hughes, F.H. Todd (a future Superintendent of the Tank), H.C. Garlick, J.J. Cross, F.J. Rayment, A.C. Rixon and J.F.C. Conn, all of whom were to serve with distinction for many years before retiring or moving elsewhere. Selman's interest was in small fast craft and when he met H. Scott-Paine, the builder and driver of *Miss Britain III* in the epic Harmsworth Trophy of 1933, he struck up an immediate affinity despite Scott-Paine's scepticism over model testing. Scott-Paine's future designs owed much to Selman and his insistence on using model data, and it was no surprise when Selman left to join Scott-Paine at Hythe and work on designs such as the successful PV70. In 1929 Miss Keary left to marry and as Mrs Smith Keary still found time to be involved for a few more years co-authoring two papers. Todd came fresh from the termination of his 1851 Exhibition Scholarship, which he had followed at Armstrong College, Newcastle, studying ship vibration.

As commercial work came in and as the various research projects were approved and initiated by the Advisory Committee, Baker directed and delegated responsibility to his various assistants. Not that in so doing he lost touch. On the contrary, nothing escaped him and his control was absolute. He expected and got loyalty from everyone and was generous in the loyalty he showed in return. The assistants called on the services of the observers for experimental and analysis duties and the workshop staff, from 1923, supervised by Dawes, looked after the manufacture and fitting of models. Although, obviously, there was a division of duties, no job was done without the consultation and involvement of all concerned including if necessary Baker himself. The decade of 1920–30 saw an average of 60 models made and tested each year, necessitating at least one wax casting per week and sometimes two. The cost to the customer for a model, plus resistance and propulsion tests in calm water, remained fairly constant at £240 during this period. The proportion of models used for research purposes varied with the demand for repayment or test work from the private firms and at times of industrial depression such as 1921 and 1930, research effort increased to fill the diminished demand for commercial work. Thus at all times the Tank stayed busy and right up until the 1970s the whole balance between test and research work shifted continually. On occasion this presented serious difficulties, since at times of depression it could never augur well if research were to become too high a proportion of the whole, unless financial support from industry could be permanently guaranteed. When DSIR was formed the new department agreed to share with industry the cost of research at the Tank. In 1922 this was estimated as £5,000, half of which was contributed by 18 shipbuilding and engineering firms, six shipowners, the Chamber of Shipping and Lloyd's Register. But by 1930 at a time of acute depression it became clear that individual firms in seeking economies chose to withdraw their support to the Research Fund. The total subscriptions received that year amounted to £1,679 and the reserve fund for research was almost exhausted. Although perhaps inevitable this was nevertheless disappointing since there is no doubt that the Tank's research during 1919–30 led and encouraged the industry to adopt new things such as aerofoil sectioned propellers, cruiser sterns in merchant ships and in certain single screw ships the use of a central stern fin.

TESTS FOR FIRMS

The work done for private firms was considerable and it is interesting to note the proportion of different ship types that were tested at this time. Taking the years 1926–28 as an example, a survey shows that 54 per cent of all such tests dealt with ocean-going steamers, 20 per cent were liners, 12 per cent cross-channel and coastal steamers, 6 per cent miscellaneous craft such as tugs and barges, 4 per cent ferries, 2 per cent paddle steamers and 2 per cent destroyers. In addition to this, 11 designs for seaplane hulls and floats were tested during the same period, some of these in support of British designs for the Schneider Trophy race. Britain won in 1927 and 1929 and at Calshot in 1929 a speed of 328 m.p.h. was recorded. Earlier, in 1920, the crash of the Felixstowe Fury flying boat led to extensive tests, the results from which were used to supply recommendations to the official Committee of Enquiry. The crash, that had occurred during take off, stimulated further research and the ACA were soon to contribute £1,000 annually to its cost (the work included both theoretical and experimental aspects, Wigley's skill being enlisted to carry out strength calculations on a flexible type of seaplane hull). The paddle steamers were notable in that fully operational feathering paddle wheels had to be made and used to propel models. One of these, some ½ metre in diameter, beautifully made by Rayment, has been preserved and can be seen in the NPL museum. Other commercial tests of particular interest were those in 1929 on the new Canadian destroyers *Sanguenay* and *Skeena*, a series of tests on Thames barges and observations of the effect of shallow and restricted water on manoeuvring which arose from an invitation Baker received to witness full-scale experience in the Suez Canal.

J.I. Thornycroft designed the new destroyers for the Canadian Navy and asked the Tank to draw up its own ideas and test both forms. The new ships had generally to be similar to the British *Beagle* or B class destroyers and capable of

35 knots. Thornycroft's design gave a waterline length of 97 metres which meant that at top speed Froude number was 0·6, well above the speed of the main resistance hump. After preliminary resistance experiments Thornycroft's design (model 1040) was better than the Tank's, particularly at speeds below 31 knots, although there was very little in it at the higher speeds. Nevertheless, Thornycroft's design was selected for subsequent propulsion and flow tests and ultimately adopted for the two new ships. The data obtained from the tests proved to be invaluable for future destroyer designs and both ships were very successful. *Skeena* achieved more than 36 knots on trial and was dubbed "the Rolls-Royce" on arrival at Portsmouth. Sadly both met unfortunate ends. *Sanguenay* was extensively damaged in the Second World War and had to be scrapped and soon after *Skeena* was wrecked off Iceland.

The tests on barges were the first of their kind done at the Tank and involved towing a train of barges behind a tug, the train consisting of two columns of three lashed side by side. Baker soon found the standard type of Thames barge to be grossly inefficient and with Miss Keary made modifications to it keeping the overall dimensions unchanged. By decreasing the angle of swim ends and side batter they reduced the pull on a barge by up to 70 per cent. Going further, a 50 per cent increase in barge length brought greater improvements such that the usual assembly of six barges could be replaced by four without changing the overall length of the train. In carrying out their tests on 1/12-scale model barges[28] Baker and Keary voiced their fears over scaling the results since a large proportion of the resistance came from eddy making. The South Metropolitan Gas Company were persuaded to make available some standard barges for full scale trials. The tug *Partnership* was used to tow four barges each laden with 200 tonnes of coal on the River Thames between Greenwich and Tower Bridge. Tank staff set up the apparatus to measure pull using a calibrated spring balance. Speed was obtained from a patent tide log towed from the end of a 3 metre boom slung over the side of a barge. The trials gave curves of pull for three speeds between 2½ and 3½ knots, which were later compared with extrapolated tank results. The two sets of curves were identical. Such agreement was hardly expected since the full size barges were several years old with surfaces which were by no means smooth but at least fears of gross inaccuracy in the model result were allayed.

The steering tests in shallow water, commissioned by Thornycroft, arose when that company was asked to carry out alterations to a ship's rudder. The ship in question had been steered up the Hooghly and Thames rivers by an experienced captain who had complained that he could not handle the ship in shallow water, refusing to take her to sea again until a completely new rudder and steering gear was fitted. Thornycroft asked the Tank to model the water depths in the Hooghly and Thames and to carry out steering experiments. A free-running self-propelled model was used and driven first of all in equivalent shoal water without side banks, rudder angle and rate of yaw being measured. It was not easy to steer the model and the captain, who was present at the tests, agreed that what he saw accorded with his experience at sea. Side banks were then added to give two channels, one deep and one shallow, each of nine ship beam widths. The yaw moment exerted during steering was balanced by Bottomley's lateral dynamometers which prevented the model turning off course. From the results and observations obtained Baker reckoned an increase in the area of the rudder would provide a satisfactory solution but the captain remained adamant in pressing for a different rudder altogether. He was finally persuaded, by seeing for himself, that a larger rudder did indeed improve matters and Bottomley's gear showed from the measurements of rudder head torque that a large rudder stock would not be needed and thus the steering gear already in the ship did not need to be replaced.

The problems highlighted by these tests led Lord Inchcape and the Australian Commonwealth line of steamers to ask Baker to gain first-hand experience of ships as they made passage through the Suez canal. Baker went on eight ships whose rudders were of the balanced or unbalanced kind. There was also a variation in the size and spread of propellers in twin screw ships. Noticeably different behaviour was seen. The best ship was a 170 metres twin screw ship with a rectangularly shaped rudder. When swung over to $8\frac{1}{2}°$ the rudder met the screw races, whereas in another twin screw ship the rudder needed to be at 26° and, not surprisingly, this ship was the hardest of all to control. Baker noticed that all of the ships as they proceeded through the canal oscillated steadily requiring constant helm correction at low ahead speeds. His observations led to a series of corresponding model tests[29] which enabled him to relate steering characteristics with size and position of both propellers and rudders.

It might be thought that the research going on attracted a glamour that routine repetitive test work lacked. This was not always so; for example, when inventors brought their ideas to the Tank for testing they could usually be relied on to provide entertaining and challenging tasks and if a new idea led to heated debate then this added spice. One such occasion occurred in 1931 when a series of tests were carried out on a controversial hull form designed by the German company Maier S.V. (MSV). Maier was an Austrian scientist who believed that if in a vessel of normal form the streamline flow could be persuaded to follow the shortest path, then reduced resistance would be the natural result. Few disagreed. But the MSV company claimed that any normal form could be altered so as to produce a path that would appear on the ship's body plan as a more or less straight diagonal. M.F. Hay presented a paper[30] to the INA, which in part was unashamed sales propaganda and stated that two model tests on normal and Maier forms had shown the latter to be 10 per cent more efficient. Reduced resistance had been confirmed by the German builders Weserwerft who had commissioned tests in six towing tanks around the world (the National Tank was not one). Ships had been built and one, the *Ile de Beauté*, a high speed passenger liner was cited as a good example with, as an added bonus, the reputation as a good sea boat. In cases of this kind a criterion which can be used to judge one design against another is usually sought and naval architects had long used the Admiralty constant, a quantity calculated from a ship displacement and the IHP at the ship's engine for an observed ship speed. Hay sniffed at the constant saying it was inaccurate but in discussing the paper Baker refuted this and went on to demonstrate how he had used the Admiralty constant of 320, as given by Hay, for longer Maier form ships and using some reasonable assumptions worked back to derive a ship Ⓒ value of 0·66. The constant was far too low in Baker's opinion and in any case he had tested many forms of similar proportions at Teddington, which had given values between 0·6 and 0·66. Nevertheless, Baker conceded that the results given in the paper for the two Maier forms were good, but then concluded scathingly that the reductions claimed could only be the result of comparing a Maier form with a "normal" form that in itself was poor to begin with. Sir Maurice Denny's tank at Dumbarton had been one of the six used by Weserwerft and the results from several model tests were to hand. Yes, some reductions had been seen but Sir Maurice was not wholly convinced. He did however think it worth paying some attention to Maier form and even suggested that an enterprising builder might like to build two ships, one a Maier to settle the argument once and for all. A cheaper solution soon emerged when Workman, Clarke and Company of Belfast came up with a spirited suggestion which they put to MSV. Workman, Clarke were willing at their expense to design and test a normal form of a single screw ship intended for 11¾ knots and invited MSV to use the lines as a basis for an alternative Maier form. Two models would then be tested at the National Tank, and if Baker at Teddington thought he could produce something better, then he would be given the chance and a third model would be tested. If Baker's results were better, then the lines would be sent to MSV, and if they so wished, MSV would be given the opportunity to pursue further experiments, this time at their expense. MSV agreed and in due course two sets of lines arrived at the Tank. Baker inspected these and then suggested his own and so three models were tested. The gauntlet had been thrown down. Model 1218B was the basis Workman, Clarke design, 1217 the Maier proposal and 1218C Baker's modification to the basis design. Resistance tests at a light draught showed 1218C to be the best of the three at 12 knots and at the load draught there was very little between the Maier and Baker forms, Baker's being about 2 per cent better at 11½ knots with the basis form a little worse than the other two. Propulsion experiments followed on the Maier and Baker forms and the improved quasi propulsive coefficient in the Baker form (0·69 against 0·65) gave it an extra edge and an overall advantage of 8 per cent. This fully vindicated Baker's view that, provided one began with a good basis form there was nothing in Maier's claims for improved performance. Unfortunately the whole affair ended in acrimony. Baker reneged on his promise to send on his lines to Maier saying:

I have a decided personal objection to being set serious problems and doing quite a lot of work on ship hulls and then to find that it is all being sent free to a continental firm.

However, the Maier S.V. company continued to promote their forms and in the years that followed became a powerful force in ship design, their Maier form bow being adopted in many successful ships.

Another claim or invention that evoked Baker's irritation concerned the corrugated ship, an idea put forward in 1920 by A.H. Hawer. Hawer had experimented with small models at Wallsend using a swinging pendulum just as Beaufoy had done 120 years earlier. Hawer claimed that corrugations 2½ per cent of the ship's beam in depth built longitudinally into the sides of the ship would reduce resistance. Baker had tried this at the Tank but had found no magical qualities. He was scornful of the whole idea and the serious limitations of the experiments dismissing Hawer's paper to the INA with:

I am sure it is always possible to find a normal form that would equal or better any of the freak designs for which inventors claimed special advantage.

This was typical of how Baker could be totally uncompromising in his views for which he gained a reputation as brusque, even rude. But his forthright and on occasion pungent comments were made whenever he was sure of his facts and there can be little wrong with that.

Since its beginning the Tank had been in almost continuous use and by the mid-1920s a strong case could be made for additional test facilities, particularly since long working hours were now a common feature of life at the Tank. And the tank itself was due for overhaul and refurbishment. Inspections were made to both it and the towing carriage. The walls had suffered no deterioration in 14 years and the quality of the soft river water used had remained excellent. The eels introduced by Baker in 1911 were still there and had been joined by carp, tench and rudd. As a result there was virtually no weed but a little copper sulphate was added as a precaution for the future. The fish shrugged this off and indeed over the years flourished to become a considerable population, one specimen, a carp, reaching a mighty 15 pounds. They were and always have been treated with affection by the staff and have enjoyed regular feeding. Leakage of tank water was found to be microscopic and temperature over the years had been within 50–62° with air remaining fairly constant at 70°F. The towing carriage had proved very successful and although experiment runs must have been short, speeds up to 7 metres per second were possible, this in fact being reached in resistance tests on a model of the racing power boat *Miss Britain III* in 1932. Flashlight photography was installed in 1925 following co-operation with the Optics Division of NPL.

The idea of a second tank took root as early as 1920 when following the war there was a steady recovery in the demand for test work. Although, as has already been noted, test work on ship designs fell away at times of industrial slump it was becoming obvious that a second tank was an inevitable requirement for the future.

The first official move came in 1923 when a proposal based on an outline design drawn up by HM Office of Works was sent to the Air Ministry. A second tank could be built alongside and parallel to the existing National Tank at Teddington, this additional facility being intended primarily as a tank in which tests on seaplane hulls could be conducted. Nothing came of this at the time although in due course RAE was to have its own tank at Farnborough. A few years later the demand for ship work had grown to such an extent that new work could not begin in a reasonable time and prospective customers were obliged to look elsewhere. The Advisory Committee, now under the chairmanship of Sir Eustace Tennyson d'Eyncourt following Sir William Smith's retirement in 1927, became concerned: it wanted the National Tank to serve the interests of all British shipbuilders. Following discussions with DSIR and with strong support from the Chamber of Shipping and the Liverpool Steam Ship Owners Association, representations were made to Government and Baker was asked to prepare a case. His approach was typically practical and in summarising it here we have a brief résumé of the state of affairs at 1929.

Baker began with a review of model test tanks at home and in Europe. In 1914 there was only one tank on the Continent available for mercantile work but by 1929 things were very different. Hamburg had two tanks (one for shallow water tests), Berlin's naval tank was working almost exclusively on mercantile designs and at Vienna there was a well-equipped tank working for German, Dutch, Italian and French interests. The naval tank in Paris was also available for mercantile work and the largest tank in Europe at Rome was nearing completion. Having listed the activity in other European countries Baker warmed to his task and continued thus:

It must be patent to anyone reading the above, that to compete with Great Britain these countries have realised that they must themselves have the advantage of tank tests for their ships, and that whereas in 1914 this country was leading and well ahead of others in knowledge of ship propulsion, it would be hopeless to suppose or to pretend that we can maintain this supremacy unless our facilities for work are increased. It must be apparent that international competition will increase in the next few years and that more and more foreign ships will be built on economical lines and so remove an advantage which has been ours up to the present.

It is a delusion to suppose that we are mentally equipped to make better progress than other nations in this scientific and practical work, and even if this were so, our present output is already less than that of the two tanks at Hamburg, and will be swamped by the Continental output when all the tanks are at work ...

Relevant to all of this was the fact that in 1929 gross tonnage of British ships stood at 20 million tons, exceeding by far any other Continental country, Germany at 4 million being next. If, with Britain's other tanks, the whole 20 million needed to be tested at the design stage, then the National Tank could not possibly cope. Baker then turned to the achievements at Teddington. In its first nine years 315 models representing 127 separate designs had been tested, an average of 31 models a year. By 1928, with propulsion as well as resistance a regular part of the test programme, the average had doubled as had income from tests. With the shift work system in operation the cost of the tests per design had remained the same since 1924. Since some firms were now withdrawing their work because of the time which had to elapse before tests could begin, Baker argued it would be quite wrong to stifle such a healthy demand for want of adequate facilities. Baker next instanced that roughly half of the designs submitted had been improved by the staff by 3 per cent or more and went on to give a vivid example of what this meant in practice to the shipowner. Taking the cost of coal as £1 a ton and the amount burnt as 1¼ pounds per IHP per hour, a 3 per cent improvement made to a hull design would save £1,500 in one year. And of course such gains accrued for the whole of the ship's life. By comparison the cost of a model test of £250 was very small beer. Baker finished by saying that a suitable plot of land was available at right angles to the existing tank at Teddington and a study had shown that a new tank capable of high carriage speeds and suited to the needs of seaplane tests would cost £40,000 plus £30,000 for a carriage and enclosing building. However, DSIR would be in the position to provide only a quarter of this amount.

The case was very convincing, in truth it was easy to make, and soon it bore fruit. Late in 1929 the Advisory Committee was pleased to report that cost difficulties had been overcome and on 20 February 1930 the Lord Privy Seal announced that a new tank was to be built at once, the total cost to be borne by the Government. Its proposed size and outline design had been approved and in addition the opportunity would be taken to provide more office and workshop accommodation.

The speed with which the final decision was made undoubtedly arose from the motives of a Government anxious to ease the severely depressed conditions that existed at the time and to stimulate employment locally. At any rate the Advisory Committee and its supporters had been rewarded for their hard work, which paved the way for a new era in the life of the National Tank.

REFERENCES

1. Riddle A.W., *Modern screw propeller geometry*, The Draughtsman Publishing Co., Rugeley, 1942.
2. Baker G.S. and Kent J.L., "Speed, dimensions and form of cargo vessels", trans. IESS, Vol. 62, 1919.
3. Skin friction Committee Report, trans. INA, 1925.
4. Hiraga Y., "Experimental investigations on the resistance of long planks and ships", trans. INA, 1934.
5. Baker G.S. and Bottomley G.H., "Manoeuvring of ships. Part I—unbalanced rudders of single screw ships", trans. IESS, Vol. 65, 1922.
6. Bottomley G.H., "Manoeuvring of ships. Part II—unbalanced rudders of twin screw ships", trans. IESS, Vol. 67, 1924.
7. Bottomley G.H., "Manoeuvring of ships. Part III—unbalanced rudders. Effect of varying fullness of form", trans. IESS, Vol. 70, 1927.
8. Bottomley G.H., "Manoeuvring of ships. Part IV—unbalanced rudders behind twin screw ships. Effect of fullness of form", trans. IESS, Vol. 74, 1930.

9. Bottomley G.H., "Manoeuvring of ships. Semi-balanced rudders of twin screw ships", trans. NECIES, Vol. 49, 1932.
10. Kent J.L., "Experiments on mercantile ship models in waves", trans. INA, 1922.
11. Kent J.L., "The effect of wind and waves on the propulsion of ships", trans. INA, 1924.
12. Kent J.L., "Propulsion of ships under different weather conditions", trans. INA, 1927.
13. Kent J.L., "The effect of rough water on the propulsion of single screw ships", trans. INA, 1931.
14. Baker G.S., "Measured mile trials and other ship propulsion data. Part I", trans. NECIES, Vol. 39, 1923.
15. Marine Oil-Engine Trials Committee, 6th Report, trans. I. Mech. Eng., 1931.
16. Baker G.S., "Measured mile trials and other ship propulsion data. Part II", trans. NECIES, Vol. 42, 1925.
17. Baker G.S., "Ship wake and the frictional belt", trans. NECIES, Vol. 46, 1929.
18. Michell J.H., "The wave resistance of a ship", *Philosophical Magazine*, Vol. 45, 1898.
19. Wigley W.C.S., "Ship wave resistance. A comparison of mathematical theory with experimental results", trans. INA, 1926.
20. Wigley W.C.S., "Ship wave resistance. A comparison of mathematical theory with experimental results—Part II", trans. INA, 1927.
21. Wigley W.C.S., "Ship wave resistance. Some further comparisons of mathematical theory and experimental result", trans. INA, 1930.
22. Wigley W.C.S., "Ship wave resistance. An examination and comparison of the speeds of maximum and minimum resistance in practice and in theory", trans. NECIES, Vol. 47, 1932.
23. Baker G.S. and Kent J.L., "Experiments on the propulsion of a single screw ship model", trans. INA, 1928.
24. Hughes G., "Model experiments on the wind resistance of ships", trans. INA, 1930.
25. Stanton T.E., NPL Collected Researches, Vol. I.
26. Hughes G., "The air resistance of ships' hulls with various types and distributions of superstructure", trans. IESS, Vol. 76, 1932.
27. Perring W.G.A., "Form effects and form resistance of ships", trans. INA, 1925.
28. Baker G.S. and Keary E.M., "Experiments on the resistance and form of towed barges", trans. INA, 1930.
29. Baker G.S., "Steering of ships in shallow water and canals", trans. INA, 1924.
30. Hay M.F., "The Maier form of hull construction", trans. INA, 1931.

CHAPTER 7

NEW FACILITIES: A SECOND TOWING TANK AND A CAVITATION TUNNEL

The specification for a second tank (known for several years as the "New Tank") was drawn up at the end of 1930 following visits to the recently completed tank in Rome and also to the tank at La Spezia in Italy. HM Office of Works' architect J. Bradley, with his assistant A.G. Ramsey, took charge of the constructional matters. With high speed testing very much in mind a long tank was wanted and it could best be fitted into the available land by building it at right angles to the existing tank. As such it would run very close to and roughly parallel to the boundary wall of Bushy Park but could not extend beyond a gate in this wall which opened on to a public footpath. Circumstances thus restricted its length to 206 metres. To achieve the carriage speeds of 10 metres per second plus that were asked for, a small light-weight towing carriage was required which led to a relatively narrow tank 6 metres wide. The continuing need for tests in shallow water persuaded Baker to include in the tank a permanent length of shallow water. The false bottom used in the main tank for such work had always given problems and there was no desire to add to these. Thus two-thirds of the tank was built to a depth of 3 metres, the remaining 54 metres shelving to 0·6 metre. In hindsight this was a mistake because 54 metres was not long enough to allow most experiment runs in shallow water to settle before measurements were taken and cutting the length of deep water led to restricted runs at the highest test speeds. In 1976, when a large programme of work in shallow water was begun, the limitations of the available length were finally recognised and 22 metres of the deep part of the tank filled in to give a continuous run of 76 metres over which water depths between zero and 0·6 metre could be arranged. This left the tank between two stools and although still useful its flexibility was reduced. Hughes' work outdoors on wind resistance had left its mark and in anticipating further work of this kind the roof of the tank's containing building was made flat without any obstructions. In fact no such work was ever done and tentative plans for offices above the tank were made but never followed up.

A small block of offices adjoining the tank which had already been authorised were built by Messrs Roll of Epsom and finished in the autumn of 1931 by which time other companies had been contracted to begin on the tank itself and associated equipment. Wilson, Lovett of Wolverhampton were contracted to build the tank and containing building and the assembly of carriage and running track was given to Messrs Markham of Chesterfield. GEC and the Brecknell, Willis company constructed the overhead power lines and collecting gear needed to drive the carriage and the Westinghouse Brake and Saxby Signal company were responsible for the pneumatic brake gear.

The space which became available between the north end of the main tank and the south side of the new was used to enlarge the existing workshop area and the transportation of models from workshop to either tank was made easier by installing overhead cranes.

As might be expected, Baker observed progress like a watchdog. Nothing escaped him and he concerned himself with such trivial details as the choice of brackets needed to mount telephones at the far end of the tank and on the carriage for communication with his office. He insisted that the unavoidable dust and dirt be cleared daily otherwise the "sweetness" of the water and the "spotless" carriage of the existing tank would suffer. He protested to architect Bradley that with just one month to go before the official opening of the new tank one plasterer only was employed to finish the rendering of the tank walls. "At this rate", he wrote to Bradley, "the work will take 60 days. We cannot allow more than 14 days for this."

At the time of the authorisation of the New Tank a distinction was needed between the existing tank and the proposed new one. It was decided in 1931 that the whole department should henceforth be known as the William Froude Laboratory and the main tank as the Alfred Yarrow Tank. The name of New for the second tank was only temporary and soon it became known simply as "Number Two tank". For many years a plaque set up at one end of the Alfred Yarrow Tank announced its origin but somehow the name never "stuck" and ultimately it was referred to as "Number One tank".

A large gathering of representatives from shipowning and building companies were invited to Teddington for the opening ceremony. As they arrived at 2 o'clock on the afternoon of 18 November 1932, they were shown some free steering experiments in the main tank on a self-propelled twin screw model, the rudder automatically controlled to produce model yaw relative to the carriage and measurements of rudder forces, etc. demonstrated. At 3 o'clock Sir Richard Glazebrook introduced the Rt. Hon. Stanley Baldwin to the assembled company and invited him to open the new tank. Baldwin, an FRS who had already served twice as Prime Minister but was now the Lord President of the Council at the time of Ramsay Macdonald's coalition Government, began his address by reminding everyone that the United Kingdom enjoyed a pre-eminent position in the art of shipbuilding. The capacity to build ships was "bred in our bones and is the product of generations of work of hand and brain". Paying glowing tributes to the genius of William Froude and the value of the William Froude Laboratory's research, proof of which could be seen in the growing demand for model tests, he emphasised that in 1932, even at a time of acute depression, the need for research:

... was as great today, indeed greater, than it had ever been. While we pass through the present crisis with courage and face the future with confidence, these days of depression are days in which we should devote ourselves to research against the days when prosperity comes, so that we might not have wasted them but be able to take the fullest advantage of the new things which science will teach us.

Such sentiments were in marked contrast to those of the 1980s Government when British shipbuilding experienced its greatest slump ever. Baldwin did go on to say research cost money and appealed to private benefactors to come forward who with the assistance of the state could provide the means for future research. He then declared the tank open and some demonstrations followed which showed a propeller being tested in open water on the recently designed propulsion dynamometer. Other items were shown and visitors were conducted around the workshop and on to the main tank carriage by members of staff resplendent in maroon NPL badges and white rosettes, splashes of colour which added to the gaiety of the occasion.

The opening of the tank attracted much national and international interest. Baldwin's views and allusions to the progress that had been made were echoed by *The Times*[1]:

One fact must have struck those who have followed at all closely the arguments for and against the completion of the new Cunarder.* The arguments against have been entirely based on economic grounds. Not the smallest doubt has been expressed of her ability when completed to regain the blue ribbon of the Atlantic. That seems to be taken as a foregone conclusion. On the other hand, when the *Great Eastern* was under construction in 1850, failure was freely prophesied and there was criticism which proved only too well justified. The contrast illustrates the remarkable progress which has been made in our knowledge of naval architecture.

Turning then to the achievements of the William Froude Laboratory *The Times* continued:

... it may be stated that as a direct result of research on cargo ship-form begun in 1911 and carried on more or less continuously ever since, the resistance to motion of a good ship-form has been improved by about 10%. The effect comes back to shipowners as a direct saving in fuel consumption amounting on a very conservative estimate, to over £1 million a year ...

The capital required for the erection and equipment has been provided by the generosity of private individuals or by the State. In present circumstances the group of firms who have for the past 10 years supported the Laboratory cannot be expected to do much more than maintain their contributions to the running costs. Until times improve the State will no doubt continue to help but the leaders of other industries benefiting from cheap and efficient sea transport may be induced to lend a hand to so essential an undertaking.

This last paragraph reiterated Baldwin's concluding remarks when he opened the tank. In lighter vein the *News Chronicle* noted that "the NPL might be called an adult scientists' playground or House of Dreams", the *Evening Standard* referred to "clever young men in grey flannels" and several newspaper reporters

* RMS *Queen Mary*, launched in 1934.

were attracted to the eels in the existing tank. "Three green eels have for ten years kept the experimental tank at the National Physical Laboratory free of water insects which would otherwise have affected delicate scientific calculations" wrote the *Daily Express*. The scavenging eels had indeed helped and more were soon caught and put into the new tank.

Amongst those present on the opening day was shipbuilder Sir James Lithgow. He was keen to see the Laboratory add to its resources by the addition of a new and different type of facility, a propeller cavitation tunnel. Lithgow's enthusiasm led him to present his plans to the visitors at the opening ceremony in November and it was not long before he became the William Froude Laboratory's second benefactor when he offered £5,000 towards the cost of a tunnel.

Sir James Lithgow enjoyed a distinguished career in shipbuilding becoming Chairman of both his own company in Port Glasgow and also Fairfield's in Glasgow. He was prominent in both World Wars. In the first he was wounded at the front, awarded the Military Cross and later recalled to become the Director of Merchant Shipping and in the second he was appointed Controller of Merchant Shipbuilding and Repair with, unusually for a civilian, a seat on the Board of Admiralty. Between the Wars he was created a baronet in 1925 and was the President of the FBI between 1930–32. Lithgow had an original and enquiring mind and was attracted to the interesting phenomenon of propeller cavitation and he became convinced that much could be learnt from model propeller tests under reduced pressure conditions in a cavitation tunnel. His generous donation was greatly welcomed and steps were taken immediately to construct a tunnel largely on the lines of his own proposals that he had demonstrated at the New Tank's opening.

The first cavitation tunnel in the world was a small piece of apparatus assembled by Sir Charles Parsons. He later used this as a basis for a much larger horizontal tunnel which he had built at Wallsend on the Tyne. But the first "modern" tunnel was pioneered by Lerbs in Germany in 1929. Lithgow was very much at the beginning of things, although by the time the tunnel which was to bear his name was completed in 1934 at Teddington, two other tunnels had appeared elsewhere in the world, at Washington and at Meguso in Japan.

Lithgow's outline was used by the staff to draw up final plans, and by 1933 a contract awarded to Markhams, who began construction in May. Space for the tunnel was found at the site of the abandoned small tank and a tall building with a floor at the level of the measuring section built to house the whole apparatus. A. Emerson who arrived at the laboratory in 1934 was given charge of the tunnel and its development and soon, with Berry, became immersed in the knotty problem of solving the many teething troubles. Both Emerson and Berry received great assistance from the skill and determination of mechanic C.C. Burgess who arrived after Emerson and became so involved with the intricacies of tunnel maintenance that he specialised in this work right up to the time of his retirement in 1960. Not surprisingly it was several years before success was reached and meaningful results published by which time a new stainless steel propeller drive shaft was fitted, its end bearing positioned outside the tunnel to avoid the problem of oil lubrication.

Two presentations by Emerson and Berry before the Scottish and NEC Institutions,[2, 3] reported that the tunnel could at last be regarded as a serious facility now ready to be used for research into propeller cavitation. These presentations in fact gave some early results on a 16 cm diameter propeller of constant pitch and circular backed sections. Curves of thrust and torque coefficient were given for a range of cavitation numbers between 0·1 (reduced pressure conditions) and 1·0 (atmospheric conditions) and photographs of the cavitation reproduced were shown. The tests were conducted in uniform flow conditions whereas a proper full scale simulation required the reproduction of the non uniform wake produced by the ship—it was not until later years that gauzes of different mesh were fitted across the tunnel section to produce velocity variations ahead of the propeller or partial ship stern shapes included in the test arrangement.

The numerous troubles which caused such a long delay before serious work could be attempted left the tunnel in danger of being regarded as a white elephant. Indeed Lenaghan in discussing one of the presentations[3] went so far as saying that at none of his visits to Teddington had he seen any work in progress and had assumed the tunnel to be redundant. The lack of success must have disappointed Lithgow who had done so much to bring the tunnel into being. His failing health forced him to withdraw from public life but at least at the time of his death in 1952 the troubles were a thing of the past and the tunnel was in regular use both for research and repayment work, a fitting tribute to Lithgow's generosity and enthusiasm.

INSTRUMENTATION AND EQUIPMENT

A resistance dynamometer similar in principle to the one in use on the main tank was built and designed with the intent that it could be capable of operation in either tank. It was completed and successfully calibrated shortly after the new tank was formally opened.

Stroboscopic lighting, so important for viewing cavitation in the tunnel, was introduced following the arrival of A.I. Williams. Williams worked with N.C. Lambourne of NPL's Aerodynamics Division to devise a clever system which owed its success to the experience of the Research Laboratories of GEC who had made high intensity flash discharge lamps of various kinds. Using one of these Williams found it possible to photograph a stationary image of a rotating propeller and designed an electrical circuit which included a condenser charged through a resistance from a source of high voltage. For a visual observation of the propeller sufficient light was obtained by successive discharges but photographs were taken by increasing the capacity of the condenser and flashing the bulb once with the camera shutter open. The visual observations possible were an extremely valuable aid to examining the onset and subsequent behaviour of cavitation on a propeller. They never failed to excite the attention of the viewer and a demonstration of propeller cavitation was always high on the list of things to be seen by visitors to the laboratory.

The dynamometer used to measure propeller thrust and torque in the tunnel was built at the laboratory, its design akin to the existing propulsion dynamometers. It was later replaced by a stronger version as the size of propellers used in tests was stepped up and torque increased.

The number of staff in 1930 was 37 and at the time of the opening of the New Tank two more had arrived. Most of the staff at this time are shown in plate 28 outside the entrance to the New Tank offices just after the opening. The entrance, a pleasing Georgian-style portal, soon became the main entrance to the William Froude Laboratory and appears the same today except that in summer it is enhanced by the proximity of a magnificent catalpa tree which over the years has grown to spread its luxurious foliage over the stream which flows under the tank at the entrance doorway.

It might be expected that the additional facilities would have led to more staff but this did not happen, only a gradual increase taking place over the next decade. From 37 in 1930, numbers grew to 39 in 1932, 44 in 1935 and 46 at the outbreak of the Second World War. With two tanks there came much relief as some work could be conducted in either and it soon became normal practice to use Number Two for openwater propeller experiments and special investigations, Number One being reserved for resistance and propulsion experiments on standard length models and for tests in waves. Overtime diminished although at moments when repayment work was at a high level the shift working system was reintroduced.

With these facilities the William Froude Laboratory was now well placed to undertake all kinds of research into ship hull design as well as support, on repayment, the needs of the shipbuilding industry. Under Baker's continuing leadership the opportunity was not lost. With devoted staff, led principally by Kent, Bottomley (sadly only for a few years after the arrival of Number Two tank), Wigley, Hughes, Todd, Conn and Emerson, there followed seven rewarding and settled years during which the reputation of the Laboratory and its staff grew.

REFERENCES

1. "Tests for ship economy", *The Times*, 17 November 1932.
2. Emerson A. and Berry L.W., "The Lithgow Propeller Water Tunnel", trans. IESS, Vol. 90, 1947.
3. Emerson A. and Berry L.W., "Experiments in the Lithgow Propeller Tunnel", trans. NECIES, Vol. 63, 1947.

CHAPTER 8

BURGEONING YEARS: 1932–1939

In May 1932 an International Congress on Hydromechanical Problems of Ship Propulsion was held in Hamburg. It attracted enormous interest, its meetings overflowing with delegates from many countries. Baker and Wigley went from the William Froude Laboratory, Wigley presenting a short paper on ship wave resistance. Both came away even more convinced that the decision to build a second tank at Teddington was right since the Conference had demonstrated very clearly the growing interest and demand for ship research throughout the world and it was obvious that competition from abroad would increase in the years to come. Even as the new tank was being opened in November, the German Institute of Naval Architects was on its way to Scandinavia in a hired liner, holding its annual meeting as it went, reading papers on shipbuilding and design matters. Arising from the Hamburg Conference (it was in fact one of its aims) was the desire for workers in the various Tanks to move towards a form of standardisation and uniformity when conducting model tests and interpreting the results to the ship they represented. At an after-dinner speech J. de Meo, an Italian consultant naval architect who perhaps had detected an inconsistency in approach when reading model test reports from different establishments, argued the case for international co-operation in ship research and advocated technical co-ordination in the shape of a Technical Marine Association. However, co-operation between Tanks was by no means uncommon. So far as Teddington was concerned both R.E. Froude and Taylor had supplied Baker with resistance data from their respective Tanks which allowed a comparison of Teddington results with those from an identical hull form run at Haslar and Washington. In 1926 Kempf at Hamburg initiated what was perhaps the first "formal" international co-operation when he proposed that a model from Taylor's propeller series should be tested in several tanks for comparative purposes. Open water tests on a 20 cm diameter propeller followed and data from Berlin, Dumbarton, Hamburg, Haslar, Teddington and Washington gave such good agreement that Kempf was able to conclude that further tests were scarcely necessary. This was encouraging to the Tanks but in later years uncertain areas arose in the whole field of model testing and so it was no surprise that de Meo's arguments found immediate support from Baker, Troost and others. Troost was new to the scene having recently been appointed to lead a new tank at Wageningen in Holland, a task which with van Lammeren he carried out so successfully that the new Dutch tank soon reached a prominent position in the Tank world. The response to de Meo's call was positive and a year later in 1933 at the invitation of the Council of the newly opened tank at Wageningen, an International Conference of Tank Superintendents was held at The Hague in July. The conference attended by 23 delegates from 11 Tanks (Baker and Riddle from the WFL) was the first of what has now become known as the International Towing Tank Conference. Three others followed at irregular intervals until at the 5th conference in 1948 it was decided to hold future conferences at three-year intervals. From 1969 its affairs have been "governed" by an Advisory Council whose membership is drawn from the heads of the principal Tanks throughout the world. From its beginning the ITTC has been loyally supported by the British Tanks and a succession of workers from BMT have served on the various Technical Working Committees.

The first conference at The Hague addressed five subjects chief of which was the choice of a standard formula for skin friction and a consistency in the presentation of model resistance results. A "Committee of Four" (Baker, Barrillon from the Paris tank, Kempf and Troost) was elected to reach decisions on the five subjects discussed. Not surprisingly most of the difficulties were left unresolved but at least the deliberations ensured a continuity of discussion at ensuing conferences and from time to time the ITTC has indeed fulfilled its purpose by agreeing and laying down principles and guidelines to Tank workers.

The growing awareness internationally of the value and importance of ship research certainly galvanised the outlook in Britain and the advent of the WFL's second tank coincided with a dramatic increase in the demand for model tests at Teddington. In 1932, the year of Number Two tank's opening, 28 ship designs were sent in for testing. Thereafter numbers increased to 45 in 1933, 60 in 1934, 73 in 1935, 88 in 1936 and 68 in 1937. Those submitted in 1935 involved tests on 160* model hulls and all through these years many of the lines plans submitted were revised by the staff before tests began, such was the accumulated experience available at the Laboratory. But the industrial slump of the 1930s was to have its effect and in 1938 Lloyd's Register of Shipping released startling figures which showed a drop of 49 per cent in the number of new ships submitted for approval in that year. This was quickly reflected in the demand at Teddington, the 1938 figure for designs tested falling to 37. A recovery set in in the following year only to be cut short by the rumblings and advance of the Second World War.

In the peak years of the 1930s demands on the staff to meet the commitments of both test and research work became so great that a return to overtime hours

---

* This is a very high number in view of the industrial slump at the time but includes modifications to some of the 73 designs submitted that year. It is probable that few of the tests carried out led to actual ship construction.

became unavoidable despite the availability of the new tank. It would have been neglect of one of the main purposes of the Laboratory if research work dwindled and the fact that it positively flourished in this period (nine papers were presented to learned societies during a 12-month period from mid-1934) is a tribute to the efforts of the staff who accepted the need for overtime without demur. And it is worth noting that no additional payment was made to individuals, extra hours worked were recovered by taking time off in lieu. The rapid production of data and reports to customers was also a tribute to both the staff and Baker's organisational powers. It became common to see a new design draughted and the model and its propeller made and tested within six weeks. Kent's success in the field of seakeeping began to bring requests for work in waves on several designs and tests in regular waves were usually completed in a day. With the demand for tests at a high level the case for more staff could not be denied and by 1935 Baker had, with the agreement of NPL and DSIR, increased the number to 44, both office and workshop departments benefiting. The ranks of the junior assistants, now graded as Assistant III were increased by the arrival of L.T.G. Clarke who although not staying long worked closely with Baker on research into propeller performance. Junior draughtsmen from shipyards in the north were recruited, W.J. Marwood, E. Laws, E. Macdonald and N.A. Witney arriving in that order to serve for long periods, contributing significantly to the work of the Laboratory. The workshops were strengthened and included the diminutive C.E. Camp, a carpenter. Camp not only went on to clock up 37 valuable years of service but lived to see his son and grandson follow him, thus beginning a family link that still continues.

From its beginning the WFL, although formally part of NPL, enjoyed a kind of independence of its own, a situation brought about by the fact that Number One tank was provided largely by Yarrow's personal donation and also, in part, by Baker's strong personality. Baker was keen to cling on to this independence; he genuinely believed that since through its own efforts the WFL had contributed importantly to improvements in merchant ship design, then "his" laboratory should have complete authority over its affairs and be free of the interfering influence of those who knew little of the work involved. In Glazebrook's time as Director of NPL, Baker's autonomous position was tolerated, the two men had great mutual respect for one another and Glazebrook had an empathy to the tank which sprang from his own involvement in its original design. However, the absorption of NPL into DSIR led to the need for a regularisation of NPL's organisation and Glazebrook's successor Petavel found himself in the awkward position of breaking down the WFL's independence and also Baker's strong will. Baker resisted the need to conform and there were heated exchanges but this was a battle that Baker could not possibly win and in due course his position of absolute authority over WFL and its staff (he had in the past sacked members of staff on the spot without recourse to official support from NPL) weakened. Soon the WFL's affairs became subject to the regulations applied to other NPL departments and organised centrally by NPL's Administration Department.

Baker's attitude was seen by his staff as staunch support as indeed it was for he never failed to recognise and praise their efforts in public. On the other hand his powerful personality and dictatorial manner could spread fear and trembling amongst those unwilling to stand up to him. This rebounded on one famous occasion when he strode on to Number One Tank to view some experiments in progress. One of the tools used regularly by experimenters when rigging apparatus to a tank carriage is the humble carpenters' clamp. Two of these had been used to secure a short plank of wood to the carriage girders on which the experimenter could sit to view the progress of the model through the water. Baker wanted to see the wave produced by the model and stepped on to the plank only to find his view impeded by one of the clamps. With the carriage at rest he turned to the mechanic Rayment who was standing by and ordered the clamp to be removed. It secured the plank on which Baker stood. "But, Sir", said Rayment "if I remove ...". "Remove that clamp, Rayment!" barked Baker so fiercely that Rayment could hardly disobey. On releasing it Baker, a heavy man, fell straight into the tank. Abbott, a moulder, seeing what had happened and sensing a moment of glory rushed up shouting "I'll save you sir", leapt onto the carriage, onto the same plank and with a spectacular splash finished up in the tank as well. With two men in the water, one the Superintendent of the Tank, priority somehow turned to the recovery of Baker which was accomplished quite rapidly in view of his size and bulk but Abbott, momentarily ignored, eventually surfaced almost unrecognisable with his overall covering his head. Fortunately, although visibly shaken, both recovered to see the funny side. The potential dangers of working above water had always been recognised by the provision of rescue apparatus such as life-buoys, ropes, etc. Happily no serious accident has occurred over the years although it must be said that A. Jenkins who came to Teddington in 1945 tried hard. He easily holds the record with four descents into one or other of the tanks, once with almost serious circumstances as on returning to the surface he was trapped for a few seconds beneath the model fixed to the carriage. Number One tank has claimed most victims, about 10 by 1988, Number Two has six but, surprisingly, only one member of staff has fallen into the largest of BMT's tanks, the recently destroyed Number Three at Feltham.

Just before the opening of Number Two Tank, the WFL received an unusual award of the Bronze medal and Hors Concours certificate from the organisers of the International Colonial and Maritime Exhibition that was held at Antwerp in 1930. The Laboratory had been asked to send a display describing its work and a wax model fully equipped with its self-propulsion gear evidently attracted much interest from the hundreds of visitors. Exhibitions of this kind, national and international, often sought displays from the Laboratory and there have been several instances when both apparatus and staff have been sent to such events. One of the largest of these was the Empire Exhibition in Glasgow in 1938 when a large display was brought together in the Government Pavilion. Actual working models of a towing tank and cavitation tunnel were built, the latter proving so useful that it was afterwards reassembled at Teddington and used for a few years to study by photographic means the distribution of wake around ship sterns. London's Festival of Britain in 1950, which was really an exhibition of technology, had a working model of a towing tank on view that was made at Teddington and demonstrated by G.B. Pearce of the Tank staff.

TESTS FOR FIRMS

Test work which as noted reached a peak in 1936 covered practically every type of ship. Designs of tankers, tramps, cargo liners, large passenger ships, paddle steamers, tugs, coasters, naval ships including destroyers and higher speed craft and, in diminishing numbers, seaplane hulls, were regularly tested from 1932 up to the outbreak of the Second World War. A huge number of designs were tested for most British shipbuilders and owners as well as many from abroad, all of which boosted considerably the income of the Laboratory. Success was high. At a time when much emphasis was being placed on economy in ship performance, advances were made in design knowledge which became reflected in higher than usual Admiralty constants in new ships (410–430 were being obtained on trial, 360 in service). Of the dozens of well known ships that were tested in model form were the "Castles" (*Athlone Castle, Roslin Castle, Stirling Castle, Warwick Castle*, etc.), the "Cities" (*City of Benares, City of Bombay, City of Karachi*, etc.) and Blue Star Line's *Doric Star* and *Trojan Star*. In the late 1930s one of the outstanding ships of the century, the quadruple screw *Mauretania* became due for replacement. She was built in 1906 four years before Number One tank and R.E. Froude had carried out model experiments at Haslar. These were followed by tests on a large 15 metres man-driven model on the River Tyne when different propellers were tried. The second *Mauretania* was slightly shorter than the first. Built by Cammell Laird at Birkenhead, who commissioned exhaustive tests at Teddington in 1937 (model 1695), she was launched just before the war and this together with the diminishing role for large passenger liners afterwards prevented her from enjoying the illustrious history of her predecessor. Plans for a new liner of similar dimensions for the Canadian Pacific Steamships line were also in hand. This vessel was intended for the Southampton–Quebec run and a series of model tests on a quadruple screw design (model 1886) were completed in May 1939. It was largely due to the amount of work that these two models and their variants generated that indications of an upturn in test work were seen at this time. A number of high speed tests, for which the longer Number Two tank was very suitable, were carried out for the British Power Boat Company and led Baker to run a small research series of high speed round bilge forms. These and the tests for the BPBC established the reputation that the Laboratory has enjoyed ever since for tests on high speed ship forms. An unusual and demanding design concerned the Southern Railway train ferries. The concept of a train ferry across the channel was finally realised in 1936 and the night ferry London Victoria to Paris Gare du Nord became a civilised mode of travelling which to the regret of its patrons was axed by British Rail in 1980. The first of such ferries, *Twickenham Ferry*, *Hampton Ferry*, etc. built by Swan Hunter on the Tyne had to carry a train consisting of 12 sleeping cars plus two luggage wagons, 500 passengers and also cars which were placed in a garage above the train deck. The size of the train imposed limitations on the choice of ideal dimensions for the ferry and led to a fine hull of block coefficient 0·53, unusually wide in the beam and of shallow draught. The WFL was asked to draw up the lines and succeeded in producing a very successful design which was based on a barge-like underwater form.[1] The ferries were twin screw and had to be capable of an ahead speed of 16½ knots, 11 knots astern. Solid bossings were chosen to enclose the propeller shafting and there was much debate at the Tank as to how the bossings should be designed in order to minimise vibration. In such a wide and shallow vessel there was a danger of cross flow into the propeller. Several bossings were tried on the model and after a series of resistance and propulsion tests a preferred design was reached. On trial the *Twickenham Ferry* delighted her owners achieving its speed in both directions and was completely devoid of any vibration. Baker was quick to underline, in the discussion of "Channel train ferry steamers for the Southern Railway"[1] the value of model experiments in such an unusual design, for five different models had been required (the last, model 1318, being 16 per cent better than the first) and extensive steering tests were needed to demonstrate the suitability of the bow and stern rudders that were fitted.

There was also a growing demand for the calibration of flow meters, Number Two tank proving ideal for the purpose. The meters which included Amsler, Ekman, Gurley and Ott types were lowered into the water from a simple gallows set up on the carriage and calibrated over specified ranges of speed. Hundreds of these current meters were issued with a calibration certificate for a small fee from 1935 onwards until this work was taken over by the Hydraulics Research Laboratory at Wallingford in about 1962.

By 1938 the much modified and finally refurbished Lithgow cavitation tunnel was being commissioned by several firms for tests on new propeller designs. Such tests were soon to become commonplace and a natural addition to a programme of tests for new ships.

The claims and designs of inventors were always part of the scene, the WFL being regarded as a national facility where new ideas could be tried out and independently assessed. As such there was an obligation to examine everything plausible that was submitted. Some extraordinary ideas appeared and one in 1935 was for a marine propeller. A spiritualist fresh from a seance at which there had emerged an odd drawing was convinced that it represented a propeller blade with unique properties. Baker was reluctant to hear more but when the drawing arrived with a request to convert it into a propeller it was given to Riddle with every expectation that even his experience would show it was an impossibility. But somehow Riddle managed to superimpose the shape on to a helical surface and produced a blade which looked for all the world like an elephant's ear. A propeller was made and tested in open water but the spiritualist's hopes were dashed when he found it to be of ridiculously low efficiency.

RESEARCH

The fluctuation in the demand for test work which mirrored conditions in industry brought its problems. In good years the fees received together with the annual contributions from industry to the Research Fund placed the WFL in the position where only a small request to DSIR for guaranteed funding was needed. In 1938 when a sudden drop in test work was seen, more time became available for research. This was fine so far as research was concerned but in 1937 £2,278 had been received into the Research Fund compared to a cost of the anticipated increase in research in 1938 of £8,000. Even with guaranteed support from DSIR a serious shortfall would soon appear once the reserves in the Research Fund had been exhausted. The Advisory Committee launched an appeal and were soon grateful to one of its members, W.C. Warwick of the Chamber of Shipping, who rallied the industry to the tune of contributions amounting to almost £4,000 in 1938, an 80 per cent increase on the previous year. Also Warwick persuaded organisations to pledge a further £7,600 over the next five years. His efforts and the response from industry carried the WFL forward with some confidence until the changing circumstances of the Second World War.

Research flourished and throughout the period 1932–39 it was led by Baker, Kent, Wigley, Hughes, Emerson, Conn and Todd who pursued topics both old and new. New areas included an investigation into the backing of ships conducted by Conn and some studies on the effect of changing the shape of a ship's bow by Wigley and Emerson. Wigley looked into the theory and practical application of bulbous bows and Emerson when free from his duties in the Lithgow cavitation tunnel carried out a series of resistance experiments on models with different bow profiles. Emerson also found time to conduct important full-scale manoeuvring trials on the *Beacon Grange* and Todd began model experiments aimed at understanding better a particular ship type, the coaster. The old areas were a continuance or completion of topics begun earlier and in particular the advantages of adopting cruiser sterns in many ship types were demonstrated. Baker continued his research into propeller design, propulsion and wake, Kent pursued seakeeping aspects, Hughes completed his work on wind resistance and a return to the skin friction problem was made by the WFL's latest 1851 Exhibition Scholar, H.C. Lackenby.

Propellers

Baker's research produced three very valuable papers on merchant ship propeller performance and propulsion. Also a smaller separate study looked into the effect of inward and outward turning propellers on efficiency and steering.[2] This was requested by a member of the Advisory Committee and logically added to the earlier experience gained in 1924 by Bottomley in his manoeuvring experiments on a twin screw form. Apart from his famous book on Ship Design which appeared as two volumes in 1933, Baker's greatest output at this time was the three papers on propellers.[3, 4, 5] Their great value came from the use of large 30 cm diameter propellers which virtually eliminated all scale effect problems. In "Design of screw propellers with special reference to the single screw ship",[5] some of the propellers were used to propel a larger than usual (7⅓ metres long) single screw model. It will be remembered that Baker in beginning this research in 1928 had favoured aerofoil sectioned propellers and had, in certain circumstances, demonstrated their superiority over circular backed sections. Now he designed his B series of propellers, which consisted of 37 models, to examine the effect of other geometric changes. From a basis propeller successive propellers introduced systematic changes in section shape (both aerofoil and circular back), blade outline, pitch, pitch distribution, rake and number of blades. All were tested in open water and the results given in two important papers [3, 4] before the INA, joint offerings with Riddle. In presenting their results the authors chose Taylor's approach in preference to that recently used by R.E. Froude and so the results were plotted in terms of a power factor, B_p and a diameter constant, δ. The resulting $B_p - \delta$ charts soon became a format that was to be adopted universally. It was shown that the commonly used circular back type of section was inferior to aerofoil sections for lightly loaded (low slip) propellers and that reduced pitch at the propeller boss led to improved efficiency compared to propellers having constant pitch at all radii. This latter fact soon influenced propeller designers and it became normal to reduce pitch by about 20 per cent at the root radius. Both papers were received enthusiastically, Kempf emphasising the value of the results from such large propellers which he indicated must be free of the effects of scale. The great achievement in this work was the highlighting of the characteristics which led to greater propeller efficiency for a given set of operating conditions. In later years Troost, in developing his famous methodical series of propellers, from the $B_p - \delta$ charts which are still in use today, was thus able to choose a parent propeller of sound basic design in cognisance of the advantages found at Teddington. Moving next to propulsive aspects, Baker tested the large model (nicknamed Big Ben) fitted in turn with several of his B series propellers in a single screw configuration. In some cases two different fore and aft positions of the propeller were tried and the large amount of data obtained allowed some useful conclusions to be reached.[5] Improved propulsive efficiency was found in propellers with rake aft and it was confirmed that the best results came from propellers with reduced pitch at the root. The idea of reduced pitch came from Baker's awareness of the variation in wake velocities at the stern of a hull, variations which were a maximum at the propeller tip and a minimum at the boss. He urged the case for wake adapted propellers arguing it was necessary to have a good average positive slip angle to ensure that it remained so in all positions during a revolution. Thus at the boss he reckoned reduced slip would be best and indicated a preferred 20 per cent reduction in pitch, a figure which was largely confirmed in the experiments. However, the model propulsion results, although of considerable value indicatively, must today be treated with some reservation. The very large and heavy model used was really too big for Number One tank, long periods of oscillation being experienced at the resistance dynamometer which led to difficulties in deciding the mean of the written record of resistance. Measurement of resistance by a spring introduces problems in models of high inertia and when large 9 metre models were tested in BMT's Number Three tank in the 1960s the same difficulty arose, which was never satisfactorily resolved and acceptable records were obtained in this tank with such large models only by virtue of the very long runs that were possible.

Ship Trials

Trials at sea on new ships were never easy to come by. Owners, keen to take charge of their ships, were usually reluctant to allow a ship to linger long once acceptance trials were out of the way and so when Houlder Brothers offered the *Beacon Grange* to the Laboratory for two days the chance was gratefully accepted. *Beacon Grange* was a 135 metres twin screw motor cargo liner with a top speed of 16 knots. Emerson was given the task of carrying out two sets of measurements, normal straight line speed and power trials over the Whitley Bay measured-mile distance and steering trials during which continuous readings of rudder angle, shaft torque (from Siemens-Ford torsionmeters), propeller r.p.m. and ship speed (from a Walker log towed astern) would be made. The weather was kind and excellent speed and power runs were obtained which later added valuably to the fund of ship-model correlation data. On the second day steering trials consisted of two half circles around a fixed buoy and four turning manoeuvres carried out along the measured-mile course. In the circle tests ship angle of yaw was determined from plottings of the ship position at given instances of time. Again excellent measurements were obtained which provided unique data for a merchant ship. In the laboratory Emerson first ran comparative speed and power experiments reproducing the exact ship trial draughts at the model. He then, by towing the model at fixed angles of yaw measured the water forces on the hull and somewhat ambitiously attempted to use these to estimate the behaviour of *Beacon Grange* during a given manoeuvre including in his analysis the known wind velocity, derived propeller thrust from the torsionmeter readings (using wake and thrust deduction values obtained from the model propulsion experiments) and the rudder forces estimated from Bottomley's work. When he presented his results[6] A.P. Cole, who had had considerable experience of similar trials at sea on destroyers, chastised Emerson gently saying that model test results from a restrained model were hardly satisfactory for use in estimating the turning properties of a ship, free-running tests with the model travelling on a curvilinear path were needed. Of course they were, but Emerson was working in the days before sophisticated apparatus was available to conduct such tests. The great value of Emerson's work, he received the Institution's Gold medal for his efforts, was the release of full-scale data for a merchantman. The variations of r.p.m. and torque that occur in port and starboard shafts of a twin screw ship when turning were seen and Emerson concluded that since a small angle of yaw affected ship resistance by only a small amount then only small rudder angles should be used when checking yaw.

Baker's research into wake which had started in 1928 with the full-scale experiments on *Snaefell* and *Ashworth* continued when the Furness Withy line offered the *Pacific Trader* for further trials. The earlier work had demonstrated the influence of scale on wake from comparative model-ship data but measurements had been made over only flat parts of the hull and Baker was now keen to see what happened in the after body where there was curvature in the surface of the hull. He took measurements of wake velocities in the after body of *Pacific Trader* but before these, two models of common forebody shape but different after bodies were made and tested. The two different shapes aft were produced by redistributing the area curve and wetted surface to give a wall-sided model with a deeply immersed stern and the second with curved buttocks and much reduced stern immersion. It was hoped that the changes would show the effect of the free surface on wake. Pitot tube measurements on each model produced curves of wake variation[7] which showed a difference in characteristic shape. On the *Pacific Trader* readings were taken in two positions in the after body and the results, which appeared good, were compared with the characteristic wake found in the models. But Baker could draw only general conclusions from full-scale results that were not as comprehensive as he would have liked. It is significant to note that he made no attempt to make and test a model of *Pacific Trader*. Nevertheless Baker's earlier conclusion that ship wake was lower than its model was confirmed and he went further, somewhat bravely, when he suggested that ship wake was of the order of 3–4 per cent lower than the model, if the form was full, and 6 per cent lower if it was fine. This was a difficult research; so much depended on the amount and accuracy of the ship measurement and also the scale effect found in a particular ship-model comparison could hardly be applied across the board to any type of ship. Allan and Cutland returned to the subject several years later following Allan's arrival and the whole problem of wake scale effect has occupied many workers since, who have used both theoretical and practical approaches, but a satisfactory solution has still to be reached. Before leaving the subject of wake it is worth recording that Baker threw additional light when returning to tests at sea on *Ashworth*, he was able to show the effect of hull roughness on wake. He went aboard *Ashworth* twice, first when the ship was 108 days out of dock with a relatively clean hull surface and second after *Ashworth*'s passage to Mauritius when she was then 242 days out of dock with her hull fouled with a thick weed.

Each time measurements were taken at the same position on the hull and showed very clearly an increase in wake velocity for the rougher surface.

Baker's Textbook and Bulbous Bows

Baker's second book published in 1933[8] is classic and of enduring value. It expanded considerably on his first and drew on the knowledge and experience gained from a large number of model experiments that covered all types of ships except large warships. With the wealth of data at his disposal Baker was able to separate merchant ships into five different categories of specified fullness and show how variations in beam, parallel body, entrance, run, distribution of area, etc. affected resistance. In volume 2, propeller theory and propulsive aspects for single, twin and multi-screw arrangements were covered. It is a pity that the rather crude diagrams spoil the book's presentation but this does not detract from the fundamental truths and design guidance given which are still largely appropriate to today's modern ships. The absence of up-to-date information on propellers and the lack of bulbous bow data is simply due to the changes in demand and fashion seen since 1933. At that time little was known of the possibilities of fitting bulbs to bows although Baker mentions them in his book. Now in later years with fuller ships being built, bulbs have become a regular feature. William Froude in the very first tank at Torquay carried out some early experiments on so-called "Swan" bows which reduced resistance at high speeds and at Teddington tests were done in 1912 following Rayleigh's suggestion of hollowed bow lines, but these showed no improvement. Coincidentally at the time Baker was writing his second book there was a renewed interest in bulbs. E.M. Bragg had carried out model experiments at Washington in 1930 and Hogner and Weinblum were carrying out calculations. Weinblum at the Berlin tank added to his calculations model experiments with different types of bulbs, the results of which he was soon to make public and Wigley also began a study at about this time following a visit to Berlin where he exchanged friendly discussion with Weinblum. Both men took a theoretical approach. Wigley would hardly have chosen otherwise despite Baker's habit of reminding him (and others) at the start of a research project of the importance of the practicalities involved. At such times Wigley, whose temper was short, would reply dismissively insisting he was "a mathematician not a bloody naval architect".

We have already noted that Wigley was much influenced by Michell and Havelock's theoretical approaches to wave resistance. Havelock in a communication to the Royal Society in 1934 outlined a way in which the combined resistances of a hull and an added bulb could be calculated, a method which Wigley found attractive. In adapting it he was able to show that the reduction in resistance due to a bulbous addition, when it occurred, was due to the interference between the separate wave systems caused by the ship's hull and the bulb. Whereas Weinblum was content to exploit Michell's theory alone in examining bulbous bow wave resistance, Wigley preferred to follow both Michell and Havelock using their approaches separately to calculate the wave resistance caused by hull and bulb. He returned to his earlier mathematical model (model 829 in his 1927 paper) and sketched on several alternative bulbous additions, varying length, depth and cross-sectional shape of the bulb. Havelock had shown in his Royal Society paper that the energy expended by a body in overcoming its wave resistance was equal to the energy reappearing in the wave profile found well astern. Wigley proceeded to calculate the separate wave profiles of hull and bulb and by addition arrived at their combined effect. His results showed the best position of the bulb and Wigley was pleased to report[9] that subsequent model experiments had verified the trend in his calculations. He concluded positively saying that the useful speed range for a bulbous bow lay between Froude numbers 0·24 and 0·57 and that greater reductions in total resistance were possible with an added bulb when the wave making of the hull alone was particularly high. Provided hull lines were not too hollow Wigley advised a bulb that projected ahead of the hull bow profile. It was hemi-spherical in shape and the reduction in resistance Wigley found for it varied with its fore and aft position. The agreement between calculation and measurement was impressive but the results, promising as they were, related to a mathematically defined hull and extreme bulbous shapes. Also beam to draught ratio of the model and its prismatic coefficient were seldom reflected in real ships so that too much could not be read into the results. Payne in discussing "The theory of the bulbous bow and its practical application"[9] described some of the experience gained at Haslar with warship forms. R.E. Froude had found certain advantages for ram bulbs which had been fitted to older battleships, not incidentally for the primary object of reducing resistance, and recent work confirmed some of Wigley's findings. Payne had found reductions with a bulb but only over the mid-point of the speed range stated by Wigley. However, Wigley was rightly encouraged by his results particularly as the calculated and experimental correspondence had turned out so well and his paper was certainly well regarded—it received the M.C. James Memorial medal. But Wigley was still anxious to remove or reduce some of the assumptions made in the mathematical treatment. The neglect of viscosity effects was probably the main reason why a better agreement between calculation and measurement could not be reached. Wigley embarked on a carefully considered study and eventually proposed a semi-empirical correction to allow for the interaction of viscous and wave flows.[10] He introduced this to the IESS in 1937 and demonstrated some success by recalculating wave resistance for his earlier mathematical forms using the correction procedure he had found. In one of these (model 1008) the model measurement had shown wave resistance to be much higher at low Froude numbers than Wigley's original calculation in 1930 but now, using his correction, the comparison of measurement and calculation at speeds up to a Froude number of 0·24 was excellent. At higher speeds the corrected calculations showed a smaller discrepancy and still left a large difference which at the main resistance hump (Froude number 0·5) showed calculation to be 12 per cent lower than the measured value. But progress had been made. Unfortunately the Second World War stopped wave resistance research in its tracks but before hostilities began Wigley summarised his and other workers' progress in a state of the art paper read at the International Congress of Naval Engineers at Liège in 1939.

Bow Shape

The Advisory Committee at the time did not think that reductions in resistance due to bow shape would necessarily come from bulbous additions alone, the degree of fineness of the bow might be important and rake introduced into the bow profile was worth investigating. Up to about 1860 forward slanting stems were normal in ships and evidently Scott Russell approved judging from his remarks on the subject in his *Naval Architecture* published in 1865 when in typical uncompromising style he wrote:

... men who hesitate to give the stem a decided character, express their imbecility by leaving it perpendicular.

Quite apart from any possible reductions in resistance that raked bows might bring, the cut away, easily introduced below the waterline, improved steerage. But opinion changed as builders disliked long unsupported weight forward. E.J. Read in 1875 used rearward slanting stems in warships and the U-shaped bow sections advocated by Froude involved a near-perpendicular stem. Now, in the 1930s more information was needed. Emerson was asked to look into these things and tested a series of 27 models of constant after body shape. Six of these were low speed forms, eight faster cargo liner types and the remaining 13 were finer forms allowing tests to be carried up to even higher speeds. Within these models fore bodies were changed to give variations of entrance angle and bow profile. The changes introduced affected the shape of the shoulder forward and the waterline endings which became either convex or hollow depending on the variation adopted. Resistance experiments were carried out on each model and on some, with a single screw arrangement, propulsion tests. Emerson published his results in a trilogy of papers, the first[11] in 1937. As expected, low entrance angles were good although they could not be reduced too far without forcing a change in the shape of the shoulder and model resistance was found to be sensitive to such changes whereas small changes in bow endings or bow rake were found to be of little consequence. Thus bow rake appeared to offer no real advantage but if used it did allow the upper deck lines to have lower entrance angles which were preferable in heavy seas. Emerson's work which he completed in two more papers in 1939 and 1941 highlighted the importance of entrance angle and, perhaps more surprisingly, forebody shoulder. It also indicated how the degree of wave-making could be influenced by both.

Propeller Shaft Bossings

Hughes' completion of his wind resistance research[12] added little to the earlier work. He was awarded an INA Premium for his paper but its discussers were less than enthusiastic, doubting the necessity of the elaborations that Hughes had pursued. Of much greater value was his latest research begun in 1935 which was a much needed investigation into the propulsion of twin screw ships. It included a study of shaft bossings and was the first on this subject since Luke's work in 1910. Hughes' findings proved to be of special value to designers of twin screw vessels and his publications[13, 14, 15] became and remain standard works of reference. Taking a design for a typical 180 metres intermediate passenger liner of 18–20 knots speed he tested a model ringing the changes between propeller spread and immersion, fore and aft positions of the propellers and also tried A brackets as an alternative to solid bossings. 13 propellers of different diameter and pitch were made and fitted, which covered a considerable range of tip clearance/diameter ratios, the clearance between propeller tip and hull being kept the same in all cases. Cross, who had joined the staff in 1928 was Hughes' principal assistant, drawing and fairing the bossing shapes and conducting model resistance and propulsion tests. To assist in the design of the bossing shape and its alignment with the hull, preliminary streamflow experiments were done over the after body using "flags" to record the direction of flow over the model surface. The results Hughes presented, mainly propulsive, indicated that provided propellers of normal size were used their position in the transverse plane (or spread) had no great influence over propulsive efficiency so long as the immersion remained sufficient. Valuable diagrams showed the importance of immersion and these diagrams could be used to estimate the speed of a new ship at its full draught from trial results usually obtained at another. As regards A brackets, existing knowledge seemed to be limited to naval ships whose propeller centres were at a relatively low height above the keel. In such cases A brackets were reckoned superior to bossings. Hughes' experiments confirmed this but they also showed that bossings could be slightly better for higher propeller heights, provided again that good immersion of the propeller was chosen. F. McAlister waxed so enthusiastic in discussing all three of Hughes' papers that at the last one, in suggesting that the future might demand higher ship speeds and power, he hoped that Hughes "might find the time and opportunity to give the profession generally as notable a series on triple screw propulsion as the series he has now virtually completed on twin screws". Unfortunately the chance never came.

Seakeeping

Model tests in waves begun in 1922 by Kent continued with a large programme of research concerning three models of fine form, all of which were towed and self-propelled through calm water and regular head-on waves. Cutland worked

Plate 1.
William Froude FRS, LLD
Pioneer of ship model research
1810 – 1879

Plate 2. National tank (later Number One) after construction.

Plate 3. National tank (later Number One) and carriage on completion.

Plate 4. Small tank shown empty. The main tank can be seen through the arches to the left.

acting on a horizontal arm, to avoid sag of spring. The
convenient thing would then be to use the same arm for
the calibrating weights. The upshot would be, for the
indicating lever) something bearing a very strong
family likeness to our present "thrust lever" of the
Kewaffs? except that the latter has a leverage (top arm
apt. bottom one) of 8 to 1, which is much more than we
now want. In the sketch in margin
I have made this leverage 4 to 1; but
if height admitted, it might perhaps advantageously be made
less still, by making the upper
arm of the lower lever longer

than the lower one, thus making the lower lever take
a share in the magnification

I am here supposing the towing knife edge (& the model)
to travel 2" for the max. resistance extension, which is about
the model travel for max. extension in our existing apparatus.
In my letter of yesterday I spoke of about 1" as the variation in
model position; but that is because the levers are buffered
so as not to be able to indicate much less than half
the maximum extension. I imagine it would be
advantageous to pursue somewhat the same plan in
the kind of arrangement I have proposed, with the
object of diminishing the total range of angle of the indicating lever, & so mitigating various errors. ~~the thing
be required~~ It is undesirable to make experiment with the
same spring for runs of which the resistance differ
more than 2 to 1. And should it be desirable for
some special purpose to measure a low resistance without
change of spring, it would always be possible to do it
by hanging on a weight.

An arrangement such as I have suggested in this
letter, ~~~~ promises to be simpler & easier to make
than what we have got; & I should say, better as well.

Yours very truly

R E Froude

Plate 5. Extract from R. E. Froude letter, 10th August 1910.

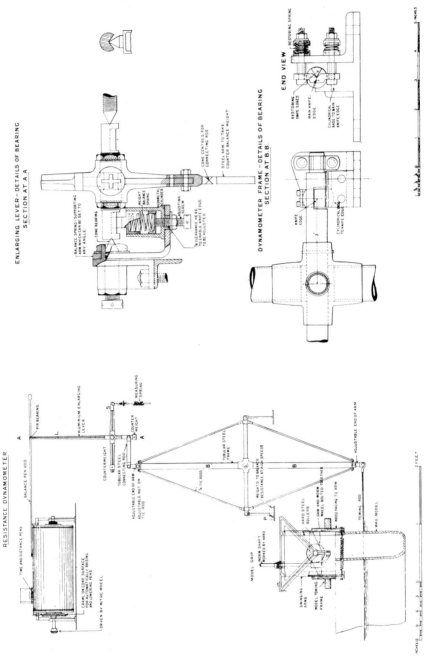

Plate 6. Resistance dynamometer, 1901.

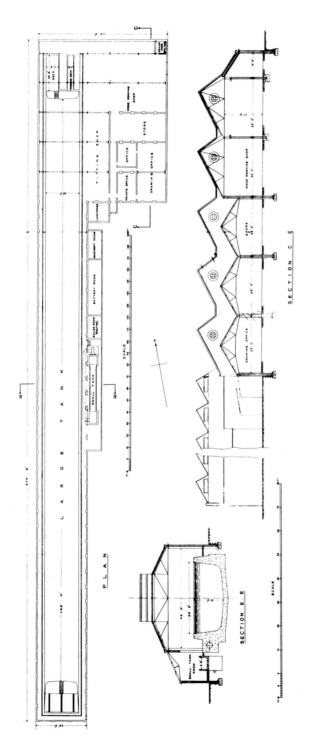

Plate 7. Layout of Number One tank and buildings, 1910.

Plate 8. Opening of the National Tank: Sir Alfred Yarrow addressing guests.

Plate 9. Opening of the National Tank: On carriage: far left, Lord Rayleigh; on right, Richard Glazebrook.

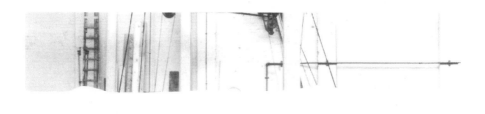

Plate 10. Flow detection methods: model with flags.

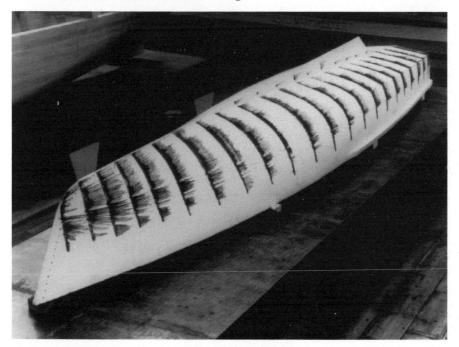

Plate 11. Flow detection methods: flow of paint on model surface.

Plate 12. Model of E Class submarine.

Plate 13. Torpedo fitted to model of *Hood*.

Plate 14. Full scale testing: C.E.I. Seaplane awaiting trials off the Isle of Grain.

Plate 15. Seaplane model under test.

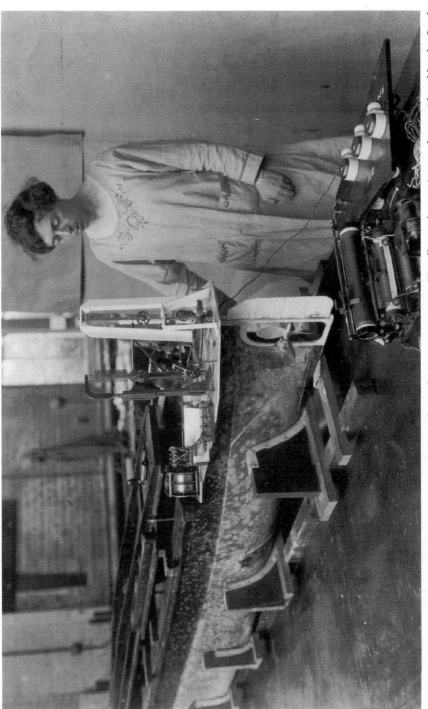

Plate 16. Rudder head torque apparatus: Miss Keary checking electrical power to apparatus. Propeller can be seen in stern frame with rudder also fitted.

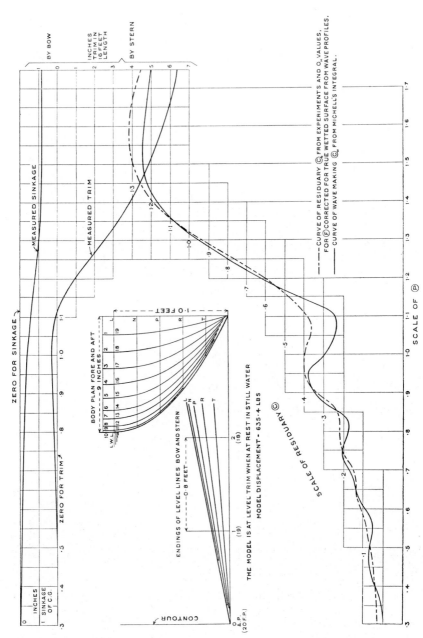

Plate 17. Resistance due to wavemaking: Body plan of Wigley's mathematical model (number 829) is shown. Lower curves compare Wigley's calculations with wavemaking resistance derived from the model measurements.

Plate 18. Experiments with Mauritania model: model is shown mounted on measuring apparatus on tower in the open air.

Plate 19. Ships tested in model form: RN Destroyer, *HMS Ambuscade*, 1926.

Plate 20. Ships tested in model form: *SS Seatrain*, rail carrying ship for Havana – New Orleans service, 1928.

Plate 21. Ships tested in model form: Twickenham Ferry, 1935.

Plate 22. Number Two tank: shallow end and shelving completed – December 1931.

Plate 23. Number Two tank carriage.

Plate 24. Opening of Number Two Tank. On carriage: from left, Sir Frank Smith (Secretary, DSIR); Sir Richard Glazebrook; Rt. Hon. Stanley Baldwin.

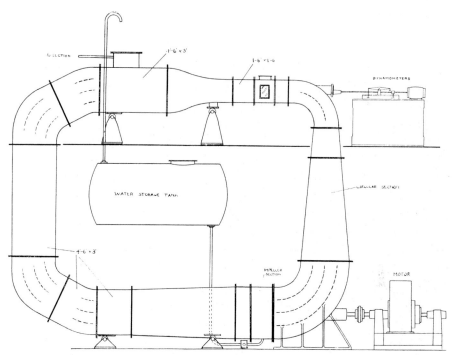

Plate 25. Lithgow Water Tunnel. Arrangement of pipe circuit.

Plate 26. Lithgow Water Tunnel. Before installation – 1933.

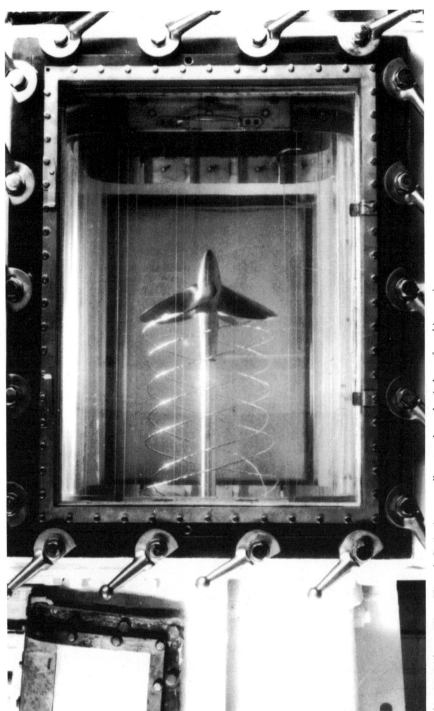

Plate 27. Lithgow Water Tunnel. Cavitating propeller seen through window of working section.

Plate 28. Ship Division staff, 1932. On extreme left of front row is Todd, followed by Kent, Baker, Bottomley and Riddell. In middle row, Cross is on extreme left, Wise is fourth from left, Cutland sixth and Dawes seventh. Extreme right in this row is Berry. In back row, Rixon is fourth from left and Rayment fifth.

PIERS FOR USE ON BEACHES

<u>C.C.O.</u> or deputy.

     They must float up and down with the tide. The anchor problem must be mastered. Let me have the best solution worked out. Don't argue the matter. The difficulties will argue for themselves.

30. 5. 42.

Plate 29. Prime Minister's memo concerning floating piers for Mulberry Harbour.

Plate 30. Large Phoenix breakwater for Mulberry Harbour. Breakwater in place before tests in waves.

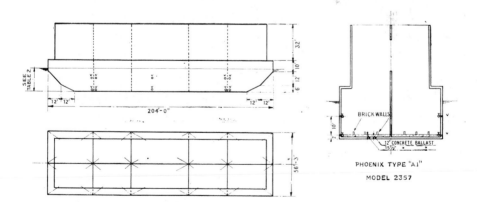

Plate 31. Drawings of Phoenix type "A1".

Plate 32. Towing tests on beetles for Mulberry Harbour. Towing with beetles swivelled fore and aft.

Plate 33. Towing configuration actually used.

Plate 34. Mulberry units. Large Phoenix under tow to Normandy.

Plate 35. Mulberry units. Gooseberries and Phoenix breakwaters shielding inner harbour.

Plate 36. Mulberry Harbour at Arromanches. (a) Floating bridge supported on Beetles.

(b) Large Phoenix pontoons sunk to form arm of harbour.

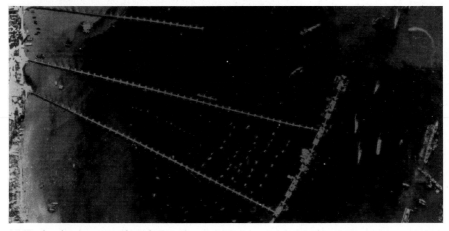

(c) Pier head pontoons and roadways.

Plate 37. Grain "Mac" ship *Empire MacCrae.*

Plate 38. Partially fabricated ship.

Plate 39. High speed craft tested in model form, c. 1940. 44 knots PV70 for British Power Boat Company.

Plate 40. High speed crafted tested in model form. Vosper MTB.

Plate 41. NPL Sports Day, 1947: Final, 200 yards. Runners in dark shorts (from left, Witney, Emerson, Cross).

Plate 42. Tea break, Teddington drawing office, 1950. Second from right is Cutland, third is Mackenzie; fifth from left is Cross, sixth is Macdonald, seventh is Marwood, eighth is Laws.

Plate 43. Some ships tested in model form, 1946 – 1959. (a) Chinese passenger ship *Democracy No. 10* (model 2913).

(b) *Lucy Ashton* – before conversion.

(c) *Lucy Ashton* – after conversion (model 3100 and others).

(d) P&O Liner *Canberra* (model 3869 and others).

with Kent and both faced the difficulties of interpreting the results obtained from the mechanical resistance and propulsion dynamometers used. The problems were particularly acute in the wave tests at moments of synchronism between the natural period of the model and its period of encounter with the waves when very large pitch and heave motions and extreme oscillations at the resistance dynamometer occurred. Measurements at synchronism had to be neglected and in other experiments reasonable mean values of propeller thrust and torque could be obtained only by repeating each experiment three times; patience and persistence were obviously the order of the day. The models used were deliberately chosen to be fine forms so as to contrast with Kent's earlier results on fuller ones in 1930. A parent form was selected which represented a typical twin screw ship of cross-channel type and two derivatives obtained from it, one having V-shaped sections forward, the other U-shaped. Initial resistance tests showed the parent to be slightly the best of the three in calm water and in waves. Higher speeds were run since the hulls were fine and tests extended to a Froude number of 0·4 at which an unexpected fact emerged. There was only a very slight increase in resistance due to waves. Experience in later years has confirmed this with the well established trend of reducing increments of resistance due to waves with increasing speed. Advantage of this is rarely taken in practice since the large motions experienced before higher speeds are reached generally lead to a voluntary reduction in ship speed. The resistance tests were followed by self-propulsion experiments on the three models and again the parent showed to advantage both in calm water and in waves. Propeller efficiency, shown to be lower in waves in Kent's 1930 work, was this time only marginally lower so that the increase in power due to waves arose almost entirely from increased resistance. Pitch and heave reached a maximum at a period of encounter of about 5½ seconds and further data including propulsive components were given in "Self-propelled experiments in smooth and rough water made with models of high speed ships".[16] In discussing the results A.M. Robb (later Professor of Naval Architecture at Glasgow) was critical of the results obtained arguing that if the model was driven by a constant speed motor (a correct assumption), propeller revolutions would also be constant for a given model speed whereas the characteristics of the propelling plant in a ship would be totally different. A ship's engines would labour in the sharply varying conditions as the ship pitched, the propeller might emerge from the water and race. How, Robb asked, could such conditions which must lead to a material effect on propulsive efficiency be represented in a model test? The answer was, and still is, they cannot. Kent in agreeing with Robb's reservation was however quick to refer to his earlier model-ship comparisons of power in waves which had turned out so well, sufficient justification of the value and main purpose of model tests in waves. The final phase of this research[17] looked at the effect of small but important changes in hull shape. The three models so far tested had raised sterns and the parent was taken and modified to give it a cruiser stern. In doing so waterline length increased a little and this with the extra streamlining possible eliminated eddies in the dead water, just as Kent had demonstrated a few years earlier, and reduced resistance and power by 9 per cent in calm water. Most of this gain was however lost in waves, particularly at the higher speeds tested but overall there was no denying the advantages found with the cruiser stern confirming once and for all its superiority. Thereafter very few ships were built with raised sterns.

Backing of Ships

The great advantage of a research laboratory is the opportunity it provides to research thoroughly subjects which might otherwise receive only superficial treatment as part of *ad hoc* studies. One such area of work was an understanding of the behaviour of ships when backing. Nothing was known of how propellers, designed to drive a ship ahead, would influence the speed and braking distance of a ship when reversed or by how much propulsive efficiency would be affected by the obvious increase in ship resistance when going astern. The investigation was given to Conn who completed a very thorough research publishing valuable data[18] that are still used today. He began by examining the performance of a number of propellers in open water under the different conditions of zero speed of advance, ahead and astern speeds of advance. The propellers used were all from Baker's B series and were chosen so that the changes in efficiency due to pitch, blade shape and section, rake and blade number could be seen. As expected efficiency in astern operation was consistently lower than in the normal ahead mode and it was noticeable that high rake (30°) gave poor results. Next, four model hulls, one a single screw form and the others twin screw, were tested for resistance and propulsion in ahead and astern directions of motion. Again, as expected, propulsive efficiency astern was lower due to increased resistance astern but Conn could now give actual figures for the differences between ahead and astern running. To determine the braking effect complicated experiments were necessary. Each model was towed at a constant speed ahead and a predetermined propeller r.p.m. was set and maintained during a particular experiment but r.p.m. was successively changed so as to cover those required to propel the model ahead to approximately the same r.p.m. in the astern direction. The thrust and torque reading obtained thus passed through zero values into negative regions whilst the reading at the resistance dynamometer represented the actual resistance to motion or the braking resistance. Conn analysed his results in the form of non-dimensional coefficients for braking resistance, thrust and torque respectively and produced diagrams which showed pronounced humps at zero propeller r.p.m. The different curves demonstrated how different propellers affected the results. The differences in propeller geometry included changes in diameter and Conn showed that stopping or braking power depended very much on diameter. Excessive rake, already shown to be unhelpful in open water conditions, reduced braking power. The time taken and the distance covered in bringing a ship to rest could be determined from the curves of braking resistance provided allowance was made for the virtual mass. Conn's paper became famous, not only did it contain unique data from model experiments but operational considerations had not been forgotten and the ability of different types of prime mover in the ship when driving or reversing propellers were discussed in the light of possible stalling of the propellers.

Singing Propellers

A few years later Conn was to become involved in a tricky problem which was causing some concern at the time—the singing propeller. It is now generally accepted that the cause of singing, a high pitched note emitted just before the onset of propeller cavitation, comes from flexural vibrations of propeller blades. Older propellers were usually of cast iron, a material with self-damping properties able to resist vibration but by the 1930s many propellers were being made in manganese bronze to keep pace with faster-running machinery and it was at this time that the phenomenon of singing was first noticed. In 1936 the INA set up a singing propeller committee to look into the question and Baker was asked to be its secretary. Soon the WFL and The Royal Technical College at Glasgow were asked to carry out studies and both organisations began by gathering evidence and going on board ships to witness the curious noise. Baker, Conn, and Emerson went on several ships but were unable to make any physical measurements because so much other noise occurred as the ships made way. The onset and characteristic sound of singing was noted and its variation with propeller speed. For each ship, its lines and fitted propeller were examined against the observed singing. There was a popular belief that since singing had not been experienced in other propellers (these propellers having circular back section shapes) the aerofoil sections now being introduced to new propellers were responsible. Blade section shape was clearly important and the two studies naturally concentrated on propeller geometry but came up with different conclusions. The WFL's effort was led by Conn who produced a brilliant paper[19] giving an analysis of the phenomenon and a proposed solution. J.F. Shannon and R.N. Arnold at Glasgow arrived at their recommendations[20] from a highly praised series of wind tunnel experiments on three different types of blade section. Both papers were presented before the IESS on the same day and attracted a great deal of discussion, no fewer than five university professors contributing. Conn in presenting his paper argued that singing arose from the combined effects of the shape of a ship's stern and its propeller. Of these, stern shape was of prime importance since it produced variable wake velocities into the propeller and thus to reduce the problem of singing every effort should be made when designing a stern to iron out these variations. The non-uniform wake if unavoidable would transmit to a rotating propeller varying hydrodynamic loads and impart twist to the blades causing vibration. Conn calculated the natural frequency of several propellers and showed that singing was caused by torsional vibration of the blades. He suggested that this could be cured by using sections in which pressure and flexural centres coincided, or nearly so, thus eliminating blade twist. Such fixed centre of pressure sections had been tested in America by Munk and had shown a small reduction in the maximum lift coefficient over the more usual aerofoil type, a penalty that would have to be accepted if such sections were to be used. Shannon and Arnold thought singing was caused by propeller cavitation brought about by the choice in manufacture of excessive propeller edge thickness. They correlated this with the erosion seen on several ships' propellers that had been in service. Their wind tunnel tests produced comprehensive pressure readings over the blade sections and led them to recommend a drastic thinning of the edges of propeller blades. Both papers advanced very considerably the existing knowledge of the subject and influenced propeller designers. In practice, to eliminate or reduce the noise, the quickest and cheapest route was usually taken, that of thinning the trailing edges of propeller blades, sometimes with successful results. Conn received a well deserved award of IESS' Gold medal for his paper; it was the first time for six years that the Gold award had been made.

Coasters

Research into hull design had in the past tended to neglect the shorter ship such as those which operate in coastal waters. An attempt to rectify this began soon after Todd's arrival at Teddington. An initial study in 1929 looked into the general effect of hull dimensions and fullness on the resistance of coasters. These ships tended to be relatively broader than ocean-going types and for a given length and fullness were required to make a faster speed. To provide some systematic data for coasters Todd compiled and tested a small model series.[21] Resistance and propulsion data were collected in calm water and there was a distinct falling off in performance in the fuller forms and in most of these Todd observed the very poor flow at the sterns by dropping small pieces of paper into the water which were sucked into the propeller disc. The flow became even worse at low speeds when air was drawn down into the screws. From his results Todd gave the recommendation that coasters should not be designed with a prismatic coefficient greater than 0·75. Logically he then turned his attention to stern shape and flow and tested three further models, one with a raised stern and the other two with cruiser sterns of different immersion. Builders and designers of coasters were beginning to work towards the use of higher speed engines which were attractive not only for their decreased weight but for a reduction in first cost. Todd in his next series of tests[22] reflected this by using smaller faster-rotating screws. Fitting these to the cruiser stern models he found the power required to meet a certain speed was 7 per cent less than larger slower-rotating screws fitted to the raised stern model, an improvement that arose entirely from the reduced resistance of the cruiser stern due to its better-streamlined shape. Todd's work was welcomed by the industry who responded by building some very successful ships. *Moira* is a good example built by Swan Hunter in 1935 after model tests at Teddington a year earlier. *Moira* was one of the first ships of her type to have a welded hull. Todd continued, now with the help of Weedon, to do further experiments on the faster passenger/cargo vessel and the slower collier. From tests on four models, all with raised sterns, the maximum prismatic coefficient for good resistance qualities was found for a range of operating speeds and by propelling one of the models with a succession of propellers the range of r.p.m. characteristics of modern engines was covered. Todd and Weedon in presenting their results[23] said it did not pay to allow propeller r.p.m. to be too high, they had in extreme cases measured a 23 per cent reduction in propulsive efficiency. Again, as with the coasters, over half of this could be recovered if a cruiser stern of large immersion was used with a smaller propeller. The case for the cruiser stern was becoming ever more powerful.

Drifters

Whilst this work was going on Todd became involved with an even smaller type of ship, the drifter, a boat used for drift net fishing. The herring fishing industry in this country had fallen on hard times and the government appointed the Herring Industry Board to investigate the causes of the depression and to assist in its rehabilitation. Although the Board concentrated on marketing aspects, technical matters were also examined which included an enquiry into the efficiency of existing steam drifters and the Coal Utilisation Council became involved. So began a co-operation between J. Edward of the Coal Utilisation Board and Todd. Three drifters were made available and were specially chosen as being representative of the very best, having been maintained well above the general average. All operated from Great Yarmouth and two, *Ocean Reward* and *Ocean Rambler* were of pre-First World War vintage. The third, *Ocean Vim* had been built in 1930. Trials at sea were conducted continuously for several hours on each ship and measurements made of speed (from a log previously calibrated over a measured-mile), power, coal consumption, flue gas temperatures and so on. So far as engine performance was concerned *Ocean Reward* was very similar to the newer *Ocean Vim* both requiring about 15 pounds of steam per horse power whereas *Ocean Rambler* was heavier on fuel. Following the sea trials Edward considered possible improvements to boilers and machinery and Todd began some model experiments to seek a better hull form. Taking the lines of *Ocean Rambler* he made a model and drew up an additional alternative form keeping length and beam the same. The revised form had reduced prismatic coefficient and a completely different bow and stern. A cruiser stern replaced the older elliptical type and a much reduced waterline entrance angle produced a finer fore body. Calm water resistance tests on both models showed the revised form to be dramatically better at all speeds. At 9 knots, a typical working speed for *Ocean Reward*, effective power had been cut by 38 per cent. Both models were then self-propelled using a model of the as-fitted screw on *Ocean Reward* and a smaller faster-rotating one designed for use on the revised hull form. It was expected that lighter faster-speed engines would be available for future drifters. Open water experiments showed the smaller propeller to be 4 per cent better and this helped the revised form but the overall increase in propulsive efficiency of 14 per cent over *Ocean Reward* was nevertheless largely due to the reduction in resistance. Wave tests followed and because large sea states had to be reproduced Todd was forced to use very small 1½ metres long models to match the capability of the wavemaker in the tank. Being small the models could be towed through waves only from a bridle but it was possible to test two side by side so that comparative observations could be made in the same waves. Realising the importance of freeboard and aware that his revised form had less than *Ocean Reward*, a second revised form with greater freeboard was drawn up. Draught aft was increased to make it more representative of a standard drifter. In making these changes the fineness of the form was not compromised. Regular wave tests immediately demonstrated the importance of freeboard, *Ocean Reward* and Todd's second revised form remaining dry whereas the first revised form sank. In irregular waves the second revision was somewhat better than *Ocean Reward* indicating that its considerably finer fore body caused no problems. Edward's study of engine and boiler efficiency allowed him to offer several recommendations for improvement and between them the authors produced a very valuable paper.[24] All the more surprising therefore to read that it was greeted by its discussers with faint praise. The advantages of changing to a different form of hull were enormous yet failed to be appreciated by an audience too resistant to change, particularly over the acceptance of a finer fore body, and obsessed with practicalities. To be fair owners of small vessels are much concerned, and rightly, with seaworthiness. For their relative size, small ships can work in very severe seas. But many owners in the 1930s thought that large buoyancy at the fore end was a prerequisite for good seakeeping, an opinion which had survived from the time of the old sailing ships. Nevertheless good sea-kindly trawlers had recently been built with finer bows and the results now provided by the authors showed the Tank's finer revised form to be better in waves than existing drifters. Edward and Todd were blunt in their reply to the discussion and summed up by saying:

We have attempted to show how an economical, seaworthy vessel may be designed, and it is for the owners and builders of drifters to translate the experimental results into facts, and not to be deterred in their work by the prejudices which they will inevitably encounter in their task.

Skin Friction

The line of 1851 Exhibition Scholars was continued when H.C. Lackenby arrived at Teddington in 1935. He was attracted to the long-running debate on skin friction resistance and in pursuing a painstaking study he returned to William Froude's original data and reanalysed the results. Lackenby plotted

Froude's results with those of other workers to a base of Reynolds number and was able to show in a very convincing way that the "perplexing anomalies" mentioned by Froude in his original reports were due to a mixed or transitional flow that occurred between laminar and fully turbulent regimes.* He argued that Froude's results from his shorter planks would have been subject to laminar flow and if due allowance was made then the results fitted quite well with those from Froude's longer planks. Emboldened by his discovery Lackenby then proposed[25] a formula for the friction coefficient at any Reynolds number which fitted the experimental evidence. His formula was never accepted. Maybe, as a humble student, Lackenby was at a disadvantage when working in the shadow of luminaries such as the Froudes, Hiraga, Prandtl, Schlicting and Telfer. Not that he or his work were brushed aside. On the contrary, Lackenby went on to become a highly respected naval architect following most of his career at BSRA. As an offshoot of Lackenby's study and in the interests of acquiring more knowledge of the effects of roughness on skin friction, the WFL began to take measurements of hull roughness on new ships and by 1938 11 ships had been surveyed.

Ship Vibration

In the same year the Advisory Committee initiated research into ship vibration. A general theory for hull vibration was extant and the first efforts at Teddington were directed at checking this theory by tests and calculations for a variety of ships. Measurements of ship vibration using a vibrograph had in fact been carried out on about six ships from 1936 and in some of these critical hull vibrations had been identified. For ships with deck erections which were short in relation to the length of the ship itself, calculated and actual frequencies were found to be in fairly good agreement but difficulty was experienced in determining to what extent longer continuous superstructures acted as part of the main elastic structure of the ship and the damping effect of entrained water. Data from ships with long superstructures disposed about midships were thus badly needed. Todd who had pursued his 1851 Exhibition Scholarship in a study of ship vibration was the obvious person to lead the research but found insufficient time before the outbreak of the Second World War to make much headway. He did however, present a paper to the Engineering Section of the British Association[26] on the subject of ship vibration in general but it was not until post-war years that real progress was made. Parallel with Todd's work was the continuation of Conn's study of singing propellers and propeller blade vibration. Baker saw the importance of this and persuaded the Physics Division of NPL to combine with the WFL in a study of the various modes of vibration that could occur over the blades of a propeller. Physics Division developed an electromagnetic method which produced resonant frequencies over model

* For a fuller discussion of laminar and turbulent flow see page 162.

propellers the iron castings for which were provided by the North Eastern Marine Engineering Company. Once excited, the nodal lines were recorded by means of sand patterns on the two-bladed propellers that were used in the tests.

INSTRUMENTATION AND EQUIPMENT

The need was seen for a large open water propeller dynamometer to allow tests on both larger and faster-rotating model propellers and a start was made on the design and construction of a new piece of apparatus which proved to be the genesis of the very large 15 h.p. dynamometer that eventually appeared after the war.

The limitations of the wavemaker in Number One tank were becoming all too apparent and steps were taken in 1937 to begin a design for a replacement. A specification was drawn up but it was by no means certain that sufficient money would become available for the construction. As the Second World War approached matters were held in abeyance but the need remained.

In the early part of 1939 work followed its usual course and the WFL was beginning to detect an upturn in the number of requests for model work until the outbreak of the war when an entirely new state of affairs arose. It is interesting to contrast the conditions at NPL in 1939 with those at the time of the outbreak of the First World War in 1914. At that time NPL was much smaller and held a unique scientific position in that it was a national organisation which placed research, as distinct from technical development, in the forefront of its activities. As the First World War progressed the potentiality of NPL became more and more apparent and it was called on to assist in several of the unusual problems posed by the war. The intervening 25 years between the two wars saw a change in outlook whereby industry had established its own research laboratories and each of the Fighting Services had created strong research departments. When war began in 1939, NPL's Executive Committee did not expect the work of the Laboratory to be converted to a war footing, at least not straight away. But soon a number of new problems were submitted not only by the Services but also by the Departments of State concerned with Civil Defence. As a consequence of this it was decided not to allow any dispersal of the scientific staff although a number were lent for periods to other establishments and others redistributed within NPL. Todd was seconded to Durham University in 1940 returning two years later, Conn whose experience with propeller vibration had not gone unnoticed was transferred to the NPL's Aerodynamics Division to work on flutter and Sargeant went to Engineering Division's drawing office. Conn returned in 1943 but Sargeant remained in Engineering until the end of the war when he and Clarke left. NPL's Metrology Division had, since 1937, dealt with the inspection of production gauges and at the outbreak of war the numbers sent in rose sharply. Garlick, who had shown a propensity for the design and calibration of resistance and propulsion dynamometers, was asked to help and transferred to Metrology in 1940. So intense was the work (almost two million gauges passed through Metrology's hands in five years) that Garlick was needed for the whole of the war and did not return to the Tank until 1946. Cross joined Garlick but returned in 1942 to become a member of the team working on the Mulberry Harbour project.

As a result of the necessary reorganisation of staff the order of priority in which research was regarded, was affected. Inevitably some subjects had to be postponed to happier times; the progress of others would depend on the demand for war work.

REFERENCES

1. Westcott Abell, Sir, "Channel train ferry steamers for the Southern Railway", trans. INA, 1935.
2. Baker G.S., "The efficiency and steering effect of inward and outward turning screws", trans. I. Mar. Eng. 1931.
3. Baker G.S. and Riddle A.W., "Screw propellers of varying blade section in open water", trans. INA, 1932.
4. Baker G.S. and Riddle A.W., "Screw propellers of varying blade section in open water—Part 2", trans. INA, 1934.
5. Baker G.S., "Design of screw propellers with special reference to the single screw ship", *Ibid*.
6. Emerson A., "Special trials of the *Beacon Grange*: the effect of steering on propulsion", trans. NECIES, Vol. 55, 1938.
7. Baker G.S., "Wake", trans. NECIES, Vol. 51, 1935.
8. Baker G.S., *Ship Design, Resistance & Screw Propulsion*, Vols. 1 and 2, Published by Charles Birchall & Sons, 1933.
9. Wigley W.C.S., "The theory of the bulbous bow and its practical application", trans. NECIES, Vol. 52, 1935.
10. Wigley W.C.S., "Effect of viscosity on the wave-making of ships", trans. IESS, Vol. 81, 1937–38.
11. Emerson A., "The effect of shape of bow on ship resistance", trans. INA, 1937.
12. Hughes G., "The effect of wind on ship performance", trans. INA, 1933.
13. Hughes G., "Model experiments on twin-screw propulsion", trans. INA, 1936.
14. Hughes G., "Model experiments on twin-screw propulsion—Part 2", trans. INA, 1939.
15. Hughes G., "Model experiments on twin-screw propulsion—Part 3", trans. INA, 1941.
16. Kent J.L. and Cutland R.S., "Self-propelled experiments in smooth and rough water made with models of high speed ships", trans. INA, 1936.
17. Kent J.L. and Cutland R.S., "Further experiments in smooth and rough water with a model of a high speed ship", trans. INA, 1938.
18. Conn J.F.C., "The 'backing' of propellers", trans. IESS, Vol. 78, 1934.
19. Conn J.F.C., "Marine propeller blade vibration", trans. IESS, Vol. 82, 1938–39.
20. Shannon J.F. and Arnold R.N., "Statistical & experimental investigations on the singing propeller problem", *Ibid*.
21. Todd F.H., "Screw propeller experiments with models of coasters", trans. INA, 1933.

22. Todd F.H., "Screw propeller experiments with models of coasters—the effect of a cruiser stern on propulsive efficiency", trans. NECIES, Vol. 52, 1935.
23. Todd F.H. and Weedon J., "Further resistance and propeller experiments with models of coasters", trans. INA, 1938.
24. Edward J. and Todd F.H., "Steam drifters: Tank & Sea tests", trans. IESS, Vol. 82, 1938–39.
25. Lackenby H.C., "Re-analysis of William Froude's experiments on surface friction and their extension in the light of recent developments", trans. INA, 1937.
26. Todd F.H., "Vibration in ships", *Engineering*, 1938, 146.

CHAPTER 9

THE SECOND WORLD WAR

The reorganisation of the staff at the outbreak of war left the WFL with a total of 44 people under the leadership of Baker who in 1939 was 62 and thoughts of retirement could not have been far from his mind although his involvement was so great and the requirements of the Second World War so challenging that he was loathe to give up completely. However, in 1940 a severe bout of influenza which developed into pneumonia affected him badly and by September 1941 he decided it was time to hand over the reins but agreed to stay on to advise and support the needs of unusual war projects. It was fortunate for the WFL at such a critical time that a natural successor was on hand in Kent whose 30 years' experience made him an automatic choice. He was appointed Superintendent at the end of the year and led the WFL through the remaining years of the war.

Baker's leadership and control of the WFL since its beginning had been strong and forthright, his contribution to its work immense. He lived in an authoritarian age and acted that way making decisions which were rarely questioned even by NPL officials. Yet he extracted maximum co-operation and loyalty from his staff, a reaction brought about largely through his continuous interest and involvement in everything that went on. Leading a small work force (never more than 50) he was of course in an enviable position compared with later years when future superintendents had no option but to become managers of a growing research group that reached a peak under Paffett in the 1970s of roughly three times Baker's charge. Baker's greatest achievement was to establish from scratch a ship model testing establishment of the highest quality which soon achieved an international reputation. The research done was the first of its kind in this country relating to merchant ship hull design and many doubting British shipbuilders became convinced of the value of model testing in advance of a completed ship design. That alone assured a succession of regular work and brought in appreciable money to underpin in a valuable way the necessary costs of sustaining the research facilities of which he had proud charge. His own contribution to ship design was vast, 43 papers to learned societies, three books (one in two volumes) and an active involvement in fostering research. He was the first to show the importance of a Reynolds number presentation in relation to skin friction resistance and forcefully advocated and defended the $\textcircled{P}$ theory introduced with Kent soon after the

Tank had begun its work. He entered enthusiastically into INA affairs becoming a member of its Council and Vice President and took a very prominent part in the ITTC particularly in its early years. His death in 1949 brought many tributes. Amongst these Professor Troost of The Netherlands speaking at an INA meeting in Copenhagen in 1949 said:

I feel that I may speak in the name of all foreign members of the Institution when I say that the loss of Dr. Baker ... is felt by all of us as a personal loss. It is not only a national loss for you in Great Britain, but an international loss ...

After referring to Baker's visit to Wageningen in 1930 when advice had been given at the time of the building of the Dutch tank there, Troost went on to describe the human side of Baker's character:

... I remember especially that in those very strenuous and difficult years, 1939 and 1940, when he saw the dangers ahead he often asked me to leave Holland and to go with my family to his house and to live during the war with him. I will never forget his repeated invitations. But, of course, it was impossible to accept them, for my duty kept me in my own country. I want to tell you about it in order to show what a great-hearted man he was.

He was indeed a great man for the WFL and a Superintendent the like of which was never to be seen again.

The 44 staff in September 1939 were boosted in 1942 by the return from secondment of Conn, Cross and Todd and, three years later, newcomers J. Dawson and J.R. Shearer had arrived to swell the ranks of Assistant. Numbers in the workshop had remained fairly static so that at the end of the war in 1945 the total staff was 50. It is remarkable in view of the vast quantity of work undertaken throughout the war period that it was accomplished by such a small band of workers, particularly when it is realised that several volunteered to man the Civil Defence brigade formed by NPL to help in the protection of the laboratory from enemy attack, a task which required both day and night periods of duty. Such output would have been impossible without long hours of overtime work—15-hour working days were not uncommon.

The immediate effect of the impending conflict on the staff occurred before Britain and France declared war on Germany in September, 1939. At the time of the Münich crisis NPL was alerted to take steps to assist in the protection of its staff and buildings. A volunteer fire brigade within the laboratory had already been in existence for a few years to provide help at an emergency in advance of the arrival of the local National Fire Brigade and now it was decided to expand the NPL brigade and call for additional volunteers. Five came from the WFL: Berry, Conn, Emerson, Marwood and Witney. Shelter for staff from possible attack from the air had to be provided and the hot summer months of 1939 saw members of staff from all NPL departments digging trenches in the grounds of the laboratory. The WFL was allocated a space on the lawn between the entrance to the Tank and what is now NPL's central library. The trench was covered with wooden boarding taken from the false bottom used in Number

One tank and earth thrown on top. The crisis at Münich passed and the trenches were forgotten, never to be used, but they were soon replaced by concrete air-raid shelters constructed by the Office of Works. A Home Guard unit was also formed and when air raids over London, just 15 miles away, became a regular feature, teams of fire watchers were formed. Members of the Fire Brigade had most to do. They were drilled once a day for an hour and paid 10 pence each per drill. Members needed to be familiar with the layout of every NPL building, its gas and water valves, electrical switches and so on. In addition, fire-fighting equipment had to be understood, exercised and maintained. After each morning drill members returned to work but would report as quickly as possible to Headquarters at the sound of a warning siren. The fire watchers were on duty after laboratory hours and were split into groups of six stationed in various buildings. Two from each group kept watch for two hours and considerable organisation was needed to arrange these things, hot meals being cooked by members' wives at night, sufficient rations somehow materialising. Sleeping accommodation was arranged in suitable buildings such as wind tunnels where there was plenty of spare space. As the war progressed, occasions where there was any danger to the immediate locality of NPL were few although the sirens sounded often enough. Staff went straight to the shelters and did what they could (Baker knitted). Soon, after so many false alarms, Baker tired of so much wasted time, ordered certain corridors within the Tank buildings to be reinforced with wooden beams and thereafter nobody left for the official shelters. During the hours of darkness it proved impossible to "black out" the Tank buildings completely but the side windows along Number Two tank were obscured and the Number One tank carriage caged in by curtains and blinds.

Despite these precautions little could be done to prevent attack from the air and the work of the WFL might well have come to an abrupt end in 1940. It was the time of the *blitzkrieg* on London and during the night of 29 November there was a concentrated air attack on the Richmond, Twickenham and Teddington areas. As with the familiar pattern of such attacks a preliminary raid dropped incendiary bombs and a follow-up one, helped by the light of the fires started, picked its targets easily and dropped high explosives. The Baltic Timber Company in Stanley Road, Teddington, about ¼ mile from the Laboratory was soon ablaze and the occupants of nearby houses were evacuated to the NPL shelter next to the Engineering Division building. Tragically, in the attack that followed, the shelter suffered a direct hit killing everyone in it except a Laboratory gardener who was standing just outside the entrance. Emerson, too, had a narrow escape. He was on Fire Brigade duty and managed to crouch behind a pump as the bomb fell. It was one of a group which straddled the NPL and another which was heard to come down was thought to have fallen in the laboratory grounds. It had failed to explode. A search was made the following morning and a small hole was found between Number Two tank and its boiler house. Although only a small hole, experts believed that at least a 2,000 pound bomb was somewhere beside or under the tank. The offices near Number Two tank and the workshop were evacuated and WFL staff accommodated in other buildings although some stayed to continue working in the offices next to Number One tank. An Army bomb disposal unit arrived and began to dig. They followed the course of the bomb six metres underground into London clay where they found it had changed course and come to rest about 4 metres beneath the tank. It was an anxious moment. Working in continuous danger and having to pump water from the hole all the time since the clay was impervious and water had drained to its level, they carefully removed the bomb. It was 2 metres long and ¾ metre in diameter. Transporting it with great care to nearby Hampton the Disposal squad steamed out the explosive by a method which coincidentally had only just been developed by NPL's Engineering Division. Sir Charles Darwin who was NPL's Director during the war years had been called to Washington but was anxious to be informed of developments. A telegram was duly sent which said:

Tank baby safely delivered—weight 1¼ tons.

The excavations caused a local sinkage of the tank and the carriage rail on the north wall sank 3 mm. All of the windows were blown out by the blast and a few weeks after the bomb had fallen, in a spell of very cold weather, the tank water froze. Altogether five months of work were lost in this tank but fortunately work in Number One was undisturbed. The shell of the bomb was kept and placed in the entrance hall to the WFL, serving as a grim reminder of what might have been.

The war itself got off to a slow start—the "phoney" war, the only serious fighting in the first six months taking place at sea. The serious threat of the brilliantly organised German U boat force very soon became apparent when the liner *Athenia* was sunk the day after war was declared. 14 days later the aircraft carrier *Courageous* perished and shortly after that a U boat penetrated Scapa Flow and sank the battleship *Royal Oak*. The urgent need to protect ships from torpedo attack focused attention on the possibility of net defence and it was essential to carry the fight to these elusive craft. U boats were rampaging all over the Atlantic and to attack them mobile seadromes, to be used as bases for bomber aircraft, were considered. These two aspects of U boat warfare, torpedo net defence and large floating structures, brought immediate involvement for the WFL and experiments were soon put in hand.

WAR PROJECTS

Protection of Ships

Net defence for merchant ships giving them protection against torpedoes had already been attempted towards the end of the First World War and the experience at Teddington described earlier was of material help in the selection and arrangement of booms and netting. That war ended before the idea could be seriously tried but now there was renewed interest and following a long series of complicated experiments at the Tank, nets were indeed fitted to a large number of slower British and American ocean-going merchant ships. The system that finally emerged was a rather simpler arrangement than earlier in that it was possible to do away with an otter board which hampered handling and the streaming of the nets. As before, steel nets were supported by booms attached to the ship. The nets were streamed along each side of the ship and had to remain stable, maintaining their shape and depth at a ship speed of 9 knots. To do this the forward bottom corner of the net was "anchored" by a kite whilst a drogue kept the aft end taut. Earlier work at the Tank in 1915 on the *Oropesa* mine sweep system had been much concerned with kites and drogues and this experience proved valuable although the design of the kite was troublesome and needed several weeks of long hours each day to get it right. The successful version was largely designed by Baker and comprised rolled circular arc sections fore and aft which acted as depresser hydrofoils to give the required downward force. The nets themselves received special attention with regard to the size and shape of the mesh. A torpedo on striking the net was brought to rest by a resistant slipping of the points of contact of the mesh which were held by grips so designed to destroy the inertia of the torpedo. The grips were tested and perfected by NPL's Engineering Division who used full-scale versions in their experiments. Torpedo heads were either hemispherical or pointed in shape and the latter type was more likely to penetrate the net. Mesh configuration was therefore important and experiments were next done in the shallows of Number Two tank where model torpedoes of different nose shape were fired at different nets. The torpedoes were fired by compressed air and a diamond shaped mesh having a 2:1 ratio was found to be best. The final arrangement was towed and streamed in the tank and its resistance measured to enable an estimate of the speed loss in a ship with nets fitted. Austin P. Farrar representing Rear Admiral Mackenzie's Net Defence Department at the Admiralty was seconded to the Tank for all of the experiments and worked alongside Hughes, Cutland and Riddle, the four wrestling with and arguing over the many problems. These were eventually solved and sea trials quickly arranged during which, in calm weather, full spreading and streaming of the nets were achieved with little difficulty. The resistance of the nets reduced the ship speed from 11 to 9 knots in a British ship and from San Francisco the Americans reported a 1½ knots loss in one of their 10 knot ships. In moderate weather things were not so promising. As the vessel pitched and rolled the alternate slackening and tightening of the leaches caused fatigue in the meshes which eventually broke. Further tests were put in hand with the net oscillating as it was towed in Number Two tank. To do this a frame was built and fitted to the carriage outrigger and the frame driven in simple harmonic motion by a motor. The experiments looked at different shapes of nets and net behaviour with modified drogues fitted. By introducing ball drogues at equally spaced intervals along the foot rope and by changing the shape of the after ends of the nets a workable solution was reached and the foot rope remained taut. This final design, if a little more complicated than was hoped, proved reasonably successful at sea despite trouble with the heavy ball drogues. Fortunately the nets could be easily mass produced and many were subsequently made and fitted to ships (Farrar instances 768 British and American ships). Professor Robb in discussing Hughes' description of the work before the IESS[1] questioned the justification for nets and said that shipowners had complained about the delays caused due to fitting and changing them and the reduction in carrying capacity in their ships. He also said that he knew of three ships that had been saved by nets but it is sure that there were many more than that.

Seadromes

In the early stages of the war, convoys were at exceptional risk to submarine attack in the Atlantic because they were outside the range of land-based air cover.

The idea of the seadrome, code named *Habbakuk*, a massive floating mobile platform that could be used as a base for bombers brought forth some extraordinary proposals. Geoffrey Pyke a talented yet eccentric scientist suggested that large floating airfields could be constructed cheaply from reinforced ice. His first suggestion was to detach a piece of polar ice-cap, an idea that was criticised on the grounds that ice would be extremely vulnerable to fracture from bomb or torpedo attack. Pyke countered this by proposing that the ice be reinforced with a small addition of wood pulp and he christened this new composite material "Pykrete". Overcoming much scepticism he eventually persuaded Combined Operations Command to proceed with the design of "mammoth unsinkable vessels" 600 metres long. A quotation from the prophet Habakkuk: "... for I will work a work in your days, which ye will not believe, though it be told you" inspired the choice of code name and Project Habbakuk (the incorrect spelling passed unnoticed and was perpetuated throughout the 21 volumes of the Habbakuk documents) was born. Both the Engineering Division, NPL and the WFL were asked to carry out tests. Engineering Division evaluated the new material whilst WFL looked into the hydrodynamics. The evaluation tests, done in a cold store at Smithfield market, produced impressive figures, tensile and compressive strengths of Pykrete at $-15°C$ being similar to concrete. Other tests showed the material to have penetration and crack resistance higher than pure ice. Not so impressive were the figures from the Tank. A wall-sided shape with a 360 metres long rectangular middle body 40 metres wide was submitted. Triangular ends brought the overall length to 400 metres, much shorter than Pyke's original plan, yet at a draught of 45 metres the whole structure displaced 2¼ million tons. The seadromes were to be built in Newfoundland where there was an abundance of the raw materials needed (sea water and wood pulp) and then towed to the desired sites and held steady there against prevailing tides as high as 7 knots. Anchoring was out of the question in waters over a mile deep. With raised eyebrows the Tank staff built and tested the monster structure to a 1/80-scale. Resistance experiments gave excessive values of tow rope power and although modifications were made without sacrificing the simplicity of the design or overall dimensions and 30 per cent reduced resistance obtained, the figures were still ridiculously high and calculations showed that to tow the seadrome at 3 knots no fewer than 65 tugs each of 650 h.p. would be needed. With only six tugs available of the requisite horse power the idea was scrapped and attention turned to an alternative structure in wood. A flight deck 450 metres long and 75 metres wide was to be supported 25 metres above the bottom of four 20 metre high floats, the floats themselves being 460 metres long, 4½ metres wide and spaced 17 metres apart. This meant that the total beam of the seadrome at the waterline was 66 metres, the whole structure weighing 156,220 tons at a draught of 12 metres. To give strength and rigidity the floats were connected at their bottoms. This could either be a continuous floor or a series of wooden cross girders spaced intermittently along the length. Resistance experiments on a 1/48-scale model showed that with or without a continuous floor total resistance was a little greater than a calculation for skin friction would suggest. With intermittent strengthening resistance was almost three times greater and emphasised the importance of reducing head resistance of such structures. Experiments in waves followed at 3 knots and the increase due to rough water was as expected with no abnormalities in pitch or heave. The design appeared to offer some promise and calculations showed that a single Bustler tug of 3,000 h.p. would tow the seadrome at 3½ knots and two tugs could reach a towing speed of 5 knots. Alternatively, eight propellers installed at the end of the floats would need a total of 8,000 horse power to reach a speed of 5 knots.

A smaller raft-like structure intended as a landing field was next tested, an idea of its inventor John Mason. This consisted of an assembly of small blocks attached to the upper and lower surfaces of a sheet of thin celluloid. The raft would flex under an applied load and in waves. Deflections in two directions were measured in tests over a range of static loads and with the raft afloat in a passing train of waves. The 1/12-scale model in waves 12 cm high and 1½ metres long flexed easily and quickly but the upper surface of the raft was continually awash so that any idea of it being of use as an aircraft landing area was dropped.

In the event seadromes were never used and the turning point in the battle of the Atlantic was reached in May 1943 when sufficient aircraft-carrying ships became available to supplement the surface escorts to the convoys. At the same time net defence was dropped but it had played an important part. The whole battle was a close run thing and experts believe that the loss of merchant ships up to May 1943 was so severe that the allies were never far from ultimate defeat. Figures speak for themselves. By the end of the war 2,828 merchant ships had been sunk by U boats against a total of 782 German and 85 Italian U boats destroyed by the Allies.

Aircraft-carrying Ships

The race to provide enough aircraft-carrying ships led to the conversion of existing tankers and new purpose built ships that could be used to carry both cargo and aircraft. These unique ships known as "MAC" ships[2] superseded those merchant ships that had already been fitted with catapults which although capable of releasing aircraft could not thereafter recover and land them once airborne. The MAC ships had to be 14–15 knot ships and long enough to accommodate a flight deck at least 120 by 16 metres with hangar space for four Swordfish fighter aircraft. Whilst taking part in convoy protection they had also to carry a cargo of grain. Three British yards were capable of building prototype cargo vessels 140 metres long to which flight decks could be added. Their hulls had already been tested for resistance and propulsion at Teddington a year or so earlier and the forms considered to be good. Further experiments were now needed at a new design draught as well as tests in waves. To complete a comprehensive programme, steering and wind resistance tests were added, the latter following Hughes' 1930 approach when a model of the ship's superstructure (with and without a closed hangar) was towed upside down in the tank. Bottomley's gears were used in the steering experiments and gave the turning moments on the ship's hull for various rudder angles and torque at the rudder stock. From the complete set of data the effectiveness of the rudder under different wind and sea conditions could be judged, important considerations in view of the need to land aircraft on to a moving platform. Towing tests at different angles of yaw with the model hull in its upright position gave the resultant water force and centre of lateral resistance on the vessel under all service conditions. The closed hangar configuration improved the manoeuvrability and reduced total resistance particularly at higher wind speeds. The only snag which could not be overcome was the severity of the ship motions in the waves selected for the tests which of course related to the length of those expected in the north Atlantic. Quite simply the ship was too short. Nevertheless a building and conversion programme began and 13 ships (9 were conversions of existing oil tankers) were produced. Plate 37 shows *Empire Maccrae* the grain ship built by Lithgows in 1942 and tested as a MAC ship at Teddington. The pilots of the aircraft carried on these ships deserved sympathy and came in for high praise as they overcame the tricky conditions of landing in rough weather.

Barrage Balloons

Another early problem concerned barrage balloons. Set up by the Civil Defence Department in and around the cities and ports of Britain as protection against low flying aircraft they frequently went out of control in cross-winds on being pulled back to the ground. At a certain height above its mooring the balloon would become unstable and swing about its anchorage. The problem which might have gone to the Aerodynamics Division of NPL was more suited to the

Tank because a larger model could be made and higher Reynolds numbers achieved. A wooden model was made with lead inserts to give the right distribution of weight and correct inertia characteristics, suspended by its cable upside down in Number Two tank and run over a range of speeds. Instability was confirmed and alterations to the tail shape indicated an improvement. But Baker hesitated before making a recommendation because an actual balloon would flex whereas the wooden model could not. He ordered it to be cut into sections and reassembled so that it could move under the forces experienced. This was difficult and the workshop staff could not find a way and reported their problem with reluctance to Baker. "What's wrong with French letters?" came the reply and an embarrassed Wise was sent out to buy large numbers, exhausting the local chemist's stock in a single visit. Cutting them into strips and gluing them to the sections of the balloon did the trick and when the experiments were repeated there was no need to change Baker's original recommendations.

Limpet Mines

Apart from the need to develop new methods of sweeping and destroying enemy mines, attention was also given to the improvement of existing and new types of mine. An interesting but simple study concerned the limpet mine. These were used with some success on a number of occasions by the sabotage squad. Using a magnet to fix a limpet to his breastplate a saboteur would swim out to a moored enemy ship which was waiting for darkness before proceeding on her voyage. Sliding it off his breastplate the saboteur attached the limpet to the ship's hull at a vital spot such as the propeller shaft. After a time delay the limpet exploded as the vessel was under way damaging her sufficiently to bring her to rest, a sitting target for bombers in daylight. The War Office wanted to know at what speeds such limpets would be washed off a ship's hull since this would dictate the strength of the magnet required. Six full-size limpets were tested in the tank and held by their magnets to two plates, one smooth and freshly painted, the other rusty. Towing speeds were increased until the limpets detached themselves and it was found that the better-shaped limpets reached $9\frac{3}{4}$ knots, the worst only $4\frac{1}{2}$ knots. The measurements of resistance through the water helped to determine the best design of the limpets selected for use.

Minesweeping and the Destruction of Mines

So far as the destruction of mines was concerned the painstaking work of the WFL in the First World War contributed to the success of the *Oropesa* system of sweeping and cutting moored contact mines. By the end of that war the new system which could be operated by a single minesweeper was successfully put into operation and gradual improvements were made in later years. At the beginning of the Second World War, mines themselves had become more sophisticated in design and new mines of the magnetic, acoustic or pressure type were soon in use and posing a severe threat to the safety of shipping. To destroy floating magnetic mines a new sweeping system was required and non magnetic wooden minesweepers were built. In 1940, following tests at Teddington, the "LL" sweep was introduced. The idea was to explode magnetic mines at a safe distance astern of a pair of minesweepers working abreast by generating a magnetic field which actuated the firing mechanism in the mine. By good fortune German mines had been washed up on British shores and their inner electrical secrets discovered. The necessary magnetic field generated by the minesweepers came from two buoyant cables with electrodes, the ships providing the electrical current which travelled along the cables thus setting up the magnetic field. Two minesweepers towing the cables were able to clear a passage wide enough to give a safe lane for a convoy of ships through a minefield whereas a single minesweeper using an L sweep swept a narrower lane. The problem brought to the Tank was to find a means of supporting the sweeps. The rubber covered cables were 60 mm in diameter and 130 to 750 metres long. During sweeping the cables were towed some 200 metres apart at speeds between 15 and 20 knots. Their lowest point had to be seven fathoms below the water surface. Maximum tension could not exceed four tons and good directional stability was needed in adverse weather conditions. Thanks to the experience gained with the *Oropesa* sweep and the torpedo net defence experiments a quick solution was reached. Tests in Number Two tank confirmed that a support unit would work well if it was made up of a hydrofoil with struts, a split sleeve and bush on the cable and a vertical fin. For 400 metres of cable it was reckoned that nine units would be needed but to be certain of this staff at the Tank went to sea and carried out full-scale trials. The LL sweep was very successful and although the degaussing of ships which was introduced at the same time reduced the danger, mines had still to be located and destroyed wherever possible. Moored mines were still in use and improvements or alternatives to the *Oropesa* sweep were sought and led to further tests on scale models of a double sweep wire 250 and 280 fathoms long to be towed at 5½ knots from sea kites attached to two ships steaming abreast and 300 metres apart. Drogues and then small spherical floats were attached to the sweeps and the pull on the wires, their distance below the water and the stability of tow were all measured at various speeds and depths. This was a lower speed sweep system and again existing expertise in kite, drogue and float design helped in its development and it was not long before a successful arrangement was found. The float was special in that its buoyancy was sufficient to support 250 metres of sweep wire at rest. When attached to the sweep wires it remained on the surface under all speed conditions, towed steadily and stably and gave the required supporting force by hydrodynamic lift. Another slow speed sweep system, the "AA" sweep required a different type of float which this time ran below the water surface. The solution was not easy; the float had to meet several demanding requirements. It had to tow stably up to 6 knots, have a static reserve buoyancy of 112 pounds and, most difficult of all, exert on the sweep a decreasing total lift force as speed increased. After much thought and experimentation a float 400 mm in diameter with a hemispherical nose on a cylindrical middle body 400 mm long was chosen and fitted with two tail fins and a deep keel fin. The position of the centre of gravity of the whole float was critical so far as successful towing was concerned and the experiments, in examining different CG positions, established the best location as well as the preferred arrangement of towing bridle. The pivot of the bridle was selected to be 12 mm forward of the static neutral equilibrium position which was calculated from the weights, displacement, CG and buoyancy of the float. The float, as finally designed, ran quite stably and at 6 knots produced a lift three quarters of its static lift at rest.

With these sweeping devices in use and many ships degaussed both types of magnetic mines were virtually neutralised but acoustic and pressure mines were very troublesome, particularly the latter. The acoustic mine was largely overcome by simulating the noise of a ship's propeller from an electrically driven hammer in a box fitted ahead of the bows of a ship. This crude and dangerous procedure seemed to succeed, the vibrations of the hammer setting off the mine at a safe distance from the mine hunter. Pressure mines which were laid on the sea bed were extremely difficult to sweep. Dropped from aircraft into shallow water they were exploded by the pressure field set up by a passing ship. Many ships were sunk by these ground mines and there was little the Tank could do to help except to provide knowledge of the pressure variation set up by a moving ship in shallow water. Model experiments were being conducted at Haslar[3] to provide similar data and Cutland using a typical model hull ran it over different depths of water in Number Two tank. Electrical pressure transducers, the first to be used by the WFL, were set up on the tank bottom and recorded the variations of pressure with ship speed and water depth. Cutland found the level of pressure dropped off very markedly at low speed and the information collected no doubt supplemented that at Haslar and helped in the selection of a safe speed at which a ship could proceed in a known depth of mine infested water. The information was also of use for mine hunting ships as they began using the sonic devices which were gradually being introduced. Once mines were located they were destroyed by frogmen.

Buoys

Towards the end of 1940 there came the request to test and observe the behaviour of a floating signal buoy that was to be dropped from aircraft into the sea. Afloat it had to stay upright from its mooring with a wireless mast extended in tidal speeds of up to 7 knots. To make detection from the air difficult the water disturbance from the buoy should be minimal. The sinker mooring cable and other apparatus were stowed inside a cylindrical buoy limited in size and weight for ease in air transport. This was a demanding task. Tension in the mooring cable was unknown and there was little or no knowledge of how an upright cylinder would behave under the force exerted by such a strong tide. At the Tank it was an easy matter to determine the force in the cable and experiments gave values for different depths of buoy over a range of tidal speed. However, as anticipated, an upright cylinder proved totally unstable and despite attaching plates and lifting surfaces, different tow points and the centre of gravity of the buoy, instability could not be eliminated. Naturally such a wildly oscillating buoy exaggerated surface disturbance and even though a reduced length of mooring cable and a double bridle reduced the instability such an arrangement was hardly a practical solution. Kent suggested a buoy which would float with its axis horizontal. This would mean a completely new design including a rearrangement of mast, sinker weight and mooring cable within the body of the buoy. Such a buoy would need a streamlined nose at its forward end and the Tank staff drew up plans. The mast was stowed in a groove in the upper surface of the buoy, the keel weight in a space flanked by buoyancy chambers, while the sinker weight and mooring cable were stowed in an open skirt at the after end. Experiments then looked at different nose designs, towing points and length of mooring cable. Success was reached and in the final design the buoy ran steadily on the surface at all the required speeds and if submerged it remained stable with its axis horizontal without oscillation. Only a slight feather of foam appeared in the submerged condition and the buoy now satisfied all transport, laying and working requirements.

Oil Booms

Burning oil on the surface of the sea was a likely occurrence and extremely hazardous if unchecked. The Home Office were using floating oil booms to confine burning oil and prevent it spreading. The boom was made up of 12 metre baulks of timber flanked by steel skirting bracketed to the timber. The exposed surfaces of the baulks were occasionally set on fire and a simple effective means of preventing this was required. Experiments were made with a ¼-scale model boom. At the suggestion of the Home Office, conical holes were bored through the boom with the aim of producing fountains of water spraying the deck as the boom moved in rough water. Although two types of hole were tried, experiments in waves showed the idea to be useless except over a small range of wave length. The skirting was removed from the weather side of the boom and replaced by an inclined plate and after many experiments the best angle (12½°) was found which successfully deflected water and flooded the wooden deck of the timber baulks in all of the likely wave heights and lengths expected. However, practical objections were raised to fitting the inclined plates and a compromise reached whereby after replacing the skirting the deck of the timber was trimmed so that it sloped to the water's edge along its length. Flooding was satisfactory but the loss of freeboard endangered the transverse stability of the boom. By changing dimensions slightly and the shape of the baulks, an arrangement was reached so that a heavy man could safely board the deck from the skirting, without danger of capsizing it, and the oil booms were made to the laboratory's final design.

Army Tanks

The Army was working hard to improve its equipment. Tanks would be more effective and versatile if they could be made to operate across rivers or (as became necessary during the invasion of Normandy) stretches of the open sea. There was no shortage of ideas or inventions aimed at using the tank's tracks to propel it across water but the speeds achieved were pitifully low. Serious attempts were made to propel a tank by a marine propeller working in a tunnel, the power to the propeller coming from the same engine which drove the tank on land without pausing to change driving gears when passing from land to sea or vice versa. The Royal Marines produced a design for an amphibious assault craft and a model was made and tested. The full-size craft was 13 metres long and when afloat it displaced 46 tons. On land at full power it could be driven at 30 m.p.h. and afloat a speed of 10 knots was required from a single screw housed in a semi tunnel. The resistance results from the model were high and propulsion experiments indicated poor efficiency and a speed much lower than 10 knots. Changes to the tunnel shape were suggested and to improve the chances of reducing resistance, screens around the tank's tracks were fitted. A new propeller was designed following cavitation tunnel tests and when all three major modifications were tried the power requirement for 10 knots was reduced by 40 per cent and this speed with the available power at the tank's engine was now a distinct possibility. The powering experiments were followed by steering experiments which despite a further tunnel modification failed to show manoeuvrability other than sluggish, in fact steerage astern was poor. A second design was for a smaller tank 10 metres long and this was proposed by Commander Warrington Smythe. The bow of the craft was shaped like a sea sled and before experiments began the Tank staff suggested lengthening this. A 1/6-scale model was tested but the required 10 knots was not feasible. Changes to the shape of the tunnel did not help until a substantial alteration was made, replacing the single screw by twin propellers. The steering characteristics of this revised design were rather better and a prototype was built and tried out at sea with Tank staff in attendance. One of the recurring problems in such amphibious craft was the prevention of internal flooding but in due course a Sherman class tank, modified to include the idea of twin propeller propulsion at sea included a collapsible buoyancy screen raised around the waterproofed body of the tank. These tanks were very successful on the invasion beaches, only two of the 33 Shermans used sank and the others "swam" a mile to the beaches giving fire support as they went to the infantry wading ashore from their landing craft.

An even more challenging task so far as tank propulsion was concerned was when the Army wanted to ferry tanks across difficult stretches of water. A typical 14 ton tank was supported by two 4 metre pontoons floating at ½ metre draught and placed one at each side of the tank. The Army had fitted short pieces of 50 mm angle iron on every fourth link of the two tracks and reported that with the tracks driven at full power they could make way across water at only 1½ m.p.h. At least 3 m.p.h. was required. 11 full-sized units of tank track were brought to Teddington and fitted to a plank and towed in Number One tank at 300 mm immersion. Resistance was measured and close observations led to step by step experiments, which showed lugs rather than angle irons were the preferred shape. More importantly the best spacing for the lugs was found and in the end it was shown that 3 m.p.h. was a possibility with the existing power available. Even better, by dispensing with lugs altogether and propelling by a 600 mm diameter screw behind each pontoon, higher speeds were possible. However, since the tank's engine had to provide the power, the drive mechanism to the propellers was too complicated and the idea was not taken up. Such tests at the WFL were a new departure and were followed soon after the war by a very large programme of work conducted periodically for the Fighting Vehicles Research Establishment as new and better amphibian craft were developed.

Large Concrete Floating Structures

In 1942 military ports were required in Scotland to supplement British civil ports and in the Middle East extensions to ports were needed to offset the possible closure of the Mediterranean. Huge concrete structures were proposed and these were intended to form part of the ports. The largest of these, code named *Hippopotamus*, was a concrete pontoon 60 metres long and 7½ metres deep with a large steel girder superstructure 20 metres high erected on it. Ideally these *Hippos* would be built in dry docks where they could be floated out but with docks in great demand it was necessary to build some of the pontoons on land. One was under construction on the banks of the river Conway in North Wales and due to restricted water space had to be launched sideways. The War Office was concerned for the safety of houses on the opposite bank, a structure weighing over 3,200 tons launched into a river only 120 metres wide would create a large disturbance and very possibly cause flooding in the houses. The Tank was asked to look into two things, the modelling and simulation of an actual launch observing wave formation and the towing of the structure once afloat.

A model pontoon was made in wax, correctly ballasted and launched into the shallow end of Number Two tank along model ways corresponding to those at the building site at Conway. Great difficulty was experienced in reproducing the right frictional resistance between pontoon and launching ways. Experiments by the War Office using samples of the launching grease to be used indicated a coefficient of friction of 0·025. Using this, calculations showed that the likely speed of the pontoon down the ways would be 6 metres per second but in the model launches this speed could not be produced to scale despite trying different types of grease. Of course the pressure per unit area exerted by the model would be much less than full scale and so grease was abandoned and a roller bearing sliding device used instead. The top surface of the model standing ways was covered by a thin steel strip and sliding ways fixed to the underside of the model were made up of two small square iron bars inset with roller bearings. A launch speed gave a corresponding full-scale speed of 6¼ metres per second, a little too high. To reduce this, weights were dragged behind the model and released by an automatic trip just before the pontoon entered the water. The whole arrangement worked well. Experiments could now begin in earnest and a series of launches was made, continuous measurements being taken of the speed of entry into the water and thereafter until the pontoon came to rest. Heel was measured, the time of arrival of the waves to the opposite bank and, crucially, the farthest point ashore reached by the water. With some relief it was seen that there would be no need to build a breakwater; a few sand bags at garden gates would be sufficient. The War Office co-operated fully and allowed Tank staff led by Todd to observe the actual launch on the Conway. Measurements were made and the whole event filmed by photographers from NPL Physics Division installed in a boat nearby. Model and full-scale results agreed extremely well, the speed during launch of the actual *Hippo* being 5 per cent slower than that scaled from the model results and the predicted length of travel of the *Hippo* from the start of launch was within 10 metres. The request for towing tests came after the first *Hippo* had been launched for it was soon found to be longitudinally unstable, not even seven tugs could control it. The War Office suggested three modifications to the shape of the pontoon and model experiments at a corresponding towing speed of 4 knots were conducted on the original shape and the three suggested alternatives. In each case instability persisted with large transverse oscillations. Attention turned to the actual method of tow and a Dutch tow (towing on a bridle from tow points fore and aft) worked well. However, a side pull on a tug would be unbalanced unless two similar pontoons side by side were towed together. Lee boards were next tried on each quarter of the model pontoon with their forward edges 2 metres from the surface of the pontoon and after edges one metre from the hull. This arrangement when towed by a single wire reduced instability considerably and a simple modification to the lee boards removed it altogether. Additional towing tests in waves were successful and lee boards were fitted to full size *Hippos* which were then successfully towed hundreds of sea miles to Scotland in early 1943, each *Hippo* requiring one tug.

The *Hippos* were in fact the precursors of the concrete caissons that were used as breakwaters in the *Mulberry* harbour project and just after the tests on the model *Hippos* serious thought was given to the construction of artificial harbours for use by an invasion force. There followed further launching tests on pontoons which were envisaged as floating pier heads to be used as a jetty for ships unloading cargo. Many of these pontoons would be side launched. A prospective builder, Wates at Marchwood on Southampton water would use this method but this time there was no danger of wave disturbance flooding waterside buildings. However, variations in the local tide could be important. A typical design, was brought to the Tank and a model made and launched into Number Two tank shallows over a range of different conditions of tide expected at Marchwood. The higher the tide the less the distance travelled by the pontoon and its sliding ways before entering the water and so the speed of entry would be lower. The reduction in speed was surprising. In a tide of $3\frac{1}{3}$ metres the speed scaled from the model test was 3·7 metres per second whilst in the higher tide of $4\frac{1}{3}$ metres it was only 1·4 metres per second, which indicated that if the pontoons were launched at high tide on a cold day, when the friction would increase, there was a danger of the pontoons sticking on the ways due to an insufficient speed of entry. The Tank thus sent a recommendation to the War Office that launches should be carried out well before high water. Full-scale launches were witnessed at Marchwood and measurements taken. Again excellent correspondence between model and full size was found.[4] At low tide when the water depth was slightly different to that set at the model the speed of the full size pontoon just as it entered the water was 3·84 metres per second compared to a predicted 3·93.

Mulberry Harbour

In parallel with these experiments on proposed pier head pontoons were tests on floating bridges which were intended to be connected to the pier heads, acting as roadways. The bridges, built in 25 metre spans, were supported on small pontoons and it was required to determine the pull on the anchors and cables needed to moor the bridges against a tidal flow which could be in a direction normal to the run of the bridges. Two spans of a bridge were modelled and supported on pontoons. Towing the assembly down the tank at an equivalent tidal speed of 5 knots enabled the best length of cable to be decided and the best kind of anchor. Because of different heights of tide a quick solution was not reached particularly with regard to the anchor and much debate and uncertainty grew between Kent and the War Office. A final decision was left in abeyance until the choice of a preferred invasion plan was reached. Discussions took place amidst mounting pressure for an invasion of Europe and Prime Minister Churchill knew that a landing in Normandy depended on the successful capture of a channel port or, if this failed, the establishment of a temporary harbour at which troops and equipment could be disembarked. The experimental raid on Dieppe in August 1942 was disastrous and ruled out the capture of a port as a prelude to invasion. The combined task force used at Dieppe of almost 6,000 suffered appalling losses, 3,600 men, a destroyer, 30 tanks and 33 landing craft—all in a single day. Channel ports were heavily fortified and if one had been captured the Germans would have wrecked port installations making the subsequent battle in Normandy even more difficult. The alternative, the germ of which had just been tested at the Tank, was to construct artificial harbours made up of individual units which could be floated and towed across the Channel and then assembled offshore to provide breakwaters, floating pontoons and roadways which would run straight to the shore. But there were snags. Beaches were mined, safe landing could be attempted only at low tide and so pontoons and roadways had to be moored with sufficient length of cable to allow rise and fall with the tide—hence the earlier feasibility tests. The units had to be towed to the invasion beaches at night under the cover of darkness which meant a towing speed of 5½ knots. The resistance of each unit was therefore critical. But this was meat and drink to the Tank and once the decision to proceed with the whole project, code-named *Mulberry*, had been reached at the Quebec conference in August 1943 (from that moment time was of the essence), the knowledge at the Tank and the solution to the mooring problem already found enabled the extensive series of model experiments which followed to get off to a flying start. There was nevertheless much to be done both in designing suitable units and the testing of them for resistance and seaworthiness. Urgent talks took place at Teddington between War Office staff led by Brigadier Sir Bruce White and Kent and Todd who led the laboratory effort.

It had been decided to construct two harbours. One, 60 miles south of Cherbourg for the western invasion beaches Utah and Omaha where US forces would land and the other, for British and Canadian troops, further east at Arromanches at Gold, Juno and Sword beaches. These locations were such that the harbours could be laid out to give entrances to small ships berthing at the floating pier head pontoons. Unloaded cargo and vehicles could then proceed ashore along the floating bridges connected to the pier heads. To give sheltered conditions within the harbour, breakwaters would be necessary. The work at the Tank was directed in turn to the design of suitable breakwaters, pontoons and bridges which would fulfil the required functions and also have tow rope powers within the capability of existing tugs (about 2,000 h.p.).

With respect to the breakwater there were four known methods of destroying approaching waves, a vertical wall, a long sloping beach, a porous obstruction or the emission of compressed air from a submerged pipe. The first was the only realistic choice and to begin with the War Office wanted floating breakwaters with vertical sides. Kent and Todd did not dispute vertical sides but said that no floating breakwater would be of any use unless it could be made to remain at rest. Whereas floating breakwaters would have certain advantages they would lead to insuperable mooring problems, difficulties which were soon demonstrated by tests which followed a few days later. It was therefore agreed that a ring of breakwaters would be made up of concrete caissons (*Phoenixs*) sunk end to end on the sea bed and supplemented by scuttled redundant ships. An outer ring of breakwaters for added protection comprised floating steel structures anchored in the deeper water. The height of the tide and anticipated waves fixed the maximum height of the *Phoenixs* as 20 metres, some could be shallower and narrower, and it was decided to make them 60 metres long. Civil Engineers and contractors were consulted and briefed on the requirements for the whole construction programme for *Mulberry*. The immensity of the task can be understood only when it is realised that about six miles of breakwater, 500 pontoons and over 150 *Phoenixs* were needed plus long stretches of bridges or roadways along which thousands of equipped men with tanks and lorries could travel to the shore. All this was needed quickly against a background of shortages of labour and materials. Simple straightforward designs of light structure were essential. By using concrete for much of the construction relatively unskilled labour could be used and many firms (over 200) around the country unspecialised in ship construction enlisted to build. Since it had been agreed that the *Phoenix* breakwaters were to be sunk to sit on the sea bed, an arrangement for flooding the units had to be worked out and while this was being considered the Tank began testing various designs of breakwater for wave-breaking and towing properties. Contractors had sent in a number of outline designs, some with solid continuous walls, some with openings and models of 12 of the most promising proposals were made and tested. The workshop could not cope with so many at once and several of the contractors, notably Holloways and McAlpine and also the Army shared in making the models. For simplicity many contractors chose rectangular shapes but Kent and Todd realised that the resistance under tow of such shapes would be excessive and in view of the modest speed required, advocated swim ended shapes along the lines of existing Thames barges. Some thought ship rather than swim ends ought to be considered so models in three different categories were tested with several variations in each. But first, to choose between solid or walls with openings models were placed across Number Two tank and subjected to waves of chosen height and length. Number Two had to be used because of the need for shallow water but this tank did not have a wavemaker. By borrowing motors, gears and ancillary equipment, a successful plunger type was built at the deep end of the tank and put into operation in just three days. The movement of the water on each side of the different wavebreakers was recorded visually and it was seen that solid walls were best although small openings on some of the designs tested did not cause undue water disturbance behind the wavebreaker. The towing experiments that followed produced no surprises. Resistance was very high but swim ended shapes gave lowest values at 5½ knots. The results from model 2305A (swim ends), model 2305B (ship ends) and model 2305C (square ends) show marked differences and even though the values for 2305A were clearly superior they were still extremely high, some eight times that of a conventional ship hull of the same length. After scaling the model result, 2305A gave a resistance of 16 tons for the full size *Phoenix* at 5½ knots. Behaviour during tow was obviously important and it was seen that 2305A did not tow quite straight but oscillated about a mean track. The towing wire was fastened through a bridle to towing points on the two forward corners of the *Phoenix*, the two arms of the bridle and the distance between the towing points forming an equilateral triangle. This was satisfactory but did not prevent the small amount of yaw. A cure was found by fitting two lee boards but unfortunately these increased resistance so much that in the final *Phoenix* design they were scrapped and the yaw accepted. Before tests in waves, the preferred swim ended shapes were rigorously examined again for their wave-breaking ability since it was realised that square ended units would give the best results of all. Two models were placed end to end and spanned the full width of the tank. Model ships and a pier head were moored at a distance from the breakwater and waves sent down. When unprotected by the breakwater the pier head was swept away and barges and motor boats swamped. With the breakwater in position, even at a water depth corresponding to high tide, only a little spray fell on the inside and there was no disturbance of the craft moored there. To complete the tests both the larger *Phoenix* designs and the smaller ones (these were needed in areas of shallow water) were towed through regular waves of 2 metres corresponding height. Resistance was high, 37 tons for the large *Phoenix* at 5½ knots compared with 16 tons in calm water but pitching was small. In fact waves tended to break against the fore end as though it were a breakwater and only a small amount of spray fell on the decked in forward compartment. The smaller breakwater, models 2312 and 3, pitched rather more and shipped a great deal of water in waves. No decking aft of the forward compartment had been included in the design of these smaller *Phoenixs* and it became necessary to include complete decking with hatch covers.

The design and towing arrangement for the *Phoenix* breakwaters was now settled. The largest was over 60 metres long, 17 metres wide and floating at a draught of 5½ metres it displaced 5,340 tons; the smallest a little shorter, 8 metres wide displacing 1,451 tons at a draught of 3⅓ metres. They were to be towed 100 miles to the invasion beaches, manoeuvred into position and then sunk by admitting water through sluice valves. The metacentric height of the *Phoenix* when afloat was relatively small and there was a risk of instability at some stage during the sinking operation. Experiments were put in hand and a special 1/24-scale model of the largest *Phoenix* was made. To ensure that the flooding of the compartments and subsequent behaviour of the model was representative of the full-sized *Phoenix* it was essential that the arrangement and capacities of the internal compartments and the position of the centre of gravity of the model should be exactly to scale. A wooden model was built, sheathed with lead and after various adjustments the correct total thickness of walls, hydrostatic characteristics and internal capacities were achieved. The large *Phoenix* had a continuous watertight centre bulkhead fore and aft (plate 31) and 10 separate watertight compartments. Each of these was fitted with two valves for flooding, one ⅔ metre and the other 4 metres above the bottom. Experiments were carried out in a corresponding water depth of 15 metres with the *Phoenix* in its original designed condition, GM being 0·28 metre. Its inside was completely dry, the water in the tank perfectly smooth and the model upright. The valves were then opened and the model allowed to sink. Despite the ideal conditions the model soon heeled and as the deck edge entered the water the instantaneous loss of stability due to the loss of waterplane area caused the model to heel over to 46°. At such an angle the valves on the emerged side were out of the water so that further water entered at the immersed side only, thereby increasing heel. The experiment was stopped otherwise the *Phoenix* model would have turned over and come to rest on its side on the bottom of the tank. The very large angle of heel was caused initially by the small GM and exaggerated by the free surface effects of the water in the compartments which rapidly reduced GM to a negative value. This behaviour could have been anticipated and the heel controlled if selected compartments were flooded in turn but this would have led to a longer sinking time and the need for considerable skill and judgement on the part of the crews in charge of the sinking. In the face of enemy action, speed and simplicity of operation was vital. The whole question of stability was absolutely crucial and Kent urged this on the War Office offering two alternative suggestions. First, to lower the CG, concrete should be added as ballast at the bottom of all compartments and to reduce free surface effects three longitudinal dwarf walls built into each compartment (plate 31). Alternatively, without the dwarf walls a thicker layer of concrete ballast should be used. Experiments on both of these ideas showed a preference for the first. When the bottom valves only were opened the model sank on even keel until the deck edge entered the water when loss of stability caused a 6° heel. As the model continued to sink it slowly recovered and the whole process of sinking took about 37 minutes (full-size time). The experiment was repeated, this time with all valves open. Behaviour was generally the same and sinking took just over 19 minutes which was considered satisfactory. It was always possible that the units would arrive on site with a list and to show the effect of this on sinking an experiment was conducted with the model pre-set to an initial heel of 10°. The head on the valves on each side of the *Phoenix* was now materially different and caused the heel to increase rapidly by the inrush of water on the lower side. After only 28 seconds the deck edge entered the water with a dangerous heel of 25°. At the moment the bottom corner touched the tank bottom the angle was 33° after which the *Phoenix* slowly settled to an even keel. In view of this it was decided to increase the thickness of the ballast and the War Office made sure to include in its instructions to crews a clause to the effect that if any unit had a list on arrival, this was to be corrected by allowing water to enter the centre compartment on the high side only, before commencing to flood all compartments. In making these suggestions the Tank emphasised that everything depended on the accuracy of the estimated height of the CG of a *Phoenix* and that an early check should be made on its calculated value. The War Office agreed and in due course Laws and others from the Tank conducted inclining experiments on the first three *Phoenix* units built, a small one at Middlesbrough in January 1944 and on larger units at Portsmouth and London two months later. At Middlesbrough the estimated CG above the base of the *Phoenix* was 4 cm below the measured position and in the larger units the difference was about 18 cm. These differences were not serious but it was important to ensure that the personnel who were to man the units should gain some experience in sinking and be warned of the dangers of careless handling. Crews drawn from the Royal Engineers and sailors of the US Navy were sent to the East India Dock in London where 10 large *Phoenix* units were being built in the dry. The men went up and down ladders working the valves without sinking the units and generally got the feel of their "ships". Next, to see what would happen in practice, crews came to Teddington to witness and carry out sinking tests on the *Phoenix* model. Tank staff demonstrated that when sinking, the unit would take up a list of 5 or 6° as the deck went under water, but that this would correct itself on further sinking and was no reason for alarm. On the other hand the differences possible if flooding started with an initial list of 10° were shown. The sappers and sailors tried all these things and with their existing knowledge of the valves a drill was worked out. Neither time nor opportunity was available to practise sinking the actual *Phoenixs* except on completion when they were partially flooded and "parked" at two assembly areas off the south coast of England to await D Day but there is no doubt that much of the success achieved at the invasion beaches had its foundation in the demonstration tests at Teddington.

The floating pier heads presented a different problem. They had to be anchored securely and rise or fall with the tide. As with the floating bridges the best way to do this led to much debate and uncertainty. An apparent obsession with detail irked Churchill as his terse memorandum (plate 29) shows. A solution was reached that drew on the experience of *Lucayan*, a dredger that was built in 1923 for the Bahamas. She had three legs or "spuds" which were lowered onto the sea bed and held *Lucayan* firmly in position against the heavy seas frequently experienced. Four spuds were placed at the corners of the pier heads which themselves were steel Lobnitz pontoons 60 metres long. The conspicuous spuds were raised to their highest point during tow giving a maximum draught of 2 metres for pontoon and spuds. On site they were lowered to the sea bed and anchored. At the same time they allowed an up or down movement of the pier head with the tide. The Tank was asked to design a buffer for the pontoons which would take way off a vessel coming alongside; it was possible that on contact the force of a ship striking the pontoon might shift the pier head off its spuds. Kent's idea was to fit a floating "door step" in the form of a hinged wedge. As a ship approached, its forefoot would run up the inclined surface, depress the pontoon and the energy absorbed would bring the vessel to rest. Calculations indicated the dimensions of such a wedge to be 20 × 20 × 2 metres at its thick end and model experiments confirmed these as adequate and showed that a typical landing ship tank (LST) could approach safely at up to 4 knots. Buffers of sufficient strength were designed which were accepted and at Arromanches proved particularly successful in speeding up operations during the disembarkation of troops and stores.

The floating bridges set up inside the *Mulberry* harbours and attached to the pier heads were, as already noted, made up in 25 metre spans. A complete bridge was about a mile long and carried a 3 metres-wide road. Each end of a bridge span was supported on a small pontoon (*Beetle*) which when fully loaded displaced 46 tons. The *Beetles* which ultimately were built in both steel and concrete were arranged to carry a number of spans thus forming separate trains. At the extreme after end of these trains a circular erection cylinder supported the rear span above the level of the *Beetles*. The trains were then towed to the beaches and on arrival the higher end of the span was manoeuvred to the *Beetle* at the lower end of the next train and the erection cylinder flooded to lower its span on to the waiting *Beetle*. The *Beetles* themselves were rectangular in shape with chamfered corners. They had flat bottoms, vertical sides and turtle decks. Models of the bridge spans, *Beetles* and erection cylinders were made to a 1/10-scale and the support of the bridge ends was arranged to give 3° of movement by fitting pairs of universal joints. These reproduced the actual pitch and roll motion of the full-size bridges when towed through waves. The War Office were hoping that as many spans as possible could be towed satisfactorily in a single train and the model experiments began by towing a single span, progressing in steps to a train of 5 bridge spans and an erection cylinder. Complete bridge spans were not made except for the leading two. In these, plywood sides were fitted to represent the side girders in order to observe how high the waves would come. There were immediate problems. A single pontoon carrying a load corresponding to a bridge span buried its head at 4½ knots and swung from side to side during tow and when a complete train of 5 spans, *Beetles* and erection float was towed the whole assembly was so unstable that the train drifted so far off course that it had to be fended off from each side of the tank. Again lee boards came to the rescue and after many experiments a solution was reached. A lee board 2 metres long fitted to each side of the last span just ahead of the erection cylinder and immersed 3 metres proved very successful and enabled 5 spans and an erection cylinder to be towed stably at all speeds up to 6 knots and the arrangement was adopted in the full-size bridges. The Tank considered the resistance of the *Beetles* to be too high and suggested either fitting fairing pieces or arranging swivels so that they could be rotated to face fore and aft during tow and once on site returned again to their best position of flotation. Swivels were fitted to the models and reorientated *Beetles* achieved a 25 per cent reduction in resistance at 6 knots or in other words the towing speed could be increased to 7½ knots. At this higher speed there were no signs of instability even in fairly high waves. However the War Office were loath to introduce changes which might lead to operational difficulties and with the continued need for simplicity in construction rotatable *Beetles* were not used. Neither were fairings to the *Beetle* shapes despite achieving similar reductions as in the tests with swivelled *Beetles*. Later *Beetles* were made in concrete and were symmetrically shaped and these different but simpler shapes became the subject of even more tests.

All now appeared ready and it is remarkable how rapidly such a large and extensive range of unusual experiments was completed. The Tank staff worked willingly and for very long hours and received maximum co-operation from the War Office and contractors. All told over 40 models of *Phoenix* breakwaters, pontoons, *Beetles*, bridge spans, etc. were made, tested and reported on in a period of seven weeks. Tests proper began in September 1943. After the war much of the Tank's work on this momentous project was described by Todd[5] and Sir Bruce White who had been the Director of Ports (War Office) and in charge of the whole operation discussed Todd's paper and was glowing in his praise to the Tank and its workers:

It was indeed a great team: in all my long experience I do not think I have ever met a more willing or more capable team than that at Teddington including Mr. Kent, Dr. Todd and his assistants. I readily say that without that assistance we should not have done what we did.

In a sense, as Churchill said in another context, this was the WFL's "finest hour" so significant a part did it play in the realisation of such a stupendous engineering achievement the like of which had never been seen before.

The story of the invasion, operation *Overlord*, has been told often enough. Crucial to its success was the naval phase (*Neptune*), the greatest armada the world had ever known—almost 5,000 ships and 200,000 men. *Overlord*, perhaps the most closely guarded secret of the war, was planned for May 1944 but forecasts of bad weather led to agonising debate and delay until D Day was finally chosen as 6 June. Five days earlier an odd collection of ancient ships set sail for the invasion beaches. These were the supplementary breakwaters and once on site would be deliberately scuttled and sunk alongside the *Phoenixs*. These Gooseberries as they were called were ancient expendable freighters and warships manned by skeleton crews sufficient to manoeuvre them into position. The first *Mulberry* units towed by 150 tugs were preceded by warships and minesweepers under powerful air cover. After a difficult crossing in awkward seas during which a *Phoenix* struck a mine, the Omaha and Utah units had arrived by dawn on 7 June to face heavy shelling from German shore batteries. A day later the Gooseberries were in place and scuttled and on 16 June, 10 days after D Day the whole western harbour was in place and 78 tanks had been unloaded from LSTs and driven ashore over the floating bridges. The Germans who had certainly been hoodwinked and unprepared for the invasion to take place where it did were baffled by the Gooseberries and the enormous concrete structures which they took to be self-propelled quays. Yet Goebbels the German propagandist sought to make capital over the sinking of the Gooseberries. "Our glorious Luftwaffe", he cried "have today destroyed a battleship of the Iron Duke class and of its complement of over 1,000, only 70 were seen to survive." The 70 were the crew which brought the *Centurion* to the scene and who left after scuttling her. The second harbour at Arromanches followed. The surrounding terrain gave a certain natural protection not available at Omaha and Utah and assembly was easier. In both harbours the breakwaters with the Gooseberries were very successful as the contrast in the surface of the sea shows in plate 35. Sinking time for the *Phoenixs* never exceeded by more than 10 per cent the time predicted from the model tests and during tow none of the units gave any trouble. Today some of the *Phoenixs* are still in the sea at Arromanches and worthy attempts to conserve them are being made by the Arromanches 93

Association. If successful they will form an outline of the breakwater that will be visible to the thousands of tourists that go to Arromanches each year. The floating bridges once in place also behaved beautifully and in all tidal conditions. What could not be catered for was the unprecedented storm of gale force that broke out two weeks later. It was particularly severe at the western beaches where there was less protection. Outer breakwaters broke loose and the *Phoenixs* were pulverised. Ships were hurled against them and enormous waves broke over the Gooseberry superstructures. Damage to both inner harbours was considerable[6] but fortunately the majority of troops were already established and advancing into France. Nevertheless replacement units were needed urgently and further experiments were put in hand because in order to speed up production, swim ended shapes had to be given up and substituted by heavier square ended units. Displacement increased by 23 per cent and this plus the square ends resulted in a huge increase in resistance over the earlier swim ended *Phoenixs*. To reach a tow speed of near 5 knots, fairings had to be fitted and experiments showed these to be essential and they were adopted and replacement units put into commission.

PLUTO

With the harbours established and troops and equipment ashore a continuous supply of fuel was needed to sustain them and when Cherbourg was captured on 27 June a pipe line was laid on the sea bed between the Isle of Wight and Cherbourg. This remarkable achievement was code named PLUTO for Pipe Line Under The Ocean. Cable laying of itself was not new but some of the cables now required had to be steel pipes and very much stiffer than those hitherto handled by existing Admiralty and Post Office techniques. Two methods of laying were used. The steel cable was wound on a drum which resembled a cotton reel of immense size. Called a *Conun* it was 15 metres in diameter and mounted either in a hopper barge or floated and towed by tugs. Having anchored one end of the cable to the shore it was then unwound as the barge or tugs moved forward. It was anticipated that the drum would rotate faster than the desired unwinding speed due to water forces acting on the drum during forward motion and that as a consequence some kind of brake would be needed. Paddles were suggested which would "grip" the water but Kent thought these would increase the resistance of the drum which because of its size and unusual shape was bound to be high anyway. He proposed a water brake designed to work inside the drum and this idea was accepted. To see how fast the drum would rotate during tow a model *Conun* was made and tested without a cable unwinding from it. Surprisingly the drum did not rotate at all until a towing speed of 8 knots was reached. This was welcome news since the required laying speed of 5 knots would mean that a brake need not be considered. Attention now turned to the resistance of the *Conun* and the tension in the cable as it unwound at different laying speeds. Resistance was extremely high yet within the capability of existing tugs at 5 knots. Two ways of unwinding were tried and it was found that if the cable was unwound from the immersed side of the drum the tension in the cable was less than if it were unwound from the emerged side. The ends of the drums were conical and such a shape appeared to influence the longitudinal stability under tow. Altogether six variations of *Conun* shape were tested. The request for the work came to Teddington at a time when the staff and the two tanks were already overstretched by the *Mulberry* project and other work in progress at the time. Subsequent experiments on five variations of *Conun* were conducted at Haslar and concentrated on refining the shape particularly with regard to the conical ends and the depth of a flange that was needed to eliminate all tendency to yaw during tow. For the longer stretches of PLUTO, the towing method using tugs was chosen whilst shorter runs were laid by the converted hopper barge *HMS Persephone*. In the former the technique of towing was complicated and difficult. Two tugs stationed 400 metres ahead of a *Conun* to reduce the effects of wash, towed the drum on a bridle whilst a third tug at the rear of the tow first anchored the free end of the cable to the shore and then helped to control the whole operation as towing and unwinding began. This was certainly tricky particularly if a strong tide was running. Exhaustive sea trials were carried out between Tilbury and Southend and NPL photographers from Physics Division took film records. Contrary to the model test behaviour the *Conuns* did in fact rotate due to forward motion. Fortunately they did so slowly and the laying procedure was not seriously affected but discussers of Purvis' paper,[7] which described the whole *Conun* development, could not understand why the model tests had failed to reproduce what was thought to be a certainty. The trials also showed the importance of the impingement of screw wash on the *Conun* and helped to decide the best position of the tugs during a lay. In the event, a PLUTO was successfully laid 65 nautical miles from Cherbourg to Shanklin on the Isle of Wight. *Persephone* was really used as an experimental ship and capable of laying only smaller-diameter cables. Nevertheless she carried a *Conun* and laid 1650 mm pipelines code-named SOLO across the Solent. These brought oil onshore at Thorness near Cowes to a pumping station and from there oil was pumped through a buried artery across the Island to TOTO, a 620,000 gallon tank at Shanklin. Over 50,000 gallons of oil a day were pumped from Shanklin through the PLUTOs to Cherbourg.

Bouncing Bombs

Before D Day arrived extensive bombing of Germany had begun. Indeed there was a school of thought that reckoned wholescale bombing rather than an invasion would bring ultimate victory. Barnes Wallis, an aeronautical engineer working at Weybridge was designing super bombs. One, the massive "Tallboy" was used to sink the *Tirpitz*. There came the desire to attack three great dams in the Ruhr at Eder, Möhne and Sorpe and Wallis conceived his famous bouncing bomb. The approach to the dams was on a very narrow and extremely difficult flight path yet Wallis thought an attack would be possible if low-flying aircraft could release bombs at a critical height (to be determined) which would bounce to their target. As is well known, Wing Commander Gibson leading 18 Lancaster bombers in three squadrons succeeded brilliantly, breaching the Eder and Möhne dams and damaging the Sorpe in May, 1943. Although the raid caused much destruction it did not deal the mortal blow to the Ruhr's power and water supply that had been intended. It did however catch the public imagination for its combination of scientific planning and sheer courage and has passed into RAF mythology. To confirm the whole idea as workable, Wallis needed to carry out tests over water and approached the Tank. Extremely busy with projects already under way, Kent agreed to release Number Two tank for a fortnight handing it over to Wallis. Kent was surprised at Wallis's demand for complete and utter secrecy—the Tank was used to the needs of war projects and had always followed normal precautions. Nevertheless Wallis insisted that one end of the tank should be screened off and, as further evidence of his independence, he brought his own assistants. Film records were needed and photographers from NPL's Physics Division were borrowed and Conn was appointed as liaison between Wallis's team and the Tank staff since a great deal of support was needed in the intricate experiments that followed. A catapult was set up over the dock of the tank and model bombs the size of billiard balls were fired at a model dam set up further down the tank. Different heights and speeds of release were arranged and photographic filming recorded the progress of the bomb as it bounced over the water and struck the dam. The underwater path of the bomb after it hit the dam and before detonation by hydrostatic fuse was critical since to be most damaging the bomb had to explode near the bottom of the dam. The underwater photographic records thus became valuable evidence and again under the veil of great secrecy (every unwanted frame of film record was burnt) it was rushed to the War Office. When 10 years later the makers of the *Dambusters* film arrived to shoot the scenes of Wallis's tests they chose to film in Number One tank because the natural light there was preferred by the cameramen.

Smaller Projects

There were several very odd projects in which the Tank was to become involved. These included midget submarines and strange devices to deflect torpedoes from their target. Midget submarines came into serious consideration following the success of the Italian "pigs" which contributed notably to the sinking of the battleships *Queen Elizabeth* and *Valiant*. British designs emerged as battery driven 12 metre submarines crewed by four men and capable of 5½ knots. They carried detachable explosives fitted with a time delay and six of these X craft, as they were designated, achieved great success in the pursuit of the German battleships *Bismarck* and *Tirpitz*. *Tirpitz* was so crippled by X craft that to seek repairs she was forced south from a remote Norwegian fjord. Then, within range of bombers, her end was not long delayed. An even smaller submarine, the *Welman* type, was designed and built and one was brought to Teddington and tested in Number One tank in an attempt to reduce its resistance. Lieutenant Morris who came too, climbed aboard and drove the midget down the tank before an incredulous staff. He manipulated the controls and held the submarine on a straight course both vertically and horizontally as a series of entertaining experiments were made during which resistance was measured with the submarine driven on the surface. Speeds of up to 4 knots were reached. The explosive device in this one-man submarine was fitted to the fore end and experiments were conducted with and without a dummy in place and led to suggested changes in hull shape and a revised propeller design. Both were successful and reduced the power required and increased the submarine's range. There was however a disturbing tendency for it to dive but Morris managed to control this and then when he did submerge it and drove it underwater he reported with satisfaction that directional stability was good. Despite the apparent success very few of these craft were built and there is no service record of them. Nevertheless they were capable of detaching and fixing a 560 pound charge to a target.

German U boats were beginning to fire "homing" torpedoes. The torpedoes were steered to their target by a clever sound device carried inside the body of the torpedo tuned to the noise of a ship's propeller. When such a torpedo arrived at a certain distance of its target, it altered course automatically with telling effect, guided by the sound from the ship's propeller. A counter-measure was needed and "Foxers" or noise producers were devised. Crude but effective—if dangerous—the Foxers were made up of loosely jointed rods which gave out a similar noise to a ship's propeller as they were towed underwater at a distance behind the ship. The noise from the Foxers was so intense that the torpedo followed them and not the ship. The first Foxer assembly disintegrated quickly and the Tank was asked to find out why. Two full-size Foxers, one a four rod British design, the other a two rod American version were provided by the Admiralty Mine Design Department and towed in Number Two tank much to Riddle's annoyance whose reaction to undue noise was to go home immediately. A glass observation plate was attached to the carriage and gave clear views under the surface of the action of the rods. Their distortion and vibration was filmed by a high speed camera which helped towards a new configuration that extended the life of a Foxer and the rearrangement of rods suggested was incorporated in the final design.

TESTS FOR FIRMS

The demands of war were not of course confined to such unusual and hitherto uncharted areas of work. Ships were being lost and had to be replaced rapidly. Existing ships were taken over and converted by the Admiralty for use as armed merchant carriers, troop carriers, hospital and depot ships and so on. Small ships too, including the *Tids*, a new breed of tug, were designed and built in record time and several designs for fast motor boats emerged. Resistance and propulsion tests on practically all types of craft for the Director of Mercantile Shipbuilding were carried out at Teddington and brought a continuous flow of routine test work to the Tank. In many cases hull lines and propellers were designed by the WFL staff.

The MAC ships already described were an example of ship conversion and in 1942 the Furness Shipbuilding Company was involved in something similar when they were asked to produce fast cargo vessels which were to carry small ships such as tugs, lighters and launches as cargo. An existing 150 metre single screw design capable of 15 knots was available and its capacity rearranged to accommodate the size of the specific cargoes involved. Furness wanted to examine the alternatives of geared turbine engines with water-tube boilers and diesel engines. Changes to the hull lines of the original design could not be avoided and after an initial set of model experiments the Tank were able to suggest modifications to the submitted after body form which succeeded in bringing resistance to a satisfactory level. However, the competing types of engine involved a different propeller speed and altogether four different model propellers were made and tested. Kent, with Baker, urged further hull modifications including extra parallel middle body and a shift forward of the LCB and at 15 knots succeeded in improving overall efficiency by 6 per cent with the preferred propeller. The final configuration led to the selection of geared turbines which were eventually used in the ships. The lines, as finally designed by the WFL are shown in Butterwick and Morison's paper[8] that also gives a detailed description of the whole development.

To replace lost tramp ships a standard vessel was conceived in which much of the structure was to be prefabricated. Its design was based on the best available in 1939 and the prototype produced included defensive armament and increased cargo handling appliances. These partially fabricated (PF) ships emerged as three types, PF (B), PF (C) and PF (D) and 68 such ships were built,[9] the first appearing in early 1941. All were 130 metres long, 17 metres beam with a block coefficient 0·78 and capable of 13 knots. In 1942 when vehicles of all kind needed to be carried the PF(B)s were superseded and design modifications introduced a longer parallel middle body and softer turn of bilge. Prefabrication was confined to the parallel middle body of the hulls which in the PF(C) was about 45 metres. Use was made of 1915 data when Baker had tested designs for a standard ship of straight line frame and chine construction. He had shown in such forms that it was perfectly possible to reach satisfactory propulsive coefficients. The subsequent model tests on the PF(C) design were encouraging and useful reductions in resistance were obtained as the bilge radius was increased to give a softer turn to the middle sections of the ship. In fact these results exposed a flaw in the earlier 1939 design. For such a slow speed design (Froude number 0·2) the 1939 ships with harder bilges had too low a prismatic coefficient. As the ships were built the WFL was asked to carry out full-scale trials. Measurements were taken on the PF(B) *Empire Irving* and on PF(C) *Empire Prospect*. The PF ships were undoubtedly successful and their utility was summed up by an enthusiastic *Canadian News* as:

The standard tramp vessels are capable of carrying in one voyage enough flour, cheese, bacon, ham, canned and dried foods to feed 225,000 people for a week; 2,200 tons of steel; enough bren gun carriers, trucks and motor cycles to motorise an infantry battalion; enough bombs to load 1,000 bombers; 2 complete bombers on the after deck, and enough aluminium to build 659 fighter planes.

The model experiments on the PFs were followed by tests on a coaster, called the *Icemaid* design and a coastal tanker. The *Icemaid* ran to tests on four models (2287, etc.) and the best form included additional parallel middle body, increased bilge radius and zero rise of floor. The coastal tanker (60 metres long, block coefficient 0·72 and 10 knots) taxed the Tank, six model variants being needed before the right design was reached.

As D Day approached smaller ships such as tugs and coasters to carry petrol and solid cargo to the invasion forces in France were needed very quickly. With time short, simplicity in construction was essential and a prefabricated form of building inevitable. The War Office demand for tugs was blunt:

Design, organise and start work immediately towards achieving in the shortest possible time, the delivery of one tug per week, using in the process, little or no shipyard labour.

One tug per week, no shipyard labour, made it imperative that orders for work should be placed with many different firms unused to shipbuilding practice. Each would build a part of the ship and final assembly could then be done at a shipyard. The concept was agreed and a simple design conceived. Beginning with the lines of a 20 metre "shipshape" form of known good performance, straight line sections were superimposed. The midship section comprised five straight lines and the shell was in five panels, each with simple curvature in one direction only. There was, therefore, no twist needed when shaping the hull plates which led to minimum assembly work. The straight line form was tested at Teddington and showed a poor propeller efficiency due to insufficient draught aft which did not allow a large enough propeller to be swung. This was overcome by adding a shrouding over the propeller position which allowed the fitting of a larger propeller and prevented air drawing. A significant improvement in propulsive efficiency was obtained. Compared to a normal shipshape alternative the simplified hull was less efficient but only above 7½ knots. The towing speed of the tugs had to be 5 knots and their free-running speed 7 and so there was no problem. These were the famous *Tids*.[10] Manufacture went extremely well. Eight separate units were built and welded together and at the peak of production one tug was launched every five days, an impressive achievement. Many were built and then came the demand for small coastal lighters. These 42 metre *Chant* series of ships were needed to carry petrol in bulk or cans. Once PLUTO was successfully in operation they switched to carrying solid cargo. They had to be capable of grounding on beaches and their closely sub-divided holds were constructed independently of the hull. The approach to their design was similar to the *Tids*, straight line frames being used with swim ends forward. Tests at Teddington showed resistance to be much higher than conventional hulls which was disappointing and the only way to an improvement was to do away with the swim ends and ease the forward shoulder thus reducing wave-making. The flat of bottom was widened and the whole modification was better but not yet acceptable. By adding a second chine forward it was possible to ease the sharpness of the lines and further tests showed a good improvement and a result comparable with a shipshape form. Again manufacture went well, one coaster being built every three–four weeks.

As already mentioned, developments in small high speed craft flourished during the war.[11] In particular, the RAF air sea rescue launches were good examples. The British Power Boat and Fairmile Companies were greatly involved and with Samuel White and Camper and Nicholson brought designs to the Tank for testing. Fairmile designs were light displacement craft 33 metres long and capable of 25 knots. 12 of these were built in African mahogany and later destined for conversion to minelaying duty. Much faster 35 knot designs came from the BPBC who brought their own models to the Tank. Selman, an ex-member of staff who had resigned just before the war to work with Scott-Paine at BPBC arrived at Teddington with the models which included designs for hard chine motor torpedo boats 18 metres long. These were fitted with two lattice-work girders hinged on the deck aft to form an extension of the torpedo runways. BPBC also produced the 21 metre PV 70 boat that reached over 44 knots on trial. Tests at the Tank on all these specialised craft were handled by Conn and Marwood, resistance data being collected in most cases. The high speed series run by Baker in earlier years proved a valuable reference point and information on the selection and positioning of spray rails, extensively studied by Baker, was provided since many of these designs generated huge bow waves at top speed. The intense competitiveness that is so often seen in designers of high speed craft was evident in these war years. Designs, particularly those from BPBC, were jealously guarded and good rapport between Tank and designer, so desirable for progress, was not often seen. As a result the Tank found time to run some designs of its own which were considered relevant to the current requirements. One of these, model 2071, a round bilge hull, proved so successful and had such excellent resistance characteristics that it was later chosen to be the parent model of the NPL high speed series run by Bailey in the 1960s. Other high speed work included tests on destroyer forms. As successors to the Hunt class, HMS *Brecon* and *Brissenden* were built in 1942 to Barnaby's lines following a long series of model tests in Number One tank.

During the war uses were often found for barges and the Admiralty requisitioned many of those that existed so that by 1943 replacements were needed. Port of London regulations were more or less inflexible and existing quays could not be changed and the scope for improving existing forms was limited. Rivetted construction of ships was gradually being overtaken by welding and this at least offered a chance of reducing resistance. Tests on a new generation of dumb barges were conducted at Teddington[12] and it was found that there was no substitute for existing swim ended forms but attention concentrated on the slope of the endings since it was found that resistance was proportional to the angle. Also, as a means of ensuring directional stability, a plate was added. Overall, useful reductions in resistance were achieved compared to existing barges and the new design was 18 per cent less resistive at 5·3 knots. It was also shown in the experiments that the total resistance of a train of barges would be less if barges were towed in pairs close up to the stern of a tug.

The many ship designs tested during the war years represented a diverse range of ship type and shape. Emerson with Witney in the last year of the war brought together the results from 64 models collapsing the data to a common ship length. Their paper[13] is a good summary of resistance and propulsion tests on merchant ships in this period and important empirical formulae were deduced giving estimated values of propulsive coefficient and propeller speed as a simple function of ship length. The formulae proved immensely useful in post war years and to some extent continue to give excellent guidance in modern forms.

On the subject of propellers, tests under cavitating conditions in the Lithgow tunnel had by 1946 reached a sound basis and confidence in the results was growing although a few years were to pass before tests on a model propeller for a new ship became routine. Emerson and Berry whenever there was a lull in war projects, modified and improved the tunnel gradually and the first serious results were obtained. With the demand for the towing tanks so high Emerson saw no reason why open water propeller tests should not be done under non-cavitating conditions in the tunnel and set out to demonstrate this so that Number Two tank could be relieved of such work. A series of comparative tests showed good correspondence between tank and tunnel, provided the propellers were not more than 170 mm in diameter. Larger propellers were subject to a tunnel wall correction. Kent was reluctant to accept the tunnel results as definitive open water data and the use of the tunnel for such tests was never in fact taken up. Tests on hydrofoil struts could be satisfactorily handled in a tunnel and a force balance was designed and fitted for use at this time.

RESEARCH

With so much work for the war occupying both towing tanks it is hardly surprising that research work was limited. When Baker relinquished his post as Superintendent in 1941 he stayed on for a few years and was able to write up his researches with Clarke which had been completed during the "phoney" war. Time was also found to fit in additional experiments with large-scale propellers and two papers of importance emerged. Baker began his last book[14] at this time which was published three years before he died. In it he indulged himself in the general subject of ship design and on matters important to a satisfactory and seaworthy ship.

Propellers

The two papers with Clarke,[15, 16] were Baker's last major offering. R.E. Froude in his work on propellers in 1908 had ignored fine-pitch screws of pitch ratio below 0·8 because of their lower efficiency. Baker and Clarke, using a series of high speed propellers of pitch ratio 0·5 to propel the large 7 metre "Big Ben" model,* showed for the first time that a 20 per cent loss in open water efficiency over a coarser screw could be recovered by an increase in hull efficiency. This could be raised to 1·2 if the wake also increased. Since propulsive coefficient was proportional to hull and open water efficiencies, a poor propeller could, if accompanied by increased hull efficiency, produce a satisfactory quasi propulsive coefficient. The second of the two papers[16] presented open water data from over 30 model propellers most of pitch ratio 0·5. Blade area, section shape, pitch distribution and blade number were varied. The results showed the importance of aerofoil shape,** the size of the gap between blades in relation to cascade effect and also highlighted certain instances where low pitch screws should be avoided. These *Lancer* tests as they were called were carried out on a revised open water propeller dynamometer which remained in use until about 1955. Faster internal combustion engines were being developed for ships and the application of higher r.p.m. propellers of low pitch could now be seen to hold promise.

Wave-making Resistance

Wigley, too, was active and of all the workers at WFL he alone managed to press on with his researches for most of the war. A new worker had appeared in the field of wave resistance, Rene Guilloton. His paper before the INA in 1940[17] was an original approach to the problem and Wigley was pleased to introduce it by adding a foreword to Guilloton's paper. The method allowed for the first time the mathematical calculation of a three dimensional hull form by dividing the hull into a number of wedges in which straight lines could serve as approximations to actual curvature. Increments of pressure due to forward motion could then be integrated which were additions to the hydrostatic pressure. Guilloton did not of course claim a complete solution and the neglect of viscosity as made by Michell was necessary but certainly Wigley found the method attractive and welcomed it.

Wigley's own work in this period was largely directed at advancing his own

---

* These tests were the culmination of those begun earlier; see page 102.
** The results are complementary to Baker's earlier findings; see page 75.

methods of calculation. They were accompanied as usual by comparative model tests. In a paper to the INA in 1942[18] he made calculations and measurements on six forms covering changes in hull geometry and showed how these changes affected the results. He was working towards a technique, later to be greatly improved by Gadd, whereby calculations could be used to indicate performance differences due to changes in hull shape even though, as he readily admitted, the mathematical approach could never replace the experimental result. A second paper two years later[19] attempted to predict the best position of the LCB in a given form by successive calculations on arbitrary changes of the position. Sadly this was to be his last paper emanating from the WFL for after a senseless haggle with NPL's Administration Department, who insisted he should sign an attendance book each day, he resigned. Snapped up quickly by the Admiralty tank at Haslar he continued to work in his eccentric way for several more years as a valued researcher and consultant in the field of work that had so fascinated him and published further papers of considerable merit. Wigley will always be remembered for his inexhaustible approach to linearised wave resistance. He used the theory to its utmost, indeed it was the only practical approach possible at a time when powerful high speed computers were not available. He himself summarised the state of the art at 1949 in an article[20] for the French Maritime and Aeronautics Association.

Singing Propellers

The problem of singing propellers had not entirely gone away and towards the end of the war Conn and Hughes returned to the subject. Conn[21] drew from air screw design theory concerning aerodynamic flutter. He had gained valuable experience of this when seconded to work with Goldstein in the Aerodynamics Division of NPL at the beginning of the war. Now he took a heavily loaded wide bladed destroyer propeller and calculated blade deflections to be a not inconsiderable one degree of angle. Hughes on the other hand embarked on an enormous study and followed a different approach producing a very lengthy paper.[22] He developed his own theory attributing singing to the local breakdown of flow on the back of a propeller blade near its leading edge. He stipulated a criterion Q for a quiet propeller which comprised the angle of incidence (defined in a special way) plus a correction angle for cascade effect minus an average angle of incidence in the mixed wake for the radius under consideration. His idea, like the title of his paper was complicated and wordy and Professor Burrill in discussing Hughes' paper thought the "complex calculations" unnecessary.

Seakeeping

Although Kent had succeeded Baker in 1941 and become more involved with organising the whole affairs of the Tank, his interest in seakeeping never waned and he encouraged Cutland to pursue their earlier work in waves. There was little available time, yet somehow Cutland ran and propelled a model of a single screw 12 knot cargo ship through regular head waves in Number One tank and followed this by additional tests on the same model with six different screws which covered variations in mean pitch and diameter. Three different lengths of wave were chosen each with varying height and measurements taken of pitch, heave and added resistance in waves as well as the propeller forces needed to keep the model at its self-propelled condition under tow. The experiments were conducted using mechanical type propulsion dynamometers as was the case in earlier work done prior to the war. Propeller thrust and torque were derived from the analysis of a spring recording and a very stiff spring would have been used to dampen the fluctuations in waves. The results were presented to the IESS in two papers[23, 24] and continued to give the industry useful data which could estimate the additional engine power required in rough weather and to establish sensible margins of power.

With so much activity at the Tank and with so many war projects involving the whole of NPL it was not surprising that a Royal visitation came to Teddington to see and encourage the work in progress. King George VI and his Queen were welcomed by Sir Charles Darwin, Director of NPL and spent the day touring various divisions of the laboratory. At the Tank, tests on one of the high speed launches were in progress and the King watched the carriage accelerate away at the beginning of a resistance test (naturally, for maximum dramatic effect, a very fast speed was selected) and an exciting run down the tank seen. There were of course many other occasions when VIPs appeared. Lord (to be) Mountbatten came, high ranking officers from all three fighting services and Departmental ministers, but not Prime Minister Churchill.

At the end of hostilities in Europe (May 1945) the WFL had come to the end of six years intensive work. As in so many other fields of activity a renewal of peacetime conditions heralded great changes and the WFL and NPL were by no means unaffected. Already in 1944 NPL (with WFL) staff had been assimilated by the Civil Service into a revised grading structure which divided scientists into three distinct categories or classes, Scientific Officer (SO), Experimental Officer (EO) and Assistants (ASO). Each was split into different levels of seniority and individuals were placed at the various levels in the different classes largely on the grounds of academic qualification and experience, which many saw as invidious. Anomalies arose, not least in the WFL, where it became difficult to assess the shipyard draughtsmen there who had been recruited in the 1930s. Such a grade did not exist in NPL at the time and an argument developed between the WFL and DSIR over the level at which such people should be placed. Eventually agreement was reached to assimilate at the EO level. The WFL itself was to an extent unique in that, as has already been seen, it enjoyed a sort of independence from NPL, a situation Baker was always keen to preserve. NPL's Administration Division were determined to run the whole laboratory in a consistent way and following the regrading of staff the WFL was absorbed as a Division of NPL and thereafter called Ship Division. Standard rules and regulations were introduced which were of course no more than an application of existing Civil Service codes of conduct and conditions of work. All staff were now required formally to record their arrival and departure times each day, a rule Wigley just would not and did not accept. It was well known that he, like so many in other Divisions of NPL, had on several occasions worked hours far longer than those officially prescribed and, if he felt like it, he would come in at 10 o'clock in the morning. Any suggestion of deliberate absenteeism was therefore nonsense yet rules were introduced and had to be obeyed. Unofficially, any overtime worked was not reimbursed as extra pay but could be taken in lieu by the individual at a convenient time.

At the time of WFL's absorption into NPL the Tank Advisory Committee was reconstituted as a sub-committee of NPL's Executive Committee and given the name Froude Ship Research Committee. The Research Fund available for research projects was closed and the balance of money transferred to provide scholarships in Naval Architecture under the general auspices of the INA. A further significant development was the setting up of a new organisation devoted to shipbuilding research which, although never intended to supersede Ship Division, ultimately became an important co-operating body. In addressing the spring meeting of the INA in 1944, Lord Chatfield, its President, said that currently the only research for the British shipping industry was being done at Teddington and that most of this was fostered by the INA through the Tank Advisory Committee. He felt that interest in research shown by shipbuilders and shipowners lacked determination. The Shipbuilding Conference set up at the start of the war and led by Wilfred Ayre, the chairman of Burntisland Shipbuilding Company, took a similar view and in conjunction with DSIR a recommendation was made that a Research Association, on the lines being set up by other industries, should be formed. Ayre's paper to the INA[25] describes the aims and constitution of the Association finally formed in 1945. It was named British Shipbuilding Research Association and Dr S.L. Smith who until 1944 had been the Superintendent of NPL's Engineering Division appointed as its first Director. Baker, during his retirement was asked to become a member of BSRA's Research Board and accepted to serve for a few years.

The creation of BSRA opened up the opportunity of researching many areas of shipbuilding such as structural design, welding, plastics, propulsion machinery, etc. and, so far as Ship Division was concerned, its model testing resources were to give valuable support to the various items of research followed either by BSRA itself or in co-operative projects.

REFERENCES

1. Hughes G., "Model and full-scale towing tests in connection with the net defence of ships", trans. IESS, 1946/7, Vol. 90.

2.   Lenaghan J., "Merchant aircraft carrier ships (MAC ships)", trans. INA, 1947.
3.   Gawn R.W.L., "Some model experiments in connection with mine warfare", trans. INA, 1946.
4.   Todd F.H. and Laws E., "Some model and full scale experiments on side launching", trans. NECIES, 1946/7, Vol. 63.
5.   Todd F.H., "Some model experiments carried out in connection with the Mulberry Harbour", trans. INA, 1946.
6.   White Sir Bruce, "The harbour of Arromanches", *Overseas Engineer*, October 1945.
7.   Purvis M.K., "Craft and cable ship for operation PLUTO", trans. INA, 1946.
8.   Butterwick W.T. and Macarthur Morison W., "Standard cargo liners", trans. NECIES, 1946/7, Vol. 63.
9.   Lenaghan J., "The standard partially fabricated 10,000 ton tramp vessel", trans. IESS, 1946/7, Vol. 90.
10. Aitken R.L., "Special wartime prefabrication methods employed in the construction of small vessels", trans. IESS, 1946/7, Vol. 90.
11. Holt W.J., "Coastal force designs", trans. INA, 1947.
12. Stephens E.O., "Thames (dumb) barges", trans. INA, 1945.
13. Emerson A. and Witney N.A., "Experiment work on merchant ship models during the war", trans. NECIES, 1947/8, Vol. 64.
14. Baker G.S., *Ship efficiency and economy*, published by Birchall, 1946.
15. Baker G.S. and Clarke L.T.G., "Experiments with low pitch ratio screws behind a single-screw hull", trans. INA, 1942.
16. Baker G.S. and Clarke L.T.G., "Effect of blade section and area on screw propellers", trans. INA, 1944.
17. Guilloton R., "A new method of calculating wave profiles and wave resistance of ships", trans. INA, 1940.
18. Wigley W.C.S., "Calculated and measured wave resistance of a series of forms defined algebraically, the prismatic coefficient and angle of entrance being varied independently", trans. INA, 1942.
19. Wigley W.C.S., "Comparison of calculated and measured wave resistance for a series of forms not symmetrical fore and aft", trans. INA, 1942.
20. Wigley W.C.S., "L'état actual des calculs de resistance de vagues", *Bulletin de l'Association Technique Maritime et Aeronautique*, 8, 1949.
21. Conn J.F.C., "Marine propeller blade deflection", trans. INA, 1943.
22. Hughes G., "On singing propellers—the effects of shape of propeller blade section and of fullness and form of hull after-body on singing of propellers with special reference to single screw ships", trans. INA, 1945.
23. Kent J.L. and Cutland R.S., "Experiments in rough water with a single screw ship model", trans. IESS, 1940/1, Vol. 84.
24. Kent J.L. and Cutland R.S., "Effect of pitch ratio and propeller diameter on ship performance in rough water", trans. IESS, 1942/3, Vol. 86.
25. Ayre W., "The British Shipbuilding Research Association", trans. INA, 1944.

CHAPTER 10

POST-WORLD WAR YEARS: 1946–1958

At the end of the war NPL was anxious to make the change from war to peace-time activities as quickly as it could. Requests for work from the Service and Supply Ministries, understandably high during the war, reduced considerably and the laboratory was soon able to devote more attention to basic research, long term projects and the maintenance of scientific standards. An early resumption of basic research was not however seen in Ship Division. New ship construction fuelled by the vigorous replacement of lost tonnage brought large numbers of requests for model tests and allowed virtually no spare time for research. In the first two years after the war over 300 designs were tested involving the manufacture of 320 model hulls and 277 propellers. Handling this enormous demand was a total staff that had increased by only three since 1939. A double shift working system was introduced but even so the delay between the receipt of a request for work and the start of actual tests grew to 14 months and in early 1946 the whole of 1947 and the first quarter of 1948 had been booked for future work. Little wonder that the transactions of the learned societies saw few reports on research from Ship Division workers. There simply was no room for such work at the Tank and an obvious need emerged for additional test facilities and, as a matter of urgency, staff. The shortage of staff was common throughout NPL and indeed the whole of the Civil Service. During the war many had been retained beyond normal retirement age so that at the end of hostilities immediate retirements as well as resignations reduced numbers severely. A recruitment drive was launched, the Civil Service Reconstruction Programme, which, so far as NPL was concerned, was not entirely successful and only through the use of the Central (Technical and Scientific) Register of the Ministry of Labour and by encouraging direct application were sufficient numbers of suitable recruits found.

By the end of the war Ship Division had lost Conn, Selman and Wigley but gained J.M. Downey (from Swan Hunter's), J.V. Garside (from British Power Boat Co.) and a few workshop mechanics. Soon Kent was to retire but his interest never flagged and he was often on hand to give invaluable advice drawing on 37 years experience at the Tank. Conn joined the newly formed BSRA as their Chief Naval Architect and was later appointed to the chair of Naval Architecture at Glasgow in 1957. Emerson and Todd also resigned.

Emerson took an appointment at Newcastle University as a lecturer where he continued his interest in propeller cavitation. He established a cavitation tunnel in King's College, a tunnel that had begun its life in Germany and which today is named after him. Todd accepted the post of Chief Naval Architect at the Washington tank. It was said that he was greatly disappointed at not being offered the post of the next Superintendent when Kent retired and when he informed NPL of the approach made by Washington, was given no clear guidance as to his future and so accepted the offer. As things turned out Todd returned 10 years later, this time as Superintendent.

There were several natural sources where suitable replacements and future staff could be found. Universities (in 1945, Belfast, Glasgow, Liverpool and Newcastle all offered courses in naval architecture) and shipyards were obvious centres, the latter including the naval dockyards. These were unique in that they had for many years employed apprentices who followed carefully structured training schemes which were the forerunners of today's educational sandwich courses. A school of naval architecture had originally been set up by the Government in 1810 at Portsmouth dockyard and after an uncertain start it became a permanent establishment 50 years later ultimately evolving as the Royal Naval College at Greenwich. Meanwhile the apprenticeship scheme had been introduced, also at Portsmouth, to be followed soon afterwards at Chatham, Devonport, Rosyth and Sheerness dockyards. Five-year apprenticeships in all the shipbuilding trades provided a combined practical and theoretical training and the best apprentices who had successfully completed the highly competitive four year course at school were selected for further education at Greenwich where they were joined by others drawn from other sources such as public schools. Those left in the dockyards formed an invaluable pool from which various organisations were not slow to draw. Local sources too were tapped and these in the main (such as the nearby Hampton and Tiffin schools) provided younger members of staff of school leaving age, many of whom took advantage of the NPL day release scheme enabling them to pursue further education at local technical colleges.

In the decade following the war several newcomers arrived from universities. Most stayed only a few years but N. Hogben spent the rest of his career in Ship Division producing work of the utmost distinction. Those from shipyard design offices included S. Grant, Miss B.J. Hales, A.J.D. Mackenzie, T.P. O'Brien, G.B. Pearce and A. Silverleaf. Silverleaf, a future Superintendent, had graduated at Glasgow and gone on to the Dumbarton tank before coming to Teddington in 1951. All of these served for many years, Grant, Mackenzie and Pearce clocking up over 100 between them. D.J. Doust and G.J. Goodrich (these two also at Newcastle University), D. Bailey and A. Jenkins, came from naval dockyards, as indeed had Baker, Cutland and Kent before them whilst D.J. Fraser, K.G. Poulton and G.A. Wenban, plus girls straight from school arrived from local sources. Doust left for Canada in 1964 and two years later Goodrich was appointed to Southampton University as the first Professor of Ship Science.

Others from this group, except Fraser who followed Doust in 1966, stayed for the rest of their careers. The recruitment of female assistants was a deliberate policy aimed at building a group of analysts to help in both experimentation and data analysis. Graded as Assistant (Scientific) their accuracy and reliability became legendary as they cheerfully tackled the often laborious and repetitive work without the help of today's computer tools. As valuable additions to the newly appointed permanent staff came students from overseas. India in particular was keen to give its new generation of naval architects practical experience and with NPL's willing compliance sent several new graduates (mostly from British universities) to Teddington for spells of up to three years.

The gradual growth in the staff took place at a time when there was a change in leadership. Kent retired in 1947 at the age of 63 and after a brief *interregnum*, when Todd took charge, J.F. Allan was appointed Ship Division's third Superintendent in May 1948. Kent's departure left a vacuum and the staff missed his impish and infectious enthusiasm. He was a small man, mercurial and energetic with a fund of stories and anecdotes about his experiences at sea, which amazed (and delayed) many visitors to the Tank. His managerial style was mild, a contrast to Baker, but he was quick to resist any high-handed interference from NPL's administrators.

Kent built for himself a huge reputation in the field of ship seakeeping and he was also a talented mathematician able to apply his skills to the important practicalities of unusual and novel experiments, particularly those undertaken in the Second World War. His great contribution over almost 40 years was recognised by the award of CBE and in retirement he produced a valuable reference book[1] published in 1958 which summarised his vast experience of model and ship behaviour in rough water.

Allan who succeeded Kent came from the Denny Shipbuilding company where he had been apprenticed. He then worked for 20 years at the Denny tank at Dumbarton and latterly was much concerned with the development of activated fins for stabilising ships. For this work he was awarded the degree of D.Sc. at Glasgow. He was also well known for his several pertinent contributions to the discussion of papers emanating from Ship Division and other sources. In 1948 at the time of his appointment the staff numbered 50 made up of six scientific grade, 18 experimental, six assistants, 18 workshop personnel and two in the Divisional office who dealt with clerical and typing requirements. Two years later the total had risen to 60 and the Division appeared reasonably staffed, yet with requests from shipyards still flooding in it remained difficult to include a research programme of satisfactory size and diversity. Again the resources at Teddington were plainly inadequate to meet the huge demand which showed no real sign of abating and the outlook for future research looked bleak. This was soon realised by the reconstituted Tank Advisory Committee. In 1945, as the new Froude Ship Research Committee, it set up a panel under the chairmanship of Dr Ramsay Gebbie to look at the possibility of new facilities. Todd was appointed to the panel and sent on tour to report on the newest facilities in America and Scandinavia. Meanwhile Kent was asked to prepare a case which could be used by the Froude Committee in its negotiations with DSIR. Kent unearthed some interesting statistics. 80 per cent of new British mercantile ship construction before the Second World War had been tested as models at Teddington and in 1945 the proportion was increasing. The favourite and convincing theme of saving fuel illustrated that reduced power requirements achieved in a model test led to an annual cost saving at the ship of roughly four times the cost of the test. Over the average life of a ship, say 20 years, the total saved became a very considerable figure. At this rate it would not take long to repay the anticipated cost of new facilities. The proposal was submitted in 1946 and received immediate approval. It called for a new 550 metre towing tank with a removable bulkhead at mid length with two carriages of medium and high speed (15 metres per second) capability, a shallow water tank, a second cavitation tunnel, a circulating water channel and a small steering pond. There followed a period of six years before any real progress was made. Suitable land proved very hard to find (it had to be within five miles of Teddington, otherwise unnecessary expense would be incurred by staff moving to and fro, and financial restraints imposed by the Government delayed matters. At last 60 acres of flat orchard land alongside the Duke of Northumberland river at Faggs Road, Feltham, 4½ miles north of Teddington and close to the burgeoning Heathrow airport was procured, with access promised for September 1954. During the waiting period Kent had retired and his successor, Allan, appointed. Allan was well qualified to take charge of preliminary design work for he came to Teddington with 22 years' experience of tank work. He chose J.R. Shearer as his assistant in drafting the original plan of towing tank and buildings and had earlier been instrumental in recruiting Silverleaf, also from the Dumbarton tank, who having quickly gained experience with the Lithgow tunnel and its recent changes was well placed to supervise the unusual design requirements for a new and very much larger cavitation tunnel.

This was a stimulating period in Ship Division's history. As everywhere in Britain, post-war years, despite their austerity, brought a surge of enthusiasm for a bright and exciting future and the renewal and pursuit of peacetime activities. Leisure and sport, hardly possible during the war, could be resumed without hindrance. These grew to unprecedented levels and it seemed that almost everybody became caught up in the feeling of confidence and freedom. Nowhere was this better seen than at NPL in the decade following the end of the war. Sport had always been important at NPL and thanks to the excellent sports field that adjoined Bushy House, most field sports had been enjoyed by staff and socially the natural mixing of laboratory staff of different disciplines often led to fruitful scientific exchange. In the early days competitive sport between NPL Divisions included rowing on the nearby Thames. Once, Baker, who had entered the sculling, became dissatisfied with his boat, trimmed it by the bow, and won with yards to spare. Stanton in Aerodynamics Division who had worked with Baker on several research projects was very keen on sport and in later years offered a cup for annual inter-Divisional competition at NPL, as many sports as possible (including indoor) being included in the final totting up of points. After the war the competition to win the Stanton Trophy reached feverish proportions. The highlight was the Annual Sports Day at which the organisers had the happy idea of awarding a point to every entrant in each event, not that encouragement was needed since competitors appeared in large numbers anyway. Cross, a fine athlete in his younger days, urged all and sundry in Ship Division to enter events they had never in their lives attempted. As a result, a motley collection appeared on the day having been cajoled, coached and timed by Cross, Downey and others. As a point of interest the clocks and watches used in the 1948 Olympic Games in London were all calibrated at NPL so it goes without saying that there could be no arguments at NPL Sports Days. Ship Division had several competent performers. Cross, Emerson and Witney could all sprint well and fought their way for several years into the final. Over the years many keen sportsmen and women came to Ship Division, most of whom appeared regularly in NPL teams. Rugby football was best served. After the Second World War, Giles, B.E. Ware and the two Williams (E.E. and G.) all played for the Laboratory. G. Williams, a brilliant scrum-half initially played for the Blackheath and London Welsh first XV's before continuing with NPL for many years. As a result, Ship Division's entry into the Stanton Trophy seven-a-side competition reigned supreme for several years. Soccer saw Cutland and Rayment figuring prominently in the original Bushy House football club, Cutland as captain. Hockey attracted both men and women. Bailey, H.J. Bowyer (Divisional clerk from 1947–1958), Silverleaf and Ware all played for NPL's first team and formed the nucleus of Ship Division's six-a-side team which enjoyed wins in three successive years. In the summer A.C. Rixon (head carpenter) who also ran the NPL Pavilion bar and Camp were outstanding bowlers and were followed in later years by J.W. English and H. Sharp. Cross, Emerson, Rayment and Witney were all enthusiastic cricketers and were followed later by Bailey. Rayment whose total service in Ship Division amounted to an astonishing 56 years, (he retired at the age of 75), played alongside E. Tyldesley of Lancashire and England who turned out frequently for NPL in 1916. Tennis was led by the stylish MacDonald who also excelled at badminton. And last but not least Downey, a scratch golfer, represented Middlesex on many occasions throughout the 1950s. The Stanton Trophy competition continues and although its popularity has waned a succession of Ship Division staff have continued to participate keenly.

Sport apart, NPL had flourishing music and theatrical societies, the latter strongly supported by Ship Division staff. Annual parties were held by all Divisions and continued every year until the early 1950s. Ship Division's (the last regular one was in 1951) was an elaborate affair at which a large bar appeared, built by the carpenters, in the form of a ship's bridge. But by the mid-1950s the general enthusiasm amongst NPL staff for these things, sport included, began to decline and there were two reasons for this. In 1956 a five-day working week was introduced and at about this time more and more people were beginning to acquire a motor car. The five-day week meant that staff went home on a Friday evening and sport next day could be more easily pursued locally than returning to Teddington, and of course the car offered extra freedom and independence. Consequently the NPL Sports and Social clubs found it hard to attract NPL staff, a situation that gradually deteriorated— today NPL Sports Club, although flourishing, draws 90 per cent of its membership from outside the Laboratory. The five-day week so far as Ship Division was concerned, although welcomed by the staff, presented problems over programming the work in the tanks; Saturday morning was a convenient time to fit in a model resistance test. Evening overtime which ironically had been relaxed in 1955 now had to be reinstated and a few years were to pass before the level of work allowed the new working hours (9 a.m.–5.30 p.m. from Monday to Friday) to become regular.

The general feeling of ebullience spilt over into the working environment. Despite long periods of apparently dull and repetitive work the spirit of the staff never faltered. The large drawing office which adjoined the workshops was typical of the atmosphere that prevailed. Morning and afternoon tea breaks were moments of universal conversation and debate on any subject under the sun. Cutland was in his element. A wonderful raconteur and mimic he would have the staff rocking with laughter as he recalled sporting events, politicians or INA meetings which to him often produced pompous discussion from distinguished men of science. All were easy prey as he poked fun.

Of course NPL provided and continues to provide a very happy environment, its various buildings set in attractive grounds. Not being a centre where secret work was undertaken many visitors were seen. Sir Edward Bullard, NPL's Director often showed his visitors around, Mathematics, Physics and Ship Division being favourite places. One visitor, impressed with what he saw, asked, "Roughly, how many work at NPL?" and received from Sir Edward the quick answer, "Oh, about half of them!" The Laboratory had always been subject to an annual inspection by its General Board and after the war it was decided to expand the occasion by inviting others from Government departments, universities and industrial organisations to see the work going on. All NPL divisions were open to visitors. Much planning and preparation was needed and staff became involved as demonstrators and guides. Open days as they were known grew into a four day event in June of each year and the last of the four, the Saturday, was reserved for members of staff and their families, thus rounding off the whole occasion on a pleasant informal and social note. Nowadays NPL open days are much reduced and BMT as a separate body takes no part. Visits from VIPs were a special occasion. In April 1952 Prince Philip, Duke of Edinburgh came to NPL. In Ship Division he was shown how models were made and at Number One tank he saw a self-propulsion experiment. There he was introduced to Jenkins the experimenter and his assistant Mavis Prince. As is usual on such occasions press photographers were close to hand and that evening the edition of the London *Evening Standard* appeared with a large front page photograph captioned "Mavis meets the Prince".

There were other occasions when Ship Division was asked to show itself to the world. NPL appeared regularly at the Physical Society exhibition and occasionally at others such as the Engineering and Marine exhibition at Olympia and the Boat Show at Earls Court. In 1950 when NPL celebrated its jubilee, an exhibition was held in the Royal Society's rooms. Stanton's work on compressible flow and illustrations of laminar and turbulent flow around ship hulls were among the exhibits. With Physics Division, Ship Division provided stands in 1952 and 1954 at Olympia showing a marine torsionmeter, a working model of a cavitation tunnel and an instrumented ship model. The torsionmeter was a new piece of apparatus for the measurement of torque on a ship's propeller shaft. It was designed by D.A. Harding of Physics Division with Jenkins' help. Two rings were clamped in halves to the propeller shaft and the relative motion of the rings under load altered the reluctance of two similar magnetic circuits. Coils linking the circuits were connected to a bridge circuit and the out-of-balance current was proportional to torque. The meter was portable and accurate calibrations could be done in the laboratory before and after a ship trial. It was however very sensitive to vibration and the damping arrangements introduced were never satisfactory yet Allan claimed a high degree of accuracy, as good ($\pm 2\%$) as the commonly used Siemens-Ford torsionmeter, a statement that surprised T.W.F. Brown of the PAMETRADA Research Station who had completed a large review of power measurement systems.[2] In Brown's opinion the Siemens-Ford was the best available and was being used by BSRA in the ship model correlation programme.

TESTS FOR FIRMS

In the Second World War over 4,000 allied ships were lost—a total tonnage of 20 million. Records list 2,828 ships (1,382 British) sunk by U boats, 520 (296 British) by mines, 300 (209 British) by surface raiders and 750 (383 British) by aerial attack. The replacement programme proceeded at such a pace that by July 1948 Britain had recovered her pre-war shipping levels, a remarkable achievement and the total in 1948 of 18·1 million was 22 per cent of world tonnage, the second highest after the USA. Developments post-war saw a growth in the tanker fleets. Reconstruction and industrial development created an oil-hungry world and shipyards everywhere were inundated with orders for tankers. It became economic sense to carry larger volumes of oil in larger ships. In 1939 the biggest tanker was 24,000 tons deadweight. A few years later this had increased to 32,000 and in 1953 the 45,200 tons deadweight *Tina Onassis* was built. All of these ships had draughts which allowed passage through the Suez canal but the crisis there in 1956 immediately disrupted the free flow of the world's oil supplies and led to the demand for even larger tankers which could work the Cape route. Thus ships over 100,000 tons deadweight became common and ultimately the first super tanker of 250,000 tons appeared. The trend was seen at Teddington in the tests that preceded these developments and the hull designs of these immense ships were being stretched beyond existing experience. It became a fertile field for the development of the bulbous bow, a successful means of reducing ship wave-making resistance and particularly effective in ships which spent much of their time steaming at the same speed. All kinds of bulb were tested ranging from the small enlargement (described as a teardrop), to the extreme "banana" bow and it could be said that one of the effects of Suez was the widespread emergence of the bulbous bow. The characteristics of many tested on tankers found application to other types of slow speed ship and today it is a rarity to see any sizeable merchant ship without one.

Whether or not the huge numbers of model tests under way at Teddington and elsewhere helped to focus attention on their accuracy is uncertain but soon an alarm was raised that reverberated throughout the whole world of ship model testing. The threat of laminar flow. Could such flow exist over the surface of a model during test and thus invalidate the results?

Osborne Reynold's historic experiments in 1883 had shown how the characteristics of the flow of a fluid through a pipe changed from streamline or "laminar" to non-streamline or "turbulent" at a critical velocity. Later it was seen that the boundary layer that forms between a surface and a fluid flowing over it could be either laminar or turbulent in nature and that the same critical velocity applied, its value depending on the smoothness of the surface. In general, the critical velocity approximated to a Reynolds number of one million and for all practical purposes a ship which operates at a much higher number experiences a fully turbulent boundary layer over its hull surface. Reynolds had also shown that the onset of turbulent flow was accompanied by a great increase in resistance. Thus, for a model test to be fully representative, flow over its surface during an experiment has to be turbulent. As early as 1925, Bairstow, expounding on skin friction and boundary layer theory, made the alarming statement that laminar flow in a model test could persist up to a Reynolds number of one million and stressed the need for some kind of turbulence stimulation at low model speeds or on small models. Baker himself was aware of the importance of laminar and turbulent flow in his work with airships but had concluded that models at Teddington were long enough to achieve a Reynolds number in the test high enough to satisfy fully turbulent flow conditions. The 5th ITTC in London in 1948 became a focus and concluded very positively that it was unlikely that complete turbulent flow existed in all model tests, particularly those run at low Reynolds number and over fuller hull forms. Evidence at once began to pour forth. Walker[3] from the Clydebank tank and others fuelled the debate and BSRA who had just started on one of its first research programmes, the collection of resistance data for a methodical series of hull forms of varying fullness, became anxious and commissioned tests on a standard model of 0·75 block coefficient. The model was tested in all the British tanks both in its normal naked or bare hull condition, and then with turbulence stimulators consisting of a trip wire fitted to the surface of the model near its bow or a strut ahead of the model. Startling results were seen. The addition of a stimulator produced a marked increase in resistance and in general improved the comparison of results from the different tanks. At Teddington in separate tests a coloured ink was released from small holes in the model surface and its behaviour photographed by underwater camera. The characteristics of laminar flow over parts of a model's forebody were clearly detected in unstimulated experiments and in fuller forms significant areas of laminar flow were unquestionably present. The need for turbulence stimulation was only too obvious and although finer forms run at Teddington prior to 1948 at Reynolds number higher than 3 million were in all probability free of laminar flow, the results from many others must be in doubt. Tank workers everywhere, with the exception of Troost at Wageningen and Weitbrecht at Berlin, who had been using stimulators since 1937, were guilty of too long a delay before taking adequate precautions against laminar flow and these latest findings were to have an immediate influence on future experimental technique. All the major British towing tanks began to fit a 1 mm diameter wire at the bow of their models girthing a section 5 per cent of the hull length abaft the forward perpendicular. Ship Division adopted the trip wire in September 1948.

The trip wire debate lasted for several months, the implication of laminar flow over ship models for years. Telfer returned to the subject frequently and in 1958 was at his most mischievous. Discussing a paper by J.B. Griffith of the Cory company dealing with Thames swim ended barges, models of which had been recently tested at Teddington, Telfer recalled Baker's earlier 1930 paper where tests on alternative designs had demonstrated savings of up to 50 per cent in resistance over standard barges then in general use. Reminding his audience that Baker's models were only 2 metres long, unstimulated and therefore prone to laminar flow, he supposed that reductions in resistance would have been as much due to stable laminar flow than the revised hull shapes that Baker had proposed. Telfer continued:

I understand that the 1930 Teddington "improved" forms were never adopted since, it was alleged, their greatly reduced resistance would have made them much more difficult to stop! Were such a barge slipped from a tow it would probably overshoot the intended landing and become a menace to river navigation. That was the story: and it would be of interest to learn from Mr Griffith the "river" version of it, as it surely must be river-lore by now. There was once a wicked model-experimenter ...

Comprehensive data from models tested with trip wires were given in 1950 by Allan and Conn[4] and Ayre[5] produced an interesting review. One of Allan's first acts after he became Ship Division's Superintendent in 1948 was to work with Hughes towards a preferred type of stimulator. This led to an important paper[6] before the American society in 1951 and the decision by Ship Division three years later to fit projecting pins or studs instead of a trip wire to all its models.

Such a system was copied by many other tanks although it came out in the discussion of the above paper that neither the Haslar or Washington tanks felt the need to adopt stimulation, a decision presumably based on the fact that most of their models were of fine form.

The studs were chosen to be 3 mm in diameter spaced at intervals along a line running parallel to the stem of the model the distance back from the stem being dictated by the fullness of the hull forebody. They projected 2½ mm from the model surface. Both trip wire and stud resistance was measured so as to determine the correction factor to be applied to the measurement of the resistance of a hull with stimulators fitted. Hughes used a special rig and for both trip wire and studs found drag coefficient to be about 0·85. In terms of the average surface area of a typical model this translated to a coefficient of 0·00002 or about ½ per cent of total model drag. The rig used by Hughes to measure stud resistance is a lovely example of his meticulous approach to experimentation. Working with D. Crewe, a high class mechanic who had joined the staff at the end of the war, an ingenious piece of apparatus was made. Several studs were fitted along the length of a 10 cm diameter cylinder which could rotate freely and vertically from two points. The cylinder was suspended from the carriage and immersed in the tank. The resistance of the studs through the water produced a torque on the cylinder which was balanced by a set of balls that ran down a sloping shute to press against a vertical plate at the top of the cylinder. The sensitivity of the balance could be varied by simply changing the slope. This clever device was really a kind of null balance. The position of the studs was always brought back to the point where the flow was tangential to the cylinder.

There was little to choose between trip wire and studs but the view was taken that studs were more effective at low speeds and could be better adapted to all sizes of model. The nett effect of fitting stimulators was of course extremely important, correct turbulent flow produced higher levels of resistance than if laminar flow existed over the surface of a model. Predicted values of propeller shaft power from model tests rose (because of increased model resistance) by anything from 2–12 per cent depending on speed and fullness of the hull form. This was alarming and the correction or correlation allowances applied to model results to achieve correspondence with the ship and which had been deduced from Ship Division's ship-model correlation research, were now in doubt and needed amendment. A further complication arose. More ships were being built with welded hulls superseding the older riveted ones. Welds produced smoother ship hulls and reduced the power at a given speed. Nothing definite could be done until comparative ship and model results on new ship construction became available and BSRA were soon to give this high priority. In the meantime awkward corrections between stimulated and unstimulated models had to be made in conjunction with amended correlation factors.

A further direct consequence of the need for stimulation was to throw doubt on the Froude skin friction correction since it was accepted that some laminar flow had existed in Froude's experiments with planks. Ship Division took this so seriously that an immediate and as it turned out important programme of research was launched. Allan with the Froude Ship Research Committee's approval encouraged Hughes, who had recently been appointed to an International Skin Friction Committee set up by the ITTC in 1948, to study laminar, turbulent and transitional flow over smooth plane surfaces. This he did with enthusiasm and was soon to produce his greatest work, a new friction formulation and method of extrapolating model resistance results to an equivalent ship.

The replacement programme already referred to included tests on all kinds of ship. Just about every shipbuilder in the land, and several from abroad, sent work to Teddington. Famous names (some alas no longer trading) such as Barclay Curle, Bartram, Bombay Port, Canadian Vickers, Cammell Laird, Cook Welton, Fairfield, Harland and Wolff, Hawthorn Leslie, Lithgows, Scotts, Thornycroft, Vosper and Yarrow were regular clients. Of the ship designs tested many were tankers of growing size (a 210 metre vessel for Furness in 1956). There were numerous passenger-cargo ships (a 90 metre twin screw vessel for Caledon, a 170 metre twin screw for Union Castle built by Harland and Wolff in 1950, and an even larger one for the same yard four years later. Ferries of different types were tested, cross-Channel ones for Fairfield in 1949, an ice-breaking ferry for Canadian Vickers in 1951 and a 120 metre twin screw train and car ferry for Alexander Stephen in 1952. Double-ended ferries and tunnelled stern vessels included a shallow draught ferry for the Argentine Government and a 40 metre ship with tunnelled stern and Yarrow flap (a device which reduced aeration in the tunnel at lighter draughts) for operation on the river Orinoco. The day of the great paddle ships had passed but there was still a demand for the smaller paddle steamer. Paddles had much to commend them. In ideal conditions their efficiency equalled the propeller and they could exert practically the same power astern as ahead. With their wide separation manoeuvrability was outstanding. However, with the ship rolling in a seaway, efficiency dropped off quickly and at light draughts paddles had little grip. On the model scale the paddles with fixed or feathering floats were works of art lovingly made by Rayment, a brilliant mechanic. One design for the Government of India proved troublesome. To determine the best position of the paddle on the hull the wave profile at the model's side was observed at 12 knots and inflow velocities at various proposed positions for the paddles. A solution was reached and the builders of the steamer, Hill's of Bristol, agreed to fit pitot tubes on the completed ship so that full-scale inflow velocities could be measured and compared with tank values. Correspondence was remarkably good. The last paddle to be tested by Ship Division was for Yarrow in 1948 (model 2846).

Smaller ships were well represented and many designs for tugs, coasters, trawlers, high speed launches, etc. were tested. Voith Schneider propellers were seen for the first time but their models were not made in Ship Division. They were provided on loan by the VS Company and the scale of the model chosen accordingly. Trawler designs came mostly from Cook Welton at Beverley and to some of these, bulbous bows were gradually being introduced. Experiments on the riding qualities of light ships, for the Commissioners of the Port of Calcutta, were also carried out. Unusual or unexpected results were thrown up on occasions. A single screw boom defence vessel which needed propeller guards at the stern was found to require 20 per cent more power with guards fitted. Such a large increase over the normal arrangement without guards was hard to accept and was an example of the problem posed when considering the scale effect of small hull appendages. In the high-speed field contrasting styles in design were seen either with or without chines and many proved very wet due to poor forebody design. Slower luxury cruising yachts such as the beautiful *Ravahine*, a 14 metre Laurent Giles design, also came to the tank for model tests.

Towards the end of the 1950s the P & O company decided to build two new 45,000 ton passenger liners *Canberra* and *Oriana* for the Australia route. These were fast ships (27 knots) and Ship Division carried out a large programme of model tests on the *Canberra* design. The high speed raised questions over stern vibration since the power to the twin propellers was very high. Stern design was thus critical and the model experiments covered both an orthodox afterbody shape and an alternative that included two very large skegs aft. The skegs were intended to straighten the flow into the propellers. Investigations of the flow on both sides of the skegs led to their modification until finally, comparative propulsion tests between orthodox and skeg stern showed little between the propulsive efficiencies of either and the selection of an orthodox afterbody was a narrow one. It was during the course of the *Canberra* project that a method was developed for measuring the velocity and direction of the flow at a specific point on the disc swept out by a rotating propeller. R. Warden in NPL's Aerodynamics Division had designed a five hole directional pitot tube and its principle was used by Silverleaf[7] to develop a tube that could be mounted at the stern of a ship model. Rotating on a shaft with the propeller removed a survey of velocity distribution in the plane of the propeller could be done to provide values of wake velocity. The values were nominal since they were obtained in the absence of an operating propeller but nevertheless such data were invaluable to the propeller designer and wake surveys became a regular part of a model experiment programme.

Before the introduction of wake surveys the majority of test programs consisted of resistance and propulsion experiments in calm water. Roughly 5 per cent of the models tested were also run in waves and, increasingly, steering experiments on completely free-running models became possible following the help received from the Vickers Armstrong Company at Weybridge who with Jenkins produced a system of driving and steering a model from a remote radio control unit. Such experiments were restricted by the narrowness of Number One tank and full turning circles impossible but the value of such tests were soon appreciated and led to considerable advances in later years.

Improvements to hull designs submitted for test, as in earlier years, continued to be made. Whereas the gains found after a hull modification were not so dramatic or frequent as in the past, clearly British ship design offices were building up data from their earlier tests, reductions in resistance of up to 10 per cent and improvements in propulsive efficiency of the order of 3–4 per cent were still being seen.

INSTRUMENTATION AND EQUIPMENT

The continuous demand for tests was perforce supported by additions and improvements to the tanks and equipment. Reliable propulsion gears were vital and Garlick worked tirelessly to achieve this. It was essential that failure of all apparatus was kept to a minimum, the smallest delay would disrupt a crowded schedule of work. Munro's were asked to build more propulsion gears and each new one incorporated a small improvement, many suggested by Garlick, until a reliable set of apparatus became available capable of accommodating a large range of propeller thrust, torque and r.p.m. requirement suited to every type of model expected including high speed. Garlick watched over the gears possessively and his attention to detail combined with the meticulous craftsmanship of the mechanics, qualities admirably suited to the need, established exceedingly high standards. He was never satisfied with "his" gears and constantly sought improvements. When in the 1960s the Munro firm went out of business, instead of being at a disadvantage, Garlick positively flourished and set about designing a new generation of gears called torque reaction dynamometers. Propeller torque was measured by balancing the drive motor reaction against a deadweight and spring system. To measure thrust the existing yoke, balance arm and sliding clutch was retained and both thrust and torque were recorded, as usual, as written records with new reservoir pens which ran without refill for several days. At the same time Garlick redesigned the shaft tube and bearing system that was cast into the wax model hull. The old method of oil lubrication was replaced by water lubrication once correct clearances between new ferrebestos bearings and the shaft were found. In the end Garlick produced a finished product that was close to the ultimate in mechanical propulsion dynamometers. They were extremely reliable and with calibration factors for gear and friction virtually constant it became possible for an experimenter to run a series of propulsion tests at one hull draught in three hours and by analysing the results as he went a prediction of ship speed was quickly reached. This was very satisfactory to visitors to the Tank who could see their model run for resistance in the morning and go away before the end of the same day with a speed and power prediction for their new ship. These splendid gears were used for a further 20 years and were replaced by today's strain gauge dynamometers only after a long period of doubt and uncertainty.

Garlick's efforts were not restricted to propulsion dynamometry. He was soon to be given the task of improving and maintaining the tanks and equipment although the Ministry of Works who supported the NPL in the upkeep of its "heavy" equipment and buildings held an overall responsibility for Ship Division's facilities, that is the buildings, offices, tanks and tunnel. It was Garlick's role to liaise and work towards further improvements by utilising both Ship Division and MoW technicians. The carriages of both tanks received fastidious attention. An automatic speed control was fitted to Number Two tank carriage in 1947 bringing to an end the need to drive the carriage from a desk at the tank side. The resistance dynamometer on this carriage was overhauled and improved whilst that on Number One was due for replacement, and a new design was drawn up by Shearer and Pearce. Garlick turned his attention to eliminating the disturbance of the tanks' water surface created by models during a test. It was normal practice to wait 10 minutes between experiments to allow the disturbance to reduce and then measure the residual current in the tank by observing the drift of a float in a graduated mirror fixed to the wall of the tank before beginning the next run. This was quite crude and a positive or negative correction to carriage speed was made to give water speed, which amounted to about ½ per cent for a carriage speed of 1½ metres per second. At lower speeds the percentage was usually higher and of significance and when Hughes began a programme of low speed measurements Garlick conceived an arrangement of curtains that could be fitted across the tank at intervals along its length. After 10 minutes in use, the drift in the tank was virtually eliminated. The curtains were successful and were soon fitted in both tanks. They were 1 metre deep and as the carriage returned after a run automatic switches were triggered so that each curtain, which was fully submerged during the test run, was lifted to break the water surface thus effectively compartmentalising the tank.

In addition to the propulsion gears a new and large open water propeller dynamometer was developed at this time. It was an ambitious undertaking intended for the testing of large 0·6 metre diameter propellers. The forces generated by these demanded a high powered 15 h.p. dynamometer, which was designed by NPL's Engineering Division with Jenkins' assistance. A heavy 2½ metre submarine shaped body housed the extension of the propeller shaft. Electrical strain gauges were used with a slip ring assembly to record thrust, torque and rotational speed. The dynamometer, packed with electronics, was supported on a triangular strut configuration at a fixed immersion, the struts connected to a four-wheel trailer which was towed by the Number Two tank carriage. The only way to install the large propellers was to build an extension to the dock of Number Two tank and by draining water from the dock and positioning the trailer over it the dynamometer could be worked on from below. The whole design was complex, extremely cumbersome and gave Jenkins endless headaches in solving the many teething problems but with perseverance and amidst much scepticism over its success he succeeded, although the dynamometer failed to enjoy a reputation for reliability or indeed accuracy and was not used for serious propeller force measurements. It did however perform usefully in 1958 when T.E. Carmichael, a newcomer that year, began a series of studies measuring the pressure field set up by rotating propellers in uniform flow.

The resistance dynamometer on Number One tank had served since 1910. Its replacement in 1956 retained the principle of allowing the model under test a small amount of fore and aft freedom but now the awkward process of adding deadweights to a scale pan was avoided by introducing a steelyard which carried a balancing weight. The weight which could be increased if necessary was driven along a lead screw by a small electric motor. The arrangement added sensitivity and proved invaluable during propulsion tests when the model resistance had to be balanced quickly against propeller thrust. The old cam operated grip that held the towed model against the acceleration and retardation of the carriage was replaced by a hydraulic brake. The behaviour of the dynamometer spring was, as in the earlier dynamometer, recorded by the movement of a pen across moving paper but an improved pen and a motorised drum were included. The whole assembly was painstakingly built by A. Dolman in Engineering Division, NPL. Dolman was an outstanding mechanic who later transferred to Ship Division on promotion to take charge of the workshops. The new dynamometer proved to be extremely rugged, accurate with good repeatability and needed the minimum of maintenance. When Number One tank was closed in 1994 the dynamometer was still available for tests on conventional hull forms.

The wavemaker was nearing the end of its useful life and was wearing out. Tentative steps to a new design had been made in 1937 but the war postponed things. In 1948, thanks to reparations, a replacement was fitted. Reparations had failed after the First World War chiefly because demands for payment of money were so unrealistic that after two efforts the whole business was dropped, much to Germany's advantage. After the Second World War the Government chose payment in kind and stipulated the transfer of technical capital equipment such as industrial plant, installations, ships, etc. to devastated countries to accelerate their recovery. The ship model testing facilities at Hamburg had already suffered indignities. The towing tank had been destroyed by the allies, its carriage broken up, put in the tank and the whole cemented over but two cavitation tunnels and a wavemaker remained. The largest tunnel was offered to Haslar and the wavemaker and smaller tunnel to NPL. Ship Division staff went to Hamburg and found that with a small modification and extension the wavemaker would fit Number One tank. Doxford's at Sunderland were asked to carry out the conversion and fitting which was completed by the end of 1948. The wavemaker of plunger type with wedge section was driven mechanically at a chosen frequency within a given range. The calibrated waves were not entirely satisfactory, although the range of height and length was greater than that possible with the earlier wavemaker. They also collapsed to an irregular formation if the wavemaker was left running for more than 10 minutes. Goodrich was soon to run some experiments on a very small model of a tank, which reproduced the geometry of Number One and alternative tank cross-sectional shape. He found that with sloping walls, as in the actual Number One tank, a certain critical wavemaker frequency produced, after a few minutes, a standing wave which grew in height. He returned to the actual tank and did the same before an incredulous audience who watched as a spectacular standing wave appeared. Garlick was not amused when, with the wavemaker left running for too long, the wave grew to such proportions as to overwhelm the carriage rails and flood the surrounding walkways. The standing wave phenomenon and the general instability of the waves generated were found to be due more to the sloping walls of the tank than the characteristics of the wavemaker itself. At the model tank if vertical walls were fitted, waves remained regular in shape and it was not possible to create any kind of standing wave. The small cavitation tunnel, that had also come from Hamburg and dismantled into several parts, lay about the Division for some time and was never erected. It was eventually taken by Newcastle University where, as has already been noted, Emerson began its resurrection.

The model cutting machine too had run its life and a replacement built by Munro's appeared in 1949. Using the same principle as the first machine but introducing a few improvements, larger wax or wooden models could now be profiled and their waterlines cut more rapidly. The new machine was used to cut hundreds of models and lasted for 40 years before being replaced by a purpose built numerically controlled machine. The wax that had for many years been used for model hulls often produced imperfect castings, tiny air holes remaining close to the surface. By adding a very small proportion of winnothene plastic (1 per cent) to the mix (49 per cent old wax and 50 per cent petroleum wax) a satisfactory homogenous material was produced which gave no further trouble.

With so many models being made the lack of workshop space became acute. This was relieved in 1947 by the construction of a separate workshop across the road from the tank buildings which was used to accommodate the carpenters and their machinery. Model hulls awaiting test or destruction were sunk and tethered along the sides of Number One tank (plate 44). This was unsatisfactory so a small storage pond capable of holding about 20 models was added at the north end of Number One tank in 1956.

The demand for model propellers was also great and at this time growing interest was being shown in the overall accuracy achieved in the manufacture of both model and full-size propellers. On the model side Marwood and Shearer began working towards a new manufacturing method for it was known that the existing method needed improvement, whilst Garlick with P.W. Harrison of NPL's Metrology Division turned their attention to the design of an optical survey instrument for use with ship propellers.

The accuracy achieved in a model propeller had always been excellent so far as diameter, pitch and blade outline were concerned. Not so good was the correct definition of blade section shape, particularly aerofoil or hollow face types. It was therefore decided to build a machine that could profile the shape of the blade at specified radii from boss to tip. There would then be positive guidance to the mechanic as he finished each blade and filed away surplus material. The established practice of casting a rough propeller was retained and for the profiling two machines were designed by Marwood and built by Gay's, a local engineering firm. The first was a pantograph device which followed the outline shape of the blade section at various radii drawn five times actual size for improved accuracy. The pantograph follower translated the shape to a cutter which machined two sets of thin steel templates, one for the faces of the sections, the other the backs. The templates were then mounted on a rotating disc in the second machine, the centre of the disc holding the shaft of the propeller model. This machine included another follower which translated the shape of the template to a high speed cutter about the size of a dentist's drill, which cut into the rough propeller blades as the disc was rotated slowly by hand. The whole process including casting, cutting, finishing and checking took nine days for a four bladed propeller. The system was a considerable advance although very precise definition of blade edge thickness (so important for cavitation experiments) was not possible and innermost radii close to the propeller boss could not be reached by the cutter, thus reducing the accuracy in this area.

The general improvement and upgrading of facilities included the Lithgow tunnel and when Silverleaf arrived in 1951 he was given the task of rejuvenating and expanding the work of the tunnel, a task he pursued with great enthusiasm. A major refit was needed for two reasons. There was a growing demand from industry for tests on propellers and a growing concern over vibration in ships which could often be traced to the propeller itself. Berry who had spent so much time with Emerson in establishing the tunnel as a reliable facility was joined by O'Brien and these two enabled Silverleaf to embark on a programme of research. But first, to improve and extend the capability of the tunnel the discharge bend was replaced by a new design and a larger test section fitted. A mitred shape was introduced to the bend and this improved the flow and under reduced pressure conditions higher test speeds than before became possible. Stronger propellers, necessary to withstand higher forces, led to a change in the material used in their manufacture. Constituents were chosen as 73 per cent tin, 12 per cent lead, 8 per cent antimony, 6 per cent copper and 1 per cent bismuth. A new 30 h.p. dynamometer was installed and by the mid-1950s the tunnel was an extremely useful facility[8] capable of the normal cavitation tests, new work covering acoustic, propeller blade deflection and flow studies. Acoustic work posed many problems. Instrumentation available at the time needed improvement and ambient noise from the tunnel during operation was difficult to isolate. The new test section was a success and could be adapted to accommodate a recently built three component hydrofoil balance which soon came into use. O'Brien took charge of most of the propeller cavitation tests and soon with Silverleaf produced a paper[9] concerning the effects of blade section shape on cavitation. In later years he led a large programme of work on a new standard series of propellers whilst Berry concentrated on developing the hydrofoil balance and investigating laminar flow on propeller blades in both cavitating and non-cavitating conditions, a task that arose no doubt from the current concern with model hulls.

It was at about this time, 1956, that the electronic computer was used in Ship Division for the first time. The Division was fortunate in having NPL's Mathematics Division close to hand. This Division had been formed in 1945 and became renowned for the discovery and development of the computer "engine", a machine capable of solving differential equations. Pioneer workers such as A.M. Turing and J.H. Wilkinson were at NPL at this time and Wilkinson with G.G. Alway finally produced the pilot automatic computing engine (ACE), component parts of which are now in the Science Museum. Months of difficulty and frustration were experienced in getting control circuits, automatic multipliers, punched card input/output, etc. to work but in May 1950 ACE worked for the first time. A program of a few instructions was inserted and amidst intense excitement the lamps on the output lit up as intended to indicate that both machine and program were working. It was the beginning of an epoch. In his jubilation Wilkinson telephoned NPL's new Director to come and see and just as Sir Edward Bullard appeared behind him Wilkinson burst out "Where's the bloody Director?" Sir Edward Bullard, an understanding man and quite unruffled, said "Here's the bloody Director". Sir Edward, although disappointed that some complicated equations that he had brought with him could not be immediately solved, recognised ACE for the breakthrough that it was—a real computer and supported its development with great vigour. An engineering version soon followed, the digital electronic universal computing engine (DEUCE) and it was this computer that became available to Ship Division workers. The world of automatic computing was of course utterly foreign but thanks to the willing help and co-operation of Mathematics Division the techniques of programming, punching cards and operating DEUCE were soon learnt by Ship Division staff. Doust, Hogben and Silverleaf were quick to appreciate the benefits and soon statistical analyses of trawler data, wave-making calculation and the analysis of flow velocity measurements became much easier. Junior staff were sent to attend courses of tuition run by Mathematics Division and gradually computational analysis replaced old manual methods. In these early days before Ship Division had its own computers the only access was via DEUCE, which was housed in Mathematics Division. A small computer group was thus formed which worked closely with Mathematics Division staff. This proved to be a good move since the group was able to keep abreast of developments in a rapidly expanding field.

RESEARCH

We have seen how immediate post-war years were barren so far as research was concerned. At last in 1949 the demand for commercial tests, although high, was beginning to reduce and a resumption in research work became possible. Tests for firms were given priority but whenever there was a spare day in the tank such research that could be done piecemeal was fitted in. Experiments on models at a specific test condition could be completed in a single day and three of BSRA's research programmes were progressed this way: methodical series work, the *Lucy Ashton* model tests and ship-model comparison studies.

Interaction

Soon after the war an urgent request for immediate tests on the *Queen Mary–Curacoa* accident enabled an earlier item of research, interaction, to be reopened and extended.

The incident occurred in October 1942 in broad daylight and in fine weather off the north-east coast of Ireland. *RMS Queen Mary* with over 10,000 American troops on board was on passage from New York to the Clyde and *HMS Curacoa*, a C class cruiser with several destroyers, escorted her across the Atlantic. As her best defence against air or sea attack, *Queen Mary*, once clear of the swept channel at New York, zigzagged continuously at 28½ knots. *Curacoa* steaming at about 25 knots kept station with *Queen Mary* throughout but suddenly off Donegal there was an appalling collision, *Queen Mary's* bow cutting *Curacoa* clean in two. Within five minutes both halves of the cruiser had sunk with the loss of 329 lives. *Queen Mary* was badly damaged but able to continue her passage to Scotland whilst the survivors, 103 in all, were rescued by the destroyers who at the time of the disaster were several miles away. An action brought by the Admiralty against Cunard White Star, owners of *Queen Mary*, alleged negligent navigation of the liner. In defence Cunard argued similar negligence and, in particular, the failure of *Curacoa* to alter course to starboard when a collision seemed likely. Although the ensuing court proceedings in considering liability were concerned chiefly with seamanship and an interpretation of the overtaking law at sea in the unusual case of a zigzagging ship, the influence of possible interaction between the two ships in close proximity could not be ignored and led to the request for model experiments. Both sides appointed technical consultants, E.V. Telfer advising the Admiralty, and Professor A.M. Robb Cunard and the judge, Mr Justice Pilcher, drew on Elder Brethren from Trinity House to act as assessors. Whereas the earlier interaction tests at the Tank in 1912 dealt with the *Hawke–Olympic* collision that had occurred in shallow water this latest collision was in deep water and many doubted that interaction forces between ships could develop in such conditions. The experiments that followed were soon to prove them wrong.

To investigate interaction between two ships on different courses really demanded a large steering pond, a facility not available at Teddington. Certain limiting factors had to be accepted. It was decided to run a *Curacoa* model on a straight course down the tank and to traverse a *Queen Mary* model across the tank at such a relative angle as to give the desired angle of convergence between the two ships. Small models were desirable to allow a long enough time before a collision and to reduce acceleration forces. On the other hand, to be free of scale effect and to ensure interaction forces large enough to be measured with accuracy, large models were best. The width of the largest tank at Teddington, 9 metres, led to 1/56-scale models. The *Queen Mary* model supplied by Messrs John Brown at Clydebank was 5¼ metres long and *Curacoa*, made at Teddington, was 3 metres shorter. Each was fitted with stern gear, twin screws in the cruiser's case, quadruples for *Queen Mary*, and internal drive motors allowed both models to be self-propelled.

The tests were in two groups. After initial calibration runs, which established propeller r.p.m. for *Queen Mary* at 28 knots and *Curacoa* at 25 knots, both models were run on parallel courses at different distances apart and at different relative positions longitudinally. *Curacoa*, attached to the towing carriage by two Bottomley gears fore and aft, travelled at the same speed as the carriage and *Queen Mary*, towed and balanced on a rope from a drum geared to an axle on the carriage, ran on a specially constructed track fitted to the underside of the carriage. The *Queen Mary* model could, with appropriately set r.p.m., either keep pace with *Curacoa* or overtake her. Next, with *Curacoa* held to a straight course, *Queen Mary* was brought in on a converging course by driving her along the track, which could be rotated to any desired angle. Two courses were selected, 23° the angle between the courses on which the two ships were reported to be steering prior to the collision and 12° an angle that assumed some avoiding action had been taken. The converging tests were extremely difficult to arrange. Having positioned the track at the desired course angle the *Queen Mary* model itself had then to be set at an angle to the trackway so that when the relative speeds of *Curacoa* and *Queen Mary* were correct, *Queen Mary* advanced directly along her course with no drift angle between her centreline and the actual track over the ground. In practice, during the initial acceleration of the towing carriage, the wave formation on either side of *Queen Mary*'s bow were not the same, a snag largely overcome by starting *Queen Mary* on a fore and aft line before swinging her to the desired angle. Also, because of the narrowness of the tank waterway, actual experiment time was very short, little more than six seconds, and vigilance was needed by the experimenters to prevent collisions since the experiments, if continued, would have made these inevitable.

The Bottomley gears measured any transverse forces set up by the influence of the pressure fields generated by each model and in the parallel tests these forces were soon evident and increased as the separation between the two models decreased. The measurements allowed helpful diagrams to be prepared which showed the changes in forces and moment occurring as *Queen Mary* overtook *Curacoa*. With the two models travelling at the same speed the dynamometer indicators responded according to the degree of interaction force and thereafter in the same experiment remained steady. In the converging tests, at the beginning of each experiment, there was a period of time when the pointers remained steady but as soon as *Queen Mary* was near enough to cause any interference, deflections were seen. Such visual proof was vivid demonstration of the existence of interaction to Mr Justice Pilcher and the KCs. However, the experiments showed that the forces of acceleration were large only when the two vessels were dangerously close to each other, about 120 metres. Of greater significance was the observation that the forces could be overcome if *Curacoa*'s rudder was swung over by only a few degrees so as to steer *Curacoa* away from the oncoming *Queen Mary*. This avoiding action was reproduced in another set of experiments by disconnecting *Curacoa* from the Bottomley gears, power to the internal motor being supplied along umbilical lines. As *Curacoa* was freely propelled down the tank and *Queen Mary* approached from her oblique course, *Curacoa*'s rudder was operated by light lines attached to the steering mechanism and controlled by an experimenter. There is no doubt that the judge was greatly impressed and influenced by what he saw for in referring to the interaction tests in his judgment he recognised that interaction forces could indeed contribute to an unavoidable collision provided the ships were close enough. Even so he stressed the fact that a small degree of rudder could nullify the forces and that in any case good seamanship should never have allowed the two ships to have come close enough for interaction to be felt. After consideration of all the other evidence presented he found *Curacoa* wholly responsible for the collision. The Admiralty appealed and a Court of Appeal reached a majority decision that *Queen Mary* was one-third blameworthy. On a further appeal the matter was next brought before the House of Lords who in a final judgment in February 1949, upheld the decision reached by the Appeal Court.

The experiments with the free-running *Curacoa* model were requested by Robb as part of his consultative work for Cunard. He later co-operated with Cutland, who had been in charge of the experiments and analysis of the huge quantities of film record that had been taken, and published a paper on interaction.[10] Despite Robb's clear description and evidence of interaction forces some discussers of his paper still expressed total disbelief of interaction between ships in deep water. The President of INA (Admiral of the Fleet Viscount Cunningham) who chaired the meeting at which the paper was read, went so far as saying that he hoped the paper would not get into the hands of captains of destroyers who take their ships alongside tankers at 15 knots. Yet any pilot in his launch approaching a large ship exercised extreme care and was well aware of the realities of interaction. Professor Havelock redressed the situation and described calculations he had made which supported interaction effects and another professor, Prohaska from Sweden, described experiments he had done following an incident between a tugboat, which overtook a dredger in the port of Copenhagen. The dredger had sheered away to strike a pier. The behaviour due to interaction was akin to that seen in the Teddington tests when *Queen Mary* overtook *Curacoa*; *Curacoa* swung into the path of *Queen Mary*'s bow and in some experiments a collision had occurred.

Methodical Series Tests on Hulls

Work on a methodical series of hulls that would yield basic hull design data for new ships was initiated by the Shipbuilding Conference in 1944 and handed over to BSRA when this body was formed. A large programme of work which took several years to complete produced resistance and propulsion data in calm water for a number of models (many but not all tested in Ship Division) in groups of constant fullness. The first group of tests concerned hulls of 0·65 block coefficient. The parent form was designed by Ship Division and the others derived from it introduced changes in bilge radii, LCB, beam/draught and length/displacement ratios. The results which provide excellent guidance to practitioners were published in two parts[11, 12] and were the forerunners of similar offerings giving data for hulls of increasing fullness (C_B = 0·70, 0·75, etc.). The whole BSRA series was carefully considered, parent forms in each block coefficient group had good hydrodynamic characteristics and the variations chosen for the various derivatives were fully representative of current ship design practice. The series was used frequently and is still a valuable reference source for preliminary hull design studies.

Sea Trials on *Lucy Ashton*

The *Lucy Ashton* programme began in 1950 and was a further attempt to measure the resistance of a ship. The main purpose of the research was to validate existing scaling laws and to investigate how different types of hull surface finish or roughness affected resistance. For maximum success *Lucy Ashton*'s resistance through the water had to be measured accurately. The earlier tests by Froude and Hiraga had measured the resistance of a towed ship and BSRA were determined to avoid the troubles that had been experienced, particulary in *Yudachi* the ship that Hiraga had towed, where it had been difficult to keep *Yudachi* to a straight course during tow. A different approach was made. *Lucy Ashton*, an old 58 metre paddle steamer, was stripped of her paddles and superstructure and four Rolls-Royce jet aircraft engines capable of a total thrust of 6 tons were mounted on deck and used to propel the ship. 6 tons was the estimated figure for a speed of 15 knots. The resistance of *Lucy Ashton* was then measured from the reaction of the steady thrust on a trunnion mounting and transmitted to pressure gauges that were calibrated at NPL. Before each trial the hull bottom was prepared to give different kinds of roughness by leaving plate edges and seams as they were, by fairing them or by using different types of paint. In later trials hull appendages such as bossings and brackets were added and their additional resistance determined. For its part, Ship Division conducted resistance tests on a series of geometrically similar models. Six "geosims" ranging between 2¾ and 9 metres in length were made and run in Number One tank and a separate wind tunnel model was tested by Aerodynamics Division, NPL. The results of the complete research published by

BSRA in a series of historic papers[13 *et al*] had far-reaching consequences. Realistic allowances for a defined hull roughness could thenceforth be included in powering estimates. The various competing methods of extrapolating model resistance measurements to the ship were brought into sharp focus and, from the model experimenters' point of view, the importance of model size was seen.

With regard to the extrapolation problem, new methods had appeared since Baker's work of 1914. Schoenherr in 1932 put forward a formulation that gained acceptance in America, a Prandtl-Schlichting line was being used by hydro and aerodynamicists and Telfer, as early as 1927, had proposed his line. All were Reynolds number based and all used the same assumptions for wetted surface as had Froude in his original hypothesis. Later, Telfer proposed a quite different type of extrapolation method. This was a brilliant conception and used the results from geosim models. Using a Reynolds number base Telfer plotted the total resistance of each geosim and was able to draw straight lines at constant speeds achieving simultaneous compliance with Reynolds and Froude laws without making any assumptions at all.

When the results from *Lucy Ashton* and the geosim models were to hand, BSRA analysed the model results using the Froude O method, Schoenherr and Prandtl-Schlichting extrapolation lines and also Telfer's geosim approach. Greatest consistency was seen with Schoenherr and BSRA came down in favour of this method of extrapolation. For the normal ship, i.e. hull with red oxide paint, sharp plate seams, the resistance above the Schoenherr "smooth" ship prediction, increased by 16 per cent or in terms of resistance coefficient the added resistance due to hull roughness, ΔC_F was 0·0004. Faired seams and a different paint reduced ΔC_F to 0·00013, clear proof of the advantage of a smoother hull. The consistency of the correlation once again vindicated Froude's hypothesis of treating viscous and wave-making resistance as independent and additive. On the debit side, Telfer's approach failed not through any fault in the method but because of invalid model resistance results. It was clear that the three largest models (6.1 metres and above) tested were influenced by the walls and bottom of Number One tank. Tank blockage as it was called exaggerated resistance and as a result Telfer's extrapolator lines at constant speeds could not be drawn in accurately. It should be remembered that models tested in Number One tank had never, normally, exceeded 5½ metres, this being the limit set by Baker in 1911 following Glazebrook's study on blockage at the time of the tank's design and it is surprising that BSRA were content to test the larger versions of *Lucy Ashton* in this tank. However, the results seen emphasised the need to know more and a few years later Hughes deduced a blockage corrector[14] based on a succession of models run in Numbers One and Two tanks.

The discussions of the *Lucy Ashton* papers make fascinating reading. Many queried BSRA's verdict in favour of the Schoenherr line, notably Hughes and Telfer. Both had vested interests but Telfer's complaint was very reasonable in view of the results from the large models. "Had the authors concentrated on the smaller models" Telfer argued, "they would have rejected the Schoenherr line in its entirety." Hughes objected to the line since the data from which it was derived had a large scatter which was not due to experimental error but a lack of geometrical similarity in the tests and he was carrying out tests on planes of varying aspect ratio to establish the effect.

Skin Friction

The *Lucy Ashton* work came at the right time for the International Skin Friction Committee who were able to digest the results in the light of the extrapolation debate. It was also able in 1953 to see Hughes' work on planes. He had begun by surveying the earlier work of Froude, Baker, Schoenherr, Gebers and others, which convinced him that it was wrong to persist with the assumption that the skin friction of a ship form could be taken as that of the equivalent plane of the same length and wetted area. He then showed from experiments on a series of two-dimensional planes how a family of friction lines could be produced by merely changing the length breadth or aspect ratio of the plane.[15] This work was the genesis of Hughes' eventual proposals on form factor and led to his proposal for a new approach to extrapolation. Before doing so he extended his earlier experiments in order to derive a basic friction resistance line for two-dimensional flow. It was an essential prerequisite that frictional resistance should be measured in turbulent flow.* Tank workers everywhere had faced the fact that accurate measurement for turbulent flow on a flat plate was not easy, certainly far harder than in a pipe (Reynolds experiments) where skin friction was readily determined from the pressure gradient. The major problem was to ensure a fully turbulent boundary layer from the leading edge of the plate being towed through water, a problem with no complete solution. Hughes was well aware of the difficulty and took great pains to stimulate and maintain turbulence by fitting stimulators (mainly studs) to the leading edges of his planes. Careful flow studies using dye confirmed that satisfactory turbulence was achieved. Working with Cross and other assistants a very comprehensive series of experiments were carried out on submerged semi-rigid plastic sheets and shallow draught pontoons. The semi-rigid sheets were between 0·23 and 1·45 metres in length and allowed very low aspect ratios (or high length–breadth ratios) to be examined. They were towed horizontally and fully submerged in Number Two tank. The pontoons, also run in Number Two, were much longer and allowed a very high Reynolds number to be reached (250 million). These were made up in 4·5 metres long units 1·2 metres wide and the longest was 78 metres. Great care was needed to achieve satisfactory joints between pontoons and very smooth surfaces. Each unit of a pontoon was built around a light cellular framework with a 6 mm plywood bottom. Bottom, sides and ends were then covered with very thin plastic sheet glued to the wood. The sheets and

* For a discussion of this see page 162.

pontoons were towed from the carriage in the usual way but a specially designed dynamometer was built which incorporated a simple weight bar supported on a knife edge. At the bottom the outer casing of a ball race was free to roll against the vertical face of a plate attached to the sheet or pontoon. With a very light spring the sensitivity of the dynamometer was 1/10,000 of a pound. Such accuracy was required in the tests with the smaller planes because of the low levels of resistance. Also the water surface in the tank had to be as calm as a mill pond before an experiment could begin. Garlick's curtains saved much time between runs but Hughes was irritated to find that small fish in the tank had multiplied to such an extent that in rising to the surface they caused frequent disturbance. A quick solution was found. Camp, a keen fisherman, knew where to find a pike, brought one to the tank and put it in. A very contented pike was removed a few days later leaving the tank completely purged.

The results of Hughes' work were published in a brilliant paper[16] which deservedly received a Gold medal award. It was essentially in two parts. First, the results from the various planes showed very clearly the importance of aspect ratio (friction resistance increased as the ratio reduced) and allowed Hughes to derive a basic friction line that could be compared with existing formulations such as Schoenherr, and second, Hughes' proposal for extrapolation, which introduced a form factor which could be derived from very low speed tests on a ship model. Hughes' basic line was at once controversial. Its level was 10 per cent below Schoenherr and Prandtl-Schlichting. This naturally led to a lower prediction of ship power from a given set of model resistance data than would otherwise be obtained using a Froude or Schoenherr analysis. Such an unexpected level of the basic line was too much for the traditionalists. In discussing Hughes' paper aerodynamicists Relf and Young, long content with Prandtl-Schlichting, and Lackenby of BSRA expressed their doubts although everyone who contributed to the discussion praised the carefully conducted work and appeared willing to believe the results. The criticism centred on Hughes' method of deriving his line from the results in which no single set covered the complete range of Reynolds number involved. The second part of Hughes' paper dealt with the actual extrapolation process. To illustrate his approach Hughes began with a simple and convincing diagram. In this he drew in a basic two-dimensional line and above it another which, if a double model of a ship were towed deeply submerged, and thus entirely free of wave-making effects, would lie above the basic line, the difference between the two being an exact measure of the effect on friction resistance due to the form of the model tested. If the total resistance of a series of geosim models were now added the curve from each would run tangentially into the single curve from the submerged double models. Hughes then assumed that the form resistance of a model (which could easily be determined from very low speed tests where wave-making was negligible) would provide a ratio of form and basic friction resistance at model Reynolds number that could be applied to the ship at its Reynolds number. The process of extrapolation would continue to follow the accepted Froude hypothesis in scaling residual resistance due to wave-making but a different basic friction line (Hughes) would be used and increased by a measured form factor. Discussers of Hughes' paper were quite happy with this, the only reservation being over his basic line. Hughes' contribution to this particular debate was undoubtedly of utmost importance. When, two years later, the ITTC skin friction committee considered competing formulations it opted for an empirical line which fell closest to Schoenherr but, so far as the all important slope was concerned, it was similar to Hughes. The "ITTC model ship correlation line (1957)", as it became known, was put to the 8th ITTC in Madrid which accepted and recommended it for future use. After a period of initial reluctance most Tanks adopted it from about 1960. At Teddington, parallel analyses were conducted for several years using both Froude O and the latest ITTC formulation, but from 1964 ship predictions were based exclusively on ITTC unless a client requested otherwise.

Interdependence Study

Whereas great emphasis was being placed on skin friction, a better understanding of the physics of ship resistance was required and led BSRA to initiate in 1954 a programme of research at NPL. This became known as a study of the interdependence of the components of ship resistance, a subject which grew over the years and to which successive workers contributed. Froude's original hypothesis that frictional and wave-making resistance were independent and separable was reasonable but needed investigation. As a start, tests on a mathematical model were conducted in both water and air. In the tank skin friction resistance in the presence of waves was derived by subtracting measured pressure resistance from the total resistance obtained at the dynamometer. A large number of pressure points were fitted to the surface of the model and pressures measured on a water manometer. An integration of these pressures gave the total pressure resistance. A double model was then made and tested in one of Aerodynamics Division's wind tunnels. These experiments gave a measure of the skin friction in the absence of waves. Two sets of curves could now be plotted, skin friction from air tests and derived skin friction from the tank. If the curves were the same then skin friction could be seen to be independent of wave-making. They were close but the tank curve showed undulations in sympathy with the natural wave profile seen on the hull. The programme of work extended to various types of measurement aimed at isolating other components of resistance. Velocity in the wake was determined from an array of pitot tubes set up at the stern of the model and in later years Hogben began to measure the actual waves set up by the motion of a model through the water. In the 1950s the interdependence work at Teddington was under Shearer's charge. Because he was becoming increasingly involved in the Feltham project progress was slow but received an impetus when Hogben arrived in 1955.

Hull Roughness and Wake Studies

Parallel studies were also in progress at this time which related to the effect of structural roughness on resistance. Using Hughes' pontoons Allan and Cutland simulated structural roughness such as plate overlaps, rivet heads and welds, as seen on ships, on the bottoms of the pontoons. The results,[17] which incidentally agreed well with earlier and briefer work done by Baker and Kempf, were dramatic and enabled Allan to estimate the effect of riveting versus welding on several typical ships. For example, the resistance due to structural roughness was increased by 25 per cent in a 200 metre tanker if she was of all riveted construction. This reduced to 10 per cent if half welded and if the ship were all welded then resistance increased by only 1½ per cent. Such figures were sure to hasten the change to all welded ships.

Allan and Cutland found another use for Hughes' pontoons. They had earlier carried out wake studies behind plane surfaces and now returned to the subject when two ships became available for sea trials. But first Cutland placed an array of pitot tubes behind a pontoon and measured flow velocities in its wake which he used to derive skin friction resistance comparing this with certain theoretical methods and Hughes' result. Then, at sea, Cutland made an attempt to improve on Bakers' measurements on *Pacific Trader* in 1935. Baker had fitted pitot tubes to this ship but had met with limited success. The two ships that Cutland used were the trawler *Sir William Hardy* and an ore carrier *Oremina*. Robust pitot tubes were fitted at the stern and near amidships on both ships and measurements of velocity in the boundary layer obtained at a number of positions around the two stations selected. Two sets of measurements were possible on the trawler, first with a clean hull and again at a later date when the hull had become fouled. Cutland fared only marginally better than Baker although many more reliable measurements were obtained.[18] It was difficult to draw definite conclusions. So far as the results from the pontoon were concerned these agreed well with earlier two-dimensional work by Ludweig and Tillmann but the ship results, reflecting the three-dimensional effect, showed considerable differences.

Ship-Model Correlation

Although ship-model comparisons which Baker instituted in earlier years remained Ship Division policy progress was only spasmodic. With the formation of BSRA the whole subject became of high priority. A regularised method of conducting speed and power trials on new ships was drawn up and allowed consistent data to be collected for a multitude of ships. Builders and owners were generous in their co-operation and the programme of work continued for many years. It was split between BSRA who were primarily responsible for ship measurements and Ship Division who ran corresponding model resistance and propulsion experiments in calm water. By doing these experiments after a satisfactory ship trial the exact condition of the ship could be reproduced at the model. The model propeller used in the propulsion test was copied from the ship drawing. A vast quantity of data materialised, some thought too much, to exercise the thoughts of future workers as they attempted to interpret the results and deduce reliable correction or correlation factors for use when predicting actual ship power and r.p.m. from future models tests. B.S. Bowden and R.E. Clements, who began their careers at BSRA before coming to Ship Division, were prominent in this field.

BSRA's trials procedure was painstaking and left no stone unturned. It was important to know the state of a new ship's hull before trial and a BSRA roughness gauge was developed which measured local hull roughness at 50 or more positions on a new hull. Similarly, for ultimate success in comparing model and trial, exact knowledge of hull appendages including the propeller was needed and led Ship Division to develop accurate measuring apparatus capable of surveying a finished ship propeller in order to compare its geometry with the design. The apparatus fully described in a 1953 paper[19] allowed measurements that were partly optical and partly mechanical. Very accurate determination of the shape of a blade section and the axial position of the section was possible but a tedious and time consuming analysis of some 600 observations were needed afterwards to produce drawings of the measured propeller. Altogether 20 man days were required to survey a 5½ metres diameter propeller. Clearly the method was unsuited to routine production checks but its accuracy appealed and several leading propeller manufacturers were soon installing permanent apparatus that embodied many of the principles used in Ship Division's optical method. In the midst of this activity, (over 40 propellers were surveyed), Professor Burrill of Newcastle University and consultant to the Manganese Bronze Company presented a paper[20] in Holland describing how this Company made propellers. Manufacturing tolerances were given. The paper came in for a good deal of criticism mainly over the degree of accuracy claimed. ISO had recently suggested "allowable deviations from measurements of ship screw propellers" and Professor Aertssen from Belgium appeared surprised that the tolerances Burrill had given were smaller than ISO's. K.G. Evans from Haslar doubted the stated tolerance achieved for blade thickness and M.M.H. Lips, a Dutch propeller manufacturer, reported that when ISO had drawn up its guidelines Great Britain refused to take part in discussions. Silverleaf in a written contribution added fuel to the flames with an attack on the basic methods used and suggested several possible sources of inaccuracy in the manufacturing method described. Burrill's replies could hardly conceal his anger and the furore that followed continued for months and almost led to libel action. Meanwhile the surveys by Ship Division continued and in general a high order of engineering accuracy was seen, although in nearly every case the blades of a ship screw were not precisely similar. To attempt to represent such minor differences at the model propeller was unjustified and surveys were soon dropped.

Sideways Launching of Trawlers

In 1953 an unusual request came from Cook, Welton and Gemmell, a shipbuilding company at Beverley in Yorkshire who had for many years been launching trawlers sideways into the river Hull. A trend to larger trawlers was apparent and the company was anxious to know more about the mechanics of launching so that practical limits of construction at Beverley could be established. This was a subject about which little was known, although Todd's work, during the Second World War on the launching of the Mulberry Harbour units, was a good reference point.

Ship Division was asked to attend the launches of six trawlers at Beverley and to carry out measurements. Doust was given charge of this and arrangements were made to take continuous recordings during each launch. A cine camera photographed the passage of the vessel down the ways and a gyroscope on board recorded the motions of the trawler once it left the end of the ways. After each launch an inclining experiment determined metacentric height, and GM and observed draughts determined displacement. Model experiments could then be carried out at Teddington in conditions representative of those at Beverley. Cook, Welton and Gemmell were becoming concerned during the building of new trawlers that additional weight high up on the vessel might affect stability during launch. The initial roll taken up by a vessel after a sideways launch was considerable and its variation with speed of launch, GM, etc. needed investigation. Some valuable tests were carried out. They were arranged in the shallow end of Number Two tank where, by damming a section of the tank and modelling the river banks at Beverley, scaled values for water depth and width could be set. The arrangement for launching was similar to that used by Todd in his work on the *Hippopotamus* concrete structures where the launching ways were replaced by rollers. The drop from the end of the ways to the water had also to be set as that existing at Beverley. Todd had experienced difficulty in reproducing the correct coefficient of friction at the ways and was forced to assume launch speeds for a given declivity of launching way but Doust now had the benefit of knowing the speed from the measurements obtained at Beverley. The corresponding speed for the model was arranged by releasing it from a restraining wire over a pulley activated by a cam the shape of which corresponded to the distance-time characteristics recorded at the full-scale launch. Roll, pitch and yaw of the model immediately after launch were recorded on gyroscopes. Some 600 launches were carried out covering variations in GM, drop, launch speed and depth of water and helpful diagrams drawn up showing limiting values of GM for capsize after launch.[21] Cook, Welton and Gemmell could now estimate GM during the construction of a new vessel and if this became close to the limit then any further additions to the superstructure could be left until after the launch.

Doust certainly helped to fill a gap in the profession's knowledge of this specialist subject. The data he provided were however restricted to a narrow range of trawler. Further model work was done with other ship types and a second paper,[22] this time with Macdonald, gave results from typical coaster and dredger designs.

Coasters

Coasters were also the subject of basic hull design studies. Todd's resistance and propulsion experiments in 1930 provided some of the first data for this type of ship and in 1951 Dawson began a very comprehensive programme on a systematic series of models. After a survey of existing coasters Dawson drew up a practical range of ship dimensions and service speed and by selecting three groups of hulls of varying fullness, block coefficients of 0·65, 0·70 and 0·75, 40 different designs were drawn up. A parent hull was designed for each block coefficient and from these, derivatives, covering systematic variations in length beam ratio and LCB, were produced. Resistance and propulsion experiments in calm water with specially designed propellers were conducted by Poulton and the results analysed to a standard ship length of 60 metres. Optimum position of LCB for each block coefficient group was easily derived and a combination of all of the results showed the effect on calm water performance of hull beam and bilge radius. Altogether Dawson produced four papers yet when presenting the fourth[23] discussers still asked for more.

Ship Vibration

Research into ship vibration at Ship Division which, as has been noted, began just before the Second World War, was resumed in 1946. Eight years earlier Todd had been given the task of determining the influence of superstructure on the elastic properties of a ship and up to the outbreak of war vibration measurements had been obtained on two ships at sea. With the willing co-operation of shipowners further ships were made available, and Todd with Marwood were able to complete a valuable piece of work.

The natural frequency of a ship is needed at the very outset of a new design so that appropriate engine r.p.m. can be selected to suit both the available machinery and propeller requirements without clashing with a bad period of vibration. Early methods of estimating frequency were based on an original formula put forward by Schlick which included an empirical coefficient derived from a similar ship. This was never a satisfactory approximation and the formula failed to take account of the virtual or added mass effect of the water immediately adjacent to the floating ship. Refinements to Schlick's formula introduced a term D, the depth of the ship to its topmost continous deck. This worked reasonably well for ships with relatively short lengths of superstructure but where substantial superstructure was included D needed modification. Todd therefore concentrated on passenger cargo liners since these had long lengths of superstructure. 13 ships became available and 10 of these had superstructures extending for more than 40 per cent of the topmost continuous deck. Marwood and Gridley carried out measurements using a Cambridge vibrograph or accelerometer, the latter capable of reliable measurement of horizontal and vertical accelerations with the ship pitching and rolling in a seaway. Readings were taken at the stern as ship r.p.m. were gradually increased. If a resonance occurred then the tolerant ship's master kept r.p.m. constant as Marwood and Gridley scurried along the deck taking records which could be used to determine the two-node mode of vibration that occurred. Todd and Marwood published an important paper[24] giving a new formula for the natural frequency of two-node vertical vibration which included a revised term in D that took account of superstructure height, ship displacement corrected for virtual mass, ship length and beam. All of these things were known at an early stage in the design of a ship. It was concluded that superstructures less than 60 per cent of a ship's length had negligible influence on the natural frequency and in such cases there was thus no need to modify D. From the ship measurements an extremely valuable plotting was produced which with Todd and Marwood's formula could be used to estimate the two-node frequency for oil tankers and passenger cargo ships.

Yachts

An entirely different and new area of research was begun in 1954 when Allan with Doust and Ware carried out model and full-scale tests on yachts. A Yacht Research Council was formed in this country a year earlier which soon realised a need for improved test techniques with model yachts. Before 1932 tests were confined to measurements of resistance with a yacht in the upright position, a condition unsuited to judging the relative merits of competing hull forms. Since then, Davidson in America had used two dynamometers to apply the lateral component of the sail force whilst allowing the model to trim naturally, Kempf in Germany had simulated the effect of wind by applying forces to the assumed centre of effort using a weights and pulley system and de Bella in Italy had experimented with models fitted with sails. Allan's approach was to design a special dynamometer that could simulate the behaviour of a yacht in the close-hauled and free-running conditions. Preliminary experiments established that it was possible to tow a yacht model from a point outside the model at an assumed position of the centre of effort. A tow point was arranged at this position at the top of a dummy mast and a constant torque applied at this point on a vertical axis. It was seen that a model when towed down the tank assumed a stable heeled and yaw attitude. Using this principle a dynamometer was built and fitted to Number Two tank carriage. At the top of the mast a universal joint connected with a vertical shaft through which the horizontal forces acting on the model were freely transmitted. Air bearings and two hydraulic bellows were fitted to ensure frictionless axial and rotational motion of the shaft. The bellows were sensitive to axial compression and by connecting them by tubing to a manometer the applied forces could be determined. The upper end of the vertical shaft was attached to a cross-piece running in roller bearings which allowed the model unrestrained vertical motion. Any out of balance moments were measured on a quadruple spring system mounted on the cross-piece. This was a delicate piece of apparatus that required careful calibration. In each experiment the leeway or lateral force was balanced against a selected wind force that was applied by adding a small weight to the dynamometer. Small 1½ metre wooden models were used and the measurements obtained gave a series of curves for a range of heel angle.[25] Gimcrack sail coefficients were then applied and values of the driving force from the sails estimated, which was used with the measured hull resistance to determine the balance point, leeway and speed made good to windward when the yacht was sail propelled. Later full-scale verification was sought and *Yeoman* a 5½ metre yacht was instrumented and tested in a nearby reservoir. Good agreement of speed made good was seen for wind speeds up to 9 knots but at higher winds the model results over-predicted those on *Yeoman*. Allan's paper attracted a good deal of interest not least from W.A. Crago and P.R. Crewe of the Saunders Roe (later BHC) tank in the Isle of Wight, who in subsequent years continued with tests on model yachts. Ship Division's interest lapsed until, over 20 years later, a great renewal of interest was aroused by the latest America's Cup races.

Work Followed by Research Scholars

Research effort on a smaller scale was done from time to time as Ship Division continued to welcome research scholars. J.F. Leathard, an 1851 Exhibition scholar, came to Teddington in 1950 and studied flow in the slipstream of a propeller using a hot wire technique. He was followed in 1952 by the first Froude scholar, R.L. Townsin, who was sponsored from the funds left over when the Advisory Committee was superseded by the Froude Research Committee in 1945. Townsin studied low drag hydrofoils and demonstrated that they could be tested successfully in a towing tank as well as in a low turbulence wind tunnel. Tests in water were preferable because the arrangements for measuring drag were simpler. Townsin was followed by P.D. Chaplin, another Froude scholar, who did some unusual experiments on slamming. Different bow shapes of varying cross-section were dropped into the water from the moving Number Two tank carriage and impact forces and acceleration measured. A section having constant acceleration during impact was found.

Statistical Analysis of Trawler Data

The last major item of research to be started before the new facilities at Feltham were complete was Doust's review of resistance data for trawlers. With the help of the emerging computer thorough statistical analyses of model data could be carried out and the likely benefits to designers of new vessels were rapidly appreciated. Working with J.G. Hayes of Mathematics Division, NPL to decide on the best mathematical approach, multiple regression analysis techniques were used and applied to model test data to produce regression equations containing hull parameter terms. Not only could the resistance of a form be estimated with a good degree of accuracy but the effect on resistance of changing any parameter could be quickly calculated. Doust produced a pioneering paper[26] that took the industry by storm. Other workers were soon to take advantage of regression techniques and Doust having gained a reputation in trawler design continued with further analyses which introduced propulsive elements into additional regression equations he produced.

Returning to the events that led up to the realisation of new test facilities at Feltham, a working party was formed which included staff from Ship Division, Ministry of Works and others such as Sir William Halcrow and Partners who advised on engineering matters. With the site now settled, positive progress could be made but a hiccup brought an immediate revision of the plans. An estimate of the cost of building came out well above the target figure of £2 million and all ideas of a shallow tank, two carriages for the main tank and a steering pond had to be abandoned. The only way £2 million could be reached was to shorten the tank to 400 metres and build it above ground thus saving an expensive excavation into ground which had a high water table. A revised proposal and cost estimate was submitted to the Treasury and final agreement to proceed was received in 1954 with the promise of further finance at a later date for the provision of a circulating water channel. The main contract was let to Sir Robert McAlpine and Sons in the autumn and on a blustery morning in March 1955 a group of Ship Division staff with the Director of NPL and members of the Froude Committee gathered around Sir William Stanier, the chairman of the Committee. He stood at the spot that marked one end of the huge tank that was to be. A stainless steel spade was handed to Sir William and with due ceremony the first sod was cut.

In 1956 the new facilities at Feltham were just two years away and Allan realised that a reorganisation of the scientific staff would become necessary to meet the new challenge as well as to maintain fully the capability at Teddington. It was also clear that supervision by one man of all the work in progress, as in Baker and Kent days, was now unrealistic. Some delegation had in fact already taken place such as to Hughes in his friction work and to Silverleaf on cavitation tunnel work. Calling his senior staff together Allan devised a system of working groups, each of which would concentrate on a specific type of work and be led by a group head who would become responsible for the work done. In January 1956 the scientific staff totalled 41. Ten were in the SO class, 23 EO and eight Assistants. They were now split into six groups headed by Hughes, Shearer, Dawson, Doust, Goodrich and Silverleaf. Dawson led a team of 14 which carried out commercial test work and the remaining 27 concentrated on different areas of research and development. This surprised the staff since it seemed that most would be involved in research work only. It also caused some resentment amongst those placed in the commercial group since it was inferred that more interesting and glamorous research work, as it was seen by most, would be denied them. In fact the whole plan was intended to be flexible and soon it became inevitable, due to a continuing heavy demand for commercial work (in 1957, 43 model hulls and 58 propeller models were made and tested for firms), that some of those on the research side became involved in commercial work from time to time. For example, if these included experiments in waves then those engaged in seakeeping research did the tests. As the new arrangements settled a drive for more staff began in anticipation of an expansion in work when the Feltham facilities became available. The workshops, at least for the time being, with 28 mechanics and semi-skilled workers were reasonably staffed but both the research and commercial sides needed strengthening.

Soon after the 1956 reorganisation T.E. Carmichael, J.W. English, J.A. Ewing and B.N. Steele arrived straight from University. Carmichael had done postgraduate research in association with BSRA and on arrival at Ship Division began propeller vibration studies which were sadly curtailed on his unexpected death at the early age of 29. English and Steele worked with Silverleaf, English soon becoming attracted to propeller design problems. Both stayed to serve for many years. Ewing, a pure science graduate from Glasgow, had pursued postgraduate work in mathematics at Birmingham and it was not long before he became involved in waves and wave-making. Developments in measuring apparatus and instrumentation were expected and with electronics, a rapidly emerging field, expertise was needed. Garlick, whose great experience lay in mechanical devices, needed support and two newcomers already at NPL were transferred to Ship Division. These were H.B. Boyle, a mechanical engineer who was allocated to Silverleaf's group and later headed a design team and H.G. Loe to Shearer's where he began to establish a small group of electronic engineers.

Allan had laid the foundation for the organisation of work at the emerging new facilities. Before Feltham materialised the Division received a shattering blow when he died of a heart attack in June 1957 whilst on holiday in Suffolk. At the height of his powers it was tragic that the realisation of such spectacular new model test facilities was denied him. It is certain he would have led the Division into a new era with confidence, and his practical grasp and appreciation of the needs of the shipbuilding industry would have been valuable assets in balancing the conflicting demands for commercial and research work at a time when the fundamental principles of ship model testing were being challenged. He handled potentially awkward situations with the newly formed BSRA with skill, particularly over the allocation of work in collaborative projects. Allan was a sociable man with a twinkle in his eye and was never happier than when entertaining the many visitors to the Tank. He supported the ITTC staunchly and was keen to see co-operation between British tanks as a way to a consistent approach to model testing. Such co-operation was formalised in 1958 with the setting up of the British Towing Tank Panel. Superintendents of the principal ship model testing establishments agreed to meet occasionally and discuss matters of mutual interest and the BTTP grew to include other smaller organisations involved in model testing. Without funds it nevertheless found opportunities to pursue research work such as resistance and propulsion tests on a standard model run in each member tank in turn.

It was a critical time to look for a new Superintendent. In the interim Hughes was asked to take charge. Todd who had left for the Washington tank in 1948 was approached and after some uncertainty accepted to become Ship Division's fourth Superintendent. No doubt the opportunity of being associated with the launch of modern facilities was irresistible but Todd nevertheless stipulated certain conditions, mainly over being free to undertake consultancy work. Subsequently these were either unfulfilled or seen to have been misunderstood, a situation that contributed to his short stay as Superintendent. In 1961 he accepted an invitation to return to Washington. Todd's credentials were of course superb but when he took office in 1958 it was not long before he applied a managerial style that was quite unknown at Teddington, which many thought had its roots in American practice. The group system was given every encouragement to the extent that any communication was transmitted up or down the hierarchical line with little direct contact with the staff. Baker would have looked on in disbelief. Perhaps numbers speak for themselves; Baker had a total staff of 18 in 1918; 40 years later Todd had 93. But exciting times were imminent. The new tank and workshops were soon to be completed.

REFERENCES

1. Kent J.L., *Ships in rough water*, published by Nelson, 1958.
2. Brown T.W.F., "The measurement of power", trans. INA, 1955.
3. Walker W.P., "Detection of Laminar Flow on Ship Models", trans. INA, 1949.
4. Allan J.F. and Conn J.F.C., "Detection of laminar flow on ship models", trans. INA, 1949.
5. Ayre A.L. Sir, "Some observations concerning resistance and propulsion", trans. INA, 1950.
6. Hughes G. and Allan J.F., "Turbulence stimulation on ship models", trans. SNAME, 1951.
7. Silverleaf A. and Bailey D., "Wake traverses and alignment of stern appendages", NPL, Ship Division Report 5, 1959.
8. Silverleaf A. and Berry L.W., "Recent work in the Lithgow water tunnel at NPL", trans. IESS, Vol. 100, 1956/57.
9. Silverleaf A. and O'Brien T.P., "Some effects of blade section shape on model screw performance", trans. NECIES, Vol. 71, 1954/55.
10. Robb A.M., "Interaction between ships", trans. INA, 1949.
11. Almy N.V. and Hughes G., "Model experiments on a series of 0·65 block coefficient forms", Part I, trans. INA, 1954.
12. Ferguson J.M. and Meek M., *Ibid*, Part II.
13. Conn J.F.C. *et al*, "BSRA resistance experiments on the *Lucy Ashton*. Part II. The ship-model correlation for the naked hull condition", trans. INA, 1953.

14. Hughes G., "Tank boundary effects on model resistance", trans. RINA, 1961.
15. Hughes G., "Frictional resistance of smooth plane surfaces in turbulent flow", trans. INA, 1952.
16. Hughes G., "Friction and form resistance in turbulent flow and a proposed formulation for use in model and ship correlation", trans. INA, 1954.
17. Allan J.F. and Cutland R.S., "The effect of roughness on ship resistance", trans. NECIES, Vol. 72, 1955/56.
18. Cutland R.S., "Velocity measurements in close proximity to a ship's hull", trans. NECIES, Vol. 74, 1957/58.
19. Harrison P.W. and Garlick H.C., "A new method for checking the profile of large marine propellers", Symposium on Engineering Dimensional Metrology, NPL, 1953.
20. Burrill L.C., "On propeller manufacture", trans. INA, 1954.
21. Doust D.J., "Side launching of ships—with special reference to trawlers", trans. INA, 1955.
22. Doust D.J. and MacDonald E., "Further experiments in sideways launching—Series 2 and 3", trans. INA, 1957.
23. Dawson J., "Resistance and propulsion of single screw coasters. Part IV, L/B = 5½", trans, IESS, Vol. 102, 1958/59.
24. Todd F.H. and Marwood W.J., "Ship vibration", trans. NECIES, Vol. 64, 1947/48.
25. Allan J.F., Doust D.J, and Ware B.E., "Yacht testing", trans. INA, 1957.
26. Doust D.J., "Statistical analysis of resistance data for trawlers", *Fishing Boats of the World*, 2, 1960.

CHAPTER 11

A THIRD TANK AND MORE

In 1763 Major General William Roy who had just left the Army for whom he had surveyed and superintended road buildings for troops, was asked by the Government to determine the relative position of the Observatories in London and Paris. Using the technique of triangulation he constructed a series of triangles from London to Dover beginning from an accurately measured base line which he chose to lay down on Hounslow Heath. The terminal points of Roy's base, marked by cannon barrels set into the ground, were at what is now Roy Grove in Hampton, Middlesex and a point near Hatton at one corner of the Heath. Jesse Ramsden designed and delivered to Roy a 120 cm diameter theodolite (now preserved at the Royal Society) which was required to measure the included angles in each triangle. The length of the base was measured three times by Roy over a three month period in 1784 using cased glass tubing, deal rods and a coffered steel chain. The measurements were within a few centimetres of each other and their mean established the length of the base as 8,352 metres. The whole exercise aroused a great deal of scientific interest and the King with several distinguished savants visited the site. Roy's triangles later became the foundation of topographical surveys of Middlesex, Surrey, Sussex and Kent. How fitting then, that 170 years after these famous measurements new facilities for scientific excellence were to be built to cross Roy's base—the mid-point of the new towing tank would intersect Roy's line. Not that this was a deliberate choice because, as has already been noted, several sites for the new facilities were considered before the land at Feltham became available. Three of these were rejected; at Ham common near the suspension bridge at Teddington, at Sunbury near a disused Thames barge terminal and at Hanworth where the old airport there had what appeared to be ideal land. Borings at Ham and Sunbury showed unsatisfactory soil and unfortunately at Hanworth it had already been decided to run a new water main across the preferred run of the tank. However, the land at Feltham was equally good with sufficient flat terrain for the size of the proposed buildings and plenty to spare for possible extensions at a later date. Whilst permission to begin building was being awaited, records of ground temperature variation and fluctuations of soil water level were taken, and A.E. Hewitt in describing constructional aspects of the new laboratory building[1] reported that the highest recorded water table in the subsoil was only 2½ metres below the ground. This was important and in the cost saving exercise of 1952 it became clear that the tank should be built above ground despite the disadvantage that this would bring when transferring large ship models from ground floor workshops to the test tank some 10 metres above.

As has already been seen, the overall length of the tank was limited, also for reasons of cost, to 400 metres. The effects of tank blockage on model measurements which had been thoroughly researched by Hughes helped to determine width and breadth. The prospect of a large tank offered a real opportunity to reduce model scale effects which were particularly troublesome in tests on multi-screw hulls. Thus larger models than those normally used at Teddington could be considered. Although 12 metres was envisaged but never in fact realised as normal practice, a 7¼ metres long model was taken as typical for the new tank. Such a model would normally have an underwater cross-sectional area of 0·4 square metres. Hughes had shown that interference from the boundaries of a towing tank was within acceptable limits of experimental accuracy if a model's area was less than 0·4 per cent of the tank cross-sectional area. A satisfactory tank area was thus 100 square metres which for a breadth/depth ratio of 2:1 gave a 14 metres × 7 metres tank. The final dimensions chosen (14.6 metres × 7.6 metres) included a small margin and meant that the tank breadth was twice the length of an average model and 15 times its beam. Also for a depth of 7·6 metres the speed of the wave of translation was 8·5 metres per second and this critical speed was well above that needed for tests on 7¼ metre models of merchant ships. For high speed craft which would reach such a speed and beyond, models, for practical reasons, would be smaller and with 7·6 metres of water beneath them (a length/depth ratio of about 0·5) bottom effect would be negligible.

The dimensions of the tank were thus settled as 400 metres × 14·6 metres × 7·6 metres. Carriage speed was the next consideration, a maximum capability of 15 metres per second over a reasonable length being required. To achieve and maintain this for say five seconds within the length of the tank would depend on carriage acceleration and braking distance. As at the time of the design of Number Two tank carriage, rubber wheels were considered since these would give a greater acceleration compared with steel. However, the loads expected on a carriage with a span of 15¼ metres ruled out the idea. With dry polished steel wheels running over steel rails it was considered that an acceleration of 0·1 g or 1 metre per second squared would be possible without slip and if braking acceleration was 0·25 g then a 15¼ metres long carriage weighing 40 tons would travel 180 metres in accelerating to 15 metres per second and 61 metres in coming to rest. With a margin of safety of 33 metres this left a distance of 110 metres over which the carriage would run steadily at its top speed, or seven seconds. For a more usual top test speed of say 6 metres per second, 300 metres of steady run was possible which for experiments in waves seemed acceptable.

The fundamental design and specification for the new tank, workshops, and buildings progressed in parallel with a study of the needs of the new cavitation tunnel. Silverleaf was faced with severe requirements. To test 60 cm diameter propellers which would produce a thrust up to 2 tons was nothing compared to the decision to build a huge U section which would act as a giant resorber slowing the circulating water in the tunnel and subjecting it to a high hydrostatic pressure so that bubbles of air produced by a cavitating body would be forced back into solution. But this is what Silverleaf's design study[2] showed and the specification for the tunnel asked for a complete circuit 55 metres tall capable of circulating water up to a maximum speed of 15 metres per second with an automatic control system that would vary the pressure in the tunnel circuit. As in the towing tank blockage was considered and the size of the working section was chosen in the light of experience gained in the Lithgow tunnel. Here it had been seen that a 25 cm diameter propeller experienced little interference from the 45 cm square working section and this ratio of propeller/working section was taken for the new tunnel. A circular section was preferred and chosen to be 1 metre in diameter. Its length was 2¼ metres.

With the specification for the new facilities settled and a budget of £2 million agreed building could begin in earnest and even as Sir William Stanier was completing the ceremony of cutting the first sod bulldozers were clearing the top soil to make way for the foundations of the tank. The architect (H.A. Snow of the Chief Architects Division, Ministry of Works) produced a design that was modern, functional yet uninspiring. To achieve an appearance aesthetically pleasing was difficult but not impossible. The site, apart from the pear trees that remained from the orchard land and which were very attractive in springtime, was dull as were the immediate environs. More important the extreme dimensions of the tank unbalanced the whole design and of course there were budgetry constraints. The unimaginative design that emerged looked like so many other office blocks that were becoming popular and could have been improved if the long unrelieved façades to tank and offices had not been adhered to and if traditional building materials particularly brick had been used. The large areas of corrugated asbestos cladding and the regimented rows of identical steel framed windows detracted rather than added to the overall appearance. Within, the building was more successful. Beginning at the entrance, a reception area decorated on one wall by a mosaic opened to a curved staircase which led to first floor offices and a library. The mosaic, a symbolic representation of the work of Ship Division was either admired or hated. J.H. Nichols who in 1978 became the first Administrator to take charge preferred to cover it with display boards describing current work in progress. A door from the reception led to a large assembly area the east side of which was the high end wall, almost entirely glazed, of the tank building. A futuristic flight of steps with a lift nearby led up to the tank itself with its carriage, a sight that rarely failed to impress. Elsewhere, model storage and manoeuvring tank, workshops, etc. all gave an impression of space and flexibility. Soon after construction began, Allan described the new facilities to the INA.[3] His paper, read a few months before his death, dealt with technical as well as constructional details and it was greeted with much enthusiasm in anticipation of the opportunities for research that lay ahead. Progress in building was good. From the start in March 1955, a target for completion was set for the spring of 1959. This was met comfortably and by late 1958 Shearer and Giles had moved to Feltham and were followed by several others who began moving and testing equipment ahead of an official opening that was arranged for October 1959.

By April 1958 all the buildings and tanks were finished and a start was made on the long and demanding task of laying the carriage rails and installing the carriage. The carriage was being built by Craven's at Sheffield and sufficient length of rail for a 550 metres long tank was made by the Lanarkshire Steel Company (the spare rails in 6 metre lengths were eventually stored behind the tank wavemaker). The rails were a heavy section rolled at 260 pounds per metre and three 6 metre lengths were welded together and then placed on top of the tank wall and laid on chairs at 1 metre centres. Each 18 metre length was aligned to the next before welding both together and so on for the entire 400 metres run of the tank. The whole operation and setting took six months, alignment being so precise that the rails followed the mean curvature of the earth—the deviation in straightness over 400 metres was 3 mm NPL's Metrology Division checked this and pronounced accuracy to be within $\pm$ 0·03 mm a remarkable achievement that bore fruit when the carriage was later seen to run exceedingly smoothly without serious vibration at all speeds.

The design of the carriage and, in particular, its drive and speed control system was far from straightforward. A rigid instrument platform was required with visibility to the water below unimpeded by too many structural members. It was designed to tow models up to 5 tons in weight. Four girders formed a framework 15¼ metres square, open inside to give an 11 metres square space into which a dynamometer and instrumentation beam could be placed longitudinally. The beam could be set at any transverse position or removed altogether if necessary. The carriage structure was made up of triangular frameworks of steel tubing and the whole assembly carried propulsion motors, speed control gear and carriage brakes. When moving, the carriage would experience loads from acceleration and retardation forces and also a certain amount of lift from towed bodies. Vertical vibration would be excited at some speed within the range and although small it might be magnified by the carriage structure, perhaps by a magnification factor between 50 and 100. A study examined the case of a two-wheeled bogie running over rails supported by chairs and showed that vibration could be reduced by careful selection of wheel and chair spacing. The preferred arrangement found was for the carriage to be driven by four two-wheeled bogies located at the corners with wheels spaced at two thirds of the chair spacing (70 cm). The choice of 68 cm diameter wheels meant the gap between each pair was just 2 cm.

Power to drive the carriage at its top speed was calculated to be 1,200 h.p., 200 of this to overcome the wind resistance of the structure. Four 300 h.p. DC motors, one at each corner, were connected in series parallel and supplied by a

Ward Leonard set located ashore. Speed control was vital and an accuracy of $\pm$ 0·1 per cent was called for using an automatic system similar to those already in successful use on the carriages at Teddington. Normal regenerative braking was selected for speeds up to 6 metres per second but for higher speeds spring operated mechanical friction brakes were used. These were held off the brake rails (which ran parallel to the carriage running track) pneumatically so that the arrangement would fail to safety in the event of loss of air supply. As an emergency measure, an aircraft arrester gear was fitted. The gear and its shock absorbing nylon harness was obtained from the aircraft carrier *Hermes*. Apart from initial tests, which were restricted to a speed of 12 metres per second for fear of distorting the carriage, it was never used.

The dynamometry for calm water resistance measurements and seakeeping experiments was the responsibility of Ship Division. The resistance dynamometer was built along the lines of that in Number One tank except that it was much larger and capable of a maximum measurement of 100 pounds. A heavy balance beam 1 metre long carried a weight which was driven along the beam by a motor and the spring response was transferred electrically to a Honeywell Brown recorder. The seakeeping dynamometer which permitted pitch, heave and surge but restrained the model in yaw, sway and roll was fitted into a longitudinal runway which allowed a generous amount of surge. This greatly assisted control as the model was propelled and accelerated with the carriage to the test speed. Pitch and heave were obtained by potentiometer and a wave probe fixed to the carriage in line with the model gave continuous records of wave height met by the model.

The towing tank was completed by the addition of a wavemaker at its west end and also by beaches. With the wavemaker in operation a beach spanning the tank at its east end was required and disturbance from a towed model in calm water had to be damped by a second similar beach at the other end and also by smaller beaches along the sides of the tank. The side beaches were simple curved flaps 60 cm wide and hinged to the wall above the water so that they could be raised clear when waves were generated by the wavemaker. The transverse beaches were larger versions of that in Number One tank and fabricated on 2 metre diameter tubes which acted as carrying beams and buoyancy tanks for use when raising or lowering. The specification for the wavemaker called for the generation of uniform trains of parallel waves up to 12 metres long and ⅔ metre high. Larger height/length ratios or steeper waves could be chosen by shortening the wave lengths. The defects of the wavemaker at Teddington had been identified by Goodrich who had also noted the need for vertical sided tank walls. It was concluded that of the different kinds of wavemaker available the plunger type was preferable. A deep wedge was designed with a hollow face of exponential form. It was fabricated in steel and set on guides into vertical rails fixed to the end wall of the tank. Hydraulic rams driven by a pump displaced the plunger up and down, the pump operating on a sinusoidal pressure cycle to give a regular series of waves. By varying the pressure cycle irregular waves could be produced.

The original proposal for a manoeuvring basin was for an area of water about 1,500 square metres. In the cost saving exercise this was reduced by the needs of a storage space for models. This left a 30 metre square for manoeuvring once a dividing wall had been erected and the south and east walls of this area were strengthened for the installation of plunger type wavemakers. It was planned that these would be articulated to enable a confused sea to be generated but at the last moment there was not enough money for this. The wavemaker that did appear on the south wall was, as a result, built to a strict budget. A wedge shaped plunger was mechanically operated by an adjustable crank and driven by an electric motor. Waves up to 5 metres long and 0·2 metre high were possible but never proved to be of ideal form. The control of models by radio link had been successfully developed by Jenkins and the same principle was tried at Feltham. However, the radio control system that had performed reasonably at Teddington refused to work under the aluminium roof at Feltham because of low signal strength. Loe faced a difficult problem which he overcame by fitting an array of parallel overhead aerials. This was a partial solution and with the assistance of NPL's Control Mechanisms Division a better system was finally found at the same time as the development of a method for tracking the paths of models as they manoeuvred around the basin.

The new cavitation tunnel was housed in a separate building and the outstanding feature of the tunnel was its resorber. One of the problems of cavitation tunnels is the maintenance of clear water of defined air content during cavitation tests. Bubbles arising from the cavitating body unless forced back into solution reappear at the test section with the recirculating water and hinder visibility. As mentioned, Silverleaf's study[2] had concluded that a deep resorber circuit of large volume was needed laid out in the form of a U tube.

A photographic laboratory complete with dark room was built alongside the cavitation tunnel building. The demand for photographs had grown to such a level that a permanent photographer was required and arranged by the secondment of a member of NPL's central photographic department.

By late 1958 most of the construction work was finished and efforts could be turned to an official opening of the new laboratory. Before describing this event it is of interest to review the number of towing tanks that existed worldwide at the time of the appearance of Ship Division's third tank. In 1960 there were 34 tanks of length 60 metres or more in existence. Britain had nine, two at Haslar, one each at Clydebank, Cowes, Dumbarton and St. Albans and now three at NPL. Abroad there were five in the USA, three in Germany, two in France, Holland, Japan and the USSR whilst Austria, Canada, India, Italy, Norway, Spain, Sweden, Turkey and Yugoslavia each had one. If 12 smaller tanks were included an impressive total of 46 was reached and Britain enjoyed a dominant share, almost 25 per cent. And more were to come. Within a few years the MoD had added a very large manoeuvring basin to their facilities at Haslar, Ship

Division would soon boast its promised circulating water channel and abroad several new tanks were on the drawing board.

The formal opening of such imposing facilities was rightly considered an important event in British shipbuilding. An approach was made to Buckingham Palace for a "Royal" opening for it was hoped that Prince Philip, the Duke of Edinburgh would agree to perform the opening ceremony. As he had already visited Ship Division seven years earlier it was feared that he might decline, but such worries were quickly dispelled by his obvious interest in ships of all kind. A date was agreed and there followed intense preparations, both organisational and technical in nature. Although it was unrealistic to expect all the facilities to be fully operational it was important to put on a "good show". Nevertheless demonstrations of tests in each facility did not come easily. At the last moment essential gear failed to work. The crane needed to lift the 7 metre model to be run in the tank broke down and was repaired only the day before the opening, the difficulties of controlling a free-running model in the manoeuvring tank already referred to were resolved only at the 11th hour and at the cavitation tunnel a build up of pressure blew out a window in the test section and the propeller shaft was found to be out of true. The blow-out could have had serious consequences. As it was adjacent offices were flooded by escaping water and fortunately nobody was injured. The shaft was rushed to a nearby engineering company and returned and installed 24 hours before the opening.

In the morning of opening day, 19 October 1959, some 90 representatives from Industry, Universities and Research organisations were welcomed by the Director of NPL and shown around the facilities. The Duke with his equerry were expected after lunch and were preceded by Lord Hailsham, who just three hours earlier had been sworn in as Britain's first Minister for Science. Precisely on cue the Duke arrived to be welcomed at the entrance gates by a contingent of 70 sea cadets from Feltham who handled his personal Standard on the flagstaff. Received in the reception area by Lord Hailsham he was conducted to a special platform erected in the assembly area before which were waiting 150 additional guests and about 100 Ship Division staff, an audience of almost 350. After an introduction by Lord Hailsham the Duke delivered a typical speech in which he stressed the importance of achieving the right balance between fundamental research into ship design and solutions to everyday practical problems in an environment that was becoming increasingly competitive in shipping and shipbuilding industries. He argued that liaison between the research scientist and the user was important and recommended that "every scientist working here should be forced to make at least one journey by sea, say across the Atlantic and back, every year". Such utterances by royalty are not taken lightly and the Duke's recommendation was in fact followed up soon afterwards when a few members of staff were allocated passages across the Atlantic to gain first hand experience. Having unveiled a plaque set up behind him, the Duke declared the new laboratory open and was then presented by Todd with a memento of his visit, a paperweight in the form of a model of one of the propellers of *HMS*

Magpie, the Duke's first independent command. There then followed a tour of the laboratory. At the tank the Duke was shown a 7 metre model of a cable-laying ship running in waves. From there a short walk to the tunnel to see an experiment on a cavitating propeller and finally, at the manoeuvring tank, a trawler model was being driven remotely in calm water. This demonstration proved specially attractive. After watching Lord Hailsham's clumsy (deliberate?) attempts at controlling the model the Duke brushed him aside to take control amidst much hilarity. The Duke had clearly enjoyed his visit and in a letter of thanks his equerry wrote to say that "the Duke was delighted with his *Magpie* propeller and had discussed cavitation in the car all the way home".

The new facilities occupying as they did a separate site five miles from Teddington were initially given the title Ship Hydrodynamics Laboratory, SHL, a name which did not, however, stick. It did perhaps suggest a laboratory quite separate from NPL or Ship Division, which of course it was not. The new experiment facilities quite naturally became known as Number Three tank, Number Four (the manoeuvring tank), Four A (storage pond) and the new cavitation tunnel, Number Two tunnel.

Opening day had been an unqualified success and after the excitement staff set about the teething problems that inevitably arose from sophisticated facilities. There were four main sources of trouble, difficulty in tracking models in Number Four tank, speed control of Number Three tank carriage, the wavemakers and the propeller shaft in the cavitation tunnel.

At the time of the opening, the sonic system for tracking models had not been developed and even the control of models using the last minute overhead aerials worked fitfully. A new approach to the latter was needed and Loe began using low frequency and induction equipment with a synchronous system that controlled by relays the rudder and drive motor in the model. This took almost four years to perfect. Meanwhile manoeuvring experiments were filled with frustration and breakdown.

The successful control of carriage speed also took a long time. Speed holding between 1½ and 6 metres per second gave no problem but at speeds above and below these limits an accuracy of only ± 0·25 per cent in actual speed obtained was possible and there was also some variation during a run. The propulsion system for the carriage was a complex, high-gain servomechanism and it was difficult fully to align and adjust the electronic control. English Electric, the contractors, seconded an engineer to the tank who spent almost 18 months trying alternative circuit and valve arrangements before an acceptable ± 0·1 per cent was reached. Had more been known of solid state systems then a suitable one would almost certainly have been tried at the outset.

There were problems with the automatic control of Number Three tank wavemaker. It was important that the plunger fitted closely to the side of the tank with no misalignment between the two hydraulic rams. During operation it was soon obvious that this was not so and the rams could not be made to work in complete harmony. As a consequence, inconsistent waves were produced.

The servomechanism associated with the drive gear gave similar problems to the carriage control and ultimately a contract was let in 1960 for the development and manufacture of a different type of servo to control the motion of the plunger and an harmonic synthesiser which combined simultaneously 16 frequencies at fixed relative values. At the same time improvements were made to the alignment problem. A year later with the synthesiser installed things were better but not perfect. Irregular waves were limited to peak accelerations in the synthesiser which if exceeded cut out and stopped the wavemaker. Nevertheless a good range of regular and irregular waves were possible and the peak accelerations could often be avoided by careful selection of model scale and the resulting maximum wave height requirement.

The completion of the cavitation tunnel equipment was severely delayed by engineering difficulties. It was not finally accepted from the contractors until late 1961. Experiments were possible between delays but were restricted by whirling in the propeller shaft. An alternative support arrangement for the shaft which consisted of five rather than three bearings was considered and some model experiments done on a small rig. But the three bearing system was retained after many modifications. Silverleaf who played such an important part in the commissioning had accepted a post as visiting Fellow to the California Institute of Technology. His absence for six months from the end of 1959 delayed the solutions to the problems at the tunnel, but by 1962 Ship Division was able to state in its Annual Report that both tunnels (the Lithgow tunnel had in the meantime been dismantled, modified and re-erected next to Number Two tunnel in the same building at Feltham—thereafter it was called Number One tunnel) had operated well during the year. Spectacular examples of cavitation could be demonstrated in the large tunnel as for example the super cavitating propeller in plate 58. This photograph became much sought after and was reproduced on numerous occasions in brochures and technical magazines.

Soon after the opening, in the spring of 1960, the INA celebrated its centenary. It had just received a Royal Charter and as the Royal Institution of Naval Architects it asked to include a visit to Feltham in its celebrations. Some 200 visitors invited by RINA arrived in the morning and after lunch in a marquee set up in the grounds a conducted tour was arranged. On view for the first time was a $\frac{1}{10}$-scale model of a circulating water channel, the prototype of the promised facility. The model was used to provide information on sump and pump layout and to try out different circuits for the circulating water. Steele had taken charge of the model and with Cross was measuring velocity distribution in the working section. The results[4] later formed the basis of the full-size channel. The model was so useful for other work, for example the calibration of hot wire probes that it was kept and is still in use today. In the morning of the RINA visit Ship Division was delighted to receive the award of RINA's Gold medal. This was unique since it had been the Institution's practice to award the medal to an individual but now it had been given to the whole staff of Ship Division for, in the words of Lord Runciman, RINA's President, "the outstanding contribution it had made to objects which are precisely what the Institution exists to promote". In accepting the medal Todd acknowledged the Institution's role in bringing into existence Ship Division's first tank 50 years earlier (Ship Division itself was celebrating its jubilee) and the fact that RINA retained a presence on the Froude Research Committee as well as administering the Froude Research Scholarship which brought its recipient to Ship Division for at least a year. Ship Division had always supported RINA and Todd was able to recall that over its 50 years the Division had contributed 76 papers to the Transactions of the Institution.

With Feltham now established and most of the teething problems out of the way it was essential that sufficient staff were available to man all the facilities. When Todd began as Superintendent in 1958 the total staff was 93 of which 25 were in the workshops. This was by no means enough when Feltham materialised, and a drive to recruit people was launched with the approval of DSIR who had committed itself to increases in hydrodynamic and aerodynamic areas. But with the expansive 1960s not yet reached it was difficult to obtain suitable candidates. Three stalwarts in the EO class were however recruited at this time, D.W. Strike and G.L. Taylor from Devonport dockyard and S.P. Ghosh who had been trained at a shipyard in Calcutta. All three spent the rest of their careers in Ship Division amassing in the process almost 100 years of service between them. From 1961 there was a larger influx and by the time Todd resigned in 1962 numbers had grown to 122, an increase of 29 in four years. In 1961 the Division welcomed G.E. Gadd on transfer from NPL's Aerodynamics Division. Gadd had been at NPL since 1950 and had rapidly built a reputation as a fine theoretical and practical aerodynamicist, qualities that were to prove ideal to Ship Division's needs. In a quiet and unassuming way he contributed importantly in extending Wigley's earlier work and in opening new frontiers in numerical analysis as applied to hydrodynamic flow and basic hull design. A third Froude scholar, J.F. Wellicome from Newcastle University arrived in 1961 to work on the measurement of model wakes and eventually became a permanent member of staff. Newcomers included G.P. White who worked with Dawson for a few years.

The workshops with Dolman in overall charge supported by artificers Camp and Oinn who supervised model manufacture and wood working, had 47 mechanics. Altogether in 1962 there were 14 SO, 37 EO, 16 Assistants and Tracers and 5 secretarial posts. Plate 60 shows the staff gathered before the staircase to Number Three tank with Dr Sutherland, Director of NPL alongside Hughes and Todd.

Apart from 1959 when a noticeable drop in the demand for routine tests was seen, work for firms continued unabated. During 1959–60 the manufacture of models was gradually transferred from Teddington to Feltham. The first wax casting at Feltham was on Christmas Eve 1959 and the last at Teddington in the following March. The recovery in demand in 1960 saw 76 wax models made and tested in the year. Most of these, and all future models, had to be transported to Teddington by road but any subsequent hull modification or the fitting of propulsion gear was done at Teddington. Until such times as models were made larger than the normal size for Teddington there was no point in running them at Feltham unless experiment programmes could be speeded up by conducting more than one experiment in a single run down the long Number Three tank. This of course was possible and attractive, but a dilemma arose. The correlation factors used in final estimates of ship power had been derived from work on normal size models in Number One tank and could not, with confidence, be used for larger models in a different tank. It was becoming clear that Number Three tank was destined to become a research facility and a place where high speed tests and unusual work could be done. Meanwhile at Teddington, 1961 and 1962 were very busy years. Number One tank was fully booked with some evening work needed.

TESTS FOR FIRMS

A wide range of ship type was tested including the emerging ro-ro ferry, larger tankers and Great Lakes steamers. Useful improvements were still being achieved after hull modification and in several cases reduction in power up to 12 per cent were obtained. It was at this time that the first tests on Cunard's *Queen Elizabeth II* were done, the design at the time being known as Q3. In Number Two tank, propeller tests in open water, current meter calibrations and experiments with tracked vehicles for the Fighting Vehicles Research Establishment occupied most of the available time. The work on amphibious tanks had been going on for some time and Poulton faced many problems in these awkward tests. Special investigations were made from time to time such as towing tests in 1962 on a section of the new Severn bridge. These experiments helped to solve the problems when floating the sections into place. An unusual project ideally suited to Number Three tank was the idea of transporting oil by flexible barges, the dracone. Experiments in waves with the dracone partially filled showed that with its skin lightly loaded at rest flexibility in waves improved to give a better ride except when waves approached head on to the dracone. In this case the fluid surged longitudinally alternatively pressurising the nose and tail. An awkward snaking and whiplash motion developed and led to attempts at reducing this by fitting stabilising rings around the dracone. Also in Number Three tank some very demanding tests were done for the Ingersoll Kalamazoo company on a high speed amphibious vehicle. To provide sufficient propulsion power to the model at the high test speeds a small lightweight model was necessary. To keep hull weight to a minimum the model was made in balsa, the retracting wheels and hinged flap aft being excellently crafted in the wood shop. At speed the less than robust model failed to withstand the vibration from the propulsion gearing and only by valiant and determined efforts by Crewe and Wyatt was the model kept in one piece for the duration of the tests. At such moments of exasperation those involved hated to be defeated and this particular job with its continual breakdown saw experimenters and all concerned working in the tank past midnight on several occasions. The extreme depth of the new tank made it particularly suited to tests on submerged bodies. Government and Service Departments hired the tank, bringing models and sometimes full size objects for test.

In 1961 the first experiments on an offshore structure were done in Ship Division, in Number Four tank. A deep sea platform *Triton* designed to be supported on a triangular buoyancy chamber 25 metres below the water surface was to be moored by three weights anchored to the sea bed. The behaviour in waves of such a structure was examined on a model the size of which was tailored to the depth of water in Number Four tank. Different wave conditions were produced, film records taken and predictions reached for the behaviour of the prototype platform.

RESEARCH

Statistical Analysis of Trawler Data

Doust continued with his analyses of trawler performance data. Concentrating on model resistance data from NPL archives he carried out further statistical analyses and developed a method of minimising the resistance equation whereby, for a given speed, optimum hull parameters could be found which would give superior performance relative to earlier results.[5] If such a method worked then a powerful tool for design had been discovered. Doust tested the accuracy of his prediction of resistance by running models having the optimum hull parameters. Agreement was remarkably good and convincing evidence of the power of regression analysis techniques if used properly, i.e. with hull forms of similar character. Doust next turned to propulsive aspects and produced further equations for propulsive coefficient. The hull parameters included in the analysis needed careful selection and the standard error in the prediction of QPC of only 1½ per cent was an impressive result. Doust's progress was being followed with interest. It was supported by the advantages of the new computer technology. Unfortunately for Ship Division, and the industry, Doust's departure to Canada in 1964 cut short his opportunities for further research but in later years others, notably Holtrop at Wageningen, recognised the value of such analysis and began applying the technique to other ship types.

Hull Resistance and Tank to Tank Comparisons

The tests on BSRA's methodical series continued with models of 0·80 block coefficient and a general research into measured model resistance was initiated by the BTTP. A standard model (model 3933) was made in glass fibre and tested in each of the Clydebank, Dumbarton, St. Albans and Teddington (Number

One) tanks. This aroused interest worldwide and copies of the model taken from the same mould were made and tested in 12 foreign tanks. The results were reported to the ITTC and gave very comprehensive tank-to-tank comparisons and information on day-to-day variation in measured resistance.

Seakeeping

Perhaps the most important item of research during this period was that followed co-operatively by AEW (Haslar), BSRA, the National Institute of Oceanography and Ship Division. This dealt with the seagoing qualities of ships and had a threefold purpose. First, an investigation of full-scale seagoing conditions would be made on ships. Second, methods of simulating these conditions in the towing tank would be developed which would allow the third objective, a fundamental study of ship and model performance in waves, to be followed. The full-scale trials were handled by BSRA with AEW and Ship Division assistance and NIO supplied a wave-measuring buoy and also advised on analysis methods. The simulation of specified waves in Number Three tank obviously concentrated effort on the capability of the wavemaker and led to Goodrich becoming involved in the synthesiser control system already described. The weather ship *Weather Reporter* was made available and Hogben joined the BSRA trials party led by H.J.S. Canham which carried out 13 separate manoeuvres with the ship covering head, following, bow and beam sea directions. The ship was instrumented to measure wave height, pitch, heave and roll and taken to the north Atlantic in the autumn of 1959. In later years similar work was done on the cargo ship *Cairndhu* on passage to and from Montreal with Hogben again in the trials party, and also on the research trawler *Ernest Holt*. Much full-scale data were collected and the first set, from *Weather Reporter* together with corresponding model results formed the subject of a joint paper[6] published by members of the co-operating bodies. Kent's earlier pioneering work had failed to produce accurate and comprehensive data since adequate instrumentation was not available to him but the latest wave data from *Weather Reporter* enabled NIO to develop their techniques for determining the three-dimensional wave spectrum which defined the sea state, a major advance. The subsequent model experiments were in two parts, tests on a towed model and tests with the model propelled. Calculated values of the ship motions using the Korvin-Kroukovsky equations developed in 1957 were obtained and very satisfactory comparative diagrams produced. These were still early days in the seakeeping field and further advances came in later years, but the research could hardly have got off to a better start.

Tugs

Another item of research supported by BSRA was an investigation into tug propulsion. It was a popular view that buttock-flow lines at the stern of a tug would increase bollard pull. Dawson and Miss Hales began a series of tests on four different hull designs. Beginning with a conventional design, three others were developed which included a form with an enlarged aperture capable of swinging a large propeller, one with a buttock-flow stern and one whose forebody was also designed on buttock-flow principles. Resistance and propulsion experiments covered the static bollard condition, towing and free-running speeds. The results[7] confounded the advocates of buttock-flow. For all conditions hulls with conventional sterns gave a better performance and in the free-running condition the buttock-flow forms required about 12 per cent more power.

High Speed Craft

In the high speed field it was becoming obvious that systematic hull resistance data were needed for fast displacement craft intended to reach speeds up to a unity Froude number. Data existed but it was by no means extensive enough to satisfy current trends in building. This was appreciated by Marwood and Silverleaf at a symposium held in Holland in 1960. They had presented a paper[8] which included random resistance and propulsion data from hulls tested at NPL. Following approval from the Froude Ship Research Committee a start was made on a series of model tests on round bilge types of fast displacement craft. Marwood with Bailey searched Ship Division's records for a suitable form which could be used as a parent hull from which others could be derived. Model 2071 tested in 1941 as part of the effort at the time directed towards improving RAF rescue launches had all the right characteristics and its design in Ship Division had been based on one of Baker's earlier high speed forms. It was selected as the parent for a new series and as time permitted 21 additional forms were derived and tested in Number Three tank.

Todd who had been Superintendent during vital years that had seen the commissioning of the new facilities decided in 1961 to accept the post of Scientific Advisor to the Commanding Officer and Director of the David Taylor tank at Washington. He thus returned to where he had gone 13 years earlier. At Ship Division the time was ripe for energetic leadership and it came when Silverleaf was appointed as the fifth Superintendent in February 1962. His enthusiasm for everything he did was abundantly clear to all and he was utterly convinced of the value of research to shipbuilding and very keen to see the industry flourish. The task before him was large and the challenge to take the Division forward, in particular guide Number Three tank to its full potential, daunting.

REFERENCES

1. Hewitt A.E., "The design and construction of the new Ship Hydrodynamics laboratory buildings and tanks at Feltham, Middlesex", *The Structural Engineer*, April 1959.
2. Silverleaf A., "The design of a resorber for a water tunnel", NPL, Ship Division Report 1, 1958.
3. Allan J.F., "National Physical Laboratory. New Ship Hydrodynamics Laboratory", trans. INA, 1957.
4. Steele B.N., "A design study for a circulating water channel", NPL, Ship Division Report 26, 1962.
5. Doust D.J., "Optimised trawler forms", trans. NECIES, Vol. 79, 1962/63.
6. Canham H.J.S. *et al*, "Seakeeping Trials on O.W.S. WEATHER REPORTER", trans. RINA, 1962.
7. Parker M.N. and Dawson J., "Tug propulsion investigation", trans. RINA, 1962.
8. Marwood W.J. and Silverleaf A., "Design data for high speed displacement type hulls and a comparison with hydrofoil craft", 3rd symposium on naval hydrodynamics, Scheveningen, 1960.

CHAPTER 12

AN EXPANSION IN RESEARCH

With a brand new laboratory and 50-year-old facilities five miles away at Teddington, an immediate problem over the location of staff arose. As has been said, Feltham was not a particularly attractive place to be and many staff who had worked for so long in the pleasanter surroundings at Teddington preferred to continue there. Suddenly, five miles seemed a very long way away. Silverleaf was quick to see the danger of a dichotomy that could arise with a staff split between two sites. In striving to achieve a cohesive unit he decided to accommodate all but a very few at Feltham and to make the new laboratories there the Headquarters of the Division. The small computer group under Wellicome, which had grown in numbers, depended on close contact with Mathematics Division and its computers and it was logical that it remained at Teddington. Also Garlick, two carriage drivers and a few workshop staff essential to the efficient operation of the tanks were asked to stay.

By August 1962 the move to Feltham was complete. The original design of the buildings had not included accommodation for so many people and as a temporary measure the large hut used by the contractors during building was converted into several separate rooms and a drawing office. Eventually a matching extension to the ground and first floor offices in the main building was built and this at once relieved the congestion. The advantage of having practically all the staff together, apart from cohesion, was that the Division's customers and others knew where to come. A serious disadvantage, the full implication of which was not seen until later years, was that the removal to Feltham became to all intents and purposes a removal from NPL. Contacts with staff from other divisions that had proved so valuable on so many occasions in the past gradually weakened and newcomers to Ship Division in coming straight to Feltham saw little of NPL. Inter-divisional contact had often been made socially, for example in the Sports Club or over lunch, but again five miles was a long way away.

Silverleaf's reorganisation went further. Proper support for new areas of work as well as good management of the traditional ship model test arrangements at Teddington was needed, particularly now that all models were being made at Feltham. Silverleaf split the Division into branches. A Contracts branch led by Dawson dealt with ship design and experiments paid for by firms at home or abroad. Hughes took charge of an internal branch that dealt mainly with the research programme. He himself devoted much of his time to his own studies on skin friction in which he received staunch assistance from Cutland who was reaching the end of a distinguished career. Shearer was asked to head a Special Projects branch formed to deal with the increasing number of requests to investigate hydrodynamic problems not directly associated with new ships and finally an Equipment group under Marwood became responsible for the development and supply of instrumentation to all projects in progress. Marwood was also asked to organise the programme of work for all the experimental facilities except the cavitation tunnels that now came under English's control. There was of course some overlapping. Ship-model correlation, officially a research item, was handled by the Contracts branch, manoeuvring and experiments in waves by Hughes' branch. Goodrich concentrated on seakeeping research and W.E.A. Acum, newly transferred from Aerodynamics Division, began hydroelasticity studies. Also transferred, this time from NPL's Autonomics Division, was D.V. Blake who began developing data acquisition techniques in readiness for the time when model measurements would be largely in the form of electrical responses and amenable to on-line computer analyses.

More staff arrived in 1962–63. A year earlier a large contract of work was commissioned by the Ministry of Aviation to begin research into the hydrodynamics of hovercraft. Fundamental research into the hovercraft principle was a new departure for Ship Division and a special team of workers was needed. It was anticipated that the MoA contract would continue for several years and with tests on commercial hovercraft designs also expected a 10 per cent increase in staff, about 12 people, was planned. In fact such an increase never materialised. Initially Hogben led the work and later J.T. Everest and two others arrived to comprise a group that from time to time needed to be bolstered by existing members of staff who were enlisted for short periods. Special rigs and dynamometry were made, additional offices erected alongside Number Four tank and space found for the assembly of a static ground rig.

Altogether in 1965 Silverleaf had 140 staff (52 under Dolman in the workshops), an advance of 18 over the 1962 figure. The recruitment of scientific staff was relatively easy, clearly Feltham was gaining a certain attraction, whereas difficulty was found in encouraging workshop mechanics of good quality to join the new laboratory. In addition to those recruited to work on hovercraft projects, B.S. Bowden from BSRA joined Dawson's branch and R.J. Jacob, from the St. Albans tank, Goodrich's seakeeping group. Both were ex-Royal Dockyard apprentices, Bowden from Devonport and Jacob from Chatham, and graduates from Newcastle University. On the workshop side Dolman needed some relief in supervising workshops that were becoming more diverse and W.S. Nunn, an artificer from NPL's workshops arrived to share the responsibility. On the debit side the Division was saddened by the loss of Downey and Rixon. Downey, who had established himself firmly in Goodrich's group, died at the early age of 40, whilst Rixon, the head carpenter, died a few years before he was due to retire. E.J. Neville, a recent newcomer, was drafted into the seakeeping group and Oinn succeeded Rixon. A new post, that of Librarian, was established in 1965 and technical records, equally important to Ship Division's workers were filed and recorded by a succession of people none of whom were able to devote all of their time to an apparently dull consignment. Riddell, in his last working years, set the standard for the organisation and retrieval of historic model data but sadly this was never continued.

Hovercraft work, which eventually became too large for Ship Division to handle, is but one example of the great expansion in research stimulated by the new facilities at Feltham and over which Silverleaf presided with such vigour and enthusiasm. In the decade following the Feltham opening new areas of research in addition to hovercraft reflected the changes seen in shipbuilding. Large super tankers were appearing, a direct economic consequence of the closure of the Suez canal. Very large crude oil carriers, the VLCC up to 275,000 tons, and ultra large ULCCs of 400,000 tons represented an astonishing increase in the size of ships. All were full-formed and ideal subjects for bulbous bows, but poor flow in the afterbodies of some designs gave problems. Trawlers were changing. Fishing nets habitually worked over the sides of vessels were, in the interests of improved stability, superseded by deployment over the stern, and on-board refrigeration plant for freezing catches were being introduced. These things led to changes in hull shape. The desire for high speed cargo and the emerging containerships increased the possibility of vibration in ships which saw research into propeller-excited vibration and, so far as propellers were concerned, interest in fully cavitating and ducted types was growing. Existing topics of research were not forgotten; studies of wave resistance, components of resistance, seakeeping and ship-model correlation were by no means exhausted and continued to flourish. A proliferation of reports on these and other subjects poured forth and were available free of charge to the industry, universities and other interested parties. All of this and the regular repayment work on a wide variety of ship designs as well as special projects brought an extremely high level of activity and kept Ship Division in the forefront of maritime development.

RESEARCH

Hovercraft

The work on hovercraft was both novel and exciting. The concept of air lubrication for ships, which would reduce resistance by eliminating friction drag, offered hopes of very high speeds over water, but efforts at lubrication had failed. Whereas a supply of air to the underside of a vessel was easy, its maintenance there as the vessel moved ahead had never been achieved and air escaped only too readily from beneath the hull. Sir Christopher Cockerell's brilliant yet simple invention in 1953 at last solved the problem. He found that by injecting air through inward facing nozzles, which extended around the circumference of a craft, an air curtain seal could be formed. Cockerell's idea was recognised and supported by the National Research Development Corporation in 1958 and a new company, Hovercraft Development Ltd. was created. HDL controlled Cockerell's patents and issued licenses to build hovercraft to interested companies such as the Denny shipbuilding company at Dumbarton, BHC (a merger between Westland and Vickers-Armstrong interests), Hovermarine and Vosper Thornycroft. HDL with Denny took up Cockerell's first suggestion for a prototype vessel, which emerged as the 18 metres long D1 hovercraft. This was in fact a non-amphibious craft since Cockerell had preferred to incorporate side walls that projected downwards containing the air by these and transverse air curtain seals fitted fore and aft. Propulsion and steering came from two 50 h.p. outboard motors. D1 was succeeded in July 1962 by a larger version, the D2 and this became the subject of the first commercial hovercraft tests at NPL. Experiments in Number Three tank showed severe bow impact in head waves with heavy spray and led to a completely revised bow design which after further tests proved satisfactory. Further developments on side wall craft were seriously delayed when Denny's went into liquidation in late 1962 and efforts shifted to amphibious craft. In these, flexible peripheral extensions or skirts to the bottom of a hull were used and in later years considerable design and refinement led to different types of segmented and bagged skirts. Notable amphibious craft that appeared were the SRN series. The first cross-Channel passenger/car hovercraft, the SRN4, was 39·7 metres long and 23·5 metres wide and could carry either 610 passengers or 256 passengers and 30 cars at 55 knots. Progress with side wall craft continued with the Hovermarine and Vosper Thornycroft companies.

The MoA contract with Ship Division began with a study of the wave resistance of hovercraft and an experimental investigation into the basic theoretical assumption that the wave height at any point in the pattern of waves produced was proportional to the air cushion pressure. A simple shape was taken to represent the theoretical concept of a travelling circle of uniform pressure. Thus a circular model 1 metre in diameter was made and fitted with a single peripheral jet set at 45 degrees which, when air was pumped in, gave a circular cushion of air. Pressure in the resulting air cushion was measured at a number of points in the circle and the model supported on a dynamometer capable of measuring lift. The model was set at fixed attitudes above solid ground to give a range of hover height and trim, air being supplied from a centrifugal fan through overhead ducting. This preliminary work on the static rig was followed by experiments in Number Two tank where the model with its trunking, looking more like a giant vacuum cleaner, was set and fixed at a given attitude and towed over a range of speed in calm water. The surface wave pattern produced was measured by a series of probes set in the tank following an arrangement recently introduced by Gadd and Hogben.[1] The results of the experiments were encouraging and showed that the wave-making drag determined from the wave pattern measurements was fairly close to that from measurements of the total forces on the model system obtained from strain gauge flexures. A further comparison with the theoretical prediction was also good and as a result a clearer understanding of the influence of trim on drag was reached in terms of the airflow momentum effects. From these initial tests the next five years saw studies of cushion wave-making, jet and skirt behaviour in calm water and experiments with models in waves. A dynamometer was built to cater for partially restrained models towed in calm water and in waves in Number Three tank, the work in calm water giving data on wave-making.[2] It was soon discovered that unless a model was allowed to surge freely over a long distance forces could build up to produce a dangerous bow down trim at speed which if unchecked would cause the model to dig its nose into the water. The large operating area within the carriage structure with the instrumentation beam removed proved ideal for these tests and some 9 metres of surge was possible, a distance that was needed when controlling some models during acceleration and stopping. These experiments were some of the most dramatic seen in Ship Division. The models, works of art in themselves, included lifting fans, skirts of different kinds and superstructure roared into life as the fans driven by a generator on the carriage lifted them from the water. With the desired hover height set the model was then towed down the tank at great speed (often up to 12 metres per second or 30 m.p.h.). Accidents occurred, usually brought about by a rapid ditching in some designs, and also, it must be said, by faulty towing arrangements. At least two models were written off completely, disintegrating as they accelerated out of control and once Giles, who was close to a model, narrowly escaped injury as it suddenly stood on its head before his eyes. But valuable information was obtained, not least resistance data at the important hump speeds. Fundamental studies continued when Everest began a series of tests on another simple planform shape. Shallow water measurements were taken over a range of water depth including zero, which represented conditions a hovercraft would meet as it approached and landed at a terminal.[3]

The whole field of hovercraft development was highly competitive and at times relations between NPL, HDL and BHC were not entirely harmonious. There was much at stake amongst rival companies and alternative craft, but for its part Ship Division had no axe to grind and happily tested the various designs with an independent mind. At the same time it gave every support to basic research, either that perceived as desirable by Everest or Hogben, or from HDL and MoA requests. The MoA contract terminated in December 1964 but research and tests on models continued. In 1966 the British Hovercraft Association staged a Hovershow 66 at which hovercraft were operated over land and sea and research projects described. Soon after, the national programme of hovercraft research and development was reviewed and for a few months Ship Division's role became uncertain. Eventually as the emphasis of work shifted to developments at full-scale and measurements at sea, HDL became rather more involved. At their Headquarters at Hythe on Southampton water HDL possessed a small tank where models could be towed in rudimentary fashion and preliminary assessments made of new designs. Experiments continued at Feltham with Ship Division acting more in the role of a hirer of its Number Three tank to either HDL or commercial firms. Hogben and Everest have summarised Ship Division's research into hovercraft hydrodynamics[4] from its beginning to 1967 and in the same year they also presented a major paper[5] to the RINA.

Seakeeping and Wave Data

An important co-ordinating committee made up of representatives from BSRA, NIO and Ship Division had been formed in 1961. Its formation was a natural extension of the work carried out earlier on the weather ship *Weather Reporter*, and it sought to organise a programme of seakeeping research which would help future model tests and respond to the growing demand for the collection of sea state data. Knowledge of operating conditions was essential to seakeeping research and the object of collecting data was to provide statistical information on wind and wave conditions all over the world especially along shipping routes, fishing grounds and, with hovercraft in mind, coastal areas. The information would come from weather ships and on-board observations from ships in operation. By 1963 information covering most of the principal shipping routes had become available and were the beginnings of a massive assembly of data published four years later by Hogben and F.E. Lumb of the Meteorological office. This large book[6] soon became a "Bible" for those seeking sea state data and remained the definitive source for several years. For the model experimenter it gave information on the average wave conditions likely to be encountered at any time of the year for most sea areas in the world and helped in the choice of waves to be reproduced in the tank. Ewing worked with Hogben in this painstaking exercise and on related matters and several preliminary reports were produced in advance of Hogben's and F.E. Lumb's book. Later, using the sea state data obtained, wave energy analyses were made which led to definitions of sea state energy spectra appropriate to open-ocean or coastal water environments. Thus, in model tests on a ship intended for operation in an ocean the appropriate spectrum was chosen and reproduced to scale by the wavemaker in Number Three tank. The waves generated were uni-directional and of course not fully representative of a real sea where a directional spread of waves combine to give confused seas. Nevertheless, they did give conditions where maximum pitch and heave would be seen in models towed or driven through waves coming from directly ahead. Ship Division had to wait several years before confused seas could be reproduced in a redesigned Number Four tank. It was important to discover what influence different wave forms had on model behaviour and Ewing carried out experiments to examine these effects[7] reporting his findings just before he left Ship Division to join the NIO at their Wormley laboratories in Surrey.

Running in parallel with the collection of sea state data was the development of procedures for predicting wave statistics from wind histories. For example, working with Professor Darbyshire of the University of North Wales, a prediction of waves in coastal waters was seen to compare favourably with measurements on lightships in the Morecombe Bay and Dover Straits areas. Although little direct seakeeping research using model tests was done at this time some general conclusions could be drawn from the various tests carried out for firms and Goodrich was able to isolate the effects of hull freeboard on deck wetness.[8] He also became involved in the design and improvement of that simplest of all roll reduction devices, the passive roll stabiliser. Its principle was based on the absence of moving parts or power supply. A tank fitted high up inside a ship was filled with water to a depth such that the motion of the water lagged behind the roll of the ship. At least a 50 per cent reduction in roll was possible. A patent application was filed in 1965 and a demonstration on a model rolling in beam seas in Number Four tank attracted many British shipbuilders and owners. Some legal arguments over patent rights arose in later years with J.J. McMullen Associates, who were producing their own versions of stabiliser, and press statements released by the Government department Mintech had to make it clear that passive roll stabilisers could be designed by NPL without infringing any existing patent rights. Many inquiries were received in the months that followed and soon several ships fitted with NPL stabilisers went into service and reports received that performance at sea agreed well with model predictions. Although simple in conception, refinements became necessary to suit the needs and characteristics of different ship types and work continued for several years and further patent applications made.

Bulbous Bows

Tankers and bulk carriers, now much fuller in form, presented a new challenge. It was not easy to optimise hull resistance and the design of the afterbody in these ships was hindered by the possibility of poor flow due to steeply sloped waterline endings. In bad cases separated or reverse flow increased hull resistance and reduced propulsive efficiency. On the other hand the full forms were ideally suited to bulbous bows. With so many of these ships in demand a full blown research into bulbous bows seemed called for and a programme of work appeared likely when BSRA initiated experiments on several 0·8 block coefficient forms fitted with small bulbs, but oddly this work was not sustained. Substantial efforts were made to understand bulbous bow action and *ad hoc* studies helped to gather experience but no systematic work was planned. Tests in 1966 on the largest tanker to be built in the UK at the time are a good example of the *ad hoc* study. The ship was the Harland and Wolff-built 305 metres *Myrina* of 200,000 tons deadweight and model tests were directed at the design of the best bulbous bow. This emerged to be one with a pronounced ram which, with the ship operating at its ballast draught, gave an appreciable gain in speed. Two years earlier claims from the Far East of very high performance in tankers fitted with ram bulbs excited Ship Division's attention and doubts and experiments were put in hand. As in *Myrina*, immersed rams projecting beyond the forward perpendicular of a hull confirmed reduced resistance at ballast but not load draughts and it was evident that bulb immersion was a critical factor in wave cancelling. Further work by White extended the application of ram bows to high speed cargo forms.[9] Again, White found draught forward important in relation to the immersion of the ram, which meant that in a given ship its range of operating draughts would influence and complicate the choice of ram. The reward for good design could be considerable. Reductions in resistance of almost 25 per cent at ballast draughts were possible. Cylindrical bows were also tried,* optimum bow radii being about 1 per cent of hull length. These bulbs appeared best suited to vessels that spent most of their time at loaded draughts. A complete understanding of bulbous bows whether teardrop, ram or cylindrical in shape has never been reached and successful design depends as much on experience as logical explanation. Ghosh in Dawson's branch demonstrated a flair that was based on instinct yet on several occasions he succeeded where others failed.

Flow Over Hulls

The suspicion of separated flow in a full afterbody arose after trial results on the twin screw bulk carrier *Hallfax* revealed an alarming discrepancy between ship power and that predicted from the earlier model test. A trial speed of 11·67 knots was woefully short of the predicted 13¼ knots. *Hallfax* had a block coefficient of 0·86 and there is no doubt its afterbody lines were poorly designed and responsible for bad flow. Clements conducted some flow studies on a model run at a draught that corresponded to the trial. A new technique of studying flow was used. Woollen tufts 5 cm long were stuck to pins which pierced the surface of the hull at several points such that each tuft projected about 2 cm from the surface of the model. An underwater camera photographed the behaviour of the tufts as the model moved through the water and prints showed very clearly that erratic and separated flow existed at the lower part of the hull. Vortex generators (fins of aerofoil section) had been used by Aerodynamics Division to prevent separated flow in the diffuser of one of their wind tunnels and Clements borrowed the idea. His generators were simpler, being triangular in shape with a chord height ratio of 2½ to 1. Eight of these, four port and four starboard, were fitted close to the base line of the hull and some 20 per cent of the hull length from the stern.

The results from the model tests had given the direction of the local

---

* See also Wigley's theoretical work, at pages 105 and 106.

streamflow and the fins were aligned to this. The fins did their job and produced vortices which supplied energy to the area of separated flow but their parasitic drag was high. Further experiments with half the number of fins, which were also made smaller, gave a compromise whereby satisfactory flow was obtained at the expense of some increase in hull resistance. With high hopes fins were fitted to *Hallfax* and additional sea trials run. Clements in publishing the results of his study[10] reported with commendable honesty that no improvement at all was found in ship speed. An interesting discussion followed. Boundary layer thickness at a model was known to be thicker than the ship and it was suggested that the improvements at model scale could not be expected to be seen at the ship. If so it might be concluded that models rather than ships were more prone to separated flow. Canham from BSRA, who had attended the ship trials, described them as of poor quality, *Hallfax*'s engines were not in good condition and a less than satisfactory measured-mile was used. Also the ship had steered badly—no skeg or bilge keels were fitted. Perhaps cross-flow from the poor steering cancelled any improvements from the vortex generators. Whatever the reservations placed on Clements' work there was no doubting the potential advantages of adding fins and in later years Gadd exploited them with success but in a rather different way. Sometimes the vibration in a ship could be traced to the presence of sharp wake peaks in the plane of the propeller. Using fins as flow deflectors Gadd succeeded in reducing such peaks.[11]

Trawlers and Ducted Propellers

Trawler research was in two parts. On the hydrodynamic side with the change to using nets over the stern and the gradual introduction of processing and refrigeration rooms aft it was important to provide the steadiest possible platform in this region of the ship. To reduce motions the centre of pitch of the vessel should move aft and fortunately Doust's statistical analysis showed that hull resistance was reduced if the centre of buoyancy was placed in the afterbody. New trawler designs aimed to do this and at the same time centre of pitch moved in the desired direction. Model experiments in waves concentrated on hull section shape and V shaped sections at the stern overhang were best and helped to increase pitch damping. Damping was also increased by the addition of a bulbous bow and in some hulls bulbs gave useful reductions in power as well. A delighted owner of a fleet of trawlers designed by NPL which included a bulb wrote to say that in a recent gale their ship with its catch reached port many hours in advance of its competitors! The other item of research was a departure for Ship Division and was carried out with the White Fish Authority (WFA). This was a technical and economic assessment of the future requirements for the fishing industry. There were contradictory aspects. Catches of larger deep sea trawlers were becoming smaller due to restrictions imposed on some fishing areas and skippers were going further afield. If "wet fish" trawlers were used they had to land their catches within 16 days to avoid spoilage. Higher ship speeds were therefore needed but alternatively if ships were equipped with quick-freeze plant, higher speeds were not required. The assessment examined technical and economic data received from the WFA and companies operating fishing fleets and estimates were reached on the profitability of fishing vessels in terms of their dimensions, machinery power, speed, displacement, catching rates and fish prices. The principles used in this approach to ship design were described by Doust[12] at a conference in Newfoundland shortly after he left NPL.

Work on trawler design also included research into propulsion devices. As was well known, a shroud or a duct added as an enclosing ring to a propeller augmented overall thrust to the ship by exploiting the accelerated flow produced by the duct. A ducted propeller could be of particular use in vessels called on to produce higher thrust than, with reasonable efficiency, was possible in a propeller working by itself. Trawlers and tugs with two different modes of operation—trawling or towing and free-running, were obvious candidates. So too, as they became larger, were tankers and bulk carriers—full load and ballast draughts brought vastly different working conditions. With no restrictions the most efficient propeller was in general large in diameter and slow in rotation. However, draught limitations in some ships restricted propeller size and diesel engines imposed a limit on propeller revolutions. So it was that attention turned to special propulsion devices some of which had in fact been tried before 1960. The Froude Research Committee appointed a Marine Propulsion Devices panel in 1966 to look into the various possibilities, most effort being placed on ducted propellers. English and O'Brien looked at propeller and duct design and as various ship designs fitted with ducted propellers came in from firms the Contracts branch tested several models and random data was obtained but again no systematic programme of work was put together. It was considered that the inflow characteristics at the ducts were important to ultimate performance and so flow was examined closely in experiments using tufts, paint and probes. The superiority or otherwise of a ducted propeller over an ordinary propeller was not easy to judge, particularly in full form ships. A ducted propeller working behind a model of a 100,000 tons deadweight tanker gave a better answer than an alternative propeller provided the overhang of the hull at the propeller position was large. This was contradicted when in tests on a larger 167,000 tons tanker the ducted propeller was better only if the overhang was small. It was thought that meaningful comparisons could be reached only by examining the results from one specific hull but even so the issue was clouded by uncertainties when analysing the model results. Although ducts were fitted with propellers in open water tests and duct as well as propeller thrust measured it stretched even more the assumptions in Froude's engineering solution to the dynamic differences between ship and model running conditions when two measurements of thrust were combined in the ensuing analysis. A torque rather than thrust identity assumption gave sensible answers but an acceptable analysis procedure has still to be agreed and occupies the thoughts of current ITTCs.

Other alternative propulsion devices were considered including a brief revival in interest in contra-rotating propellers. Garlick produced a special mechanical dynamometer for use in propulsion tests but it was used only rarely. The controllable pitch propeller was becoming increasingly popular; it too was ideal in ships with two different modes of operation. In making models the propeller blades were machined separately and set, with a rotational ability, into an enlarged propeller boss. The open water tests became an extensive requirement to collect data for all four quadrants of operation at each of several pitch settings.

Bow Propellers

Unusual devices were not confined to a ship's stern. In 1955 a bow propeller had been tried on the Canadian ferry *Princess of Vancouver* to assist in getting the ship away more rapidly from a quay. Bow propellers were seen as aids to improved manoeuvrability but with a ship under way the efficiency or lateral thrust dropped away very quickly. English began a research in 1961 and two years later published some of the first data covering the performance of bow propellers.[13] It so happened that model tests on a new NIO ship *Discovery* were in progress at the time and *Discovery* was to be fitted with a lateral thrust unit. English used the model to measure the side force acting on the hull at forward speeds with the LTU in operation and confirmed straight away the drop in sideways thrust for a given LTU rotational speed. At an ahead speed of only 2 knots it had fallen by half from the measured side force at zero speed. He found that it was important to ensure that the suction generated at forward speed was kept to a minimum and clearly the shape of the hull opening in which the LTU was placed had to be carefully designed. This early work gave an indication of the extra resistance produced by the hull opening, a matter that would receive considerable attention in later years.

Conventional Propellers

The 1960s saw large efforts devoted to propeller design using conventional as well as new techniques. O'Brien had for several years been involved amongst other things in collecting data from 60 propeller models which made up three separate NPL series, the Blade Section, Blade Thickness and Standard Series.* His output was enormous and culminated in a fine book[14] published by Hutchinson in 1962. In this, O'Brien reviewed information on all aspects of conventional propeller design describing all the well known tests on methodical series emanating from Haslar, Teddington, Washington and Wageningen. Similarly, cavitation data according to Burrill, Gawn and others were given and

---

* These together with Baker's earlier data (see pages 101 to 103) are a significant contribution to worldwide data on propeller performance.

presented in usable form. Of great value to the practitioner were several worked examples showing the processes involved in designing propellers for cargo vessels, passenger vessels and trawlers. Many of O'Brien's other publications were ideally suited to the propeller designer and found a popular outlet in the technical press. For example, three related articles[15] dealt with the designs of propellers for tugs. He also produced valuable papers showing the influence of changes in the principal design parameters on performance, a typical example being his 1965 paper in Newcastle.[16] It was largely due to the accumulation of such data that Ship Division at this time was able to offer a short cut to firms when commissioning model propulsion experiments. Hitherto every propeller designed for a ship had been made at model scale and used in the experiments. By 1965 with so many model propellers available it became perfectly reasonable to chose a suitable one for tests on a new ship model, tailoring the size of the model so that ship and model propeller diameters corresponded. A simple empirical rule, found from O'Brien's work, gave a correction to propeller r.p.m. as measured in the model test which took account of the pitch differences between the chosen model propeller and the design propeller intended for the ship. This technique which became a common practice at other tank establishments saved much time and money. Unfortunately O'Brien was soon to suffer a mental illness that kept him away from Ship Division for long periods and he was sorely missed when eventually he had to give up and accept an early retirement.

English concentrated on newer methods of propeller design and in 1962 was working on a simplified lifting surface technique[17] which later found favour with workers at MIT. He also, as has been noted, took over the responsibility for the cavitation tunnels when Silverleaf was appointed as Superintendent. Before that, Grant had been moved to work on the tunnels and became a leading experimenter in this specialised work. Poulton followed Grant a few years later and worked with English on several projects including the development work on simulating irregular ship wakes in both tunnels. This was achieved by inserting gauzes upstream of the working sections in a trial and error fashion until the irregular flow produced matched that measured behind a towed model in the tank. Silverleaf had started the first basic investigation in Number Two tunnel in 1961 and examined the effects on a cavitating propeller of changing air content in the tunnel water. The large resorber in this tunnel was ideal in that it allowed a very wide range of air content to be set. Tests gave measurements of propeller forces and cavitation patterns and it was found that air content could have an appreciable effect on propeller forces but only a minor influence on cavitation patterns. Clearly the composition of the tunnel water was important, a fact that was to assume even greater importance when measurements of noise from a propeller and studies on propeller-excited vibration began.

There was growing interest in propellers that operated with cavities completely covering the suction side of blade surfaces. Cavities occurred either naturally (plate 58) due to high speed or could be induced artificially by ejecting air through the blades into the region where small cavities formed. A design procedure for such screws was extant but it needed improvement to take account of the shape and thickness of cavities. Such information could come only from tunnel experiments and work was put in hand in Number Two tunnel. However, this was soon curtailed when it was found that the cavity formed affected the water-lubricated bearing of the propeller shaft. In fact the whole bearing system was the Achilles heel of the tunnel and despite modifications in 1961 had never behaved satisfactorily. After time consuming efforts spent in seeking a solution an entirely new arrangement became unavoidable and was specified and ordered in 1967.

Propeller-Excited Vibration

A demanding area of work was that of propeller-excited vibration, PEV. Propellers operating behind a ship not only created their own variable pressure fields but faced irregular inflow over their blades due to the non-uniform wake produced by the hulls they were driving. As a consequence the forces generated by propellers fluctuated to excite propeller shaft and machinery vibration or hull vibration through shaft support systems. In an attempt to understand the mechanism of PEV and to measure fluctuating forces an ambitious programme of model and full-scale measurement was begun in 1961. Carmichael, using the large 15 h.p. open water dynamometer as a prime mover, had already investigated the pressure field set up by a rotating propeller and now Silverleaf, before he became Superintendent, expanded the work in an attempt to predict thrust and torque fluctuations for ship propellers from measurements on ship models. Following measurements at sea on five ships a method of measuring fluctuating propeller forces was designed and used in experiments on models of two of the five ships. The models were self-propelled by propellers in the usual way and towed in Number Three tank. The ships tested at sea were two sister twin screw passenger liners, a large quadruple screw passenger liner, a single screw tanker and a single screw oceanographic research vessel, the last also being the subject of comprehensive vibration trials carried out by BSRA. Boyle designed the measurement arrangements at ship and model and used silicon strain gauges to record axial and torsional strain in propeller shafting from which the fluctuating propeller thrust and torque were derived. At the model a similar approach was used but to avoid bearing friction and extraneous noise very small strain gauges and a slip ring unit were installed inside the propeller boss. Other steps had to be taken to reduce the effect of the elastic properties of the propulsion system and shafting. A flywheel was fitted inside the model close to the propeller to increase the natural frequency of the whole measurement arrangement above that of the fluctuating forces and as a final precaution against hull vibration, lest it influenced the dynamic behaviour of the propeller and shaft, the complete system including propeller, shaft, flywheel and shaft supports was attached to a rigid frame isolated and suspended from the hull itself. It is hardly surprising that many difficulties were experienced taxing

Boyle's ingenuity to the full but results were obtained. Silverleaf, Marwood and Boyle who worked together on this difficult task brought together their ship and model results to publish them in what they properly described as a progress report[18] only to run into a barrage of criticism. Most of this came from BSRA. Perhaps the Association viewed Ship Division's work as an intrusion, BSRA had after all, by 1964, carried out full-scale vibration measurements on 53 ships. The full-scale results obtained by Ship Division conflicted with current knowledge principally over the relationship between propeller r.p.m. and blade number, peak responses at odd orders of frequency occurring in propellers with an even number of blades. The contributors to the discussion of Silverleaf et al's 1964 paper[18] were unwilling to believe this and blamed inadequate instrumentation. The point was also made that conditions at the model, for example variation in wake velocities, were different to the ship and would inhibit the achievement of representative measurements as would the usual scale effect problems. This of course was well appreciated by Silverleaf before he began but the aim of the work was to try to account for these differences in the prediction method he was hoping for.

Drag Reduction

An intriguing research that was taken up enthusiastically by Gadd was the notion of reducing drag by adding long chain molecular substances to water. Since a large proportion of ship resistance arose from turbulent friction then if turbulent flow could be converted to a smooth laminar condition the prize would be great. Gadd experimented with a fine wire and found that the frequency of eddy shedding was much reduced if a certain concentrate of polyethylene oxide was dissolved in water. The amount of concentration was critical and best results were found when it exceeded 20 parts per million. There was a danger of degradation when after a while drag reduction effectiveness was lost and a search was made for other substances. Those with low molecular weight were promising and Gadd discussed some interesting findings.[19] Drag reduction was undoubtedly possible but only if very large quantities of the chosen substance were used and to do this continually from a moving ship was uneconomic.

Interdependence Study

The work on the interdependence model described in Chapter 10 had taken a long time to complete. It was a large programme of work, problems were encountered in the tank when measuring total pressure resistance and L.F.G. Simmons who was responsible for the wind tunnel tests died unexpectedly before the measurements were analysed. However, by 1965 Lackenby from BSRA and Shearer were able to give complementary accounts of the whole research.[20] Shearer's derived skin friction curve for the model undulated whereas the wind tunnel skin friction curve obtained in the absence of waves ran above and parallel with the Hughes and the Schoenherr two-dimensional extrapolation lines. Thus the effect of wave-making on skin friction appeared to show interdependence and the undulations appeared to be in phase with wave-making phenomena. Lackenby concluded that despite the interaction between viscous and wave-making components at model scale there seemed to be no reason why such interaction should not also occur at full-scale in which case the existing method of predicting ship resistance from a model test using Froude's hypothesis of independent and separable components was sound. There remained uncertainty over a complete understanding of skin friction and so far as wave-making resistance was concerned it was fortunate that a new technique was becoming available in which this component could be determined directly.

The implementation of this technique in Ship Division was due to Gadd and Hogben following the latter's work with the circular hovercraft model. The principal tool for calculating wave resistance was linearised wave theory which although thoroughly explored by Wigley had made no great advance by 1965. The alternative route developed by Gadd and Hogben and based on Eggers' work in Germany applied theoretical equations to the experimental measurements of the free surface elevation of the wave system set up by a moving model to calculate wave resistance. However, the early measurements of wave pattern resistance used relatively crude methods of measuring the waves by manually set probes, and it seemed that full use could not be made of the method until better techniques had been devised. However, the value of these additional measurements was soon appreciated. Good hull design had been assisted by comparing total resistance with similar data from earlier models. Now, the effect of changes in hull shape relative to wave-making resistance could also be seen and strengthened considerably the hand of the designer.

Geosim Model Results and Extrapolation

In reviewing the current position of the extrapolation problem and noting that by 1962 many results from geosim models had been published throughout the world Hughes took the opportunity of carrying out a rigorous analysis of all the data in the hope that a more precise definition of the extrapolator slope would be reached. In doing so he corrected all the model resistance results for the effect of tank blockage using the correction method he himself had proposed a year earlier. There were seven sets of geosim model data available. These were for a 0·75 block coefficient form tested at Teddington and in Norway, the *Victory* ship (Gothenburg, Teddington and Wageningen), *Tina Onassis* (Madrid), *Simon Bolivar* (Wageningen), a 0·55 block coefficient steamer (Hamburg and Teddington), a cruiser (Hamburg and Teddington) and *Lucy Ashton* (Haslar and Teddington). Altogether 40 separate models were involved and in addition, since uncertainties existed over some of the original *Lucy Ashton* model results,

Hughes made another three models and ran them in the large Number Three tank where they were certain to be free of blockage effects. Hughes' extensive analysis[21] gave correlation lines for each set of geosims and the slopes of the lines Hughes found to be independent of Froude number and dependent on the viscous resistance coefficient. This being so he concluded that there was complete harmony between the correlation of ship-model resistance and the correlation of flat plate friction data. As a result of the analysis Hughes decided to modify slightly the correlation formulation he had given in his 1954 paper and, as a final statement, Hughes proposed that model and ship viscous resistance should be correlated by the formulation $C_V = 0.062r(\log R_N - 2.18)^{-2}$ where r was a form factor expressed as the ratio of the actual viscous resistance and that from a two-dimensional flow formulation. Hughes then went on to describe how form factor r could be obtained from low speed model resistance experiments. However, in carrying out early analyses Hughes soon realised the dangers in collecting data at very low test speeds where very careful experimentation was necessary if the desired accuracy was to be achieved. The determination of true speed through the water was difficult and laminar flow, if present, would wholly invalidate results. He thus chose a different method which combined calculation with resistance measurements taken at low and moderate Froude number. Returning to Froude's original circle constant notation he split total resistance Ⓒ in the usual way into separate components, his formulae for which contained constants x and y in the viscous and wave component equations respectively. x included the effect of form in a given model and from the model measurements x and y could be found after a somewhat complex but workable process of calculation and plotting. In 1966 with the results from 150 models analysed in this way Hughes described the analysis method and gave some preliminary results.[22] He was confident that for normal operational speed ranges his formulae for the viscous and wave components expressed with fair accuracy the total resistance. He also expected, and this was of potential value to hull designers, that derived values of x and y would show the dependence of resistance on hull parameters.

Hughes' papers always produced interesting discussion. Telfer was a regular contributor as were Lackenby, Wigley and others. Telfer, although never slow to criticise Hughes' general philosophy or approach to extrapolation, respected Hughes for the conscientious and meticulous experimenter that he was. J.R. Scott from the St. Albans tank was also attracted to Hughes' work but became a regular critic and sceptic. His utterances were always coolly and sometimes loftily deflected by Hughes. Scott, a physicist by training, was a knowledgeable statistician and aimed most of his criticism at Hughes' analysis techniques, in particular the degree of accuracy achieved. Hughes for his part had little knowledge of modern statistical methods but was fortunate to be able to turn to members of NPL's Mathematics Division for expert advice. Nevertheless Scott's attacks were relentless and a running battle was conducted over several years as successive papers by Hughes appeared, so much so that the casual reader would be excused if he turned first to the discussion to be entertained by the latest instalment of Scott versus Hughes. The essential difference between the two was that Scott was convinced of the power of correctly applied statistical methods to problems whereas Hughes preferred to look for physical reasons when interpreting his results.

Ship-Model Correlation

Ship-model correlation studies were a continuing task and the emergence of fuller form ships almost certainly meant that correction factors currently in use would be affected. In such ships, comparative tests were already showing that higher power factors were needed at ballast draughts than at the deep draught for the same ship. Efforts to use correlation factors in a consistent way were first made by Allan in 1951 at a time when changes in construction from riveted to welded ship hulls were seen. Summarising Ship Division's correlation data and making allowance for hull roughness following his own work in this area, Allan produced a graded system of correlation factor whereby ships were grouped into broad categories depending on their hull surface finish and length. The factors were by no means definitive but served until further results from ship-model comparisons became available. By 1959 Clements had worked on further data and six years later he joined with Canham of BSRA to present an analysis of data for one type of ship, the single screw tanker[23] drawing on results from 125 ship and model trials obtained by Ship Division, BSRA and other sources. BTTP had a great interest in this work and in parallel with the Canham and Clements work conducted a separate analysis (carried out by Scott)[24] on most of the results available. Canham and Clements used statistical methods to derive correlation factors at load draughts. With the power and propeller r.p.m. correlation factors as dependent variables, no fewer than 19 independent variables were used in the regression equations covering such things as hull roughness, ship speed, shallow water effects, etc. The derived factors were found to be influenced most by Reynolds number scale effect, hull roughness, time the ship was out of dock before going on trial, shallow water and the measured-mile itself. The equations produced were never adopted by Ship Division but were an indication of how things might develop when more data from different ship types became available, indeed Scott favoured the approach and was later to produce equations for power and r.p.m. factors which were functions of the environmental conditions met on measured-mile trials with new ships. For the time being BTTP chose to make recommendations based on a practical consideration of the two analyses. The use of equations was eschewed and factors for power were plotted quite simply to a base of ship length, different curves distinguishing between standards of hull roughness. The factors shown were obtained from a traditional Froude 0 analysis. When, in 1964, Ship Division began to use the new ITTC friction formulation, equivalent power factors were required which were obtained from a simple relationship between the two formulations. The ITTC factors with similar recommendations for r.p.m. were used by Ship Division for several years until Dawson and Bowden returned to the subject. By then practically all ships were of welded construction and although surface finish varied and was a very important factor, the amount of variation seen from ship to ship was not so great as in earlier days when the presence of riveted or partially welded ships led to a wide dispersal in the data used.

Standardisation of Measurement and Analysis

BTTP was also keen that tank establishments in Britain should carry out ship-model experiments in a standard way and, so far as resistance and propulsion tests were concerned, Silverleaf with Moor from the St. Albans tank worked together to produce a detailed and authoritative document which covered recommended practices on model manufacture, test procedures and analysis,[25] a manual which is still used today by BMT. Relevant to this was the vexed question of day-to-day variations in measured resistance and BTTP work on the standard model had monitored resistance and propulsion measurements for the past four years. It will be remembered that Baker's regular running of an *Iris* model had been discontinued in 1919. His conclusions then were confirmed when during the four years of repeat testing of the fibre glass standard model Hughes found resistance remained constant within 1 per cent. As a result it was decided that there was no basis for applying a correction to model resistance in general and there, so far as Ship Division was concerned, the matter rested. Nevertheless there was always the possibility of biological contamination in the tank water and although Silverleaf was fairly sure of the stability of the water in the Teddington tanks he welcomed the chance of carrying out a survey in Number Three tank. I. Hartley from Salford University was asked to do this and produced a fascinating report[26] which identified seven classes of living organisms in the tank water including, briefly, one specimen known to be a potent drag reducing organism. All were truly microscopic. Hartley analysed the water over a four month period in a poor summer looking for the fluctuation in numbers of algae, ciliates, etc. and Gadd made turbulent friction measurements by determining the pressure drag along a submerged tube through which water was pumped. Neither set of observations showed any abnormal variation and Hartley concluded that the chances of friction-reducing contamination in the tank were very small although he did warn that in better summers more hours of sunshine could have an effect. Gadd retained his measurement device for use in any Ship Division tank should any suspicion of irregularity arise.

High Speed Craft

A large project on hydrofoil performance was carried out over a five-year period from 1961. Hydrofoil ships were by 1961 well established; Russia had several hydrofoil ferries in operation and the Supramar company led by Baron von Schertel was producing craft in Western Europe. The Canadian Navy had started on the design of a hydrofoil anti-submarine warfare ship, a canard type craft intended for 60 knots. Silverleaf had an abiding enthusiasm for the hydrofoil concept (he had worked with Allan at Dumbarton on a Grunberg type during the Second World War) and was pleased to offer the ideal facilities afforded by Number Three tank for experiments on the Canadian design. He and Steele worked alongside B.V. Davis of the De Havilland company to conduct a large programme of tests on models of bow and stern surface piercing foils as well as a 1/16-scale model of the hull plus foils, all of which were supplied by De Havilland. Early results led to a need to modify the geometry of both foils and helped significantly to improve the overall performance of the ship, *Bras d'Or*, that finally emerged from the experimental study.[27] *Bras d'Or* was a 200 tons craft which, although designed to reach a high speed, was also intended for long periods at slow speeds during which it would be hull borne. In the experiments on the foils measurements of drag, side force, lift and pitch, roll and yaw moments were required for a range of pre-set attitudes of pitch, roll and yaw. Silverleaf and Steele designed a multi-component balance that consisted of two parallel flat plates separated by three bars that acted as flexure elements. Each element responded to bending in two normal directions and to axial tension or compression. Resistance strain gauges measured bending forces and semi-conductor gauges the axial forces. Each foil was attached to the balance, set to a selected attitude, and towed down the tank over a range of speed covering both hull borne and foil supported speeds. It was found that ventilation of the foils through the free surface could occur and to prevent this fences were added to the foils. On the other hand to maintain an effective air supply to foils designed to operate with large vented cavities, spoilers in the form of a step were added to the upper surfaces of the foils. On the carriage a high pressure air supply was fed to the model foils to give artificial venting when required. To assist in the design of a fully wetted foil section running below the free surface, over 70 pressure measurements were taken. Finally, with the preferred configuration of foils decided these were fitted to the displacement hull and spectacular experiments in calm water and in waves followed. The results obtained led to a further modification. Pitch motions in head waves were high but were reduced by changing the tandem foil arrangement. There was a danger of flutter in the bow foil and further experiments were arranged. Excitation of the foil came from an electro-magnetic vibration generator and measurements of the response of the foil to excitation were obtained from strain gauges built into the foil. They were not entirely successful and had to be replaced by accelerometers to record horizontal and vertical accelerations. To complete the comprehensive series of tests a propeller was tested in Number One cavitation tunnel. Following experiments in uniform flow English fitted a wake simulator in the form of three struts covered by gauze ahead of the propeller to reproduce a more realistic inflow to the propeller. This was the first attempt at wake simulation, a technique that was to become common practice in later years. The work for the Canadians was followed a few months later by tests on ventilated foils for the Supramar company.

Apart from work on hovercraft and hydrofoils, tests on high speed displacement craft were frequent. The collection of calm water resistance data for the NPL round bilge series proceeded and was attracting the attention of shipbuilders. The market for high speed craft of patrol or small warship type was expanding and in this country Brooke Marine at Lowestoft and Vosper Thornycroft were quick to take advantage. When the first report[28] on the NPL series work was published the timing could not have been better and copies of it were soon exhausted as many smaller firms and individual designers sent in requests. The influence of the series forms tested began to be seen in patrol and offshore craft built worldwide and resistance and propulsion tests for firms at home and abroad soon reached peak levels. Tests in waves were also requested and these were a challenge to the experimenter due to high model speeds and severe motions. Planing craft, even faster in speed, although not so numerous, were also tested and the expansion in work focused attention on the need to collect correlation data for these specialist craft. Excellent co-operation in making ships available for trials at sea was received from Brooke Marine, Cheverton, Vosper Thornycroft and others. Of special note was Vosper's 43 metre *Tenacity*. Built as a private venture she was a triple screw vessel designed for 40 knots. Vosper was gaining experience on new propulsion engines, and gas turbines as well as diesel engines were installed. During trials *Tenacity* was placed at the disposal of co-operating bodies who included Southampton University and a large programme of measured-mile, seakeeping and manoeuvring trials were undertaken in the Solent, which provided invaluable data to interested parties. *Tenacity* was later to see service as a fisheries protection vessel at the time of the Icelandic cod wars.

TESTS FOR FIRMS

The routine repayment work on new ship designs continued at a high level throughout the 1960s, an average of one new design per week being tested except in 1967 when a marked decline was seen. Commissioned work was bringing in an income well over £100,000 a year and the Contracts branch under Dawson developed into a highly organised unit capable of responding rapidly to the constant demand. There could be little room for inefficiency, models had to be ready on time and a rigid programme of work adhered to. Dawson was supported by a strong team of experimenters whose results were monitored and checked by the experienced Macdonald and Mackenzie so that project managers had the relatively easy task of compiling the necessary reports. Some famous ships featured in the model tests. The new Cunarder, *Queen Elizabeth II*, was the subject of very comprehensive tests. The existing *Queen*

Elizabeth launched just before the Second World War eventually began her intended service between Southampton and New York in 1946. The voyage took five days and the first class fare cost £91. An alternative BOAC flight, which lasted for an uncomfortable 20 hours with several fuelling stops, cost £93. Crossings by sea flourished (66 per cent of all passengers in 1952 used the two *Queens*) and Cunard raked in the money. In 1957 a new *Queen* was on the drawing board—the Q3. Model tests on this design had been carried out at Teddington in 1961 but by then BOAC had flown its first Comet jet to New York spelling the end for the proposed Q3. A smaller *Queen* was considered— the Q4 with draught and dimensions to allow passage through both the Suez and Panama canals. The new *Queen* could act as a cruise ship and cross the Atlantic. Seven different models were tested in Number One tank during 1965, which were by no means all of those conducted in support of this prestigious ship since John Brown, her builder, also carried out experiments in their own tank at Clydebank. It was a great moment when the third *Queen* slipped into the Clyde in September 1967 yet as Dawson and others from Ship Division watched they witnessed the end of an era. *QE II* was not to follow her predecessors and provide a regular passenger service across the Atlantic but to find a role initially as a cruise ship. Later an agreement was reached with British Airways whereby passengers could travel one way to New York by sea and the other by air, an arrangement that is becoming increasingly popular. Several designs were tested for the Ben and Glen lines, the ships *Benloyal* (in 1954) and *Benledi* (in 1964) for the former and a new Glen class for the latter. The earlier *Glenearn* class had been tested at Teddington in 1939 and four cargo liners 150 metres long were required as successors. Of unusual fineness (block coefficient 0·59), their design led to a series of model tests shared by Ship Division and the St. Albans tank. At Teddington the original hull design was refined to include a small teardrop bulb and an enlarged stern frame, which together reduced power at the service speed by 2½ per cent. The propulsion experiments with a propeller from stock were repeated in later tests at St. Albans when a model of the ship's propeller was used and run at the trial draught for *Glenfalloch*. M. Meek, who in later years joined BMT, described these interesting ships.[29] Experiments were also carried out for Yarrow on a new class of oceanographic survey ship for the MoD. The single screw design was given a Mariner or clear water stern wherein the familiar stern aperture was replaced by a cut away stern and hung rudder. Following resistance and propulsion experiments, which showed no need for any hull modification, manoeuvring and roll stabilisation tests were conducted. Results from model turning trials showed an area of directional instability but by adding a skeg at the hull centreline below the propeller shaft the instability was overcome. Tests with a passive roll stabiliser gave excellent results. Roll was reduced by 50 per cent in irregular beam seas representing Beaufort 6 conditions. B.N. Baxter in describing the evolution of these ships[30] gave trials data from one, *HMS Hydra*. Power and propeller r.p.m. predictions from the model correlated well and in zigzag trials only a very slight degree of directional instability was noted. These model tests were but one example of how the manoeuvrability of several ships was improved by fitting skegs at the stern.

The extreme size of Number Three tank was hardly intended for tests on full-scale craft. Yet this in fact happened when the Amateur Rowing Association agreed to lend three racing shells for resistance experiments. Wellicome conducted some interesting experiments which not only appealed to Ship Division but to the crew of the Nautilus rowing club who came equipped with oars and conveniently compared the speed of the three boats against the carriage as it kept pace with the crew rowing down the tank. Not only was Wellicome interested to study oar action and compare the performance of the boats[31] but Hughes could obtain valuable "end" data from extremely slender hull forms (L/B approximately 30) for use in his latest method of splitting viscous and wave drag. The three shells were a Sims boat built at Twickenham, one from Berlin by Pirsch and an Italian Donoratico hull from Livorno. So far as total resistance was concerned the Italian boat was best but it was the slenderest of the three.

The Special Projects branch under Shearer found itself with plenty of unusual requests for work. Requirements in offshore engineering brought more tests on structures and experiments with underwater bodies. An interaction study following a marine accident was carried out in Number Four tank and, offshore work saw two large projects in two years the first of which started in 1963. This was an investigation into the characteristics of a single-point mooring system for loading and unloading tankers offshore. Experiments on a tanker model moored in Number Four tank were carried out in waves. To simulate the effect of wind and tide a bank of fans was set up and directed towards the model which was built inclusive of its superstructure. The surge and yaw of the model were recorded on film by two cameras, one overhead and the other underwater whilst forces in the anchor cable and mooring lines were measured by strain gauge. The second project was tested in Number Three tank. An ocean radio station had been proposed by the MoA and the shipyard who were to build the long tubular structure wanted to tow it in a horizontal attitude to its operating position before restoring it to the vertical by transferring water ballast. Three stages were examined in the tank on two different designs. First, each model was set horizontally and towed through waves to determine a safe speed. Then, behaviour was noted in translating each model from the horizontal to the vertical. Finally, with each model upright more tests in waves indicated how the structure would behave in its final attitude. Requests for model tests in support of the offshore and gas industries that had begun in 1961 with the *Triton* platform tests were increasing but so far this was a mere overture of what was to follow a few years later.

In 1964 underwater search devices were being used for defence, oceanographic and fishery research purposes and their streamlined bodies which housed sophisticated ultrasonic transducers were towed from a parent ship. The need to keep these to a desired attitude during tow posed problems similar to those faced by Ship Division during the two wars when minesweeping techniques were being worked out. The types of body sent in by the Naval Research Establishment of Canada were of the hydrofoil depresser type as distinct from those depressed by their own weight. The six component balance already developed for the Canadian hydrofoil work was used to measure drag, lift, side force and the moments of pitch, yaw and roll. Forces were extremely high, up to 6,000 pounds, due to the large-scale models sent in. Smaller ones were also made and tested under cavitating conditions in the tunnel and following a three year programme of work the results were correlated by NRE at sea from trials on similar bodies.

INSTRUMENTATION AND EQUIPMENT

The diversity of work placed great demand on the available apparatus and instrumentation. The use of the strain gauge increased, indeed without it many measurements would have been impossible. Silverleaf was keen to develop electrical propulsion dynamometry since otherwise there could be no prospect of reducing the time needed to do propulsion experiments. Boyle and Marwood approached the design in the same way as was chosen for the work on fluctuating propeller forces—the measurement of propeller forces inside the propeller boss. This was ambitious and extremely difficult and despite valiant efforts no satisfactory way was found. The mechanical gears were continuing to serve well but in higher speed models their limitations were only too obvious and as data acquisition methods advanced along with computer technology it became inevitable that a completely electrical system was needed. In the end several strain gauge propulsion dynamometers were bought from the specialist manufacturers Kempf and Remmer and after a lengthy study of their use and application to ship model measurement they were found to be extremely sensitive and their setting into models needed careful alignment. After a long period of doubt and uncertainty—in truth experimenters in the Contracts branch, used to the very reliable mechanical gears, were sceptical of the accuracy of the new gears and unwilling to make a change—they were eventually adopted and thereafter the old mechanical gears were superseded.

An original piece of apparatus was produced at the time of the hydrofoil experiments. In these tests the distribution of pressure over the foils was required involving many measurements at different positions on the foil. Electrical transducers were used but measurements at a single point in one run down the tank would have been an extremely laborious and time consuming task. Boyle designed a scanning valve which was made in the workshop. The pressures to be measured were transmitted through water-filled leads to five banks of 18 ports around the periphery of a fixed female cone. A rotatable male cone had five ports connected to a pressure transducer. For each setting of the valve the five ports in the male cone lined up with one port in each bank of the female so allowing five simultaneous measurements. Once these were obtained it was a simple matter to rotate the male cone to the next setting and take five further measurements. This device proved of particular value in the new circulating water channel for measurements of pressure on a hull surface. The scanning valve allowed 90 measurements to be made in about 15 minutes.

The method of controlling and tracking free-running models in Number Four tank was finally perfected in 1964. Loe, whose Electronics Group had been strengthened by the arrival of M.H. Steele from NPL, had satisfied himself that radio control, after a few refinements, worked well. To track and record the path of a model as it manoeuvred under the action of its rudder a sonic plotter was designed. A receiver was placed underwater at each corner of Number Four tank and from instrumentation within the model ultrasonic pulses sent out signals which were picked up by the receivers. The distance between the model and the receivers at a given instant was measured by the times taken for a pulse to travel through the water. Distances were recorded on paper tape for a computer analysis and printed for manual position plotting. This arrangement worked well but was cumbersome and some years later it was superseded by a better overhead photographic system that was originated and introduced by Lewison.

An important change took place in 1966. For over 50 years ship model hulls had been made of wax. But now that these were being manufactured at Feltham problems arose, models cracked on their way to Teddington by lorry. Some actually broke in half. The severe vibrations of the lorry which caused the accidents were cured by stiffening the floor of the lorry and by fitting a special carrying frame. Nevertheless the problem was not entirely eradicated. Also the demands for larger models, frequent at the time when large tankers were being designed, meant that some model lengths approached 10 metres. These large wax models were prone to distortion and again there were frequent breakages. An alternative material was at once considered. It had to be light (more and more instrumentation was being added to models making low hull weight desirable), dense and of good rigidity. Marwood visited several firms who were producing different types of polyurethane foam. Most promising was a high density organic compound comprising resin and isocyanate. The Baxendale Chemical company at Accrington were making white blocks 3 metres long and Marwood ordered some to try. With the right kind of glue that avoided hard and brittle joints between blocks a 5 metre rectangular solid block was produced and cut in the machine at Teddington. The first thing that appeared was an appalling cloud of fine dust but a hull form was successfully machined and finished using normal hand tools. Understandably the prospect of working with such an unpleasant material raised a furore amongst the workshop staff. It was claimed that the polyurethane was toxic, which was not however borne out after a careful analysis. However, the unions that were called in were adamant as to possible dangers and insisted that masks and protective clothing be supplied. At Feltham where polyurethane models would be machined an enveloping blind and extraction fans were fitted to the cutting machine to control the spread of dust. Before the change from wax to polyurethane could be made with confidence, the quality of the surface finish and the general stability of the new material had to be examined. After the machining process model surfaces had a rough granular surface caused by the ruptured cells in the material. This was sealed by a coating of shellac before painting. Carefully applied a good surface finish was achieved with an average surface roughness of 50 microns and overall a completed model looked promising. It was certainly light and, with internal reinforcement, perfectly rigid. The acid test would come from comparative experiments with wax and polyurethane models. Resistance experiments were duly carried out by Mackenzie on several pairs of models each made to the same scale and the results were most encouraging. Differences between wax and polyurethane resistance curves were within normal experimental error. Distortion under load was minimal thanks largely to the internal reinforcement and even more encouraging, repeat resistance experiments after a period of a few months were very close to the original measurements, a situation unlikely with a wax model. Polyurethane soon replaced wax although ironically very few large models were made after 1967. The new material was a boon to high speed models due to its light weight and ideal for models run in waves but on the debit side the manufacturing process was long-winded and more expensive.

One of the great events in Ship Division in the 1960s was the realisation of the promised circulating water channel. Built to a cost of £520,000 this large facility, or most of it, was housed in a large extension of the existing cavitation tunnel building. Its return horizontal circuit which consisted of a 3 metres diameter tube was placed outside the building; inside the building was the contraction, working section, pump and plant. The prominent building, 15 metres high in the region of the pump, included a range of offices for staff. There were important initial design considerations. It was known that the flow of water through a channel reached a critical speed at a Froude depth number of 1·0 at which a large standing wave appeared. The first sign of a wave was at about half this number. Obviously experiments on models were best conducted at sub-critical speeds and a top limit which would give a Froude depth number of 0·5 was set. The water depth in the working section would thus depend on the average test speed. Models not shorter than 2½ metres were preferred and for most tests envisaged top water speed would be about 2½ metres per second. Thus a water depth of 2·4 metres was indicated and the overall dimensions of the channel working section chosen to be 18 metres long, 3·6 metres wide and 3·6 metres deep. The details of the whole circuit, pump, bends, etc. had to be worked out and the 1/10-scale model already referred to became a valuable prototype. Before this model was built very useful guidance had been given by J.C. Orkney at Cambridge University where a small flume had been constructed in 1954 following BSRA sponsorship. Orkney had found that the best chance of achieving good flow through the working section was to feed water to the section from a constant head tank and then break the circuit after the working section at a weir allowing the water to fall freely into a sump. This principle was followed in the design of NPL's channel.

Construction of the channel (see Technical Appendix, page 326) began in July 1962 and in March 1965 it was filled with water. Six months later, after initial trials and minor modifications, the first serious tests could begin. The initial assessments showed a very satisfactory flow through the working section. Using a current meter the constancy in speed was found to be within $\pm\frac{3}{4}$ per cent and velocity distribution across the centre of the section reasonably consistent. What was surprising was the appearance of a standing wave 8 cm high at 3 metres per second. Fortunately this speed was above the likely maximum required in normal models and at speeds below $2\frac{1}{4}$ metres per second no standing wave at all could be detected. The one serious defect in the design which became apparent in winter months was the amount of heat lost in the return limb outside the building. It had been hoped to maintain water temperature in the working section at about 60°F but the heat input from the pump did not compensate for the losses and in cold weather temperature dropped to as low as 48°F. The design and construction of this highly successful facility was described[32] by Steele and his MoW colleague R.T. Turner at a symposium on ship research facilities held at Feltham in 1967.

The impressive new facility was formally opened by the President of the Institute of Mechanical Engineers, Vice Admiral Sir Frank Mason. Sir Frank was also the current chairman of the Froude Committee. A group of representatives from the shipbuilding industry and some members of Ship Division staff assembled on the evening of 28 March 1967 for the ceremony, which was conducted on the floor space above the sump.

It was never intended that force measurements would be made on models in the channel. The great advantage of the channel was that it allowed flow to be observed over a stationary model at a given water speed for a long period of time whereas experiments in a towing tank were limited by speed and length. Nevertheless, although in future years many flow studies and hull pressure measurements were conducted, other types of experiments could be successfully carried out in the channel. Dand pursued hull interaction studies there, the modelling of canal sections and banks was possible and the Ministry of Agriculture and Fisheries brought trawl nets for observation tests. Many plankton samplers were sent in for test and calibration and the windows in the side of the channel were particularly useful in observing the behaviour of these conical devices. Even the deeper water in the contraction section proved useful for experiments with underwater bodies.

The large circulating water channel (called Number Two since the 1/10 model was retained for use and called Number One) was a major addition to the facilities at Feltham. Yet another, a small tank, was built at this time. It was 15 metres long with a constant cross-section of $1\frac{1}{4}$ metres $\times$ $1\frac{1}{4}$ metres and equipped with a small wavemaker. Called Number Five tank it was sited alongside Number Four tank and intended for studies of the generation of regular and irregular waves. Never in regular use it however proved useful to several small projects. The new channel brought the test facilities in Ship Division to five tanks (three for towing tests, one for manoeuvring or seakeeping and the small Number Five), two cavitation tunnels and the smaller channel, nine facilities in all. It might have been 10. The work on hovercraft and hydrofoils reflected what appeared to be a growing national interest in high speed marine travel and soon after a start had been made on the construction of the water channel a proposal was made for a new tank (Number Six) designed to satisfy two needs, very high test speeds and an ability to reproduce confused sea conditions in addition to the uni-directional waves presently available in Numbers Three or Four tanks. A design study was approved by the Froude Research Committee. A new tank 340 metres long, 24 metres wide with a top carriage speed of 25 metres per second was to be erected to the south of Number Three with entrance to it from the west side of Number Four. Such high test speeds led to a radical design for the carriage which was conceived as an overhead rail cantilevered from one of the walls of the building and running along the centreline of the tank. Confused seas would come from the out of phase operation of a number of small wavemakers fitted along one side of the tank. The realisation of this new facility was subject to some curious bargaining. In exchange for a new tank it would be agreed that Number Two tank was redundant and given to NPL who needed a large storage area for radioactive equipment. Eventually, once the new tank was in operation, Number One would be given up as well leaving all of Ship Division's facilities at Feltham, a neat arrangement which no doubt appealed to NPL with its growing need for additional space within a site already limited in size. The whole plan fell victim to mixed thinking, some preferred a modernised Number One tank, and in the end economic considerations brought delay, a summary halt and tank Number Six never materialised, although its plans were kept.

In the midst of the expansion in research, which was seen in other Government laboratories as well as at NPL, some very significant changes took place. To begin with a major reorganisation of the whole Scientific Civil Service followed the publication of the Trend Report[33] in 1964. This influential report proposed that DSIR should be disbanded and replaced by a number of Research Councils who would become responsible for most of the civil science carried out in this country. The incoming Labour Government of October 1964 took account of this and announced its intention of establishing a Science Research Council and Ministry of Technology, the Ministry to take over the responsibility for most research and development establishments of the DSIR. After some debate NPL with its neighbour at Teddington, the National Chemical Laboratory, NCL, were absorbed as a single laboratory into Mintech rather than the SRC. The combined laboratories under one Director (J.V. Dunworth was appointed in October 1965), took the existing NPL name. All this meant that the affairs of the "former" NPL which had been conducted through its Executive Committee now passed to a Steering Committee for the combined laboratories, an arrangement agreed between Mintech and the Royal Society. Thenceforth the new Steering Committee submitted annually to Mintech a research programme for the following year together with proposals for budgets and staff. So far as Ship Division was concerned the Froude Research Committee was re-established with Sir Frank Mason as Chairman. It continued to advise on research programmes but was now required to submit an annual report to the Steering Committee. The "new" NPL had a total complement of 1,662 staff, 140 in Ship Division, and the cost to Mintech of the combined laboratories in 1965–66 was £5½ million made up of £2·31 million for salaries, £1·28 million for the purchase of equipment and £1·91 million for support services supplied by the MoW.

Whereas changes in some of the old NPL Divisions were great (new Divisions of Chemical Standards and Molecular Science were formed from NPL and NCL staff) those in Ship Division were minimal, but such a state of affairs did not last long. Soon NPL regrouped under three main sections, Measurement Science, Materials and a Third Group the latter including both Aerodynamics and Ship Divisions. The enlarged NPL saw the appointment of three Deputy Directors. Silverleaf was selected to be one of these and not surprisingly found himself in control of the Third Group. He was appointed in September 1966 and although still very much concerned with the affairs of Ship Division it was obvious that a successor to him was needed. In the meantime Dawson was asked to handle day-to-day matters until the arrival of J.A.H. Paffett who took up the post of Ship Division's sixth and, as it transpired, last Superintendent almost exactly a year later in 1967. For Silverleaf to retain a close involvement with Ship Division was impossible given his new commitments to the Third Group. His absence was keenly felt for he had led the Division with tremendous enthusiasm and was a tireless advocate of its activities and relevance to the industry. The name of the Third Group somehow conveyed a feeling of uncertainty which was indeed true so far as both ship and aerodynamics work at NPL was concerned. Soon HDL was drawn into the reorganisation when in October 1967 it came under NPL control and renamed the NPL Hovercraft Unit. Yet another towing tank came under the jurisdiction of the NPL and at Hythe in the grounds of The Grove, a fine house used as the Unit's offices, an open-air track was laid out on which a tracked hovercraft could run. The Unit became involved with full-scale development of prototype marine hovercraft and also tracked hovercraft. A 9 metres man-carrying hovercraft (the HD2) was designed and built at Hythe for sea trials with different directional control systems installed.

Soon after the absorption of HDL, NPL's Third Group was enlarged in 1968 and given a more satisfactory name, the Engineering Sciences Group. It was intended to serve industries or technologies associated with air and sea transport and with computer usage. Thus the old NPL Divisions, Aerodynamics (under R.C. Pankhurst), Mathematics including Computer Science (under E.T. Goodwin) and Ship (under Paffett) were, with the Hovercraft Unit (under J.E. Rapson), brought together to form the enlarged Group.

When Paffett arrived he inherited a staff of about 150 which in 1967 included newcomers F.G.R. Cook, G.R.G. Lewison and A.J. Johnson. Cook, an experienced Government scientist had endured a serious illness and on return to duty was seconded to NPL. He became the secretary of a Mintech working party on hydrofoil ships and an adviser on hovercraft work until finally he became Head of the Hovercraft Unit in January 1969. Before then he had already made his mark in a splendid paper with Silverleaf,[34] a balanced review and comparison of various high speed marine craft including hydrofoils and hovercraft.

Lewison, from Churchill College, Cambridge, arrived to take up a permanent position in Ship Division after an earlier spell as a guest worker and Johnson from BSRA began by succeeding Goodrich who a year earlier had left for Southampton University. In 1969 Wellicome also left to take up a post as Lecturer in Goodrich's new Department. A little earlier Ship Division was to lose one of its finest researchers ever when Hughes who had continued for several months after the normal retirement age finally decided to leave in 1968. It is probably fair to say that research into skin friction had, at Hughes' retirement, run its course and that his departure was not as critical as it might have been had he reached retirement 10 years earlier. His contribution to the subject was immense and brought prestige to Ship Division. His final publication,[35] strangely neglected, continued from his previous pages[22] and gave the results of an analysis of 458 models tested at NPL. For hull designers at the time, and to a large extent today, it represented invaluable guidance. Published several months after he retired, its excessive delay frustrated and angered Hughes to such an extent that many thought it accelerated his departure.

Interest in the extrapolation problem did not wane at Hughes' departure. Gadd was very busy reanalysing some of Hughes' earlier results and produced a friction formulation of his own.[36] This attractive offering received a RINA Premium award but Gadd's proposal was never followed up perhaps because his formulation was thought to overestimate friction at very high Reynolds number.

The state of British shipbuilding also came under scrutiny at this time. In February, 1965 the Board of Trade appointed a Shipbuilding Inquiry Committee with A.R.M. Geddes as its chairman. A marked decline in orders for new ships in Britain had set in. From enjoying 40 per cent of the world's order book in 1952, Britain's share 12 years later had tumbled to 14 per cent with growing competition coming from yards in the Far East. It seemed that the face that launched a thousand ships would be Japanese. The committee was thus charged with the task of investigating the situation in Britain regarding organisation and methods of production in order to recommend what action should be taken to make the shipbuilding industry competitive in world markets. In preparing its report[37] the committee not only visited shipbuilding yards worldwide but spoke with Government and Research and Development organisations including BSRA and NPL. Its conclusions in 1966 make interesting reading today. It was recommended that Government should adopt a positive policy towards shipbuilding and to give additional support to research and development. It should set up a Shipbuilding Industry Board to stimulate the necessary action within the industry and administer and control Government financial assistance. So far as research was concerned the report noted with satisfaction that the research effort provided by BSRA (£1·18 million) and NPL Ship Division (£0·7 million) in 1964–65 showed, after allowing for inflation, a three-fold increase over the figures for 1958. This had been brought about largely by DSIR initiative in 1962 when it undertook to provide half of every £1 raised by BSRA from industry and offered a grant of £1 for every £1 contributed by British shipowners for research work. In the same year a strong central research organisation covering all aspects of marine engineering had been created by merging the Newcastle-based Parsons and Marine Engineering Turbine Research and Development Association (PAMETRADA) with BSRA (BSRA itself was to move from its London offices to Newcastle a few years later). The combined organisation was renamed British Ship (replacing Shipbuilding in BSRA's original title) Research Association. As a result of the merger a large Production Division was formed and allowed BSRA to reduce its activity in hydrodynamics research, a reduction that made sense and was supported by the Geddes report in view of Ship Division's recent tests facilities at Feltham. In so far as future hydrodynamics research was concerned the report acknowledged Ship Division's important contributions over the years and considered that major efforts at, for example, improving bow and stern design should receive continued support.

Ship Division's new Superintendent, Paffett, arrived initially on secondment from the Admiralty. Apprenticed at Portsmouth dockyard during the Second World War and graduating from Greenwich in 1945 he spent working periods at Bath, Malta and Rosyth engaged in the design and construction of frigates before becoming Professor of Naval Architecture at Greenwich in 1962. He was thus an ideal choice with his combination of practical and academic experience, strengths which soon became obvious and influential. Paffett soon became content to accept a permanent consignment at NPL and spent the rest of his career at Feltham. He was to preside for nine eventful years. Not only did these see further bursts of activity in existing and new fields but "reorganisation", which had already affected NPL so significantly, was soon to turn its spotlight on both Aerodynamics and Ship Divisions.

REFERENCES

1. Gadd G.E. and Hogben N., "An appraisal of the ship resistance problem in the light of measurement of the wave pattern", NPL Ship Division Report 36, 1962.
2. Hogben N., "An investigation of hovercraft wave-making", Journal of Royal Aeronautical Society, February 1966.
3. Everest J.T., "Shallow water drag of a rectangular hovercraft", NPL Ship Division Report 79, 1966.
4. Hogben N. and Everest J.T., "Review of hovercraft research in Ship Division of the NPL", "Powered lift" Committee of ARC (ARC No. 29092), March 1967.

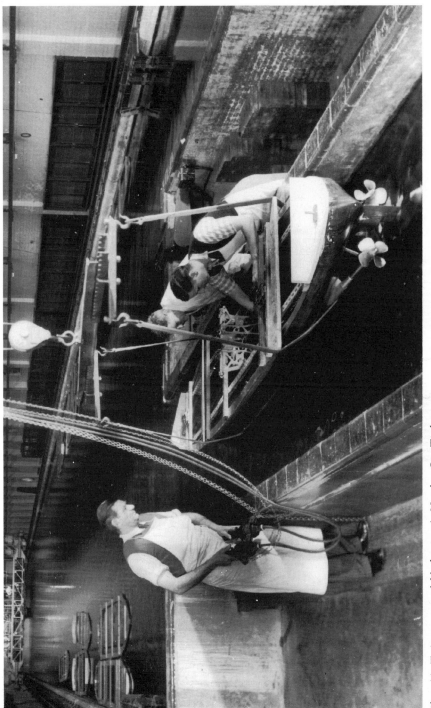

Plate 44. Twin screw model before test in Number One Tank.

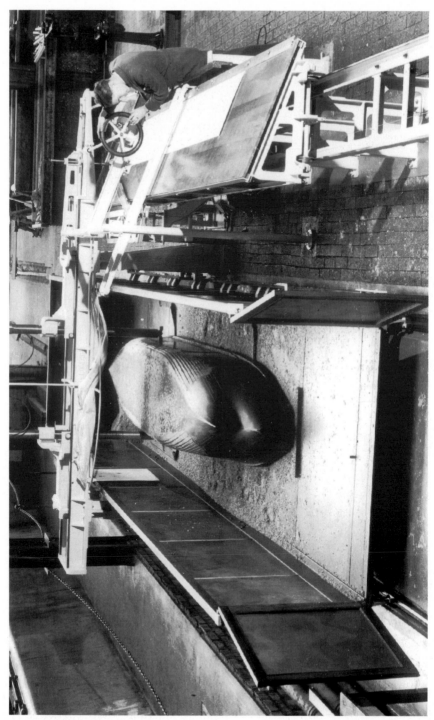

Plate 45. Model cutting machine – 1949.

Plate 46. Trawler model being launched sideways.

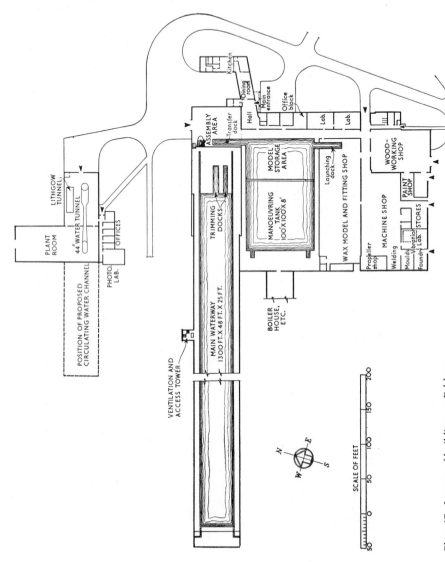

Plate 47. Layout of buildings at Feltham.

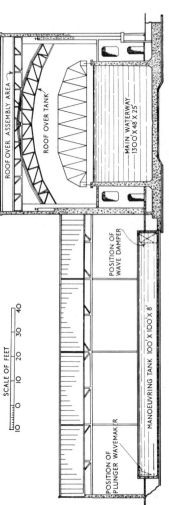

SCALE OF FEET

10 0 10 20 30 40

POSITION OF PLUNGER WAVEMAKER

MANOEUVRING TANK 100' X 100' X 8'

POSITION OF WAVE DAMPER

ROOF OVER ASSEMBLY AREA

ROOF OVER TANK

MAIN WATERWAY 1300' X 48' X 25'

TRANSVERSE SECTION THROUGH MAIN TANK AND MANOEUVRING TANK

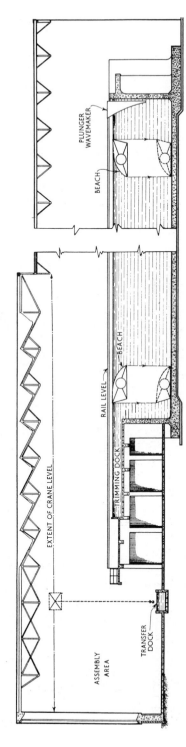

PLUNGER WAVEMAKER

BEACH

BEACH

RAIL LEVEL

TRIMMING DOCK

EXTENT OF CRANE LEVEL

ASSEMBLY AREA

TRANSFER DOCK

LONGITUDINAL SECTION THROUGH MAIN TANK

Plate 48. Number Three Tank.

Plate 49. Number Three Tank under construction, looking west.

Plate 50. Completed office buildings.

Plate 51. Number Three Tank. The two docks, in which models were prepared prior to test, are in the foreground. The model (5078), of a supertanker, was the largest (10 metres) ever made in polyurethane.

Plate 52. Number Two cavitation tunnel – model of tunnel showing vertical limbs 55 metres long.

Plate 53. Number Two cavitation tunnel – the working section to the left of the large return limb.

Plate 54. Number Three Tank – wavemaker.

Plate 55. Number Three Tank – seakeeping dynamometer.

Plate 56. Formal opening of Feltham Laboratories – The Duke of Edinburgh speaking. Lord Hailsham is on the left, Todd is on the right.

Plate 57. Opening of Feltham Laboratories – manoeuvring a model in Number Four Tank.

Plate 58. Supercavitating propeller.

Plate 59. One-tenth scale model of water channel.

Plate 60. Ship Division staff, 1962. Silverleaf is ninth from left in front row. Next is Todd, then Sir Gordon Sutherland (Director, NPL), Hughes, Dawson, Shearer and Doust. At far right in this row is Cross. In the row behind, Gadd is between Dawson and Shearer, and on Gadd's left is Ghosh, Clements, Wellicome and Goodrich.

Plate 61. Model of circular hovercraft in Number Two Tank.

Plate 62. Wave probes set for measurement of wave pattern.

Plate 63. Hovercraft model tests – model of cushion craft in Number Three Tank.

Plate 64. 200,000 Tons D.W. ship *Myrina*.

Plate 65. Model tests in waves – two different model forms are being towed in parallel through head-on waves.

Plate 66. Subjects of testing, 1965 – 1979: (a) *Tenacity*.

(b) Rowing eight in tank.

(c) *QE2*.

(d) *Benledi*.

Plate 67. Circulating water channel – working section seen beyond control desk.

Plate 68. Ship Division staff, 1972. Marwood is seated in the centre of the front row with Paffett on his right and Dawson on his left, Ritter is next to Dawson. *Sitting on the ground:* B. N. Steele is third from left; and Loe fourth from left. *In the middle row:* second from left is Rowe followed by Lewison, Hogben and R. P. Browne. *In the row behind:* Dolman is third from left, Morrall fifth, Acum sixth, Blake seventh, Mackenzie ninth. Bowden is third from right in this row. *In the back row:* Bailey is fourth from left, English fifth, Poulton sixth and Dand seventh.

Plate 69. Stability tests with damaged hull – model rolling and shipping water through damaged amidships.

Plate 70. Stability tests with damaged hull – model attached to GZ apparatus.

Plate 71. Model slamming in waves.

Plate 72. Model jet flap rudder in Number One Cavitation Tunnel.

Plate 73. Rotating cylinder rudder – final version of rudder fitted to model hull.

Plate 74. *VIC 62* turning at sea.

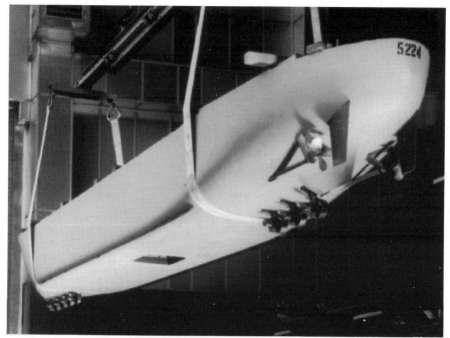

Plate 75. Thrusters fitted to model at fore and aft.

Plate 76. Model of semi-submersible "Uncle John" undergoing tests.

Plate 77. Tests in waves on tethered offshore working platform.

Plate 78. *Sir Claude Inglis* on trials.

Plate 79. Feltham test facilities from the air – 1975. To the left of the towing tank the open-air manoeuvring basin can be seen. On the other side of the tank are the cavitation tunnel buildings and the longer circulating water channel building.

Plate 80. Model of trawler *Gaul* (model 5319 – one-twentieth size).

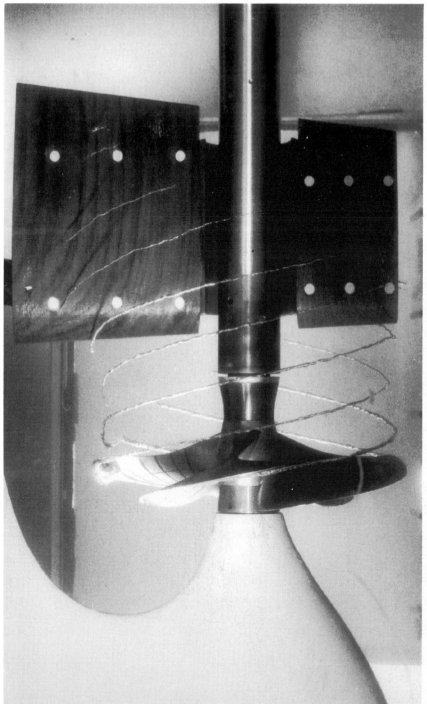

Plate 81 Tests in cavitation tunnel – dummy stern with rudder in tunnel under cavitating conditions.

Plate 82. Model ocean facility – remote controlled ship model in tank. Wavemaker in distance and computer room and control area to the left.

Plate 83. Model tests on Lena tower – at moment of launch.

Plate 84. Model test on Lena tower – tower upended.

Plate 85. Tests with ship models in 1986 – flotilla of barges under tow in Number Two Tank.

Plate 86. Test with ship models in 1986 – high speed patrol vessel in waves.

5. Everest J.T. and Hogben N., "Research on hovercraft over calm water", trans. RINA, 1967.

6. Hogben N. and Lumb F.E., *Ocean Wave Statistics* published by HMSO, London, 1967.

7. Ewing J.A. and Goodrich G.J., "The influence on ship motions of different wave spectra and of ship length", trans. RINA, 1967.

8. Goodrich G.J., "The influence of freeboard on wetness", NPL Ship Division Report 60, 1964.

9. White G.P., "Ram bows on high speed cargo liner forms. A preliminary survey", NPL Ship Division, TM 140, 1966.

10. Clements R.E., "The control of flow separation at the stern of a ship model using vortex generators", trans. RINA, 1965.

11. Gadd G.E., *Naval Architect*, No. 6, 1980.

12. Doust D.J., "Fishing vessel design and some related technical and economic factors", Conference on Design, construction and operation of small fishing vessels, St. John's, Newfoundland, 1965.

13. English J.W., "The design and performance of lateral thrust units for ships", trans. RINA, 1963.

14. O'Brien T.P., *The design of marine screw propellers*, published by Hutchinson, 1962.

15. O'Brien T.P., "Design of tug propellers", *Ship and Boat International*, issues 18 and 19, 1966.

16. O'Brien T.P., "Some effects of variation in number of blades on model screw performance", trans. NECIES, Vol. 81, 1965.

17. English J.W., "The application of a simplified lifting surface technique to the design of marine propellers", NPL Ship Division Report 30, 1962.

18. Silverleaf A. *et al*, "Some ship and model measurements of unsteady propeller forces", trans. RINA, 1964.

19. Gadd G.E., "Effects of dissolved additives on turbulent friction and physical properties of the fluid", *Nature*, 1966, 212 (5065), 874.

20. Shearer J.R. and Cross J.J., "The experimental determination of the components of ship resistance for a mathematical form", trans. RINA, 1965.

21. Hughes G., "Correlation of model resistance and application to ship", trans. RINA, 1963.

22. Hughes G., "An analysis of ship model resistance into viscous and wave components", trans. RINA, 1966.

23. Canham H.J.S. and Clements R.E., "An analysis of a sample of ship-model correlation data for tankers", trans. RINA, 1965.

24. Scott J.R., "A contribution to ship-model correlation using the BTTP 1962 data for single screw tankers", trans. RINA, 1965.

25. "Standard procedure for resistance and propulsion experiments with ship models", NPL Ship Division Report 10, 1960.

26. Hartley I., "The biology of No. 3 Towing Tank of Ship Division, NPL", NPL Ship Division Report 130, 1968.

27. Eames M.C. and Jones E.A., "HMCS Bras d'Or—an open-ocean hydrofoil ship", trans. RINA 1971.

28. Marwood W.J. and Bailey D., "Design data for high speed displacement hulls of round bilge form", NPL Ship Division Report 99, 1969.

29. Meek M., "GLENLYON Class—Design and operation of high-powered cargo liners", trans. RINA, 1964.

30. Baxter B.N., "Oceanographic Survey Ships", trans. RINA, 1967.

31. Wellicome J.F., "Report on resistance experiments carried out on three racing shells", NPL Ship Division, TM 184, 1967.

32. Steele B.N. and Turner R.T., "Design and construction of the NPL Circulating Water Channel", Symposium on experiment facilities for ship research in Great Britain, NPL, May 1967.
33. Committee of Enquiry into the Organisation of Civil Service, Cmnd 2171.
34. Silverleaf A. and Cook F.G.R., "A comparison of some features of high speed marine craft", trans. RINA, 1969.
35. Hughes G. and Cutland R.S., "*Viscous and wave components of ship model resistance*", Vol. 1—*Hull form data*, Vol. 2—*Resistance data*, published by HMSO, 1973.
36. Gadd G.E., "A new turbulent friction formulation based on a reappraisal of Hughes' results", trans. RINA, 1968.
37. Shipbuilding Inquiry Committee, 1965–66 Report, Cmnd 2937.

CHAPTER 13

YEARS OF CHANGE: 1969–1976

At the time of Paffett's arrival Government research effort in aero and hydrodynamics was spread throughout the country. Outside NPL several MoD (Navy) research establishments, some of whose work could be viewed as complementary to NPL's, had been in existence for many years. Similarly the Aero and Ship Divisions at NPL were well entrenched and the newcomer, the Hovercraft Unit at Hythe, was now part of NPL's Engineering Science Group. Aerodynamic research was also in progress at Bedford and Farnborough. Although this dispersal of effort appeared to work without serious difficulty, the Government was, nevertheless, determined to work towards greater unification at least so far as civil research was concerned and the first of several major decisions for change was reached in January, 1969. At a press conference, the Minister of Technology announced his broad objectives. These included the transfer of Aerodynamics Division aircraft research to the RAE at Farnborough leaving "industrial" aerodynamics at NPL. The word "industrial" had been coined to describe civil engineering aerodynamics which was concerned with bridges, chimneys (the helicoidal strakes fitted to circular chimney stacks to prevent wind induced oscillations were an NPL invention), tall buildings, air flow over landscapes and so on. The split up of Aerodynamics Division, which was a sudden and unpalatable shock to many of its staff, began in October 1970. Wind tunnels, such as the low density tunnel, were uprooted and re-erected at Farnborough and equipment seen to be of use to the tunnels at Bedford and Farnborough transferred. The work in NPL's Aerodynamics Division had been long and distinguished and has been reviewed[1] by Pankhurst, its last Superintendent. Well known names such as W.J. Duncan, S. Goldstein, D.W. Holder and H.H. Pearcey, to list but a few, had contributed importantly and given NPL an international reputation in aerodynamics.

The group left at Teddington was not of course devoid of facilities, some wind tunnels remained and the demand for work continued. An investigation into the effect of wind on the superstructure of an oil drilling ship and tests on the new Humber bridge are examples of the work done at this time. Nevertheless the industrial aerodynamics work appeared isolated as indeed did the work at Hythe and it came as no surprise when in April 1971 the activities of both were brought together in a new division of NPL, named the Division of Maritime

Science, DMS. Cook was appointed as its first Superintendent. The problem of dichotomy that had arisen in 1960 when Ship Division was divided between Teddington and Feltham sites cropped up again, Hythe being some 70 miles from Teddington. Silverleaf was keen to transfer all at Hythe to Feltham and, eventually, to build new offices and laboratories. Initially several members of staff as well as new recruits were accommodated in the offices built alongside the new circulating water channel but most of those already at Hythe remained. Cook needed a site manager at Hythe since trials at sea were still very much part of the new Division's work and Boyle was appointed and transferred in 1971. Meanwhile plans were drawn up for new offices at Feltham and an extensive laboratory with an elaborate arrangement for pumping air through ducting to hovercraft test rigs. The new buildings were to lie between the river boundary and Number Three tank leaving sufficient room for Number Six tank should it ever materialise. Cook, was anxious to overcome the shortcomings of the existing Feltham offices. Aircraft noise from nearby Heathrow airport had increased (96 decibels was recorded in a first floor office) and double glazing, which in fact was installed in later years, was of limited use in summer unless air conditioning was provided as well. Cook asked for a double-skinned building with air conditioning but an estimate of cost for this and the complex laboratory was far higher than the funds available and the whole idea abandoned. Efforts were then directed at improving the facilities at Hythe including a new large workshop there and Cook alternated between two offices, one in the Tunnel building at Feltham and the other at Hythe.

But to return to Ship Division and the situation inherited by Paffett. As has been said, about 150 staff were in post. Recruitment continued and in 1970 H. Ritter arrived on transfer from the Admiralty to head a branch that was to deal with a wide range of research topics within the ship propulsion and seakeeping fields. R.P. Browne and I.W. Dand arrived from Glasgow University, A. Morrall from Newcastle, S.J. Rowe from Leeds and R.G. Standing from Cambridge and Manchester Universities whilst the first of several transferred following the break up of Aerodynamics Division, G.E. Hellens, came to assist Marwood in the organisation of the facilities programme. Hellens was followed by J. Osborne who became involved with Hogben's researches and G.S. Smith an instrumentation specialist. Also transferred from NPL were R.A. Browne and F.J.M. Kirby (from DMS). By 1972 the total staff had risen slightly to 155. Of the scientists, Everest transferred to the Road and Transport Laboratory at Crowthorne and White resigned to become a lecturer at Portsmouth Polytechnic. In 1969 there came the shock news of Shearer's death on holiday. He had, before taking charge of the Special Projects Branch, been Allan's right hand man in the run up to the new facilities at Feltham and was an important link between the Division and the architects and contractors. In his last years he had been able to return to research and was pioneering with Steele the measurement of skin friction on models in the circulating water channel. Two other significant losses were Garlick and Marwood who retired within two years of one another after long years of service. Garlick's skill and dedication enabled the Division to enjoy a strong reputation in measurement and he was a tireless champion of mechanical dynamometry. Marwood was a true all rounder, his versatility proving valuable in a variety of areas, the design of apparatus, vibration work, high speed testing and, in his final working years, overall organisation of the test facilities programme and workshops.

In the 1970s there were clear signs that the emphasis in the work of Ship Division would change. The expansion in offshore engineering and the growth in the number of ships and tonnage were the main influences. Offshore, the exploitation of North Sea oil fields was proceeding rapidly and the rate of increase in new ships was shown vividly in Lloyd's statistical tables. From these the trend was as follows. In 1939 gross registered tonnage was 65 million tons spread around some 30,000 ships, in 1960, 125 million from 35,000 ships and by 1970 the total had reached an unprecedented level of 230 million tons and 53,000 ships although the large number of ships was soon to be seen as an over capacity leading to a dramatic reduction in new construction from the mid-1970s. The large numbers carrying hazardous and noxious cargoes through busy shipping lanes pointed to an increased risk of collision or strandings in coastal waters. As it was 170 collisions and 33 strandings were on record for the period 1958–1971. The *Torrey Canyon* accident off the Scilly Isles in 1967 was a disturbing example of the environmental damage that could occur. The responsibility for legislation affecting marine safety had for many years been the Government's and after the setting up of IMCO (now the International Maritime Organisation, IMO) such legislation and the associated international negotiations increasingly demanded a background of technical information. It was only natural, therefore, that Government turned to its Research Establishments and soon DMS was asked to carry out a traffic survey in the Dover Strait, a particularly awkward sea lane with a high density of passing ships, and to Ship Division for many other matters.

Formalised research by Ship Division had always been agreed annually by the Froude Committee, a committee which however included only two representatives from Government departments. From 1971 national bodies concerned with safety at sea, notably the Marine Division of the Department of Trade and Industry (DTI), were included with other Government departments in the discussions which formulated future work. In 1970 Ship Division had already anticipated the increasing hazards at sea and had sent a report to Mintech suggesting ways of reducing human failure that often led to marine accidents. As a result, later years saw an involvement in the development of ship simulators for training ships' officers and also studies on the ergonomics of ship control. Support from Government was arranged through newly formed Requirements Boards. There were seven such Boards and each placed contracts of work with the various Research Associations such as NPL. Requests to Ship Division came through the Ship and Marine Technology Requirements Board, SMTRB.

In anticipating the changes to come Paffett decided a reorganisation of staff was needed. He retained the basic structure set up by Silverleaf 10 years earlier, two Branches and a support group, but now concentrated staff in specific work areas. Branch One, as before, was headed by Dawson and dealt with the large majority of commercial test work and that part of the research programme dealing with fundamental studies of ship resistance. Tests from firms were in the charge of Bowden, Clements and Morrall with Mackenzie handling data and ship power estimates. Morrall divided his time between tests and managing the computer group, and Bailey took charge of high speed model tests, most of which were for patrol craft and small warships with occasional hovercraft models. The circulating water channel, in regular use for both research and commercial tests, needed a resident manager/experimenter. Dand controlled the facilities from 1973 with Pearce as experimenter and adviser to other users. Branch Two was headed by Ritter (Johnson had moved to DMS just before Paffett's reshuffle) and most of its work was devoted to research projects although an overlap with commercial testing saw English leading tests on special propulsion devices. In this he was assisted by Rowe who became increasingly involved in offshore tests, responsibility for which he was to assume in 1975. Acum led vibration studies and Hogben ranged over a wide field covering wave studies and loading of offshore structures. Browne and Lewison took on most of the seakeeping research and some aspects of manoeuvring whilst special investigations such as the development of the rotating cylinder rudder were led by Steele. The important support group did not have a Head as such, its responsibilities being divided between Blake (electronics) and Marwood (facilities and workshops). Loe, under Blake, controlled an instrumentation group and the large and complicated job of organising the design of new equipment, workshops and facilities to ensure the flow of work to priorities agreed by Paffett led Marwood to hold daily meetings between representatives from the various working groups. Paffett's reorganisation worked well and stayed in place in all but detail until the next change overtook Ship Division.

In August 1971, NPL bade Silverleaf a reluctant farewell as he left to become Director of the Transport and Road Laboratory. Ship Division had lost a strong voice in defence of its existence and activities—if defence was needed in 1970 (it certainly was 10 years later), although Paffett was never slow in coming forward with powerful and forthright opinion. A clear and uncomplicated approach to hydrodynamics was a Paffett hallmark seen best when speaking to wider audiences as for example in his paper "Hydrodynamics and ship performance".[2]

The test facilities, so crucial to Ship Division's output needed regular maintenance and, if occasion demanded, modification. Number Two tank presented problems. In 1965 its ageing carriage had run out of control to hit the end wall of the tank building with near disastrous results and the length of shallow water had never been adequate. When Dand began experiments with model tankers running over shallows the inability to run a good range of test speeds over a length sufficient to reach stable conditions became all too obvious.

The growing interest in ship behaviour in restricted waterways persuaded Paffett to increase the length of shallow water in the tank. Plans were drawn up by W.S. Atkins and Partners at Epsom to provide a 76 metres run of shallow water (a maximum water depth of 60 cm) shelving upwards from the rest of the tank where over a length of 120 metres water would be to its original depth of $2\frac{3}{4}$ metres. As has been noted earlier, this restricted the tank for other purposes such as tests in deep water on very high speed models. Number Three tank was of course ideal for such work but a more expensive facility. The changes planned gave the opportunity of specifying a close tolerance to the flatness of the tank bottom over the length of shallow water and this was achieved. After the alterations were complete Hogben extended the ability of the tank further when he designed a simple attachment to the carriage, which when dragged through the water generated a high steep wave. The wavedozer, as it was called, proved a valuable device for tests on models of offshore structures where a wave height greater than that available from normal wavemakers was needed. In later years further improvements were made in which a modern control and drive system for the carriage were fitted and a wavemaker capable of generating both regular and irregular waves.

At this time Ship Division acquired its last test facility, Number Seven tank. This was built ostensibly to satisfy the needs of a single project, the study concerning the enlargement of the Suez canal. The new tank had to be large enough to erect model sections of parts of the canal and manoeuvre free-running models over shallow water and it was needed in a hurry. Intended as a temporary facility it was built outdoors between the metal workshop and the south side of Number Three tank. Wooden walls with a rubber lining were built to a height of $1\frac{1}{4}$ metres and formed an enclosure 60 metres square. The tank, or rather basin, of water was not built to a high standard yet it proved to be an extremely useful addition despite being completely open to the elements. The large water area offered greater scope for manoeuvring experiments than Number Four tank and on fine days (a wind break was added along its south side) several other projects were successfully accomplished.

INSTRUMENTATION AND EQUIPMENT

Developments in instrumentation centred on the desire to replace mechanical dynamometry, the exploration of a numerical control system of manufacturing hull and propeller models and keeping pace with the developing computer. A computer was installed on Number Three tank carriage and data recorded on magnetic tape fed into it for analysis and automatic plotting. This was a great step forward and of enormous benefit to tests on offshore structures where large quantities of data were gathered. Rowe, Kirby and Neville developed the whole process of on-the-spot data acquisition and analysis and with a PDP computer installed, this extremely powerful tool was much appreciated by clients and users alike. Ship Division had, since the days of the DEUCE computer, been tied to NPL for access to a large computer. The NPL's KDF 9 computer had succeeded DEUCE but soon Ship Division bought its own self-contained computer, a Hewlett Packard, which was capable of small calculations. It was put into offices next to the reception area at Feltham at which time Neville had become manager of a computer group comprising four people. For larger computations the Hewlett Packard could be operated as a remote batch terminal over a land line connection to a commercial computer bureau.

Wellicome was the first to make an attempt at machining a model propeller by numerical control. He wrote a program for use with the KDF 9 computer which described in detail the ordinates and shape of a simple propeller blade and working with the National Engineering Laboratory in Scotland an analogue magnetic tape was produced that could be used to control a machine tool. A blade was successfully machined and only a little material had to be removed by hand to reach completion. This encouraged further work by Marwood with the ultimate objective of machining both hulls and propellers. To begin with another more complicated propeller shape was profiled on a machine in the DMS workshop and also a hydrofoil strut. At Marwood's retirement W. Pearson took over and was encouraged to carry out a feasibility study for a full manually controlled system, a task he pursued with such enthusiasm that his final proposals asked for the installation of a commercial numerical control milling machine to manufacture hulls and propellers and the requirement of a special building with accommodation for 10 additional staff permanently assigned to the task. This was hardly feasible and understandably forgotten. In the event, with few models needed in later years, the decision to abandon numerical control was wise. It could make economic sense only if large numbers of models became a regular requirement or if suitable, affordable equipment ever became available.

RESEARCH

Ship Stability when Damaged

As we have seen, from the 1970s Ship Division research was largely dominated by the requirements of Government departments. An early request was to measure the dynamic stability of a ferry in seas before and after suffering collision damage. The overall aim was to provide designers and regulatory bodies with data to assess ship safety in damaged conditions relative to sea conditions. It was thought that the 1960 Safety of Life at Sea Conference regulations for watertight subdivision left room for improvement. H. Bird of the Marine Division, DTI worked with Browne in a long programme of work chosen deliberately to be experimental rather than theoretical because of the serious lack of mathematical treatment available for accounting for the mechanics of capsize or the movement of water in and out of damaged parts of a ship as it moved in waves. Their work was thus entirely devoted to model tests on a typical passenger and vehicle ferry 106 metres long. Since many experiments were called for including frequent capsizing of the model it was decided to build the 1/25-scale model in GRP. It was divided horizontally at its main deck and below this six watertight bulkheads were inserted, four spanning an assumed area of damage at amidships and two, serving the same purpose, in the forebody. On the port side two removable watertight portions were fitted in the two regions of assumed damage to allow water to flood freely into the holed compartments during experiments in waves. The experiments in irregular waves, conducted by Jacob in Number Four tank, covered a range of intact and flooded cases with the model at a pre-selected condition of initial stability. The model was positioned beam on to the waves, its damaged side either facing or in the lee of the oncoming waves and minimum stability conditions were found which would resist capsize. For each condition of critically flooded stability, or capsize point, values of the hull righting level, GZ were required—curves of GZ and the area under them were standard criteria when assessing stability. Values of GZ were found in separate experiments using a new piece of apparatus designed by Marwood's design group. The model was connected through a hinged coupling that permitted trim and yaw, to a strain gauged member attached to a slide in vertical guides. This arrangement allowed the model to rise or sink freely in the water. The model was then heeled to a known angle at which it took up a position of equilibrium in trim and yaw and the strain gauge measured the moment on the model from which GZ was calculated. Bird and Browne gave their results,[3] which attracted much interest for they had broken new ground. Little was known of how ships behaved in a seaway when damaged and open to the sea. Unfortunately the effect of wind was not simulated in the experiments, which detracted somewhat from the conclusions reached, but the value of the paper was undoubted and recognised by the RINA in the award of its Bronze medal.

Squat

The mighty ships of 250,000 tons or more were becoming a cause for concern as they entered approaches to terminals. Hitherto the sea areas in the world were considered deep with respect to a normal tanker's draught but now in carrying much larger cargoes, dimensions, in particular draught, had increased and water became relatively shallow. Restricted water depth reduced the manoeuvrability of these large ships and hydrodynamic reaction between hull bottoms and the sea bed caused a bodily sinkage or squat of the hull which in certain cases might have led to grounding. It was not uncommon for underkeel clearance in the approaches to Southampton, for example, to be as little as a metre and squat could easily equal that at certain ship speeds. Dand measured the squat of tanker models in the shallows of Number Two tank. Tests on full forms gave measurements of the sinkage at bow and stern over a range of speed and water depth which were compared with full-scale measurements. From the model experiments Dand deduced empirical factors, which he used in a theory to predict the degree of squat, and found good agreement with measurements on self-propelled models and full-scale results. Squat was seen to increase rapidly with ship speed and for a 330 metre tanker with an underkeel clearance at rest of 2 metres, Dand's prediction showed that the ship would strike the bottom at 14 knots. Happily this was a higher speed than that at which such a ship would be driven as it approached a terminal but even at 8 knots one third of the available clearance was lost. A useful predictor had been produced[4] that could give guidance to ship operation anywhere. As regards loss of manoeuvrability in shallow water, current literature had little relevance to such full forms and with the backing of Marine Division, the Chamber of Shipping and Ports Authorities, Ship Division set out to obtain information. Manoeuvring experiments on a free-running model were carried out by A.D. Gill who arrived in 1972 and Lewison in Number Four tank with enough water drained away to give representative depths of interest. Lewison's recently introduced alternative to tracking the path of a model from exposures taken from an overhead camera set up in the roof of the tank proved invaluable since the existing sonic probes became exposed in shallow water conditions. The measurements showed a very obvious reduction in manoeuvrability with reducing water depth. With underkeel clearance of 1/10 model draught, turning circle diameter at a given approach speed was double that obtained in deep water. This was obviously serious since it implied a slower response of the ship to small rudder movement at low speeds and hence poor manoeuvrability in the approaches to terminals. Already ship owners were anxious to remove way quickly in these large ships well before harbour entrances were reached and braking devices such as parachutes were considered. Any means of improving control was keenly sought and led Ship Division to include in its researches investigations into special types of rudder.

Rudders

An interesting idea concerning the modification of a conventional ship's rudder was worked on by English and Rowe. The principle of the mechanical trailing edge flap used in aerodynamics was taken and applied as a jet of water discharged from the trailing edge of a rudder. The jet changed the pressure distribution around the aerofoil surface of the rudder and increased lift. Such extra lift exerted on a rudder was equivalent to an increased side force so that even when stationary it was feasible to move a ship laterally. In practice, slots were required on both sides of the rudder and the direction of the jet switched whenever the rudder was changed from port to starboard operation. A new technology of fluidic switching was available and the British Hydromechanics Research Association, BHRA, was contracted to carry out a special design exercise. Meanwhile tests in Number One cavitation tunnel examined the additional lift characteristics possible from jets discharged through different slot thicknesses. For a zero speed and for 35° of rudder angle, side force increased by 27 per cent with the jet operating. English and Rowe with Bain from BHRA described a system[5] that could be fitted to a typical ship and calculated the power required to pump water through the rudder stock to the jet and operate the fluidic switch. Their idea was not greeted with the greatest of enthusiasm. Ship owners were apparently quite content with bow thrusters and it was considered that to install a jet flap rudder, as it was described, would incur a high initial outlay as well as additional costs in maintaining the jets against fouling and possible blockage. As a result the idea never gained favour and attention shifted later to another form of rudder modification, the rotating cylinder rudder.

The development of the rotating cylinder rudder exploited the Magnus effect which is set up when a cylinder rotates in a fluid to generate a force normal to the cylinder, Steele began by experimenting with a conventional rudder whose leading edge was replaced by a cylinder. A small motor remote from the rudder provided the power to rotate the cylinder. In the water channel side force was measured over a range of rudder angle set against an oncoming uniform flow. A powerful side force was demonstrated and, of greater significance, unstalled flow was maintained for rudder angles up to 90°. Normally a rudder stalled at about 30–40° beyond which lift decreased rapidly. However, the rudder plus cylinder gave excessive drag and improvements were needed. The cylinder was moved to the trailing edge of the rudder and designed as a trailing edge flap, the rudder moving with the flap. This proved successful and the idea was patented. Free-running experiments with models fitted with a rotating cylinder rudder were very encouraging, dramatic manoeuvres becoming possible. With the rudder hard over and the cylinder rotating at a selected speed, models could be made to turn on their axes with a near zero turning circle. Paffett was enthusiastic and convinced that full-scale trials should begin. An elderly 200 tons coaster, *Vic 62*, a Clyde steam "puffer" was bought from the Admiralty at scrap value and refitted at Hythe. Its massive Scotch boiler (now in the Science museum) was removed and a new diesel engine installed as well as an electric generator. *Vic 62* could be used for a variety of trials at sea, indeed a floating test bed, and a ship's container was put in the hold and used as a small laboratory for whatever equipment might be needed. A rotating cylinder rudder was designed by Pearson to fit *Vic 62* and with Dolman taking charge of its construction, the two spent a good deal of time at Hythe supervising the fitting. In due course the trials team were euphoric as *Vic 62* duly turned on the spot with the cylinder rotating and a photographer was immediately despatched in a helicopter to photograph the trail of foam on the surface of the sea showing *Vic 62*'s bow moving sideways with no headway on the ship. Moreover a 90° turn executed at full engine power brought *Vic 62* to a dead stop in a very short distance and time. Much publicity followed and the BBC featured the new rudder in one of its television programmes, *Tomorrow's World*. The time was right for commercial exploitation, YARD at Glasgow handled this with Ship Division acting as consultants providing measurements from *Vic 62* for use in the engineering design work. The herring fishing vessel *Claben* was fitted with a rotating cylinder rudder in 1974. *Claben* used large Seine nets, which in harsh weather was a difficult task. The new rudder gave additional control of the ship and the stabilisation achieved in holding *Claben* on station in rough seas eased considerably the deployment of the nets. The rotating cylinder rudder worked superbly well but factors militated against its universal adoption. A special steering engine of significant power was needed to reach the large rudder angles needed as well as additional power to rotate the cylinder. And of course other devices such as the Becker and Schilling rudders were competing for acceptance. Many shipowners were delighted with the success of LTUs in large tankers, and thrusters fitted at other parts of the ship were proving their worth as English was soon to demonstrate in tests on dynamically positioned ships. Whatever the reason for its rejection the new rudder failed to enjoy further development and Ship Division's work on it was wound up in 1975.

Manoeuvring

Whereas improvements to existing steering gear were desirable the fundamental elements of ship manoeuvring needed to be more fully understood. Gill worked with Lewison to begin a study of manoeuvring dynamics to develop mathematical models comprising equations of motion for use in the simulation of ship manoeuvres, the coefficients for which could be obtained initially from captive and then free-running model experiments. Paffett became particularly interested in this for he saw the need for the development of a cheap ship simulator, a nocturnal simulator that was eventually built by Decca and used by Nautical Colleges, the mathematical model for which was supplied to Decca from the results of Gill and Lewison's work. In the corresponding experiments it was important that accurate modelling of ship manoeuvring was reproduced since the effectiveness of a rudder was dependent on the slipstream and overall propeller thrust which had to be to scale. A free-running self-propelled model gave a resistance coefficient higher than the equivalent ship. An auxiliary thruster in the form of a contrarotating fan mounted on the model was devised which was driven by a small engine installed separately within the model.

Interaction

The hazardous consequences of shallow water to approaching and passing ships were seen in 1972 when the British passenger cargo ship *Royston Grange* collided with a Liberian ship the *Tien Chee* in the River Plate estuary. The collision and fire that soon followed was severe and resulted in heavy loss of life. In the litigation that followed the DTI was asked to suggest technical reasons that may have contributed to the accident and its Marine Division requested model experiments that would reconstruct the likely circumstances of the collision. They were led by Dand and carried out in the shallow end of Number Two tank. Since the exact depth of shallow water was so important the topography of the sea bed had to be reproduced. The collision had occurred in a straight 3 kilometre stretch of the Punto Indio channel of the estuary and from hydrographers' charts the characteristics of the sea bed and sloping sides of the channel were carefully copied using granite chippings. After conventional resistance and propulsion tests, which gave estimates of the maximum possible approach speeds attainable by each vessel in the prevailing water depth, free-running experiments were conducted and interaction aspects studied. From his results Dand could do no more than suggest possible reasons for the collision since with no survivors from the *Royston Grange* there was no evidence of the circumstances that led to the disaster. He did suggest that collision could have occurred due to the excessive speeds of approach by both ships, an unavoidable sheer to port by *Royston Grange* due to rejection forces from the sloping sea bed and loss of rudder effectiveness in *Royston Grange* if, as had been supposed, her engines were stopped at a crucial moment before collision. This was an impressive and meticulous piece of work rendered more difficult by the necessary smallness of the models used in the free-running experiments. They were roughly 1½ metres long and unable to accommodate the usual radio control apparatus and batteries. Apparatus of the kind used by amateurs was bought and found to work perfectly well, the independent control systems in each model being unaffected by the surrounding metal structure of Number Two tank building.

This latest work on interaction between ships proved a spur for further work, again carried out by Dand. This time the problem of a small ship such as a tug or pilot vessel coming alongside a much larger vessel was one of the subjects for consideration. There were cases on record where tugs had actually been swept across the bow of the large ships they were approaching. The circulating water channel proved suitable for simulated experiments, its large working section being ideal for long-term layout of river banks and channels when these were needed in a shallow water investigation. Dand produced a valuable paper[6] that set out the hydrodynamic features connected with shallow water and the forces of interaction between a ship and another ship or bank that could contribute to a collision. The worth of the paper was recognised by the award of the RINA Silver medal.

Ships' Lifeboats

Requests from Government departments covered a wide spectrum, as indicated by an investigation into ways of launching and releasing ships' lifeboats. Large tankers were vulnerable to fire and under way, even at low speeds, their inertia was so great that in an emergency it took several valuable minutes to bring the tanker to rest before lifeboats could be launched. Conventionally, ships' lifeboats were lowered from davits and released by hand from their falls when afloat by an off-load mechanism. If a satisfactory on-load release gear could be designed, would it be possible to lower, launch, tow and then release a lifeboat whilst the ship was still moving forward? Bailey was asked to look into this while DTI considered alternative release mechanisms. A 1/5-scale model of a typical ships' lifeboat was made and suspended on falls fore and aft alongside a long plank immersed and attached to the carriage to represent the side of a ship. Jacob with the instrumentation group designed an ingenious release trip that could be operated remotely to release the model from its falls at any desired moment. The tests over a range of assumed ship speeds began by lowering the lifeboat, ballasted with the weight of a full complement of survivors, into the water, towing it on its falls. Even at low speeds the model yawed sharply outwards, heeled over and began shipping water. This happened soon after the model had assumed its normal draught in the water so that any idea of releasing it from its falls was fraught with danger. Drogues fitted at the stern to stream out automatically to improve directional stability under tow met with little success. A solution was found by setting the lifeboat in the falls at an angle of 10° stern down. This way its rear struck the water first and subsequent behaviour under tow appeared satisfactory and by setting the rudder hard over, the model after release moved away from the ship's side very safely. It was perfectly possible to design a release mechanism for a full-size lifeboat but the idea never gained ground, principally over fears that a mechanism could not be completely proof against failure or corrosion. Successful and rapid operation and release of both falls simultaneously was crucial to a safe evacuation from the moving ship.

DTI Ship *Miranda*

The same department was using a vessel to support trawlers operating in the harsh conditions off Iceland. The acquisition of a support vessel was a recommendation in the Holland-Martin report that said a vessel should be available in winter months to help prevent ship losses by giving weather forecasts and advice to trawlers. The Department was using *Miranda*, a converted sailing vessel with an elegant clipper bow. Clearly she had to be a good sea boat. *Miranda* was reported as seaworthy but not seakindly and Lewison with other members of staff were invited aboard to assess her performance at sea. Roll and pitch motions were recorded and found to be high and it was noticed that *Miranda* steered badly in strong winds. Ship Division was asked to suggest realistic modifications to improve matters and as a *quid pro quo Miranda* could be made available to NPL for any research purposes. Recommendations were put forward that included a new propeller, a roll stabilisation tank and, following wind tunnel experiments in 1972, a revised superstructure to reduce wind resistance. In return Lewison carried out various speed, power and manoeuvring measurements and DMS used *Miranda* as a base for surveillance by radar of shipping movements in the Dover Strait.

Flow and Skin Friction

Other research carried out at this time, with the new circulating water channel as a stimulant, was aimed at fundamental problems such as detailed examinations of the flow around ship's hulls. Shearer with Steele did this in the channel using woollen tufts, paint, hot wire probes, etc., and also attempted to measure the magnitude and distribution of the skin friction over the surface of hulls. As ships grew in size their wave-making resistance shrank to a relatively small part of the total so that the major part of their resistance due to viscous effects, principally skin friction, became of greater importance. The earlier work on the interdependence model had isolated most of the components of resistance. Total viscous resistance had been obtained from pitot tube measurements behind a model. That part of the viscous resistance acting normal to a hull's surface (pressure resistance) was obtained from pressure measurements and eventually wave-making resistance was calculated from wave pattern measurements. Now, in the new channel, that part of the viscous resistance tangential to the hull's surface (shear stress or skin friction resistance) would become available once a satisfactory way of measuring it was found. Both Paffett and Silverleaf were excited at the prospect since by isolating all the principal components the fundamentals of ship resistance would at last be open to a complete physical understanding, a situation bound to influence and help hull design. Shearer and Steele looked at existing flow measuring techniques and after a long study rejected transducers, Stanton tubes and hot film probes, the latter having been used successfully in detecting and measuring turbulence levels, for the Preston tube, a device developed by J.H. Preston once of Aerodynamics Division. This tube, connected to a manometer, consisted of a forward facing total head tube placed very close to the surface of the hull, which, with a separately measured static pressure at the same point, allowed a simple calculation of the shear stress. Successive measurements at some 100 other places gave, after integration, the total skin friction resistance over the hull. This was the first time such measurements had been attempted.

Two slender form models were chosen for the first tests and fitted with pressure points. To make sure the tubes were properly positioned preliminary paint flow tests were run to determine streamlines and the tubes aligned accordingly. The channel was ideal for the tests. The water could be allowed to circulate for fully 10 minutes before measurements were taken thus ensuring settled conditions and adequate response time for the tubes and Boyle's scanning valve allowed simultaneous readings. Pearce carried out the bulk of the experiments and handled the extensive analysis. He joined with Steele to produce a paper of utmost interest[7] which gave the results from two 0·54 block coefficient models, one of which was fitted with a bulbous bow. The distribution of skin friction was shown for each model and the effect of the bulb in changing the distribution was clearly seen. From this it was concluded that the bulb did not act solely on the wave-making resistance. Total skin friction resistance was compared to that given by the Hughes flat plate formulation. The model results straddled the Hughes line and overall were very close to it. This was surprising for it might have been expected that Hughes' (two dimensional) formulation would have fallen below the model results thus giving an indication of form factor. Reservations were placed over the successful use of Preston tubes in regions of strong pressure gradients and further experiments were conducted this time with fuller form models, a 0·8 block coefficient tanker with and without a bulb, a bulk carrier and another tanker with block coefficient 0·7. Happily, fears over the tubes were unfounded and consistent results were obtained. In these fuller forms viscous resistance was high and again the effect of the bulb was influential. Comparative wave pattern measurements with and without the bulb were virtually identical indicating that the reduction in viscous resistance found was due to the bulb alone. Shearer and Steele in presenting results[8] summarised the position and were optimistic that the new technique for obtaining skin friction data and its distribution would advance the hull design process. This was no doubt true at a price, for channel tests were a lengthy and expensive business and in fact the best use of the channel in later years was seen in specific investigations of hull flow to cure separation problems or other types of study such as Dand's interaction work. Skin friction measurements continued for a while but could never be made cost effective and in any case Gadd was soon to develop theoretical methods of predicting flow direction and assessing hull resistance which, thanks to computers, could be done at a fraction of the cost of channel experiments.

The ability to study flow under ideal conditions was attractive to others. Everest who had embarked on a research into multi-hulls used the channel to examine the changes in flow direction over the twin hulls of a catamaran due to changes in their separation. The proximity of one hull to the other was important since interference effects could sometimes reduce overall resistance. Everest found regions of beneficial wave interference at Froude numbers between 0·3 and 0·4 for optimum separation distances between the hulls. Savings of up to 50 per cent in wave resistance over a monohull were possible. This interesting research[9] was presented to the North East Coast Institution and renewed interest in the multi-hull idea. BSRA soon commissioned tests on catamarans and trimarans allowing Lackenby[10] to postulate a fast cross-Channel vessel comprising three hulls which with the right combination of fore and aft and transverse hull spacing gave a calm water resistance comparable with an equivalently loaded monohull. Lewison followed up his work on the slamming of ships in waves by running tests on a catamaran, the twin hulls of which he joined at their forward ends with a fin. In waves he succeeded in reducing pitch motion by half and eliminated water impact on the span decking.

Wave-making Resistance

A greater understanding of wave-making and its contribution to ship resistance was a continuing interest and in Gadd, Ship Division had a natural successor to Wigley. The first publication[11] to bear the fruits of Gadd's work in this field was presented in 1969. It was an attempt to improve existing wave theory by introducing second-order potential flow effects into the calculations. He used a method, that derived from Havelock's approach, of dividing the hull into a grid of rectangular panels over which wave-making sources were assumed to be distributed. The phasing of the humps and hollows in the curve of wave resistance from a mathematical form were now more accurately predicted. However, for realistic ship forms, theory had always overestimated stern waves but by introducing an empirical reducing factor, very reasonable agreement in wave resistance was reached for a 0·6 block coefficient hull. The attraction of the panel method began to be seen because hull offsets at each grid point could be easily changed and the revised wave resistance calculated quickly by computer. An early example of Gadd's success was demonstrated in a trawler, the model test for which had given a mediocre result. The lines of the trawler were modified by a rearrangement and fairing of the offsets over part of the hull. Gadd's theoretical predictions of wave resistance (C_w) for both original and modified forms showed lower values for the latter and subsequent measurements of total resistance (C_t) showed a useful advantage at higher test speeds. The improved theory would be enhanced still further if an ability to estimate the direction of the local flow over a hull could be included and Gadd's next paper[12] addressed this.

Hess and Smith in a recent publication had described a computer program that calculated in great detail the flow over simple bodies submerged in unrestricted inviscid flow. Adapting and simplifying the method to the case of a floating ship, Gadd calculated pressure coefficients and wave velocity components which after integration gave total wave resistance. From the velocity components flow directions, at each point on the same grid arrangement as used earlier, could be found. Boundary layer effects were not considered but since boundary layer thickness at the bow was not very thick the velocity components and flow directions over the forward half of a hull were an excellent approximation to reality, as could be seen when flow vectors were compared with a paint flow test on a model tanker. The calculated flow patterns had another attraction. Flow separation, or reverse flow, if a possibility, could perhaps be inferred from the flow directions, giving the chance of an early assessment of a hull in advance of a model test. However, Gadd was quick to point out that the method worked best for fine hulls, bluffer shapes being more difficult. Although his achievement was most welcomed enthusiastically by Weinblum and Eggers in the discussion of Gadd's 1970 paper[12] that followed, Gadd was aware of the need to supplement his computations with three-dimensional turbulent boundary layer calculations, and was later to achieve this in a paper[13] presented in 1978.

Wave pattern measurements initiated in Ship Division by Gadd and Hogben were being keenly gathered by Hogben, who at the same time greatly improved the technique[14] enabling automatic measurements to be made at the same time as routine resistance experiments. There was a growing belief that Froude's classical extrapolation could be replaced by the combined measurements at the model of total viscous and wave-making resistance. The addition of these were agreeing remarkably well with the total model resistance at the dynamometer. However, when Hogben and Standing collated and examined results from a cross-section of models[15] a very significant fact emerged. In full forms (block coefficient above about 0·75) or in tests at ballast draughts where bulbs, if fitted, sometimes pierced the water surface, the pressure resistance was no longer completely accounted for by the wave pattern because of the appearance of a wave at the bow which curled over to break close to the hull dissipating its energy into the frictional wake instead of into the wave pattern remote from the hull. Such "breaking" waves were unfortunate but an inevitable consequence of the fuller form and finally put paid to any hopes that a more accurate method of extrapolation could be reached from unambiguous measurements of wave-making resistance. Wave pattern measurements ceased to become part of routine measurements but were still a useful resource for hulls with low wave-making. The difficulty with the breaking wave cropped up again when Gadd tried to improve his theoretical approach to wave-making of full forms.[16] He abandoned commonly used Kelvin wave-making sources which worked well in very fine or "thin ship" theory for the simpler Rankine ones. Kelvin sources, distributed over the centreplane of a hull, as in his 1969 paper,[11] or the hull surface, as in his 1970 paper[12] satisfy free surface conditions only approximately and Gadd found that the conditions were satisfied more accurately using Rankine sources distributed over an area of the free surface surrounding the hull as well as the hull surface. Gadd was the first to use this approach which is now the most widely used technique for calculating wave resistance. In his latest paper[16] he got an excellent comparison between calculated and measured wave profiles for a 0·7 block coefficient form. Also, for the same hull, calculated wave resistance compared well with the residuary resistance derived in the usual way from the model resistance measurement. But in fuller forms still (block coefficient 0·9) his calculated wave resistance at Froude numbers above 0·14 was well below the measured result due to the observed large breaking wave, much of the energy from which could not be accounted for in the theory. Nevertheless, Gadd had shown improvements in calculated results for a wider range of hull than before. Thanks to the computer, calculations of resistance from a variety of bow shapes in a given base design could be obtained quickly and ranked according to preference.

Methodical Series Tests on Hulls

One of the consequences of very full form ships was the obvious lack of hull design data. BSRA recognised this and sponsored model tests on a 0·85 block coefficient form that were a natural extension of the already completed BSRA series. Two publications resulted from this work co-authored by Clements (who was in charge of the experiments) and G.R. Thomson of BSRA. The first of these[17] appeared in 1974. Further series work concerning high speed craft was done by Bailey. There was a gap between the finer forms of the NPL round bilge series and an American series by Yeh that dealt with extremely fine forms. Three further models were run each with a length/beam ratio of 7·5 and when propulsion, manoeuvring and seakeeping data were obtained later from some of the series models all the information was brought together and published in a monograph.[18]

Ship-Model Correlation

Correlation factors agreed by the BTTP in 1965 and used then by Ship Division were a subject for periodic review as more data for new ships became available from the BSRA programme. Of its own volition, Ship Division departed slightly from the 1965 figures in 1969, changes being made as a result of a reconsideration of power correlation factors for the shorter ship. Two years later when correlation data from larger modern ships became available it was clear another review was needed and Dawson with Bowden began a major new analysis. They were in possession by now of a huge array of data from scores of ships and could apply a more rigorous approach. Thus older, less perfect data could be ignored. Two things emerged clearly from their analysis. Hull length/draught ratio and roughness had a consistent effect on the deduced correlation factors. New formulations for the selection of the power factor, $1 + x$ and propeller speed factor, k_2, were proposed for single and twin screw propelled ships.[19, 20] The formulations were simple equations containing standard draught and specified hull roughness terms. Although BTTP had decided that the old 1965 figures should be replaced, agreement to adopt the Dawson and Bowden formulae was not reached. Nevertheless, they became Ship Division's official policy and came into use in predicting from the model result the speed and power of a new ship on a measured-mile course in ideal trial conditions. The Dawson and Bowden formulae are still used by BMT today but are not regarded as the final word since hull designs will continue to evolve with time.

An example of the differences in predicted ship power that could arise from using different correlation factors was seen in the *Priam* class cargo liners described by Meek.[21] Model tests were conducted mostly in the St. Albans tank but Ship Division was asked to carry out certain resistance and propulsion tests with stock propellers. Whereas St. Albans adhered to the 1965 BTTP factors,

Ship Division used their modified version of these. For the maximum service power available at the ship the margin of power allowing for bad weather and fouling above the predicted calm water trial condition came out at 50 per cent according to Ship Division and 45 per cent according to St. Albans. This may not have been important so far as power margin was concerned but predictions of the ship speed on a measured-mile would have disagreed by about ¼ knot. Such a situation led to understandable confusion in the minds of shipbuilders noting, as they did, different answers coming from different tanks for the same ship. It was regrettable, therefore, that at the time of Dawson and Bowden's analysis the lack of agreement within BTTP perpetuated this inconsistency.

Slamming

Cargo ships were being driven faster and soon reports came in of structural damage at the bow due to ships slamming in heavy seas. A theory was extant that showed that the impact of a plate falling on water could be controlled by trapping air beneath it. Lewison as a visiting fellow to the University of California before his arrival at Ship Division had looked into the cushioning effect of air in tests on a flat plate in a vertical drop test machine. He now applied his experience to the current problem of ship slamming. On a typical ship model he fitted external keels running parallel with the hull centreline following the experiments in California that had shown that vertical flanges helped to prevent the escape of air just before the plate hit the water. Lewison ran the ship model in high waves with and without keels fitted measuring the pressures at the hull surface in the bow region. With keels fitted maximum slamming levels reduced, but not by much. A worthwhile reduction was found when air was ejected from the model into the space created by the forefoot as it emerged from a wave. A sensor was designed to detect emergence and activate the discharge of air. Lewison certainly succeeded (with air ejection the incidence of serious slams reduced by one third) although his report[22] was hardly received with enthusiasm perhaps because of the drawbacks of fitting keels to a ship. They had to be quite long, almost half the length of the ship and fairly deep, typically ⅔ metre below the centreline keel, and since retractable keels were hardly feasible, their resistance would be a nuisance. Further complication would come from the need to install an air supply. A cheaper solution appeared to be the acceptance of slamming and to monitor it on board. The ship's master could then be warned when the frequency of slamming reached dangerous levels and ship speed reduced until frequency levels fell. The shipowning company Manchester Liners operated a weekly service of cargo liners between Manchester and the St. Lawrence seaway. Five of their ships had suffered bottom plating damage forward and the company asked Ship Division to investigate the incidence of slamming with a view to installing ship-borne instrumentation. Strain gauges and an accelerometer were fitted to *Manchester City* and wired to recording instruments set up in the bridge. As luck would have it, the ship with Lewison on board, during a double crossing of the north Atlantic, met very little rough weather and only on one evening was the instrumentation put to any real test. The gauges and accelerometer worked well but a counter device that was intended to give a statistical record of accelerations in 0·1 g steps failed at the crucial moment. Lewison returned convinced that the system, once improved, would work and a year later in 1969 a container ship, the *Manchester Challenge*, operated by the same company over the same route, became available. This time an NPL passive roll stabiliser was installed as well as improved slamming instrumentation and Lewison joined the ship for another double trip. It was February when seas in the Atlantic would almost certainly guarantee rough conditions but this was not to be. Lewison reported in his usual entertaining way that:

... it must be admitted from the outset that the presence on board of an observer who scanned the daily horizon and the facsimile weather maps for signs of a storm had a mildly disquieting effect upon the officers and crew but a profoundly calming action upon the waters.

In beam seas some rolling occurred to test the stabiliser which evidently worked well and it was only during a second voyage a few months later that heavy seas of sufficient intensity were at last met and which allowed a rigorous examination of the slamming gear. A bow emergence gauge had been added, with a counter displayed at the bridge, and a recommended number of emergences of 33 per hour stated, which if exceeded would indicate the presence of real slams and the danger of eventual damage from fatigue. During the voyage the recommended level was exceeded on several occasions. For a count of 37 the master reduced ship speed by 3½ knots to give a reduced count of 32. Seven hours later the wind had moderated and the count had fallen to 10. The ship then reverted to its full speed with no count above 30. It was a successful trip and after further slight improvements to the emergence gauge the instrumentation became a permanent installation in the ship.

Slamming produced unpleasant whipping stresses in a ship and vibration. Two node vertical oscillations of a ship's hull, often set off by slamming, were troubling several ship operators. If resonance occurred between a ship's natural frequency and the wave encounter frequency, prolonged vibrations of considerable amplitude were set up. The larger ships being built resonated at low frequencies and unfortunately, as could been seen from Hogben's ocean wave data, wave spectra at low frequencies contained significant energy. Ships were monolithic structures with little natural damping and since the mass and stiffness of ship girders were virtually fixed by design then the response of a ship in waves could be changed only by altering its natural damping. Paffett, drawing on the well-known method of reducing vibration by using a small mass on a spring tuned to have a natural frequency close to that to be damped, sketched an idea that substituted water for the mass and air (which would of course be elastic) for the spring. He conceived a simple arrangement of water sitting on a pocket of air in a U tube arrangement. A deep rectangular tank was built divided in two by a vertical wall. At the bottom of the wall a gap allowed the free passage of water from one half of the tank to the other. The U tube, one half of which was a vertical column of water restrained by the air pocket, was fixed to a table and vibrated. The oscillatory motion of the water was studied by Acum and the best proportion of water and air found that gave the desired ship frequencies to scale. But, as always, there were doubts over scaling so Paffett borrowed an old RN destroyer, *HMS Scorpion*. A trials party led by Johnson and made up of members of BSRA, NCRE at Dunfermline and Lloyd's tried out the idea on *Scorpion* which was afloat in a large dock. The NRDC financed the construction and installation of the free-standing damping tank that was erected on the quarter deck. BSRA provided a vibration exciter and this was placed at the forward end of the ship. The exciter was started and produced an alarming agitation. A two node vibration was detected and the damper activated. It proved entirely successful and very satisfactory reductions in vibration were obtained with 4 tons of sea water needed in the damper and it was a simple matter to achieve fine tuning by altering the volume of air in the tube. A patent was filed and it remains a mystery why such a simple and cheap idea (only air and seawater were required in a damper with no moving parts whose weight was a mere 1/1000 of a typical ship and its cargo) was not taken up and used in tankers for which it was intended.

Propulsors and Ducted Propellers

English's work with thrusters grew from the needs of the offshore industry. Dynamically positioned drilling ships had to maintain station over a fixed point on the sea bed without recourse to anchors and an array of small thrusters arranged in banks of two, three of four were fitted along the length of ship at selected positions. Their operation gave an auxiliary thrust to a ship and by virtue of being rotatable, thrust could be provided in any direction. The first work on such vessels with thrusters was sponsored by the DTI and led to English conducting tests on a Wimpey Sea Lab design, a project that soon attracted the interest of the GEC company. The published results[23] were the first of their kind and English followed this with another first when he gave some results[24] concerning the interaction effects between thrusters and a ship's hull. These could be large. English showed that two thirds of the available thrust from a thruster operating in open water could be lost when the thruster was fitted to a ship. Their performance and positioning became important considerations as was seen in a large project for Houlder Bros (known as *Uncle John*). *Uncle John* was a semi-submersible multi-purpose support vessel and T.O. Haavie joined English in planning the extensive model tests conducted, the results from which[25] they published in 1977.

English also continued his work with ducted propellers. Designing for uniform flow was well understood but insufficient since the presence of an irregular ship wake needed to be recognised. Interaction between duct, propeller and hull was important and led to the design of an experimental rig that could be used to measure the forces from propeller and duct and the pressure distribution over the stern of the hull, all of these things being obtained simultaneously. Propeller induced vibration studies were also done whereby the interaction forces were obtained under cavitating conditions in the cavitation tunnel. A major conclusion found that in order to arrive at a design of optimum efficiency and minimum vibration, the hull, duct and propeller should be designed as a system, not as discrete components. A symposium on ducted propellers organised by RINA in 1973 allowed English and Rowe[26] to give some useful results from the work in progress.

Offshore Engineering

The growing involvement with offshore engineering led naturally to research in this field. From 1973 NPL was being consulted more and more over the effect of wind, waves and currents on offshore structures. In the next three years commercial work included tests on the newest developments such as monolithic structures, production platforms (model 5273 was for the Thistle Field) and investigations into the towing and sinking behaviour of jacket structures. Requests for research came from Government departments, who were mainly interested in the safety of rigs in the hostile environments to be met. Rigs and platforms were to be certified as fit for use in the same way as ships, but before rules could be framed a body of knowledge on environmental conditions and the resulting forces on structures needed to be gathered. The DTI asked NPL to act as a national focus for research on environmental loading and an NPL Offshore Structures Fluid Loading Advisory Group, OSFLAG, was born, its chairman (Johnson) coming from DMS and its secretary (Standing) from Ship Division. OSFLAG set the pattern for a number of Advisory Groups in which oil and construction industries worked with Government departments and other Institutions to bring their experience of offshore activities to bear in formulating research. The SMTRB monitored research programmes in the maritime field and for offshore matters it acted on behalf of the Department of Energy. OSFLAG researches were split into modules. Ship Division became responsible for OSFLAG 1, a study of wave forces on large fixed monolithic structures and OSFLAG 10, a state of art appraisal. DMS handled OSFLAG 9, the Christchurch Bay project. This became an enormous undertaking that entailed the erection at an exposed site in Christchurch Bay of a large-scale model representing the major elements of a fixed oil production platform including a gravity base. It was to provide the vital link between theory and the laboratory to the real sea and large-scale structures. The tower had other uses, mainly in a collaborative exercise with the Building Research Establishment who wanted information on the reaction of the sea bed to the pounding load transmitted through the gravity base. OSFLAG 1, the study of wave forces, was led by Hogben.

The forces exerted by a wave on a fixed body varied and the inertia forces acting were amenable to calculation by classical hydrodynamic theory. However, a problem arose when the body horizontal dimensions became comparable with wave length, a situation seen in most offshore gravity-based structures. Some of the wave energy absorbed by the structure was re-radiated in different directions away from the body—the diffraction problem. The base of a gravity structure consisted typically of a single reinforced concrete cellular block held down on the sea bed by its own immense weight. Slender columns rising from the base supported a working platform above the water surface. The design of the base was crucial. A computer program was written to calculate the forces acting on such a gravity structure due to an arbitrary wave shape. As ever the theory needed validation and large models of simple square and circular section were tested in waves in Number Four tank. Browne from Marwood's design group built a new five component force and moment balance that was used to measure the various forces. They showed good agreement with theory and allowed the computer program to be made available to the industry through commercial computer bureaux. Hogben, Osborne and Standing presented their theory and experiment results in an important paper[27] which won RINA's Silver medal. OSFLAG 10 was carried out by Hogben and his appraisal of fluid loading on offshore structures[28] included what he had found after consulting experts in Europe and America. A paper on this same subject received from the Institute of Civil Engineers the award of the George Stephenson medal.

Ship Division research at this time enjoyed regular recognition from the learned societies. Everest's catamaran paper was awarded the Ayre Prize, English and his co-authors of the 1971 paper[5] picked up the M.C. James medal, Gadd collected two RINA premiums, Shearer and Steele, one—five awards from nine papers presented during 1967–1971. From its beginning, the Division's research had always been disseminated largely through Institutions such as RINA, but as the 1970s saw more diverse research programmes include offshore engineering aspects and ship safety, other suitable outlets were needed. To some extent these were provided by the growing number of Conferences and Symposia organised at home and abroad and, for offshore interests, the Houston Offshore Technology Conference. For ship safety matters the Nautical Institute and the Schools of Navigation were ideal bodies at which to present papers or generate discussion. 1970 also saw British industry committing itself to metrication. This had an immediate application to laboratory work and the publication of reports. Paffett was the ideal man to lay down guidelines and his 1971 paper[29] to RINA became definitive. The new *Système Internationale d'Unité* or SI system of units replaced the Imperial system and the shipbuilding industry aimed to make at least a 75 per cent change by the end of 1972. The new units caused much irritation and confusion amongst the Imperial traditionalists but the change to a more satisfactory and consistent method could not be resisted and Ship Division converted in about 1975. It would be a long time before such things as the power of a ship's engine would be quoted in kilowatts and so tabulations of both horse power and kilowatts were provided in reports to commercial customers.

TESTS FOR FIRMS

Ship model testing continued at a high level with an average of 45 new ship designs tested per year. These included large tankers, ro-ros, cargo liners, bulk carriers, tugs, ferries and container vessels. Container ships were newcomers. Following the American army's success in transporting cargo in large boxes during the Korean war the idea of door-to-door instead of quay-to-quay transport was developed vigorously by companies such as Overseas Containers, OCL and the revolution that soon followed saw the new container ships sweeping aside cargo liners. Austin Pickersgill at Sunderland also enjoyed success at this time with their standard ship designs, and models 4759, 4942 and 5035 were prominent in the development of these forms. A trio of tankers for Trident tankers (*Orissa*, *Ottawa* and *Orama*) were tested in 1968 and also the 115,000 ton tanker *Narica*. Amongst the ferries were British Rail's *Caledonian Princess* and a double-ended design for Sydney harbour. In the high speed field Vosper's 40 knots planing craft, the Royal Navy's *Brave* class (model 4959) was tested in Number Three tank and in Number Four, tests for offshore engineering clients included the semi-submersible drilling unit *Sea Quest*. These were complicated tests with the barge moored from several cables. Tensions in each were measured in wave tests as well as the motions of the barge in all six degrees of freedom—pitch, heave, roll, yaw, sway and surge. It was *Sea Quest* that found the first major oil field in the North Sea.

With many different tests now available to the industry the principal towing tanks in northern Europe and Scandinavia decided to meet regularly at a so-called "Peppermill" conference to discuss fees and consistency between tanks. Peppermill, first convened in 1963, continued for over 20 years and from 1968 Ship Division published a list of its test fees. In that year a typical 5½ metre model cost £405 and resistance and propulsion tests using a propeller from stock, £800 or £1,100 if a new propeller was made. Seakeeping experiments in irregular head seas (a second smaller model had usually to be made) cost £1,000 and free-running manoeuvring tests £615. Three years later, in 1971, income from tests had reached £140,000.

Apart from actual model tests, advisory services at the early stages of new ship designs were a growing demand. Preliminary hull lines were assessed, power estimates made and by 1970 requests from shipbuilders averaged about one a week, evidence that the depth and extent of Ship Division's historic data was a valuable aid to preliminary design. Indeed they were indispensable to those companies who had few data for certain types of ship. The job of retracing model results and calculating estimates of power for new ships fell initially to Laws who in later years was followed by Mackenzie and then Strike. Some of the advice sought concerned unconventional ideas such as the notion of using submarines instead of tankers to carry large quantities of oil. A submerged body made no surface waves and so wave resistance would be eliminated. Calculations showed that an advantage would be seen but only in a well submerged, very large and very fast body. A 100,000 ton nuclear submarine powered to give 40 knots could probably be built and operated outside the continental shelf but it was unlikely that such a vessel would be allowed to enter the English channel or European waters submerged. At the surface, performance would be far inferior to a conventional ship of equal capacity.

An unusual request came from the Hydraulics Research Station, HRS at Wallingford. HRS carried out field studies and surveys in estuaries and inshore waters and were in the habit of hiring small craft to carry its scientists and equipment to working areas. They now wanted their own survey vessel and after discarding the idea of buying a second-hand craft and adapting it, decided to have one designed and built to their own specification. Ship Division was asked to prepare a design for a 15 metre long hull capable of 12 knots. D.J. Freeman in Dawson's Branch who had, before coming to Ship Division, experience in the building of similar craft with Philip's at Dartmouth, drew up a general arrangement for a twin screw vessel based on Bailey's suggestion for hull lines to meet the required speed. Normally this would have ended Ship Division's involvement but in fact HRS asked the Division to assume responsibility for tendering, overseeing building and acceptance of the finished vessel. D. Allen from HRS was to be the master of the survey vessel and he worked with Ship Division throughout the whole project. Groves and Guttridge on the Isle of Wight were selected to build a wooden hull, which for added protection was sheathed in GRP. Freeman left in 1969 and Bailey with Allen attended progress meetings at Cowes with a surveyor from Lloyd's as occasion demanded. The new vessel was launched in 1970 and named *Sir Claude Inglis* after HRS's first Director. It was a beamy boat, deliberately so to give a good stable platform for measurements at sea, and of extremely robust construction. Opportunity was taken of including the new vessel in Ship Division's correlation programme for high speed craft, and measured-mile trials at several draughts were obtained and compared with later model experiments.

The year 1975 marked the beginning of another change. Although the demand for tests on high speed ships was strong (Vosper Thornycroft commissioned tests on a 52 metre quadruple screw patrol craft (model 5221) and their Mark 9 corvette and several tests were made on designs for firms abroad), a noticeable reduction in routine ship model tests was seen. The trend to series and standard ships and an over capacity of large ships was the main reason. On the other hand offshore tests were increasing as was work to do with the safety of ships at sea. But above all an obvious overlap in the work carried out by Ship Division and DMS proved to be the catalyst. DMS had embarked on the Christchurch Bay tower project, massively supported to the tune of £500,000 by the Department of Energy and were conducting a major survey of traffic density in the Dover Strait whereas Ship Division was much concerned with improving the manoeuvrability of large ships and had just started on OSFLAG projects. The facilities at Hythe and *Miranda* were used regularly by both Divisions and the conversion and operation of *Vic 62* involved staff from each Division. It was perfectly logical therefore to merge the two. There were political expedients that may also have influenced official thinking. The years 1972–74 spanned a period during which NPL was subjected to pressure on its resources. Total direct annual expenditure had been allowed to increase by only £0·12 million from £1·06 million in 1972, which corresponded to a decrease in real terms. The removal of DMS and Ship Division from NPL would alter the economic equation considerably and perhaps helpfully so far as NPL was concerned. The request from Government to form a separate body:

... to handle certain vital problems not previously dealt with at NPL and not receiving attention elsewhere ...

had a hollow ring, for these problems were in fact being handled by both Divisions. Nevertheless few doubted the wisdom of rationalising the position and focusing efforts in the affairs of a single entity. In February 1976, the Secretary of State for Industry, Eric Varley, announced the setting up of a National Maritime Institute, NMI to continue and develop the work carried out by the Ship and Maritime Science Divisions of the NPL. Vesting day was to be 1 July 1976. Thus the Government had a new research establishment inheriting the employees (all civil servants) from the two NPL Divisions. So far as Ship Division's future was concerned the old arrangement of a Superintendent leading a research group and participating to some extent in actual projects (in Baker's case almost exclusively so) was no more. However, the merging of a large body of scientists and excellent air, water and full-scale facilities (the sea with Hythe as a trials base) held great potential. It would need firm management and direction lest the new Institute ran out of control or over-spent public money and so an Administrator was appointed. The Director NMI got, J.H. Nichols, happily had a scientific background with maritime links. At the time of the merger Cook, who had died suddenly in 1975, had been succeeded by Pearcey, who brought with him a long experience in aerodynamics research.

J.H. Nichols had served in the RN during the Second World War and afterwards took a post in the RN Scientific Service until 1955. After six years with the Atomic Energy Authority he joined Mintech, became Chairman of the Requirements Board for Computers, Systems and Electronics before moving to the DTI as Under Secretary, Research Contractors Division in 1974. His experience in computing led to his appointment as Director also of the Cambridge Computer Laboratory.

Nichols found himself in charge of a large body of technical expertise. The total scientific staff was 140. Of the more senior (about 50), 40 were graduates, several with second degrees. Income in actual cash from commercial tests and Government research amounted to a healthy £1 million, almost half of this coming from Government departments. Test facilities were amongst the finest in the world. NMI could hardly have been better equipped to meet the technical challenges that lay ahead and during the next six years maritime research in this country was to reach a climax.

REFERENCES

1. Pankhurst R.C., "Aerodynamics at NPL, 1917–1970", *Nature*, Vol. 238, No. 5364, 1972.
2. Paffett J.A.H., "Hydrodynamics and ship performance", *Philosophical Transactions*, Royal Society, A 273, 1972.
3. Bird H. and Browne R.P., "Damage stability model experiments", trans. RINA, 1974.
4. Dand I.W. and Ferguson A.M., "The squat of full ships in shallow water", trans. RINA, 1973.
5. English J.W., Bain D.C. and Rowe S.J., "Some manoeuvring devices for use at zero and low ship speed", trans. NECIES, Vol. 88, 1971.
6. Dand I.W., "Hydrodynamic aspects of shallow water collisions", trans. RINA, 1976.
7. Steele B.N. and Pearce G.B., "Experimental determination of the distribution of skin friction on a model of a high speed liner", trans. RINA, 1968.
8. Shearer J.R. and Steele B.N., "Some aspects of the resistance of full form ships", trans. RINA, 1970.
9. Everest J.T., "Some research on the hydrodynamics of catamarans and multi-hull vessels in calm water", trans. NECIES, Vol. 84, 1968.
10. Lackenby H., "The case for multi-hull ships with particular reference to resistance characteristics", trans. SNAME, 1968.
11. Gadd G.E., "Ship wave-making in theory and practice", trans. RINA, 1969.
12. Gadd G.E., "A method for calculating the flow over ship hulls", trans. RINA, 1970.
13. Gadd G.E., "A simple calculation method for assessing the quality of the viscous flow near a ship's stern", Symposium on Ship Viscous Resistance, Gothenburg, 1978.
14. Hogben N., "Automated recording and analysis of wave patterns behind towed models", trans. RINA, 1972.
15. Hogben N. and Standing R.G., "Wave pattern resistance from routine model tests", trans. RINA, 1975.
16. Gadd G.E., "A method of computing the flow and surface wave pattern around full forms", trans. RINA, 1976.
17. Clements R.E. and Thomson G.R., "Model experiments on a series of 0·85 block coefficient forms", trans. RINA, 1974.
18. Bailey D., "The NPL high speed round bilge displacement hull series", RINA MTM4, 1976.
19. Dawson J. and Bowden B.S., "The prediction of the performance of single screw ships on measured-mile trials", NPL Ship Division Report 165, 1972.
20. Dawson J. and Bowden B.S., "Performance prediction factors for twin-screw ships", NPL Ship Division Report 172, 1973.
21. Meek M., "PRIAM class cargo liners—design and operation", trans. RINA, 1969.
22. Lewison G.R.G., "On the reduction of slamming pressures", trans. RINA, 1970.
23. English J.W. and Wise D.A., "Tank and wind tunnel tests for a drillship with

dynamic positioning control", Offshore Technology Conference, Houston, Vol. 3, 1975.

24. English J.W., Propeller Committee Report—Appendix 2, 14th ITTC, Ottawa, 1975.
25. Haavie T.O. and English J.W., "Design of a special purpose North Sea support vessel", trans. NECIES, Vol. 94, 1977.
26. English J.W. and Rowe S.J., "Some aspects of ducted propeller propulsion", Symposium on Ducted Propellers, RINA, 1973.
27. Hogben N., Osborne J. and Standing R.G., "Wave loading on offshore structures— theory and experiment", Symposium on Ocean Engineering, RINA, 1974.
28. Hogben N., "Fluid loading on offshore structures, a State of Art Appraisal: Wave loads", RINA MTM 1, 1975.
29. Paffett J.A.H., "Metrication in ship research and design", trans. RINA, 1971.

CHAPTER 14

THE NATIONAL MARITIME INSTITUTE

The decision to establish a National Maritime Institute (NMI) had not been reached lightly. Visits to the test facilities at Teddington and Feltham by Ministers of State from both Tory and Labour Governments of 1970 and 1974, the inevitable working parties, developments in the maritime world and, as has been noted, the changing role of NPL, all played their part in the long debate that ran for some five years before the final decision was made. A leading player was Sir Ieuan Maddock who as Chief Scientist to the DTI was guiding and reshaping all of the Government's research and development establishments at a time when spending on science and technology was under attack.

Two major recommendations had emerged from the deliberations. A new organisation could be either outside Government, in which case it would become a limited non-profit distributing company or a new research establishment within Government. In rejecting the former, NMI (part of the DTI) was given significant aims—greater utilisation of its large capital facilities and the levelling of realistic charges for work done. Maddock had always advocated fair financial terms for research work and long before the economics of Thatcherism were brought to bear on the expenditure on science, had introduced a system of payments under which industry was charged the full economic cost of the research done by his departments' laboratories. Incidentally it was Maddock, an earlier worker in atomic research, who found himself lined up with other senior civil servants before the newly arrived Minister in the 1970 Heath Government. "By the time I was 36", declared the Minister "I had made half a million pounds. What had any of you done?" Maddock replied, "I don't know about half a million pounds, but I had let off five atom bombs."

For NMI to achieve its aims a commercial attitude to the conduct of its business was needed, a philosophy that Nichols was keen to foster. Ironically it was precisely this attitude that Baker, and latterly Dawson had followed so successfully from the very beginning of Ship Division's activities, but a similar approach was not to be seen in other areas of NMI. A management board was appointed which comprised equal numbers of members from industry and the Civil Service with a brief to oversee the balance of research and work for commercial firms. Such a role had of course been followed for many years by the old Tank Advisory and Froude Committees but now the emphasis was shifting. Profitability, if possible, and accountability were becoming important considerations in NMI's development.

Financially, at the time of NMI's creation, expenditure was running in excess of income and the regular shortfall was to become a persistent thorn in the flesh. No matter how well the current and foreseeable climate might be for British maritime research it was hardly possible that NMI's large and expensive resources could be operated without annual loss. By 1979 yearly expenditure amounted to almost £5 million, two-thirds of which went on salaries, wages, general expenses and maintenance of facilities against an income of just over £4 million. Of this income over half came from Government research programmes. If one were to ignore these a serious deficit of more than £3 million a year might be seen, a situation unlikely to appeal to the incoming Tory Government of 1979. Difficult years lay ahead.

The combined staffs of Ship Division and DMS just prior to NMI was 265. Predictions for NMI suggested the need for many more, 400, made up of 260 non-industrial (scientific and office staff) and 140 industrial (workshop and ancillary staff). Recent newcomers included M.E. Davies and R.B. Holland. Davies was destined to play a prominent part in NMI's development and future. He began working in fluid dynamics alongside leading figures such as D.W. Bryer and M. Gaster whilst Holland started in Dawson's group before moving on to work with Dand. If NMI was to reach 400 (it never did) extra accommodation had to be found, mainly at Feltham, the chosen headquarters of NMI. Nichols, using his contacts in the Civil Service, rapidly acquired a temporary two storey building that had been used in London for a Commonwealth conference. Surplus to requirements it was brought to Feltham and re-erected at right angles to the main office block where it became known as the South Building. Fitted out and furnished in 1977 it provided generous accommodation for some 50 staff in 30 offices.

In organising the newly formed NMI, Nichols could see that its work was split broadly into four areas. These dealt with ships and shipping, offshore engineering, industrial aerodynamics and measurements at sea. Already the staff was allocated appropriately throughout the four areas so there was no need for a wholesale redistribution, although some minor adjustments were made. But an overall structure was required and Nichols created four groups. Paffett, the ex-Superintendent of Ship Division was appointed Deputy Director of NMI and also Head of a General Management group, its activities including the running of the workshops, computer and data processing policy, operations at Hythe, nautical matters, propulsion and vibration. Pearcey, the ex-Superintendent of DMS was appointed Head of a Research group, a group that would handle long-term and fundamental research topics. Dawson headed a Commercial group which continued with traditional ship model, aerodynamic and offshore structure testing. The fourth group, an Administrative group, a necessity now that NMI was a separate Government research establishment, was headed by

J.D. Thomas who came from DTI headquarters. This group dealt with administrative and financial matters and also library and information services.

NMI was to exist for just six years and three Directors were to come and go. The early months appeared to offer a most promising future. Demand for repayment work was holding up well particularly in offshore structure testing and programmes of research for Government departments burgeoned. More staff were recruited (a total of 301 was reached in 1979) and improvements and additions to facilities were made. The level of support to the marine industry particularly for research topics had reached unprecedented levels. The only blot, despite efforts at controlling expenditure, was the continuing financial deficit. The debates that had rumbled on for so long over the setting up of a research body outside Government started again. Now NMI became a prime candidate for privatisation despite the obvious financial imbalance. Before delving into the events that led to this upheaval we should look at the improvements made to the facilities and the work carried out during NMI's six-year life.

A new test facility was provided in 1977. This was a wind/wave tunnel erected in one of the wind tunnel buildings at Teddington. It was built to allow studies of the effect of wind-induced waves. A long glass-sided tank was filled with water and air blown from one end of the tank over the surface of the water which could be further disturbed by the generation of waves from a small wavemaker. The wind/wave tunnel with a test section 4½ metres long became useful for *ad hoc* studies such as an examination of the behaviour of life rafts subjected to the combined effects of wind and waves. In Number Four tank a rotating arm device was designed by Pearson. It could be quickly set up and dismantled in the middle of the tank when desired. Gill and Lewison's work gathering manoeuvring characteristics for different ship types was speeded up by using this rotating arm. It was a light structure comprising four arms at right angles, one of which was instrumented and held the model under test, constraining it to move in a circular path at a selected and fixed angle of yaw. The arm could accommodate models up to 4 metres long and could be set to operate in a range of different water depths. Modifications to one of the wind tunnels, Number Seven, were substantial and produced a facility that could provide air flows representative of atmospheric wind in terms of speed profile and turbulence properties. The large test section was equipped with a turntable capable of carrying topographical models and special provision could be made to study the dynamic responses of structures to wind.

TESTS FOR FIRMS

Turning now to the work carried out during this period and looking first at the repayment work for new ships it is noticeable that most of this concerned designs for container ships and high speed craft. Each of the Bay, Boxer and Tackler class of container ships involved large numbers of tests whilst other types of ship included GEC's supply vessel *Star Hercules* and the single screw cargo vessels *Maron* and *Mentor* for Scott's. In the high speed field, patrol craft, corvettes, a frigate (this, in 1981, a very large project for the Canadian Navy) and minehunters were subjects for test. A major hull design study was requested by the RNLI who were developing a new class of fast slipway boat. Fully protected in a boathouse when not in use the lifeboat would be launched down a steep slipway, recovered and hauled back after a mission. It was essential that the twin propellers were fully protected against damage and so a deep tunnel stern design was necessary. Bailey based the design on the NPL high speed series and, following flow calculations by Gadd, added tunnels optimised to give as good a flow through them as could be arranged within the geometric restraints in the design. The large programme of model tests including free-running tests in the Solent were an essential prelude to the successful design that eventually materialised.[1]

A dramatic development in the history of model testing at Feltham was seen in the mid-1970s as a great surge of activity in offshore engineering began. A few model test programmes had been undertaken since 1961 and the OSFLAG research already described was well into its stride by 1973 but the large expansion in repayment work for builders of offshore structures and their consultants began in 1975. The challenging demands of the rigs in overcoming unique design problems and the harsh environmental conditions of the North Sea brought many requests for model tests on these spectacular structures. The benefits of Number Three tank were immediately seen. The immense structures could be well over 100 metres high and in modelling them to an acceptable size so as to reduce scale effect, large models were preferred. The generous dimensions of Number Three tank, particularly its depth, were ideal. On the other hand the capability of the wavemaker was limited and unable satisfactorily to reproduce some of the sea states required. Number Four tank also proved useful for single buoy mooring and jacket launching tests. Rowe, who in 1975 took charge of the repayment projects, was an energetic leader and he was fortunate to receive strong support from G.E. Jackson and others. Rowe's fluency with computers and data acquisition proved invaluable and Jackson who had transferred from NPL in 1975 adapted readily and successfully to the complicated experimentation.

Model experiments were diverse and covered tests on designs for offshore tubular towers, tethered buoyant platforms, gravity structures and so on. Tests on the launching and upending of production platforms were vivid examples of the engineering problems that had to be overcome. The platforms were complex jacket structures of cylindrical tubing and were carried on a barge and towed to the required location at sea. There the jacket was launched, flooded, upended and piled to the sea bed. The model experiments had to simulate towing of the barge and jacket in calm water and in waves, the launch (usually in calm water) and the subsequent behaviour of jacket and barge. Rowe and his colleagues faced many difficulties. Modelling the barge was a routine exercise for the workshops but a jacket with perhaps 500 separate cylindrical components, not all of the same diameter, had to be made to represent to scale full-size weight, inertia and buoyancy. The manufacture of individual tubing was far too expensive and time consuming so model scales were tailored to suit commercially available standard plastic tubing. Without proper welding equipment for plastic in the workshops the models were made by a specialist firm under contract but later when aluminium replaced plastic, models were made in-house. The buoyancy requirements were awkward to meet since total buoyancy and that at different levels of floating had to be right. The centre of gravity of the finished structure and its inertia had also to be to scale. By manipulating weights inserted into some of the tubes the correct characteristics were painstakingly reached. The trajectories of barge and jacket after launch were critical. The barge might be difficult to control or the jacket could strike the sea bed. On the model barge a winch mechanism, remotely controlled, pulled the jacket along the deck. As it approached the edge of the barge the jacket tilted on rocker arms before sliding into the water and naturally the forces of reaction at the rockers were important and were continuously measured during an experiment by force transducers. The friction between the sliding surfaces was rarely known in advance but realistic coefficients were arranged by allowing the jacket to slide over rollers which themselves could be set at any angle to the path of the jacket, a novel solution developed by Rowe and R.A. Browne. To track barge and jacket during and after launch, time lapse photography was used. Two cameras filmed flashing lights set up on both bodies, the lights appearing as dots on the processed negatives. Digitisation and computation then gave time history information on trajectory, speed, acceleration and the motions of barge and jacket.

The results from the model experiments were not taken at face value but were correlated with theoretical calculations and although the Reynolds number for the cylindrical members suggested scale effect problems, comparisons of trajectory were remarkably good. Quite apart from examining launch behaviour the experiments were of great value in helping to choose the best operational plan for the full-scale launch and to determine the best ballast condition of the jacket. Also, installation personnel were able to receive training for the upending procedure. Valves were fitted to the legs of the model jacket and by remote control they could be opened to admit water in a controlled way. History had repeated itself. During the Second World War crews of the *Phoenix* breakwaters had come to Teddington to learn how to flood and sink their charges.

Tests on tension leg platforms, TLPs, were quite different. These over-buoyant semi-submersibles were held down in the water by tensioned vertical tethers which prevented pitch and heave. Such platforms were described as "compliant" since they could still move horizontally under the combined action of wind, waves and current. A very large programme of tests for CONOCO and later the platform designers Brown and Root dealt with the Hutton North Sea

TLP. This was the first TLP to be built following CONOCO's initiative, and prior to its installation in 1983 NMI carried out theoretical studies followed by model tests with the aim of optimising the underwater shape of the platform and to study behaviour of risers and tethers. The 1/64-scale models used were subjected to extremely severe wave tests in Number Three tank which represented worst storm conditions expected in 100 years of operation in the North Sea. This TLP design was probably the most comprehensively tested structure ever and the use of 100 km of 14 channel magnetic tape gives some idea of the quantity of data collected. The capacity of the platform to survive severe conditions was impressive.

In six years from 1975 almost 40 different offshore designs were tested at Feltham quite apart from the research items in progress. So dramatic was the change in the type of repayment work received that by 1981 offshore projects actually outnumbered ship model tests. Work was done for companies such as BP Trading, CONOCO, Marathon Oil, Noble Denton, Brown and Root and CJB Earl & Wright.

RESEARCH

Enlargement of Suez Canal

Great activity was seen at this time in ship research projects some of which, for example the work connected with the enlargement of the Suez canal, began as *ad hoc* investigations. During the Middle East crisis in 1956 the canal was closed and blocked to traffic forcing ships to use the Cape route. When it was reopened eight years later existing ships, many now very much larger as a consequence of the rerouting, could not use it and with Egypt's economy dependent on income from ships using the canal, modifications to the waterway had to be made quickly in order to attract back the lost revenue. Before advancing money for a construction programme the World Bank requested a detailed techno-economic study. This was led by Maunsell Consultants who commissioned NMI and HRS at Wallingford to carry out model experiments with Coopers & Lybrand concentrating on the economic aspects.

Dand worked with W.R. White of HRS in a series of fascinating experiments[2] which examined the navigability of ships through narrow waterways. HRS had a large basin 90 metres long and 10 metres wide and a straight section of the existing Suez canal was modelled in the basin along which Dand and his team of workers drove and manoeuvred a large 8 metre model of a typical VLCC. An existing model of *Esso Northumbria* (model 5278) already tested in Number Three tank was used and equipped to be driven and controlled by an operator sitting on board. The object of the tests was two-fold: to see whether such a large hull could be safely navigated through the waterway at reasonable speed or if not what modifications to the size of the canal would be necessary, and to ascertain the effect such large ships would have on the canal itself such as erosion of its banks. The water in HRS's basin could be made to flow at a speed representative of the tidal rates that occurred in the canal and the model was driven either with or against the tide. Propeller forces and rotational speed, rudder angle, squat and backflow velocity (from a current meter) beneath the model at amidships were measured and in simulating a cross-wind fans were set up on the top of the model and another, positioned aft, provided auxiliary thrust to satisfy ship-model propeller thrust identity. The operator sat in a chair that was adjusted to bring the eye to its correct height to scale. Measurements were recorded for each run along the canal with the operator noting the actions needed to counteract the forces of bank rejection and wind. These experiments in a straight stretch of water were an important start but to examine navigability in curved parts of the canal a wider test area was required and led to the construction of Number Seven tank. Here curved sections of constant radius were modelled and the canal waterway could be altered when needed to give different widths and angles of bend. As in the tests at Wallingford tidal flow had to be reproduced and this was done by installing a pump alongside the tank. Two smaller models were used, a 3·7 metres geosim of *Esso Northumbria* and a single screw coaster model of similar size. Each was equipped with radio control apparatus and operated remotely by an experimenter who kept pace with the model on a walkway. The models carried a motorised camera that tracked their paths at known time intervals in relation to previously surveyed marker posts. Some interesting patterns of behaviour were seen particularly in the fuller *Esso Northumbria* model. The forces of rejection from the bank could be exploited to advantage when steering round a bend to "balance" the ship and assist its passage. Indeed in practice canal pilots could position ships skilfully, "playing" the rejection forces and cancelling any possible sheer by rudder action. However, the tests in Number Seven tank showed that in some cases this state of balance could not be held for long and the models took up an oscillatory path around a bend as rudder had to be successively applied to avoid collision with the bank. Clearly much depended on the type of bend and the great value of the experiments was seen when it was found that relatively simple modifications to a bend would allow large ships to proceed safely at reasonable speeds. Proposals were made and accepted and led to a change in the curvature of one of the canal bends and, at a more awkward stretch, a bypass at the approach to the Bitter Lakes which on completion became known as the Deversoir bypass.

Interaction and Ship Simulators

The Suez project was a good example of how NMI and HRS were ideally equipped to carry out *ad hoc* studies. This particular one stimulated further work on the overall design aspects of navigation channels. The National Ports Council had made a survey of ship behaviour in port approaches and found little of help in the current literature. Recognising this the Department of Trade (DoT) asked NMI and the Ports Council to look into unexplored areas of interest. With the Council providing technical guidance Dand began a thorough study covering four main aspects: ship-ship interaction, manoeuvring characteristics near a bank, squat, virtual mass effects of a ship at its berth and the special problem created by ships moving past a moored vessel where high tensions in mooring lines had been reported. Dand's publication,[3] which was one of several on this large subject (another on ship-bank interaction[4] gained a RINA Silver medal award), utilised his earlier work on interaction between passing ships, squat and his latest experience with the Suez project. He was able to postulate a design method for new port approaches and taking a fictitious waterway arrived at figures for major parameters such as maximum size of ship and speed for safe transit through the assumed waterway. For example, in one-way traffic a channel 16 metres deep with a bottom width of 111 metres could accept a ship up to 255 metres $\times$ 36 metres $\times$ 13.7 metres draught, whereas in two-way traffic the largest ship should be 125 metres long, 18 metres beam and 7 metres draught with a maximum approach speed of 7·8 knots. A most promising design method had been produced, although improvements were necessary. Good visibility and navigational aids were assumed and a ship simulator was needed to test the effect of these factors.

On the question of simulators the first to appear in the UK was the nocturnal simulator already referred to. It was built at the College of Nautical Studies at Warsash in 1977 and was followed by another, also at Warsash, and one in Glasgow. Their development relied on the building of mathematical models which in turn used manoeuvring derivatives obtained from Gill and Lewison's work. I.C. Millar, an ex-Merchant Navy Officer, arrived at NMI in 1975 and provided the ideal link Paffett sought in the development of simulators. The aims of these devices and the design requirements for them were described by Paffett and Millar in their 1975 paper.[5] To complement the simulators at Warsash two large 10 metre models that had already been tested for other purposes at Feltham were fitted out for operation by a two-man crew and delivered to the college. Trainee mariners could then experience at first hand the hazards and uncertainties of manoeuvring slow response full form vessels. Miller also became involved in an ergonomics study of merchant ship bridge design. This work, part of a DoI contract with the EMI Company, produced a code of practice for bridge design that was published in 1978.

Safety of Ships at Sea

Lewison also became involved with the safety of ships at sea. The extensive ship traffic surveys carried out by staff at Hythe in the Dover straits since 1967 had led to equally extensive analyses by M.J. Barratt, D.R. Johnson and others. If two ships passed within about ½ mile of one another then this was considered an "encounter" and encounter rates were seen from the analyses of traffic flow to bear a relation to collision rate. 17 collisions had occurred in a 300 square mile area between Dover and Calais in the nine years since 1967. Lewison now examined the probability of collision risks[6] in the Dover straits and found them to be much higher as visibility decreased and that the direction of encounter (head on, crossing or overtaking) had a comparatively minor effect on probable collision. He extended his study to cover other areas around the UK[7] and assembling evidence supplied from ships which included weather observations, visibility and traffic density, identified areas of potentially high collision risk. Apart from the obvious Dover straits area, where traffic separation regulations were now in force, an area off East Anglia was found to be of high risk. Lewison next turned his attention to the plight of disabled ships whilst Barratt who had transferred from the old HDL organisation at Hythe to DMS, continued with traffic flow and later complemented Dand's work on ship safety with studies such as[8] which used marine traffic statistics with mathematical models to arrive at predictions of collision rates at any location of interest.

Lewison's work concerning disabled ships sprang from the incident in 1978 when the rudder of the Liberian tanker *Amoco Cadiz* broke off leaving her seriously disabled in heavy seas off the coast of Brittany. 200,000 tons of crude oil were released from the crippled ship as it fell victim to the prevailing wind and waves. Lewison began a series of tests with a model in waves using the now familiar technique of fans on deck to simulate the effect of wind. The model was fitted with sensors to record its heading and a microprocessor which adjusted the wind effects in line with stored data obtained from earlier wind tunnel tests. His 1981 results[9] were unique and included measurements of the drift forces experienced. Lewison's paper before the RINA was well received and attracted a Bronze medal award.

Investigations into *Gaul* and *Trident* disasters

Two major disasters involving fishing vessels occurred in 1974 and led NMI into large programmes of work. The Hull trawler *Gaul* was lost with her crew of 36 near the north cape of Norway and *Trident*, a smaller inshore vessel with a crew of seven capsized and sank in the Pentland Firth. In seeking to clarify the reasons for these losses the Marine Division of the DoT commissioned model experiments. Morrall led the *Gaul* investigation and Bailey studied the behaviour of small trawlers in waves.

The formal investigation into the loss of *Gaul* had concluded that she had capsized and foundered after being overwhelmed by heavy seas. It expressed the hope that the possible causes could be investigated by naval architects with a view to promoting greater safety. As is so often the case in such disasters where there are no survivors, the exact circumstances prevailing or the precise condition of the ship at the time of loss were unknown and the investigation with models was forced to make certain, albeit slight, assumptions. However, it was clear that *Gaul* as designed and in her anticipated loaded condition had an adequate reserve of stability, especially compared with the criteria recommended by IMO. It is hardly surprising then that the vast quantity of experiments failed to show the model at risk, its survivability even when flooded artificially and tested in severe sea conditions never being threatened. Indeed on no occasion was it possible to capsize the model. Morrall's findings were consistent with the view that *Gaul* was not lost as a result of inadequate intact stability or poor seakeeping qualities and he was forced to conclude that the most probable cause of the loss was due to the effect of severe waves and wind and the possibility of meeting a large steep wave or waves in combination with some other unknown circumstances admitting water to the ship.

The scope and conduct of the experiments were impressive.[10] The programme of work included stability calculations, wind tunnel tests, tests in the towing tanks and free-running model tests at sea in natural waves. Two models were made. The smaller, to a 1/64-scale, was for wind tunnel experiments in which the aerodynamic forces were obtained over a range of wind speed and angle of ship heel. These results made clear that the effect of wind alone would have been insufficient to endanger the vessel. The larger 1/20-scale model was beautifully crafted to include trawl and factory decks, deckhouses, bridge, etc. The experiments in waves in Number Three tank that followed failed to show any danger to the ship with an intact hull. To subject the model to waves beyond the capability of the wavemaker an area in the Solent near Hurst Castle was chosen for tests in actual seas; measurements of typical waves there were equivalent in scale to a sea state expected from Beaufort wind force 10. The model behaved well and in long experiment runs not once did it appear vulnerable. It was pressed even further by assuming that water was trapped on deck due, for example, to blocked freeing ports or penetration of water to the factory deck, and after modifications to the model that simulated such flooding, further tests were done in the Solent. The enforced flooding induced very heavy heel in waves, up to 70° at times, and at last dangerous conditions were seen. Morrall's thorough investigation led to his paper being awarded RINA's Gold medal and the rigorous programme of experiments had, comfortingly, demonstrated that the intact hull stability at rest which conformed to IMO recommendations was sufficient to ensure seaworthiness. But no light had been thrown on why *Gaul* was lost.

In contrast to *Gaul*'s excellent qualities, experience with smaller inshore trawlers showed how easy it was to capsize models of such vessels in certain ship and sea conditions. As with *Gaul*, assumptions as to exact seagoing conditions had to be made but it soon became apparent that a combination of high centre of gravity and low transverse metacentric height, GM, produced little roll stiffness and dangerous conditions in beam seas. The programme of model experiments comprised a series of comparative observations using two models representing alternative designs, A and B of an inshore fishing vessel. *Trident* by all accounts had met very severe seas in relation to her size and to reproduce these in the tank small models were obligatory in view of the capability of the wavemaker. Two models about 1·7 metres long were therefore used and because of limited internal space only the minimum of instrumentation could be accommodated in each. The models were made with all essential superstructure details including freeing ports and instrumented for free-running by remote control and with a roll/pitch gyroscope linked to a telemetry recording system. Apart from roll and pitch motions the data obtained were mainly visual and cine film recordings. Being small, each model could be driven and manoeuvred into waves in Number Three tank such that in a single experiment its behaviour could be examined in all wave directions.

Although the size and displacement of the two designs were similar, the characteristics of the static stability curves showed marked differences. Design A had a higher GM and a longer range of stability than Design B.

For such vessels IMO had no recommendation regarding the angle of vanishing stability but the curves of stability for both designs satisfied the stated criteria for righting lever, etc. However, the experiments soon revealed that Design B rolled more heavily than the alternative in the same waves. Also Design B took more water on its decks which nevertheless escaped readily enough through the freeing ports. She was seaworthy and able to manoeuvre at any direction to the approaching waves which in height and frequency were representative of those assumed when *Trident* was lost. It was however very likely that breaking waves were present in the area where *Trident* was last known to be, and by manipulating the wavemaker operation waves of the required height could be made to collapse and break in a very realistic way. The Design B model in such waves was immediately vulnerable and in beam seas could be capsized if the timing was such that a breaking wave struck and broke over its bulwarks. The alternative design could be capsized too but only in additional tests when GM had been reduced by rearranging internal ballast weights. It had been shown conclusively that Design B in an assumed condition had insufficient stability at rest and that she would have been vulnerable in breaking waves of a severity which she might conceivably encounter. The IMO recommendations for such vessels appeared insufficient at least so far as the two designs examined were concerned and much of the discussion that followed when the work was described by Morrall in Glasgow and London[11] supported this view.

Measurement of Viscous Resistance

The hope of a better method of extrapolating model resistance results to the ship using wave pattern measurements had been dashed when wave breaking in fuller forms was seen. Nevertheless the ability to isolate components of total resistance remained attractive since knowledge of their individual contribution to an unduly high total resistance in a given hull would lead to solutions as to how reductions might be reached. Running parallel with Gadd's development of methods for calculating wave resistance and flow direction was an attempt to devise a quicker method of measuring the viscous resistance behind a model.

Hitherto pitot tubes had been used but were time consuming. A method that gave sufficient measurements in a single run down the tank was needed. With SMTRB funding, NMI asked Townsin at Newcastle University to look into the possibility of using tiny 10 mm diameter vanewheel anemometers to measure flow speed at specific points in the same transverse plane behind a model. Townsin's student, Wynne, produced a fine piece of research[12] that included some results from a model fitted with different bulbous bows. A large piece of apparatus was built and fixed to the rear of Number One tank carriage. A strut carrying 32 vanewheels appropriately spaced to avoid interference effects was supported on an automated frame that could position the strut at any height in a transverse plane behind the model or, if desired, in the plane of an absent propeller. Response time of the vanewheels was quick and for most model speeds, readings at different depths could be obtained in one experiment run. Gadd was quick to demonstrate the value of this new piece of apparatus by running seven models from which both wave pattern and viscous resistance were obtained. Summating the two would of course in theory give total resistance but as Gadd reported[13] he was not interested in a lengthy proof of Newton's laws of motion but rather to examine the measured components and their effects. From the viscous measurements, curves showing the distribution of viscous drag were obtained rather along the lines of Steele's earlier results from the circulating water channel. The presence of wave-breaking whenever this occurred was easily seen in the plottings by the appearance of "lobes", irregularities that had also been noted by Townsin. It was now possible in the course of a normal model resistance test to gather simultaneous viscous data but as commercial pressures built up in model test programmes little use was made of the new apparatus despite its obvious potential as an aid to improved hull design.

Ship Vibration

Vibration in ships, a recurring theme, came into renewed focus as a trend in increasing the powering of single screw ships developed. Some of these had poor flow over their afterbodies which often led to excessive variation in the wake velocities at the stern. As a result, oscillatory forces set up and transmitted by the propeller produced cracking of aft end structure and uncomfortable living and working conditions in accommodation spaces aft. Silverleaf, some 12 years earlier, had made a bold attempt to measure fluctuating propeller forces and now in 1974 a renewed attack on propeller excited vibration (PEV) was launched which started as a three year programme of work. It was jointly funded by SMTRB, the General Council of British Shipbuilding and BSRA and when later, British Shipbuilders, Stone Manganese Marine and Lloyd's Register joined as collaborators, a further three year programme was agreed that looked into the interaction between propeller and hull (PHIVE). Meek described[14] the overall aims of the whole research at a symposium on propeller induced vibration held in London in 1979.

The PEV project was a combination of full-scale measurements on 33 ships, calculations and model experiments. At sea BSRA obtained hull pressure measurements and were attempting to measure the flow ahead of a propeller using a laser doppler velocity meter. They also used an exciter on 13 ships to induce vibration, just as Paffett had done on *Scorpion*, and measured structural response. At NMI a wake survey was obtained from a model in the tank and, with the propeller fitted, unsteady forces recorded. In Number Two cavitation tunnel a start was made on PHIVE by installing a dummy afterbody shape ahead of the propeller and its running shaft. Transducers were inserted in the dummy to record the unsteady pressures at the hull under cavitating conditions. At the same London symposium English produced a fine paper[15] that placed on record and described the practicalities of testing model propellers behind dummy sterns. The problem of reproducing accurately the non-uniform flow determined from the wake traverse, largely solved by adding gauzes, was nothing compared to the need to carry out tests in water whose constituent gas nuclei were free of scale effect. Cavitation bubbles produced in unsuitable water would transmit unrepresentative pressures. English had no means of measuring nuclei although the overall gas content in the water could be controlled after measurements from standard apparatus. He was relieved to see that hull pressure measurements from tunnel tests correlated well with the BSRA ship values. This was perhaps fortuitous but suggested that the nuclei problem in the tunnel was not as serious as was feared although there was no denying the potential difficulty. Whilst measuring the pressure fluctuations English was excited to detect the existence of vortex bursting. The highly loaded propeller blades and the uneven wake led to periodic bursts of cavitation as successive blades moved into or out of areas of high velocity flow and it was noticeable that as tip vortices formed there was significant activity which led to their ultimate collapse. The pressure signals showed moments when vortex bursting occurred, the large pressure fluctuations having harmonic components at frequencies of twice and higher multiples of blade rate. English tried to reduce the high pressures by injecting air into the propeller blades and at model scale achieved considerable success.

The overall hope for the PEV and PHIVE work was to arrive at a method of estimating the pressure forces for a new ship design. Such a tool, based on theory and empiricism, would be helpful at those stages in a design where changes were still possible. The aims were not quite realised, as was shown in a later NMI report that described an extension of the PHIVE programme. By then English had left NMI to become seconded to the DoT where he acted as liaison officer in research and development projects funded by SMTRB. Davies took over the responsibilities of cavitation experiments and with Gadd and Poulton conducted tunnel tests on a single screw cargo carrier, full-scale measurements from which had recently been obtained by BSRA. This particular ship had experienced bad vibration and after recommendations by Gadd, flow deflector fins were fitted at the stern which greatly improved things. Davies wanted to see whether the benefit from the fins could be repeated at model scale. However their presence militated against successful flow representation over the dummy stern in the tunnel and Gadd proposed additional wind tunnel tests on a double hull model. The Poulton *et al* report[16] showed comparative ship and model hull pressures to be on the whole disappointing and they concluded that whereas model tests could identify a bad propeller-hull combination that would lead to unfavourable pressure variations, confidence in predicting the magnitude of harmonics was low due principally to inadequate representation of the wake field and the complications over the scale effects of bubble nuclei. However, the PHIVE work was not wasted effort. Workers at BSRA, notably P.A. Fitzsimmons, had arrived at criteria for minimum vibration levels from an assessment of wake measurements and the high pressures arising from vortex bursting were a warning, although English's idea of air injection was unlikely to be seen as a practical solution.

Offshore Engineering

Offshore engineering research was important not only to seek solutions to the many technical problems associated with the rigs but to reach an ability to predict environmental conditions. With Hogben providing the stimulus Standing worked on the difficult diffraction problem* and produced a computer program, NMIWAVE, capable of estimating forces on and the motions of specific designs including gravity structures, TLPs, barges, floating breakwaters and energy extraction devices.[17] NMIWAVE which relied heavily on earlier data collected in the OSFLAG research project proved so successful that it came to be used by industry under licence. Validation of NMIWAVE predictions with model results were excellent as was seen in a study by Rowe[18] who compared NMIWAVE calculations with test results from a model TLP. NMIWAVE also found application for ships, motions and wave forces being calculable for ships holding station in waves. As to the actual size and frequency of waves likely to strike the rigs, Hogben's earlier work with Lumb in 1967 had not correlated too well with direct measurements at sea. The 1967 data were visual observations of average wave height reported by mariners whom it seemed tended to ignore smaller waves in a given sample. When measurements from instrumented wave buoys became available, significant values of wave height corresponded more or less to the average heights reported by the mariners. Average values are, by definition, less than significant and the reliability of the data was uncertain. Hogben was aware that observed wave height should ideally be accompanied by observed wind speed and when Miss N.M.C. Dacunha and G. Olliver arrived in 1983 a major analysis, masterminded by Hogben, handled a staggering number

* Described on page 260.

of observations of wind and waves (55 million) from ships on passage between the years 1854 to 1984 and produced a data base that ultimately led to a major new publication "Global Wave Statistics". But before this stage was reached Hogben had outlined his thoughts in a penetrating paper[19] when he described the concept of wave climate synthesis, a process that derived wave statistics from wind statistics. Later, on the same subject, Hogben's paper before the RINA received the Bronze medal award.

Wind itself could influence the safety and working efficiency of the large offshore structures. Helicopter operations could be at risk and the path of the flare combustion plume might be altered by wind action. The Department of Energy (DoE) commissioned a series of wind tunnel studies[20] the results from which were summarised by Davies in 1982. *Ad hoc* studies on various offshore structures were often the subject of wind tunnel tests, and ship superstructures such as an LNG gas carrier in 1981 for the Energy Transportation Corporation were tested. In fact the wind tunnels saw a variety of work at this time. Bridges were a staple diet, topographical models frequent subjects and latterly vehicle aerodynamics were a new departure. Here, Formula One racing cars were tested on a special rolling road device set up in Number Six wind tunnel. The ground-effect downwards force and the air flow under the cars were determined and such tests continue on a regular basis to this day.

Measurements at Sea

An important ingredient of NMI's work was the ability to carry out full-scale measurements. Mention has been made of the very large programme of work on the Christchurch Bay tower and this project occupied workers at Hythe for several years with many reports such as J. Bishop's 1980 paper[21] appearing. The heavily instrumented structure provided amongst other things much needed wave force data used in the empirical design aspects in the NMIWAVE program. The requirement for supporting these measurements with reliable instrumentation was vital and Boyle developed robust packages that could be conveniently assembled. For greater mobility standard ship containers were used and fitted out as mini-laboratories, a good example of this being the delivery of a container to the *Cormorant A* offshore platform where tow force and motions of the platform were measured as it was towed out to sea by tugs. In the early 1980s instrumentation in use followed a fairly standard pattern. To measure physical quantities, analogue and digital modules included electrical transducer output in analogue form on multi-channel magnetic tape recorders. After an experiment the magnetic tape was transferred to a computer for digitisation and analysis. A gradual move to on-line data processing gathered momentum in areas where such a system proved more efficient such as in offshore projects where vast quantities of data were collected.

Other measurements at sea were conducted by J.A.B. Wills and dealt with what was described as the structure of wind, the characteristic properties of wind speed and turbulence with height above the surface of the sea. An 85 metres radio mast on the *BP West Sole A* platform in the North Sea was equipped with anemometers, vanes and temperature sensors at seven levels on the mast.[22] These and the associated instrumentation were left running and unattended for a long period of time giving at the end the wind velocity profile and gust factors with height. Data collected were then used to predict wind loads on structures at sea.

A full-scale measurement project to rival the Christchurch Bay tower work began in 1980 following an approach from Shell Research Ltd. to examine the behaviour of ignited gas at sea. This was an example of how NMI as a combined establishment covering all aspects of maritime science could tackle an unusual request. NMI was asked to supply instrumentation for measurements over a large area of sea off Shoeburyness. 70 pontoons were anchored in a circular area 2 km in diameter and a pipe running from the shore to the centre of the circle acted as a release point for either LNG (liquefied natural gas) or LPG (liquefied petroleum gas). Tons of gas were released and ignited by remote control devices on each pontoon. The measurements of radiated heat, sea temperature, etc. scanned at a rate of 10 per second, were transmitted by cables to relay stations on the sea bed. Data, collected over a six-month period as successive quantities of gas were released, were sent to the Shell company for analysis. The whole project and its planning was so successful that soon similar tests, requested by the Health and Safety Executive, were put in hand. A very comprehensive programme emerged which occupied some four years. This time the trials were on land at Thorney Island near Portsmouth with the purpose of providing a data bank on the dispersion characteristics of heavy gases released into the atmosphere. D.R. Johnson led NMI's efforts in these unusual tests.[23]

In the midst of NMI's activity, the scope of which was expanding all the time, the plans alluded to earlier for converting the Institute into a private organisation began to emerge. In September 1979 Sir Keith Joseph, then Secretary of State for Industry, visited Teddington and Feltham for discussions with senior staff and union representatives before seeing work in progress at the tanks, cavitation and wind tunnels. Sir Keith evidently went away impressed with all that he had seen and doubtless the important decisions that were soon to follow crystallised at this time. It is perhaps not without significance that many of NMI's more senior staff were approaching retirement at this critical moment. A.J. Johnson left in the early summer of 1979 to be followed by Nichols himself in September. Dawson (in 1980) was followed a year later by Paffett, Pearcey and Ritter. The only voice of protest at the proposed changes during the years of flux was Paffett's who *before* the formation of NMI sent in a powerfully argued minority report to the Department. The years 1977–1981 were not devoid of ominous signs. The UK shipbuilding industry (nationalised in 1977) which historically suffered periods of recession was showing signs of another, the offshore testing "bubble" was as likely as not to burst once oil production platforms were operating successfully and with NMI's main business narrowly based there was never any realistic prospect of profitable operation. On the other hand it was to be hoped that Government would wish to maintain its support for the whole maritime field by continuing to encourage research programmes.

Following Nichols' retirement his replacement, E.S. Mallett, took over at the end of 1979. Mallett, a scientist (almost 20 years at RAE Farnborough where he had been Head of Data Transmission and Instrumentation) had become an Under Secretary and Head of Research, Technology Requirements and Space Division at the Department of Industry (DoI). It soon became clear that his stay at NMI would be brief for he was destined to become Director of Applications in the European Space Agency, a post he took up at the end of 1980. Nevertheless he presided at a critical time and was soon to address the staff on NMI's future. In the early months of 1980 the new Tory Government had begun determined efforts at reducing the size of its civil service. NMI with other Government research establishments came under increased financial pressure and there was a ban on the recruitment of new staff. Mallett's announcement confirmed suspicions and brought into the open the official intention of privatising NMI by October, 1982. He himself was convinced that for this to be successful NMI would need an annual subsidy, indeed financial support was required anyway if NMI were not privatised. An independent enquiry into NMI's affairs, activities and prospects was to be made by management consultants Inbucon. The reaction of the staff to privatisation was mixed and, as events unfolded, tinged with apathy in the face of an irresistible tide. Most were pessimistic but some attracted by the prospects of NMI enjoying unfettered control of its affairs and the allure of higher salaries and company perquisites.

With the die irretrievably cast, NMI awaited Inbucon's enquiry with interest. In the meantime new senior posts had to be considered to replace those recently lost due to retirement. Steele, who in 1975 had been seconded to Haslar as Chief Scientist returned to become Dawson's successor and when Mallett moved on J.E. Cammell became NMI's third and last Director in January 1981. He appointed Steele as his deputy in August and then turned his attention to a restructured NMI to meet its future needs as a private company and the appointment of new senior staff. Cammell had no scientific background but his successful progression through the Civil Service was notable. He had lately worked in the Vehicles Division of the DoI where his powers and talent in negotiation (invaluable qualities at NMI's moment of severance from Government) had come to the fore.

The ominous signs for NMI were soon to become real. As a consequence of the nationalisation of British shipbuilding, major shipyards had been brought together in a common body, British Shipbuilders Ltd. (BS). The St. Albans tank, originally part of the Vickers group, was now regarded by BS as "its" tank and by 1979 it was obvious that the majority of model tests for BS yards were being directed to St. Albans despite the habits of many to place their work at

Teddington. This reduction in one of NMI's traditional areas was a blow from which it never fully recovered. Another worrying event occurred at the same time when cuts in Government expenditure saw a large reduction in SMTRB and other Research Board funding. This would almost certainly have its effects on future research programmes at NMI. And then in June 1981 the Government announced forthcoming cuts in defence. On the naval side Chatham Dockyard would close in 1984 and some 6,000 jobs would be lost at Portsmouth. Although NMI was not directly involved in UK defence work these changes had relevance to NMI's future. The idea of rationalising and combining model test facilities took root and Departmental ministers considered the merging of Haslar and NMI facilities in view of the fact that with merchant shipbuilding heading towards serious slump and with fewer warships needed there was an abundance of facilities available to serve a declining demand. However attractive the idea was to some, nothing was done and NMI was left to face its ultimate destiny. Drastic measures came in early 1982 when the tanks at BHC on the Isle of Wight were virtually closed, activity there reduced to an absolute minimum. The continuing collapse of the market for ships caused increasing difficulties with the order books at the Dumbarton and St. Albans tanks and these two tanks became vulnerable. Their stay of execution was not to last long; they were closed in early 1985.

In January 1981 Inbucon reported.[24] Their inquiry had been thorough and looked at NMI's make up and organisation against the perceived market for marine work. So far as prospects for work were concerned, Inbucon thought the demand for maritime research would continue at a high level into the 1990s. They identified the world market for ship model testing as £36 million in 1980 and thought that about £6–£7 million of this ought to be available to NMI. Inbucon thought that offshore testing would hold up well, the world market here was £8 million, and that requests for ship model tests would recover. The anticipation of a recovery in ship work was optimism on a grand scale and a serious misjudgment. Historically the demand for traditional powering tests on new ship designs was, allowing for slump years, running at a rate of about 40 per year and this included work from abroad. The maintenance of such a steady flow of work would be expected to form part of the life blood of a private company yet recent trends were obvious, of known cause, and possibly irreversible. Since the nationalisation of British shipyards in 1977 the numbers of investigations received at NMI each year for new ships were 31, 24, 7 and 3, an alarming drop in the two years before privatisation. Their optimistic view led Inbucon to conclude, with reservations, that a private NMI was feasible and a slimmer sharper organisation should move into profit by 1985. The reservations were the need of a large initial subsidy (since Inbucon could not see NMI as a self-financing body), a considerable reduction in staff and the removal of the costly support services of the MoW (now PSA).

To steer NMI towards the private sector a shadow Board was appointed under the chairmanship of J. Birks who was also Chairman of Charterhouse

Petroleum and had lately been a managing director within BP as well as a member of the Advisory Council on research and development. His experience of the oil industry was invaluable and he was supported by J.A. Derrington from the Sir Robert McAlpine organisation, R. Maybourn from BP Shipping, A.W. Rudge (ERA Technology) and B.A. Smouha (Touche Ross). Cammell and Steele completed a seven man Board. The Board's first move considered the restructuring of NMI to meet the challenge of the future, proposals for which were submitted by Cammell. Senior and managerial staff were involved in free and open discussion and by February 1982 a new look NMI was in place. The Research Group set up by Nichols was disbanded and its members distributed around three separate Technical Divisions. A fourth was responsible for personnel, finance and marketing matters, the last of these now an important new consideration. Research would continue but under strict financial control and programmes of work would be accorded the same degree of consideration as any other fee-paying activity. Pearcey retired in November 1981 but still offered his services as a consultant and by the end of the year two new senior posts were filled. Bowden became Head of a Hydrodynamics Division which would handle ship and offshore engineering model tests and Davies was appointed to head a Fluid Mechanics Division which would include in its work the physics of flow and engineering aerodynamics. The third Technical Division called Maritime Services Division was an expansion of Boyle's responsibilities at Hythe (he remained Head) to include the organisation of all workshops and instrumentation services. The Administration Division included a small section called the Ship Support Unit, a small group that had been set up in 1980 to provide direct assistance to the DoT in placing and monitoring contracts with industry for research and development projects such as ship simulators.

It was inevitable that the Heads of the three Technical Divisions functioned mainly in organisational capacities as distinct from other senior staff such as Dand, Gadd, Gaster and Hogben who remained in charge of or led specific work projects. A procedure for monitoring and costing projects within strict budgets had to be established and it was the task of the Heads to work towards this with staff unaccustomed and reluctant to accept such a discipline. The existing staff had after all been used to the more relaxed atmosphere of a research laboratory and placed the scientific and technical content of the work before the costing and accounting of every task down to the most trivial activity.

There next followed a period of transition as important matters awaited settlement. The shadow Board negotiated with Government the whole process of severance which included the transfer of assets (valued in March 1980 as £14·8 million) to the new company, the drafting of Articles of Association and re-employment of NMI staff. It was hoped that most of the existing staff would wish to continue and that as civil servants would be seconded until such times as formal contracts of work with the new company were offered. At the same time NMI was asked to prepare a business plan, a strategy document outlining its aims and aspirations for the future. Discussion followed discussion and a weekend management course was held at Warsash where some 50 senior staff were lectured on modern management methods and financial control. In June 1982 the shadow Board reported uncompromisingly. It declared staff numbers to be too high for the anticipated requirement. 76 posts would be lost, leaving a complement of 225, a figure that more or less confirmed Inbucon's view. The unions which had openly opposed the whole idea of privatisation protested but to no avail. The Board had, however, extracted an excellent deal from the Government. NMI with the curious status of a company limited by guarantee would have no shareholders, any profits being used to improve capability and facilities. If there were no profits the deficit during a crucial five-year transitional period would be met by the Treasury. Moreover in accepting the need to update and improve facilities in order that they became comparable with competitors abroad a capital investment grant of £10 million was provided. Also, positive links were to be forged between NMI and Government departments which would guarantee research programmes at NMI over the same five-year period. The position over staff was not so satisfactory. Some had little confidence in NMI or its future prospects at the end of the five-year honeymoon when the company would stand alone. The unions demanded pension and redundancy rights in line with existing Civil Service practice and pressed for staff to be seconded for a period before accepting or rejecting contracts with the new company. Secondment was not a problem but as it became clear that no formal confirmation of the agreement had been received from the Government, the unions urged staff to reject secondment until it was. With 30 September 1982, the day of the official launch of the company fast approaching, an impasse was reached in an atmosphere of total confusion and only at the last moment were matters resolved satisfactorily and even then secondment agreements had still not been exchanged.

The launch at the Millbank Tower, London took place in a blaze of publicity. The Secretary of State for Industry, Patrick Jenkin, was present with 170 other guests and representatives of the press. The new company and what it had to offer was introduced by Cammell and Steele and on show were exhibits of models that had recently been tested in the tanks and tunnels as well as films and display boards describing other activities. Later in the day a formal Extraordinary General Meeting of NMI Ltd. was chaired by its first chairman Dr Jack Birks. The momentum of the occasion was continued next day by placing advertisements in leading newspapers and a series of four fortnightly articles appeared in *British Business*. All had suddenly become real and the teething problems of a new company, to say nothing of the need to resolve the problems of staff employment, awaited immediate attention.

REFERENCES

1. Bailey D. *et al*, "A new RNLI lifeboat: the TYNE fast slipway boat", trans. RINA, 1983.

2. Dand I.W. and White W.R., "Design of navigation canals", Symposium on aspects of navigability, Delft, 1978.
3. Dand I.W., "An approach to the design of navigation channels", NMI Report 104, 1981.
4. Dand I.W., "On ship-bank interaction", trans. RINA, 1982.
5. Paffett J.A.H. and Millar I.C., "Ship simulators for the merchant marine", National Development, August 1979.
6. Lewison G.R.G., "The risk of ship encounter leading to a collision", *Journal of Navigation*, Vol. 31, September 1978.
7. Lewison G.R.G., "The estimation of collision risk for marine traffic in UK waters", *Journal of Navigation*, Vol. 33, September 1980.
8. Barratt M.J., *Encounters, near misses and collisions at sea. Mathematical aspects of marine traffic*, edited by S.H. Hollingdale, published by Academic Press.
9. Lewison G.R.G., "Experimental determination of wind, wave and drift forces on large tankers", Joint RINA, RIN and NI Symposium on the behaviour of disabled large tankers, London, June 1981.
10. Morrall A., "The GAUL disaster : an investigation into the loss of a large stern trawler", trans. RINA, 1981.
11. Morrall A., "Capsizing of small trawlers". Trans. RINA, 1980.
12. Townsin R.L. and Wynne J.B., "Viscous drag measurement of ship models : the design and use of an automated system", trans. NECIES, Vol. 96, 1980.
13. Gadd G.E., "The use of resistance component measurements as diagnostic tools in assessing the resistance qualities of ship models", NMI Report 153, 1983.
14. Meek M. *et al*, "General view of UK research on propeller-hull interaction and associated ship vibration", RINA Symposium on propeller-induced ship vibration, London, December 1979.
15. English J.W., "Cavitation-induced hull surface pressures—measurements in a water tunnel", *Ibid*.
16. Poulton K.G. *et al*, "Cavitation-induced hull pressures measured in a water tunnel for comparison with ship trials on a single screw cargo carrier", NMI Report 114, 1981.
17. Standing R.G., "Applications of wave diffraction theory", NMI Report 32, 1978.
18. Rowe S.J. *et al*, "The model testing of a tethered buoyant platform and its riser system", NMI Report 47, 1979.
19. Hogben N., "Wave climate synthesis for engineering purposes", Society of Underwater Technology, May 1979.
20. Davies M.E. and Miller B.L., "Wind effects on offshore platforms—a summary of wind tunnel studies", NMI Report 140, 1982.
21. Bishop J., "The UK Christchurch Bay project: a review of results", Proceedings Offshore Technology Conference, Houston, 1980.
22. Wills J.A.B., "The measurement of wind structures at West Sole", NMI Report 79, 1980.
23. Johnson D.R., "Thorney Island Trials: systems development and operational procedures", *Journal of Hazardous Materials*, 11, 1985.
24. "Feasibility study of the National Maritime Institute as an independent entity", Inbucon International Consultants Report, January 1981.

CHAPTER 15

PRIVATISATION

In theory, the company launched on 30 September 1982 had no staff. Employees of NMI had resisted offers of secondment on three occasions until reasonable guarantees had been received from the Department. These included the opportunity for employment elsewhere in the Civil Service for those not offered contracts with the new company during the secondment period and, in the case where a contract was offered and accepted, the availability of satisfactory redundancy terms should these become necessary at some future date. Ex-civil servants expected to qualify for the same terms of severance as those provided by the Civil Service, which were much more favourable to the individual than those available in the private sector. After two months of intense union negotiation partial agreement was reached and by November the majority of NMI staff had accepted secondment for a two-year period. The few that refused either left or, without too much difficulty, arranged alternative employment in DoI. Natural wastage occurred anyway, Lewison and Millar for example had already accepted new posts within DoI.

There next followed prolonged negotiations over the key issue of Government support to the new company and the awkward task of drawing up contracts of work for the seconded civil servants. Naturally they expected, and were promised, conditions of service, salaries, pension rights and so on to be, when taken as a whole, no less favourable than those already in force in the Civil Service. The five-year agreement over funding already described was in place but it was only too clear that a free-standing private company could never sustain the high capital costs associated with marine research at its current level. Abroad, NMI Ltd.'s competitors were enjoying government assistance and Secretary of State, Patrick Jenkin was pressed over future assurances. He refused to commit the British Government to support existing projects of work or capital costs but did promise a major review after the first three-and-a-half years of privatisation. It was beginning to be obvious to all as they pondered the prospect of employment in the private company that when this moment came the implications were likely to be dire.

The shadow Board felt confident that a two-year secondment period would give enough time to sort out the complications associated with drawing up acceptable terms of employment for the civil servants. But negotiations were difficult and complex and by May 1984, 18 months into secondment and two months after the deadline when contracts should have been offered the knotty problems of pensions and severance were still unresolved despite Cammell's determined and fair attempts to reach settlement. Another complication arose. It was now proposed that NMI Ltd. and BSRA should merge to form a single company. With this additional factor to consider individuals could hardly be expected to accept contracts until a decision on a merger was reached. An extended period of secondment was inevitable, this time to an unspecified date six months after which offers of employment would be made and accepted or refused by those concerned.

Merger talks did not last long and we will return to these. As things turned out a decision to combine NMI Ltd. and BSRA was reached and announced by Birks at Feltham on 26 July 1984 at the same time as a similar announcement was made to BSRA staff at Wallsend. Negotiations over contracts dragged on and were eventually settled by the end of the year allowing those who were offered contracts to consider them and reach a decision by the spring of 1985.

Meanwhile NMI Ltd. had since October 1982 been operating as a private company and staff were soon to see how different life could be outside the well regulated environment of a government department. Cars were offered to senior staff, bonus payments to others and the entertainment of visitors and prospective clients became far more generous than before. A game of bluff between senior management and staff developed that amused and irritated many. Of course the Board could not know in advance of contracts who would or would not sign up for the new company. The inducements which were after all normal practice in private companies were seen as pawns in a gambit that would help to oil the wheels of decision for those required by NMI Ltd. when contracts were offered. On the other hand there were some staff who were seen to be surplus to the company's future requirement and in December 1982 the first of three waves of redundancies saw some 70 staff leave. One or two others who were close to the end of their careers accepted early retirement, Clements who had fallen ill, being one of these. Not that this left the company weak numerically. Recruitment was stepped up, Hydrodynamics Division alone offering posts to 10 early in 1983.

The capital grant of £10 million was waiting to be spent and the research programmes for Government departments covering the five-year guarantee period had to be drawn up. The former began to be used to enhance equipment, instrumentation and facilities. Also a vigorous marketing policy was introduced as well as continuing recruitment although it was never intended to recover the losses due to redundancies. With regard to equipment it was one of the snags of privatisation that the valuable links with NPL's advanced computer services were weakened and eventually severed. As a result considerable capital was needed to keep NMI Ltd. abreast of the rapidly developing computer world. It was of course important to have the right kind of hardware to match the software (NMIWAVE, NMIMET, etc.) being produced by NMI workers. A triangular network of computers and terminals was established that allowed staff to work at any computer whether it was at Feltham, Hythe or Teddington. At Feltham two large Gould machines provided the main computing power and served administrative, scientific and word processing needs whilst separate PDP computers were dedicated to Numbers Three and Four tanks and Number Seven wind tunnel. At Hythe a Hewlett Packard minicomputer handled data tapes collected from field trials and terminals allowed access to other parts of the network. On the Teddington site a third Gould was used for scientific work.

A large part of the money available for improvements was directed towards facilities and instrumentation. An ambitious conversion of Number Four tank at Feltham, originally mooted in 1980, began in earnest and Number Two cavitation tunnel, in urgent need of dynamometry that could be used to measure propeller forces in inclined flow, was equipped with new gear bought from the Kempf and Remmer firm in Germany. A new and better seakeeping dynamometer was also needed. More and more models were being tested at high speed in waves and the existing wave probe that measured the waves from the moving carriage was limited to a forward speed of 2 metres per second. The design of both a new dynamometer and high speed wave probe was undertaken in-house and whereas a probe was developed almost to the point where it could be used, the dynamometer conceived by Rowe and J.R. Spouge was never completed, subsequent events unfolding such that there was no longer a demand for it. Spouge who arrived from Southampton University in 1982 was one of the new wave of recruits. He made great strides into the difficult field of seakeeping and contributed to both experimental and theoretical aspects. W.J. Brendling who followed Spouge was recruited to work mainly on theoretical studies within the Offshore Branch.

Apart from the repair and renewal of much of the roofing at Feltham, the major investment went into Number Four tank. It will be remembered that this tank was, in the original plans for Feltham, intended to provide a test area of 1,500 square metres but that as a result of the cost saving exercise at the time only part of the 49 metres × 30 metres tank became available for tests. A dividing wall had been inserted to give storage space for models leaving only 900 square metres of water for manoeuvring experiments with free-running models. Since the storage of models had never been a problem, few models were ever kept afloat or submerged in the storage area, it was decided to remove the dividing wall and open the way to a more satisfactory area for measurement. Also the installation of a new wavemaker would give the prospect of a modern facility equipped with the latest instrumentation in which either models of ships or offshore structures could be tested. The whole conversion took 18 months and cost almost £2 million, a sobering commentary on inflation when it is recalled that the entire laboratory at Feltham had been built for just about the same money 24 years earlier. It was realised that if the revitalised tank was to be a success it had to overcome the shortcomings of both Numbers Three and Four tanks. The limitation of Number Three was its wavemaker, waves from which had never been entirely satisfactory. Also tests in waves in this tank, except with small free-running models, were restricted to two directions, head or following seas which, although available in the form of regular or irregular waves, did not include the directional spread of waves that existed in real seas.

The modified tank that duly emerged had three distinctive features, a superb wavemaker, powerful computer control over waves and data acquisition and a tank floor relaid to a levelness within ±3 mm that included a 6 metre deep pit for tests on tall offshore structures. The wavemaker produced long-crested regular or irregular waves which could be set to run axially or obliquely in the tank and short-crested irregular waves which when used with a "pseudo-random noise" technique gave a multi-directional wave spectrum that was continuous in both direction and frequency. The latest in computer technology was chosen to give control of the wave field and fast analysis and presentation of data, Brendling being responsible for the writing of new and original wave analysis software. Two Digital Equipment Corporation PDP computers (one to control the wavemaker, the other data analysis) and several peripheral functions such as plotters and magnetic tape discs were installed. The computers and peripherals were installed in an air-conditioned control room on the south side under the roof, the elevation providing an ideal view of the experiment taking place below. The tight specification for the tank bottom arose from the need to extend the capability of experimenting with ship models in shallow and confined waters, Dand's work with designs for port and harbour approach channels being an expanding activity. The pit, a 6 metre cube, was fitted with a flush lid that could be removed whenever experiments with models of tall offshore structures were required.

A contract for the final design and construction was awarded to BHC who in turn led a consortium of companies responsible for individual aspects. Hydraulics Research were used as design consultants, Tilbury Construction for civil engineering work, Keelavite for the hydraulic drive of the wavemaker, and so on.

The new wavemaker was placed at the west end of the tank and spanned the full 30 metre width. It was a flap hinged at the bottom split into 90 separately actuated and controlled flap elements powered by four hydraulic pump units. Each element and the hydraulic pump functions could be electronically servo-controlled by the PDP computer. At the end of the tank opposite the wavemaker a beach having a chord of 8 metres acted as a passive wave absorber. It was inclined to a slope and depth suited to the depth of water chosen for a particular test. As a means of reproducing other environmental conditions a water jetting system was installed capable of creating a current and if wind was required portable banks of fans could be set up to blow across the model test area.

With the realisation of this improved facility a name more suited to describe its use was needed and "Model Ocean Facility" was chosen. When formally opened in 1985 it was the icing on the cake of a laboratory that could hardly have been better equipped to meet the challenge of private operation. Yet, ironically, the new facility became available just at a time when there was a slump in the price of oil, the full implication of which, so far as NMI was concerned, was a reduced demand for offshore tests.

Marketing the new company's ability was seen as crucial and a Business Management Division was formed. It included the Ship Support Unit and later expanded to cover publicity, planning and development. The latter involvement led to short management courses on modern marketing and managerial methods for senior staff and an important market survey conducted by the Stanford Research Institute (SRI). SRI began by interviewing senior staff and concluded that NMI Ltd. was unfamiliar with marketing processes and, more seriously, lacked market research data. SRI argued in an initial report that even if such data were available they would be of little use unless the inadequacies identified were rectified. The Board accepted the criticism and commissioned a further SRI investigation in which a thorough market research was requested (160 organisations at home and abroad were visited) and a marketing strategy worked out that could be followed up by NMI staff. Excluding work for Government departments sales had in 1983–84 totalled £3·1 million which came from shipbuilding, oil, civil authorities and defence industries. SRI's worldwide survey estimated that in 1985–86 NMI Ltd. could, if properly marketed, achieve £8·2 million. To support this apparently promising prospect, 250 companies were targeted as sources of future work. Of these only 23 were existing clients. SRI's final report gave recommendations for ways in which NMI's ability could be promoted and in the months that followed many visits were made to the companies listed. The success achieved in attracting new business was however minimal. It was becoming only too clear that the recession in the marine industry was by no means confined to Britain and that too many organisations such as NMI Ltd. were chasing too little work.

In early 1983 as part of the rationalisation of the activities at Hythe it was decided to concentrate effort there on services to design, development, installation and maintenance of data acquisition systems for full-scale measurements on land or sea. A new technical Division, the Capital Projects and Trials Division was formed under Boyle. Earlier responsibilities for the running of NMI workshops were transferred and the staff of 50 at Hythe who had been working together on the trials and development of hovercraft, gas dispersion and the large Christchurch Bay tower project now began to become involved in other activities such as coastline and estuarial problems. These additional areas of work were seen as opportunities for the future and soon NMI Ltd. was to set up its first subsidiary company CEEMAID (Coast and Estuary Engineering Management for the Acquisition and Interpretation of Data). The creation of CEEMAID arose from a desire to continue fruitful collaboration between NMI, Liverpool University, IOS and Hydraulics Research in work along the Wirral coastline, work that had come to an end in 1981. The Board set up to control CEEMAID was chaired by P. Cox of Rendel Palmer and Tritton and its members included Steele from NMI and representatives from Liverpool University and Imperial College, London. P.C. Barber who had co-ordinated the work at the Wirral was appointed as Managing Director. CEEMAID, seen as complementary to the CP and T Division, was able to use the latest full-scale measurement capabilities available from Hythe.

Funding for new research was now entirely dependent on the agreed five-year programme, future requests from Government departments or from consortia. The small in-house budget for research, known as Director's Research fund (before privatisation it amounted to 10 per cent of annual budget) was abolished and the organisation and content of research came under tight scrutiny. It was not long before Government-sponsored research was diluted such that industrial firms needed to contribute to costs before the rest was made up from Government funds. Research into ship safety did however attract 100 per cent funding from Government but other types of work approved by Departmental Requirements Boards (which had replaced the earlier Boards of which SMTRB was one) needed the support of industry and were difficult to initiate unless a consortium of companies could be persuaded to agree to collaborative arrangements.

RESEARCH

There were many topics of research included in the five-year programme. The largest commitment went on ship manoeuvring, NMIMET (a computer program for deriving wave climate data), research into the improved safety of ships, ROVs (remotely operated underwater vehicles) and several studies directed at offshore engineering matters.

Efficient Ship

A survey of the UK marine industry had come up with a policy paper. In it recommendations for a long term strategy for R & D programmes were given. Two committees were formed to explore proposals for resources from the sea and the "efficient" ship. BSRA became involved with the latter and NMI's Ship Support Unit canvassed the industry for ideas and support. Most were interested in seeing the replacement of ship's bridges by "high tech" cockpits, exploiting advances in micro-electronics and the adoption of more economic manning levels but other matters related to fuel saving also attracted attention. Power saving devices, simple attachments to existing ships, became popular and some odd shapes were tried amidst claims of considerable savings in power. Nozzles, curved vanes fitted close to a propeller as a means of recovering rotational losses from the propeller or improve flow were all reported in the technical press as successful. As part of the five-year programme of research some model experiments were carried out with such devices[1] but in general little was found to commend them. The asymmetric stern, another proposal for the recovery of rotational losses, enjoyed enthusiastic support and application in Germany. Model tests by Ghosh showed a slight advantage over a conventional symmetrically shaped stern but only over a limited range of speed. The idea was never followed up in Britain. On the credit side positive advantages were found whenever it was possible to replace a ship's propeller by a larger one of slower rotation. This was hardly a surprise but for successful application revised stern shapes were often necessary which in some cases could not be accommodated within an existing design.

Ship Manoeuvring

Research in this area was inspired by comprehensive sea trials on the 278,000 tons deadweight tanker *Esso Osaka* in the Gulf of Mexico in 1977. Towing tank establishments throughout the world were encouraged to run model experiments and compare results with those from the ship, a co-operation that took place and possibly the last of such exercises to be seen in the future. Dand tested two geosims, a 1/200-scale model provided by the Stevens Institute in New Jersey and a larger 1/90-scale model made at NMI. Constrained tests in Number Two tank and on the rotating arm in Number Four were conducted on the smaller model whilst the larger was fitted out as a free-running model and tested in Number Seven tank. The report[2] that followed identified areas of agreement with the ship results and also areas of disagreement, the most notable being in the measurement of sway force coefficient. One of the purposes of the work was to compare predictions from a mathematical model (in NMI's case the one developed by Gill in 1980) with full-scale and free-running model results. The latter results agreed well with steady turn data obtained from the mathematical model but the discrepancies noted when comparing the full-scale data were evidence of scale effect problems.

Wave Data

Since the publication of Hogben and Lumb's book *Ocean Wave Statistics* the methods of analysing and interpreting wave data had advanced and, as has been noted earlier, were soon to be used in the production of a major new publication *Global Wave Statistics*. Wave data came from both direct and indirect sources. Direct data giving actual measurements of waves from instrumented wave buoys were best but by no means widely available. Indirect data could be obtained by hindcasting from wind data or from visual data noted by ships in service. Hindcasting was limited to short rather than long term climate statistics and visual data, prone to unreliability, was usually confined to shipping lanes. It was against this background that a mathematical model and computer program using improved statistical methods was developed by Hogben and his assistants. The program developed, NMIMET, described in "Wave Climate Synthesis",[3] took as input, global archives of visual observations held by meteorological agencies such as the UK's Meteorological Office. NMIMET used methods based on parametric modelling of the statistical relations between relevant wind and wave parameters to derive wave data of enhanced reliability and overcame much of the uncertainty associated with visual recordings. A feature of the mathematical model was its ability to synthesise wave period statistics from visual wave heights without using any of the wave period observations, which were known to be particularly unreliable. It could also derive wave statistics from wind speed measurements or observations in cases where no wave data were available. NMIMET was an undoubted success and was extensively validated against direct instrumented data at sites in the North Sea, North Atlantic, the Pacific Ocean and elsewhere. The program paved the way to a successor to *Ocean Wave Statistics* and met the growing demand for reliable knowledge of wave climate globally. Work on the new publication soon began and its aim was introduced and described at a conference in Brighton.[4]

Offshore Engineering

The special challenges in extracting oil from beneath the sea bed led to some unusual and unmanned underwater vehicles such as the remotely operated vehicle, the ROV. ROVs were powered via tethers from the mother ship and deployed TV cameras and robot manipulator arms for survey and inspection tasks. Much needed to be understood of the hydrodynamic behaviour of vehicle and tether and a research study was set up by the Offshore Supplies Office of the DoE and carried out by a combined team from BHRA, Cranfield Institute of Technology, NMI Ltd. and NPL. NMI tested a full size ROV in Number Three tank and experiments in Number Two circulating water channel examined the behaviour and the drag of an umbilical. The ROV was propelled and controlled by side thrusters and their interactive effects were important factors in the behaviour of the craft. Tests examined both captive and free-swimming modes. In the channel, operating limits imposed by the drag of the tether and "strumming" when this occurred were found and used to supplement the theoretical studies made by BHRA and NPL.

Other research into offshore technology, also sponsored by the DoE, covered work on wave forces on cylinders including the effect of marine fouling on structural loading and an investigation of wave drift forces and their effects on moored ships and moored offshore installations. Marine growth on a cylinder quickly added to drag or wave loading. Laboratory and sea trials were put in hand on artificially roughened cylinders, the work being carried out in three parts—wind tunnel measurements in uni-directional flow, wave load measurements on vertical and horizontal cylinders in the tank and measurements at sea on vertical cylinders. In all cases cylinders were tested with smooth and rough surfaces, roughness being achieved by attaching different grades of emery cloth or actual seaweed. Increases in measured force coefficients due to roughness were found in some cases to be in excess of 30 per cent. Pearcey's report[5] brought together the results obtained from these tests with complementary measurements[6] on smooth cylinders fitted at four levels on the Christchurch Bay tower, a very comprehensive series of tests also commissioned by the DoE.

The investigation into wave drift forces was complicated and Brendling examined two different calculation approaches.[7] The forces were a major cause of low frequency response motions in both moored ships and structures and to calculate forces and responses in irregular seas it was necessary to extend the NMIWAVE computer program. Standing used the new version to calculate the motions of a moored ship and found that they compared well with corresponding model experiments[8] which gave added confidence in the use of NMIWAVE for other purposes. Reviewing the whole investigation Standing joined with E.C. Bowers of Hydraulics Research to present a paper[9] at a conference organised by the Institution of Civil Engineers in 1982, the value of which was recognised by the award of the Institution's Manby Premium.

Seakeeping

Progress was also being made in calculating the motions of a ship travelling in a seaway. Thanks to the computer and to M. St. Denis's breakthrough in 1953 when he demonstrated the technique of linear superposition[10] advances since Kent's early pioneering work were dramatic. 30 years after St. Denis's paper "strip theory" programs had been developed and improved by a succession of workers such that they could be used with reasonable confidence to estimate the seakeeping qualities of a ship at the design stage. A computer program NMISEA, largely produced by Spouge, drew on the work of A.I. Raff who had developed a SCORES program and R.T. Schmitke who had introduced to the calculation process a better treatment for roll motion. Parallel work at Haslar led by A.R.J.M. Lloyd also contributed to the program that eventually materialised. NMISEA treated a ship as 21 separate two-dimensional transverse strips and calculated the force on each strip when moving sinusoidally in calm water. Combining these forces with added mass and damping coefficients, equations of motion for the ship in regular waves were found which could be solved in two sets, one giving pitch and heave and the other roll, yaw and sway. Motions in irregular waves could then be calculated using St. Denis's linear superposition technique with response amplitude operators in combination with an appropriate wave spectrum for the ship, the response operators having been obtained from the ratio of calculated motion and wave height. The program could accommodate the effect of hull appendages such as bilge keels and stabiliser fins, these having a strong influence on roll in a seaway. NMISEA was highly successful and results from it correlated very well with many model experiments, so much so that some firms became content to use NMISEA as a cheaper substitute for the model test.

TESTS FOR FIRMS

The number of requests for model tests on new ship designs during the 1980s may have been disappointingly few but at least they did not lack variety or interest. With a slowing up in new ship construction the idea of "jumboising" existing ships became an option and led to some unusual tests. A new British challenge for the America's Cup saw tests with model yachts, the first for many years, but ship model tests during this period will be remembered for the spice provided by a large controversy that broke out over the relative merits of alternative designs for naval frigates.

In 1979 the MoD produced a Naval Staff Requirement (NSR 7069) for a new frigate to succeed the Type 22. The desire for a smaller crew, lower noise and cost led to the creation of a new design, the Type 23, to meet NSR 7069. It included an independent evaluation by YARD. At the same time Thornycroft, Giles and Associates Ltd. were promoting to Government and the national press a new design concept based on the idea that hull forms used for small working craft such as TGA's highly successful Nelson pilot launches and derivatives of these, the Azteca and Osprey patrol craft could, with advantage, be scaled up and used for larger vessels. As such, a larger frigate form would have a low length-beam ratio (about 5) in contrast to conventional forms that were much finer (typically L/B about 8). Soon TGA proposed an alternative to the Type 23, a Sirius 90 or S90 design that was assessed by the MoD's Ship Department, YARD and the Defence Scientific Advisory Council, the latter an independent body. All three were in broad agreement and considered that S90 fell short of NSR7069. As a result the MoD rejected the design. TGA would not accept the situation and continued their promotion at the highest levels with the critical advantage claimed for "short-fat forms", as they became known, that they did not obey conventional principles of hydrodynamics and further that seakeeping qualities would be superb. NMI Ltd. and others became involved to the extent of model tests and offering opinion on hydrodynamic design aspects of the short-fat philosophy.

The next phase was the creation, under the Chairmanship of Baron Hill-Norton, an Admiral of the Fleet, of an unofficial committee to report on Hull Forms for Warships. This suggested that there were indeed advantages in the choice of a short-fat design such as an increase in top speed over the maximum possible in a long-thin hull of similar size and, based on TGA's claims, substantially cheaper building costs. Such claims were bound to add fuel to the flames of a debate that had at times seen acrimonious exchanges. Naval architects who doubted the claims of a low resistance form and that hydrodynamic lift was not present were labelled as "old-fashioned". However NMI's experiments indicated S90 to be unexceptional (a comparison with series data showed resistance to be exactly as expected) and rather than experiencing lift at higher speeds, bodily sinkage occurred, again as expected. Then the final prediction of the power required at the ship's engine raised another dispute over the choice of correlation factor to be applied to the results of the model self-propulsion experiments. TGA wanted to use 0·97, the single factor derived from a correlation study conducted by NMI on *Havornen*, a ship of Osprey type. NMI preferred a higher factor basing it on a wider spectrum of results obtained from correlation exercises over the years on several similar hull forms. Whilst all this was going on the whole debate was exacerbated by litigation or threats of litigation, the worst being a breach of copyright brought by TGA against British Shipbuilders. The Superintendent of the BS tank at St. Albans had had sight of TGA's lines plan and, with BS knowledge, made a model and tested it, being very interested in the merits claimed for the design. TGA protested that the tests were done without permission and after the usual legal delays came to court. The High Court action was finally ended by an out of court settlement in favour of TGA. The arguments over short-fat versus long-thin persisted for almost eight years until at last the Government in accepting a recommendation of the Hill-Norton Committee that:

... an Official Committee of Enquiry or Investigation should be put to work at once to validate or reject our conclusions and bases for them ...

ordered a detailed investigation. The first nominee was rejected by TGA as being biased and eventually it was carried out by Lloyd's Register whose fair and rigorous report[11] appeared in 1988. It came up with very positive statements and found that the S90 hull required substantially more power to achieve a given speed than that suggested by the Hill-Norton Committee and that a Type 23 solution was cheaper to build and operate. Also a firm conclusion said:

... the Sirius design concept is unable to produce as good a solution to the NSR 7069 as the Type 23 and that MoD were correct in their rejection of the S90 design proposal in 1983.

Lloyd's had concurred with NMI's opinions of the hydrodynamic characteristics of the S90 both with regard to levels of power and correlation factor.

The idea of enlarging existing ships, jumboising, involved adding parallel middle body to a hull. Two proposals were examined in model tests. Blue Star Line was considering lengthening its container ships by adding two more holds near the amidships position. To satisfy renewed stability requirements compensatory sponsons were suggested 2 metres wide extending over half of the ship's length. The model experiments were aimed at selecting the best shape of sponson to minimise increases in resistance. Furness Withy also commissioned similar tests with sponsons added to some of their ships. Govan Shipbuilders were building large passenger-car ferries and interest was growing in radical new stern shapes. Tests were put in hand to compare performance of current designs with alternative twin skeg sterns. The success of fitting skegs depended on achieving satisfactory flow over them and several unusual shapes were tried but worthwhile gains were not found. Among the larger ships tested at this time was a design for a new Great Lakes vessel for the Collingwood Company in Canada.

In 1983 the world of America's Cup yacht racing was turned on its head when the Australian challenger *Australia II* wrested the trophy from the apparently invincible Americans. The success of *Australia II* was due in no small measure to revolutionary wing keels fitted to the hull. Designed by B. Lexcon and optimised in model experiments by P. van Oossanen at Wageningen in Holland their success served to demonstrate for the first time the important contribution model test and theoretical flow studies could make to the design of a racing yacht. Future challenging syndicates were quick to use models in the run up to their designs and suddenly towing tanks were faced with the possibility of an unprecedented demand. The Wolfson Unit at Southampton was kept busy with tests on small models and the tank at Wageningen was all but overwhelmed. At the time of the 1992 Challenge large sums of money were being poured into technical studies led by highly qualified hydrodynamicists. Italy's challenger *Il Moro de Venezia* consumed a $55 million budget and *America³*, America's successful defender was designed by a scientific team led by H. Meldner, himself the holder of four separate doctorates from MIT.

For the 1987 challenge Britain's Royal Thames Yacht Club, who were the first challengers as long ago as 1870, threw its hat into the ring. Convinced of the need for strong technological support the design team led by Admiral Sir Ian Easton and syndicated as the British America's Cup Challenges Ltd. approached NMI Ltd. in June 1984 attracted no doubt by Pearcey's enthusiasm for harnessing the combined expertise of hydro and aerodynamicists.[12] The model tests that followed at NMI were the first since Allan and Doust's work 20 years earlier with the important difference that now the advantages of the larger Number Three tank could be used to test large 1/3-scale models thereby reducing the awkward scale effect problems that would arise when small appendages such as fins and winglets were added to the hull. As things turned out 12 smaller models of 1/10-scale were also tested and complementary wind tunnel experiments run to examine the characteristics of drag reduction from bulbs, winglets and flaps.

For the work in the tank a special resistance dynamometer was required. It was designed by Poulton with assistance from the AVCO company and consisted of a four bar cage strain gauged balance with a trailing link model mounting frame. Whilst restraining the model in roll and yaw the whole arrangement allowed sinkage and trim in forward motion. The balance measured sway and surge forces and roll and yaw moments and the trailing link allowed the model to be heeled over and locked at any angle in the range ±30° or alternatively a selected angle of yaw could be set on a turntable. Tests were conducted with models set in the upright floating position and over a range of heel and yaw. Because each model was towed from a point at the centre of the dynamometer and not at the sail centre of effort a compensating pitch moment was applied by rearranging ballast inside the model to give the estimated bow down aerodynamic moment due to the sail force acting at the known sail centre of effort.

The tests were in two parts. First, a 1/3-scale benchmark model of a 12 metre yacht was built, its design an interpretation of *Australia II* minus appendages except rudder and trim tab. Next, a completely new design by D. Hollom was tested at both 1/3- and 1/10-scales. The smaller models also included hull shapes of two other designs, *Imperial* and *Royal Oak* and an earlier challenger, *Sverige*, as well as changes to Hollom's design following Gadd's wave resistance calculations that indicated possible benefits from a redistributed curve of cross sectional area. Tests confirmed the calculations and helped in drawing up a final basic hull shape that was then built to a 1/3-scale. Meanwhile Pearcey's wind tunnel tests had examined a variety of bulbs and winglets added at the base of the keel, the most promising of which were then included in Hollom's design and tested in the tank. Drag reduction achieved by any means was vital and two other possibilities were tried, special coatings and riblets applied to a hull surface. A suitable coating, thought to be a polymer based paint, held the promise of reducing turbulent friction and riblets, known to be successful on flat plates, might show a similar benefit on a three-dimensional surface. Riblets were grooves of semi-circular cross section (0·125 mm radius) set into continuous plastic strips 18 cm wide which were stuck to the surface of the 1/3-scale benchmark model. Paint flow experiments determined the run of streamlines and the riblets were aligned to these.

The results of all the experiments showed the Hollom design to have clear advantages over the benchmark. In its best form a bulb was added to the keel. The aft portion of the bulb was hinged in the vertical plane so that it acted as a kind of tail flap and a series of tests helped to determine the best angle of the flap. The improvement over the benchmark was most noticeable at higher wind and boat speeds where for a boat speed of 8⅓ knots and in a 20 knots wind an increase of ¼ knot in the speed made good was predicted. Results from the coatings were inconclusive although in one case a polymer coating gave a 3 per cent reduction in skin friction. More positive conclusions were reached in the riblet tests. Here at speeds up to 8 knots riblets, provided they were in prime condition, reduced total drag by 3 per cent.

In parallel with this work tests on another 12 metre design prepared by I. Howlett were taking place at the Wolfson Unit. Whereas Hollom's design was regarded as innovative, Howlett's was more conventional but at any rate the syndicate built two 12 metre yachts to each design and shipped them to Perth in Australia for the 1987 challenge. Delays and problems over balancing the sails plagued the Hollom design and ultimately Howlett's was chosen, racing under the name *White Crusader*. Unfortunately the challenge was not crowned with success, *White Crusader* being beaten in the elimination races. Later, in races in Sweden, Hollom's yacht performed well and it is a matter of conjecture whether it might have succeeded in Perth.

Other test work not directly related to new ships included the growing field of waterway design. Ship operators and the designers of waterways needed to know how ship behaviour was affected by the layout of shipping channels. NMI's capability had developed to the extent that either physical or mathematical modelling techniques could be used to solve a particular problem. A request to study ship handling in a restricted waterway in Hong Kong led to a series of model experiments in Number Two tank and so far as mathematical models were concerned these were now established for use in bridge simulators. Designers and operators of a proposed waterway were able, with mariners, to participate in exercises using a bridge real-time simulator. A study for a proposed shipping channel at Cape Lambert in Australia is an example of what could be done at this time and UK nautical colleges collaborated in such exercises.

Offshore work included launching and upending tests on a 1/48-scale model of the very large 24,500 tons tower installed at the Lena oilfield in the Gulf of Mexico. This steel jacket structure with some 5,000 tubular elements was developed by Exxon and had an unusual narrow base. Stability was provided by guy wires anchored to the sea bed which kept the tower upright but allowed a degree of movement in severe sea conditions. The sideways launch from the barge posed special problems of load sharing between the four tower slideways and barge rocker beams. Any difference in friction at the ends of the tower might have induced a dangerous yaw during launch and the model tests in Number Three tank were intended to examine the complex relationship between the parameters and confirm analytical predictions. Both tower and barge models had therefore to be instrumented to measure the three-dimensional motions of each, the forces at the rocker beams and the angle through which the beams rotated. Once launched further experiments checked the upending on to the sea bed and involved controlled flooding of 20 separate chambers inside the model. Finally tests in waves confirmed the survival of the tower in severe weather conditions whilst in transit to the oilfield. These unusual experiments were described by Rowe in a collaborative paper.[13]

Number Seven wind tunnel was also in demand by the offshore industry. Companies in Norway were very active and Statoil, the Norwegian national oil company, was developing the Gullfaks field. A 1/100-scale model of the platform to be used was made in the workshops and tested to investigate the safety of helicopter operations in wind and the dispersal of hot exhaust plumes.

A great deal had happened in the ship and offshore industries during the transition period since NMI's privatisation. It was clear that shipbuilding in the UK was falling into serious if not permanent decline and that British Shipbuilders (BS) would soon be in acute difficulty. British towing tanks were feeling the pinch and there was renewed talk of mergers, this time the Haslar tank and its staff with either BSRA or NMI Ltd. Nothing came of this but, perhaps under pressure from elsewhere on moves towards rationalisation, BS announced that it would close its tanks at Dumbarton and St. Albans in 1985. Led astutely by Moor in recent years the loss of these tanks with their long pedigree of excellence was an unwelcome shock to the fraternity yet, in theory, NMI Ltd. could expect to recover some of its old clients. BS went further in their desperate measures. They were currently paying BSRA a direct grant in lieu of payments received by the Association from its member firms before nationalisation. Now BS declared its intent to deal commercially with BSRA as it did with any other company. The removal of a regular subsidy that amounted to half its annual budget placed BSRA in a vulnerable position and it came as no surprise when discussions began on a possible merger with NMI Ltd. This was not the first time that the idea had cropped up; earlier proposals had been short-lived. A successful merger held great potential and it seemed that conditions in the industry in 1984 were right for the formation of a single, strong technical body to support the flagging maritime scene. BSRA, formed in 1945, had succeeded in the Government's intent as a Research Association serving a specific industry. Its early history and the merger with PAMETRADA in 1962 has been described by Darling[14] who gives the total staff, none of whom were civil servants, as 250 in 1984 although several of these were soon to leave through early retirement or redundancy. Through its recently created Production Division, BSRA had made great strides in computer aided design for ship construction and was equipped with highly developed hard and soft computer ware. This with BSRA's experience in ship design would fit naturally into NMI's and a combined organisation held the promise of developing into one of the most powerful centres of ship technology in the world. Yet this was not a view shared by all at NMI, many could see little gain from a merger. Nevertheless, agreement between BSRA and NMI Boards was reached and, as has already been noted, the intention to merge was announced simultaneously at Feltham and Wallsend in July 1984.

The first direct consequence of the merger was the arrangement for the funding of the two bodies, a matter that could now conveniently be considered by the DTI at the same time as the promised review of NMI after three-and-a-half years. What emerged was a rescheduling of the original and remaining guaranteed funding for NMI plus additional money for the combined organisations spread over five years from 1 April 1985, the day set for the launch of the new company with the name British Maritime Technology Ltd. (BMT). The agreed funding was for £18 million of which more than half was for British Government research projects. There was however no guarantee that further funding for such work would be available after five years. Included in the £18 million was £2 million which BSRA had in reserve and £1·5 million to cover the cost of any future staff severance payments. All this amounted to an excellent settlement but there was no disguising the problems that lay ahead. The combined expenditure of BSRA and NMI was £10 million a year which, in the absence of support in the future, meant this same amount had to be attracted as income from a market that could hardly be in a worse state of depression.

Leading up to the merger, changes had taken place amongst the senior staff of both organisations. At NMI, Cammell, on secondment but appointed as NMI Ltd.'s first managing director, returned to the Civil Service in the middle of 1984 and was followed four months later by Steele. Cammell's successor, M. Meek, was well known to NMI as a naval architect who had worked for BSRA, Alfred Holt and Ocean Fleets Ltd. before becoming Head of Ship Technology at BS. In a sense he came to NMI representing the customer for he had extensive experience in the commissioning and application of R & D. This was it seemed a highly appropriate appointment at the time of NMI's emergence as a commercial company. A Technical Director would be needed, a post Steele would have been expected to fill, and Davies was appointed in November 1984. Lower down, Bowden transferred to Haslar as that establishment's Chief Scientist and English who had earlier returned from secondment in London went to Korea to advise the Hyundai company on the setting up of test facilities at their new tank. BSRA had gone through a recent reorganisation that saw G. Ward and A.Y. Odabasi appointed as Technical Director and Senior Scientist respectively with D. Goodrich the managing director of the Association. Goodrich had been apprenticed at Bartram's shipyard in Sunderland before becoming a member of the Royal Corps of Naval Constructors. In 1978 he was seconded from the Admiralty to BSRA and succeeded J. Chadbund as Head of the Productions Division. In the same year D. Jeffrey had arrived as Secretary and soon Goodrich became Managing Director.

The imminent merger concentrated minds. Difficulties over contracts for NMI's ex-civil servants were at last resolved and a new set of conditions of service to cover those in the north and south had to be agreed. By no means all of the seconded civil servants were offered contracts with NMI Ltd. Those disappointed amounted to the final round of redundancies that the Board had in mind. Where possible, alternative employment was found within DTI, where not, terms of redundancy or early retirement were implemented. Of those that were offered contracts, 115 accepted and signed before the end of March. An organisational structure for the whole company with its components at Feltham, Hythe, Teddington and Wallsend had also to be agreed. The closure of the BS tanks had provided the opportunity to recruit redundant staff with relevant experience and several newcomers accepted contracts at Feltham.

The management of BMT, a new British company limited by guarantee (as NMI Ltd. had been) was vested in a main Board under the non-executive chairmanship of Birks. Deputy chairmen (also non-executive) were G.H. Fuller of VSEL and also the ex-Chairman of Council of BSRA, S.M. Tennant (Harland and Wolff) and W. Ferguson (BS). Rudge and Smouha who had been founder directors of NMI Ltd. were also included in the Board. Meek became Deputy Chairman (executive), Goodrich Managing Director (also executive) and Jeffrey the company secretary. BMT was then structured as seven operating divisions covering fluid mechanics, computing, hydromechanics, marine construction, measurement, ocean engineering and ship operation responsible to Davies and

Ward the two Technical Directors. Appendix VI shows the breakdown of the operating divisions with senior staff. At the moment of merging, over 350 scientists, engineers and experimentalists were on the books and the new company proudly described itself as the most comprehensive and advanced maritime research organisation in the world.

The inauguration of BMT took place at Feltham on 1 April 1985. The Model Ocean Facility which had in fact been in operation for two months was naturally included in the opening ceremony and Norman Lamont, the Minister of State for Industry arrived to conduct the formalities. About 250 guests attended and were welcomed by Meek. Following the inauguration ceremony during which the Minister spoke of BMT and its future the new facility was opened to a demonstration of waves which impressed everyone as they watched the dramatic behaviour of life-rafts and small ship-models in the confused seas produced. Although the new facility was the centre of attraction, other side-shows were laid on in Number Three tank and Number Two cavitation tunnel and a whole range of models from America's Cup yachts to the Christchurch Bay tower were on display in the workshops.

Thus BMT was launched to a secure five-year future after which financial support from the Government was no longer guaranteed and the real questions of survival would be asked.

REFERENCES

1. Bush R.B., "The effect of stern shape and propeller size on the efficiency of a typical bulk carrier", NMI Ltd. Report 196, 1985.
2. Dand I.W. and Hood D.B., "Manoeuvring experiments using two geosims of the ESSO OSAKA", NMI Ltd. Report 164, 1983.
3. Andrews K.S., Dacunha N. M. C. and Hogben N., "Wave climate synthesis", NMI Ltd. Report 149, 1983.
4. Dacunha N.M.C., Hogben N. and Andrews K.S., "Ocean wave statistics—a new look", Proceedings Oceanology International Conference, Brighton, 1984.
5. Pearcey H.H. et al, "Fluid loading on roughened cylindrical members of circular cross-section", NMI Ltd. Report 191, 1985.
6. Bishop J.R., "Summary report of wave force results from the second Christchurch Bay tower", NMI Ltd. Report 177, 1985. (The base of the original Christchurch Bay tower was enlarged in 1981. Hence reference to the second tower.)
7. Brendling W.J., "A comparison of two methods for calculating wave drift forces", NMI Ltd. Report 137, 1982.
8. Standing R.G. et al, "Slowly-varying second-order wave forces: theory and experiment", NMI Ltd. Report 138, 1982.
9. Bowers E.C. and Standing R.G., "Environmental loading and response", Conference on Offshore moorings, ICE, London, 1982.
10. St. Denis M. and Pierson W.J., "On the motion of ships in confused seas", trans. SNAME, 1953.
11. "Warship Hull Design Inquiry", published by HMSO, 1988.
12. Pearcey H.H., "Hydrodynamics and Aerodynamics—cross-fertilisation in research and design", Aeronautical Journal, Royal Aeronautical Society, January 1982.

13. Danaczko M. *et al*, "Lena Guyed Tower Launch Studies", RINA Symposium on Offshore Transportation and Installation, 1985.
14. Darling R.F., *40 years of progress. A history of the Wallsend Research Station, 1945–1985*, published by Clark Constable, 1982.

CHAPTER 16

BMT'S FIRST 10 YEARS AND A RETROSPECTIVE VIEW

The publicity surrounding the launch of BMT and the attraction of the new Model Ocean Facility provided much needed momentum. The recent closure of the St. Albans tank led to an influx of additional ship model tests and for a while it was almost like old times as the tanks at Teddington were kept busy with work for British Shipbuilders. Former clients returned and, as part of BMT's declared policy, inroads into obtaining work from overseas were made—a large test programme on a flotilla of barges for the J.J. Henry company in America was begun in early 1986. A wider range of tests was now possible in the Model Ocean Facility and, thanks to improved acquisition and analysis, the large quantities of data demanded by offshore projects could be handled at a faster rate than before. Sadly, however, optimism for the future was short-lived, ominous clouds were gathering which soon broke to leave BMT and maritime research seriously depleted. Before examining the reasons for this we should look at the test and research work done during the early months of BMT's existence.

TESTS FOR FIRMS

To begin with the J.J. Henry job. A dustpan dredge flotilla and pipeline pontoon was required by the US Army Corps to pump water and spoil from the Mississippi along a 250 metre pipe supported on self-aligning pontoons. Tests in Number One tank demonstrated the advantages of modifying the shape of the pontoons and tests in different depths of water on different configurations of the whole system were carried out in Number Two tank. J.J. Henry also took up BMT's proposal to write a time-domain simulation computer program in order to assess performance in deep and shallow water. The program used the data obtained from the model test measurements. This large programme of work was followed by another, for Harland and Wolff, who were building the first of class replenishment vessels (AOR) for the Navy's new Duke class frigate. A tight contract led to a demanding speed specification which was achieved only by dint of considerable modification and testing of various shapes of bulbous bow.

307

Wind tunnel tests were included to study wind flow over the superstructure and helicopter landing area.

A most unusual series of tests were carried out for Sunderland Shipbuilders. They were building the world's largest crane vessel to a cost of £45 million which was to be capable of lifting 4,000 tonnes. A novel system of motion damping and lift compensation had been built into the design that presented awkward problems in the model tests. Double skin outer shell tanks extending ⅔ of the ship's length, port and starboard, were open to the sea at the bottom, the volume of air above acting as an air spring to suppress motions (akin to Paffett's earlier vibration damping tests on *HMS Scorpion*). To give correct scaling of the air stiffness at the model, Kirby devised an arrangement of sliding inverted boxes connected to springs in each of the separate tank spaces. The model tests did not end there. The crane vessel, *ITM Challenger*, was dynamically positioned by four azimuthing thrusters which were modelled and used to measure thruster/hull interaction forces. Ordinary resistance and propulsion data were also collected in calm water.

Ro-ro and containership designs also featured as well as a gas carrier for Govan Shipbuilders. In 1989 extensive experiments were carried out on the design of a new ship to serve the island of St. Helena and tests on high speed forms saw a quadruple screw design for Brooke Marine in Number Three tank. These were followed a few years later by a design study and model tests on a new generation of fast afloat boats for the RNLI. Small Waterplane Area Twin Hull Ships, SWATHS, and catamarans attracted increasing interest and designs for these were sent in and tested.

It was one of the features of ship model tests in the 1980s that more and more unusual requirements were included in programmes of work and the *ITM Challenger* and barge flotilla tests were good examples. There was a growing demand for model tests in support of litigation cases and these too brought extra variety. The *Herald of Free Enterprise* disaster brought immediate tests for the Government's Secretary of State for Transport and research into the safety of ro-ros soon followed.

The plans for the new power station and airport for Hong Kong required a detailed marine impact assessment of what is one of the busiest shipping areas in the world. BMT's software including the simulation of ship manoeuvring and traffic movement, ideal for the purpose, brought involvement for both BMT workers and civil engineering interests.

In the offshore field things were not so good. The price of oil remained obdurately depressed and consumption per unit GNP was falling. This was quickly reflected in a slackening in demand for model tests. Competition amongst tanks for such work as there was became fierce yet BMT managed to win several orders at this critical time. Two major projects were for the Shell company and both were undertaken in the Model Ocean Facility. The first concerned the installation of the Eider platform in the North Sea and the second covered slamming tests on a floating oil storage unit. The upending procedure of the Eider platform was unusual in that the jacket was designed to turn through more than 90° during launch, upending itself to finish in a vertical position. It then had to be mated to a previously installed sub-sea template through which production wells were drilled. The docking procedure was tested exhaustively, the intensity of the forces in the piles during mating being of particular importance in different sea states. The results obtained helped to determine the weather limits to be set on the whole installation operation. The slamming tests involved a floating storage unit (a converted tanker) that was permanently linked to a single anchor leg mooring in the Fulmar field. The tanker from which oil was transferred to shuttle tankers moored in succession to its stern, suffered from awkward bow and yoke slamming in heavy seas. Model tests were put in hand and covered a number of possible modifications, all suggested by Kirby, including fairing pieces fitted to a bow box beam which supported the yoke attachment to the anchor leg buoy. The fairings reduced slamming considerably and they were fitted to the storage unit which was then reinstalled on site during the summer shut down period in 1985.

RESEARCH

A personal highlight in the research area was the election of M. Gaster as a Fellow of the Royal Society in March 1985. Naturally this brought prestige to BMT and a fitting tribute to the fundamental studies that had been in progress for some years in the Fluid Mechanics division.

Wave Data

A major item that came to fruition was the publication of Hogben's work on ocean wave statistics. The background and aims have been described (see pages 295 and 296) and the book that finally emerged was the result of a collaboration with the Meteorological Office. The need for the book was obvious since its predecessor *"Ocean Wave Statistics"* published in 1967 although out of print for some time was still in demand. The new book not only satisfied the growing requirement for wave data but provided full global cover (104 sea areas against the 50 in *Ocean Wave Statistics*). However, the arrival of *Global Wave Statistics*[1] did not render the NMIMET computer program obsolete since the latter was soon used to develop a personal computer database, PC-Global Wave Statistics, that has become popular with users who need fast convenient access to wind and wave data for the oceans of the world.

Efficient Ship

The feasibility study on an Efficient Ship undertaken mainly by BSRA was completed in June 1985 and at a DTI seminar the results were announced. The study had highlighted the dramatic decline in UK shipping instanced by the fact that in 1975 its merchant fleet numbered more than 1,600 compared with a projected 500 in 1986. Consequent upon this reduction were losses in employment and export earnings. To arrest the downward trend the study called for an urgent appraisal of the concept of an efficient ship. Abroad, development projects were already under way in Japan, Norway and West Germany. A similar study was needed in Britain and at the seminar it was announced that the DTI was launching a UK Efficient Ship Programme which called for close collaboration between individual shipowners and equipment manufacturers. It was argued shipowners would benefit particularly from advanced shipboard automation, better support and reduced manning levels. A programme of research was proposed aimed initially at a 12–14 man ship by 1990. Currently a target of 17–18 crew members was regarded as within the scope of available automation systems. It was even proposed that, following the completion of individual research projects and their trials, a trial ship should be built incorporating all the technological advances achieved. This was a bold step into the troubled future of UK's marine industry and a lot would depend, if success was earned, on the participation of industry. For its part DTI remained enthusiastic and provided project management services through BMT's Ship Support Unit and Meek's rallying cry declared that:

If all sections of the UK shipbuilding and marine industries commit themselves wholeheartedly and without delay to a national effort, the country can stay among the leaders. But if DTI's proposals are ignored there will be no second chance and UK shipping, merchant shipbuilding and associated equipment manufacturers will drift further into decline.

At about the same time as Meek was speaking thus he expanded on his views in a brilliant award-winning paper[2] before the RINA in which he charted the notable improvements made in ship cargo, fuel and crew efficiency since the 1950s and described the evolution in ship types from 1919 to the world recession in 1982. The effect of the recession so far as Great Britain was concerned was that its seaborne trade was increasingly being carried by foreign ships. Thus the UK fleet was shrinking and shipyards held only a modest share of world tonnage. The malaise was such that marine engineering and ship repair in the UK was dwindling almost to extinction. Meek asked the question, why, in view of the UK's successes in technology and innovation was there no benefit to UK maritime business? Our inability to apply technology seemed a partial answer. There was also an air of apathy surrounding the UK's future in shipbuilding. As an example of this Meek recalled a paper by A. Holt[3] to the Institution of Civil Engineers in 1877 that gave a review of progress in steam shipping and which stimulated a discussion so long that it continued over four separate evenings (124 pages in the Institution's Proceedings). Meek's own paper, much the same in length as Holt's, attracted 10 pages of discussion and he was forced to suggest that UK's shipbuilding industry was going down without a fight. There was, no doubt, much truth in this statement but in the final analysis economics, industrial relations and, mainly, the role of Government held the key, factors which were to contribute to the gathering clouds that threatened BMT.

Ro-Ro Safety

The capsize of the *Herald of Free Enterprise* focused attention on the safety of ro-ro ferries and led the DoT to request a programme of research. Building on his earlier investigation into the hydrodynamic aspects of the capsize of the *Herald of Free Enterprise* that had produced an excellent paper,[4] Dand using both physical model tests and mathematical modelling examined basic behaviour of damaged and drifting ro-ros whilst, separately, BMT also led a team of consultants who looked into the feasibility of fitting various remedial devices among which were buoyant wing spaces, transverse barriers and moveable bulkheads to vehicle decks.

This was a major research, paid for by Government in reaction to an unexpected tragedy. Apart from this, very little research in this area has been done since 1992. Such research papers that have appeared from BMT workers on this subject have been the result of spirited efforts in spare time and it is a sad commentary on the industry that so little commitment to investment for the future is forthcoming. Recently BMT has initiated an in-house research programme to address 14 areas selected from over 40 suggested by BMT Group subsidiary companies.

G.H. Fuller has recently urged that future R & D objectives must be set.[5] To support maritime transport systems he identified four key areas covering design, production, operations and maintenance.

The difficulties that were soon to beset BMT were seen a year after the creation of BMT when the stark realities of operating as a private company became all too plain. It was suspected from the start that the annual cost of facilities and staff could not be balanced by income and try as it might to cut costs the Board reported in October 1986 that losses were still running at £100,000 each month. And this after a third wave of redundancies in March 1986, that saw 40 depart from the Feltham and Wallsend sites, a development that hardly inspired confidence or morale amongst those that remained. Desperate measures were needed. If BMT were to carry on with all its resources and test facilities intact then an annual subsidy was a necessity. That one was possible—it could come only from Government—was unlikely in view of the negative attitude to science and technology in general. Evidence of this was not hard to find. Many and loud were the protests voiced throughout the 1980s. A House of Lords Select Committee reported[6] in 1985 and was sharp in its criticism of Government, noting that there was lack of a clear objective towards the marine industry. The Committee had taken evidence from the Royal Society, the Science and Engineering Research Council, DTI, the National

Environmental Research Council and others including BMT and concluded that UK marine research suffered from fragmentation, an inadequate level of funding and a lack of co-ordination of a national research effort. It was clear that the Government's view was that more industrial funding should be attracted to research, in future it would not provide cash. Since SERC was unable to give finance for basic research after 1985 and the DTI transitional funding ended in 1990, BMT's bleak situation was obvious, a fact quickly recognised by the chairman of the Committee when he commented to BMT representatives in the course of BMT's oral evidence:

The Government is rapidly pulling the rug out from under you in two directions at once—probably three if the defence squeeze comes on.

Indeed the Government was firmly committed to a political philosophy that led to a massive privatisation programme. Privatisation came to mean far more than denationalisation but rather the partial or complete withdrawal of Government involvement from many areas which had long been seen as appropriate for public rather than private action. Thus traditional cash subsidies to industries such as shipbuilding were withheld. That this was not the case abroad was a contributing factor to British Shipbuilders' demise in the late 1980s—BS found itself competing hopelessly in the world market. Universities too received reduced support and were "encouraged" to seek private funding. Government funding of science in fact fell significantly from 1981 to 1991 and the shortfall was by no means balanced by an equivalent increase in industry-funded research. There can be no doubt that scientific research through the 1980s was woefully underfunded. What possible hope therefore could BMT entertain for a subsidy? Obviously very little, yet an effort had to be made. Accordingly the Board wrote to Paul Channon, Secretary of State, arguing their case and requesting a direct annual subsidy of £1 million to ensure the continued use and maintenance of BMT's Feltham facilities. At the same time, encouraged by the DTI, an effort was made to rationalise BMT and Haslar test facilities. If the most modern facilities at each were preserved at the expense of sacrificing older ones (tanks at both Haslar and Teddington came into this category) considerable savings could be made and co-operative arrangements between the two establishments would ensure continued use of the better facilities available. Although permission of access by BMT to Haslar's facilities was agreed the whole idea of rationalisation foundered and a great opportunity was lost. Worse was to follow. The reply from Government to BMT's request was negative, no subsidy would be available and the Board was now faced with an agonising decision. Closure of the Teddington tanks (BMT was paying a rent to NPL for access to these facilities) would yield insufficient savings whereas giving up Feltham and everything there indicated an annual saving of at least £¾ million. Not only that, the site, bereft of facilities, was potentially of great value. It could be developed, planning permission provided, as a Science Park or sold. The Board had no option. BMT's future could be assured only by giving up Feltham and transferring all scientific effort there to Teddington. The decision reached in December 1986 was greeted with a storm of criticism. It was indeed a shattering blow that reverberated round the whole fraternity coming so soon after the blaze of publicity that attended the launch of BMT just 20 months earlier and the opening of the superb Model Ocean Facility. At a stroke, arguably the finest towing tank, circulating water channel, seakeeping basin and cavitation tunnel in the UK were lost for ever, there being no possibility of such large and expensive facilities being built again. In retrospect the decision was perhaps inevitable given the number of foreign countries where similar facilities were either owned or subsidised by their governments. The small circulating water channel did, however, survive to be re-erected in one of the wind tunnel buildings at Teddington.

Following the decision to vacate Feltham all staff there, except those comprising the Headquarters organisation who remained in the South Building, were relocated at Teddington. This was difficult since accommodation there was limited to a few vacant offices in wind tunnel buildings and three under-utilised offices in the tank building. As expected the closure of Feltham initiated further redundancies but even so there would be a shortage of space at Teddington for those transferring. So far as redundancies were concerned staffing levels were reviewed at all BMT sites with the result that 56 were made redundant, 39 of whom were from Feltham, 12 from Wallsend, 3 from Teddington and 2 from Hythe.

The idea of establishing a Science Park at Feltham came to nothing and soon the whole site was sold for redevelopment as a Business Centre. Fortunately new offices had recently been built at Waldegrave Road in Teddington, a short walk from NPL, and BMT bought the whole complex known as Orlando House. This enabled Headquarters staff to move in with the library services, finance division and some scientific staff which relieved considerably the congestion at the tanks and wind tunnels. The bulldozers were quick to move in and within a few months all signs of laboratory buildings at Feltham had disappeared.

The shock waves felt at the loss of these modern facilities brought the fear that soon BMT might have to give up the Teddington tanks as well. Happily this did not materialise immediately and work continued there for a further seven years. But in the early 1990s with fewer and fewer shipbuilders in the UK, orders for model test work became scarce and the tanks could stay busy only if there was a continuing demand for research. In 1990 the five-year period of guaranteed Government funding was up and although a programme of research into ro-ro safety had been ordered by the DoT there was little else that needed the assistance of model experiments.

Against this background the number of staff directly employed at the two tanks at Teddington had fallen to 15. In a sense the wheel had turned full circle. Baker in 1911 had started with a staff of nine; in 1994 a working group (the Vessel Hydrodynamics Department under Dand) comprised 15 scientific and workshop personnel. Worse still the buildings at Teddington were deteriorating. Roofs leaked, carriages and equipment suffered through inactivity and BMT would soon be faced with large maintenance bills. How did this state of affairs compare with tanks elsewhere in the UK?

The smaller facilities at universities appeared untroubled but at Haslar things were not so good. Following run-down in MoD activity research establishments such as Haslar had been absorbed into a Defence Research Agency. Haslar's first towing tank dating from 1886 had been closed and the other facilities there, although in excellent order, were being used only occasionally. A solution appeared. By keeping Haslar going under the combined direction of BMT and Haslar staff, model tests for either could be accommodated in the second tank (built in 1931) and the large manoeuvring basin. Thus an extensive range of specialist marine and technical consultancy support to both commercial and naval markets would be available at a dual Technology Centre. An agreement was reached in November 1994 and an executive management council formed comprising senior management from BMT and DRA. Thereafter the closure of the Teddington tanks was not long delayed. Sadly the end of an era that had seemed likely at the time of the Feltham closure was now a reality. The National Tank that Yarrow had inspired almost 100 years earlier would be no more. And standing beside it, Number Two tank, would also go after 62 years of almost continuous use. But at least BMT retained the ability to test models and all that remained was the satisfactory translation of staff to Haslar to continue the tradition under another roof. The facilities there were renamed as the Haslar Hydrodynamics Test Centre (HHTC).

It was a sobering moment at which to look back and reflect on the achievements of the past, reasons perhaps why BMT needed to do all it could to retain the ability to make physical measurements on models. The rewards for so many model experiments and analyses carried out since 1911 had not been inconsiderable. Our knowledge of hydrodynamics advanced and the savings in fuel costs passed on to shipowners incalculable. At the same time, improvements in test techniques and an increase in the number of test facilities were seen. The experience gained will be a lasting benefit to the model testing fraternity but there remains the question as to why so many facilities were needed.

In the years immediately before the building of the Feltham laboratories almost 20 facilities including cavitation tunnels were in regular use throughout Britain. Those at Haslar were a strong base for naval work and the tanks at Teddington, despite being regarded primarily as research tools, had become the same for merchant shipping. At first sight these two establishments might have seemed sufficient to satisfy British needs. That this was not so became clear in 1945 when the case for a third tank at Feltham was made. With tanks at private shipbuilding companies busy and companies without tanks commissioning more and more work at Teddington, prospects for future research were poor. A co-ordination of all British facilities for mutual benefit was never a serious possibility and when the new facilities at Feltham appeared it was not long before the confidence of the 1960s was being spurred by Prime Minister Wilson in his famous speech on creating a new Britain in "the white heat of the technological revolution". Research in all British industries grew and a new Government department, the Ministry of Technology, was set up with the task of developing Britain's nascent computer industry and the promotion of new science-based industries. Against this background the expansion at Feltham that included the new circulating water channel was a natural corollary and it is doubtful if all of the advances made would have been possible without a progressive supply of new and adequate facilities. A glance at Appendix IV confirms that other countries were taking a similar view.

It is of course invidious to single out all of the advances made in hydrodynamics but at least those summarised below are likely to be seen in years to come as notable. And of course the outstanding contributions to the needs of two World Wars are not easily forgotten.

— *The frictional resistance of plane surfaces*

Froude's method of estimating ship resistance depends on an accurate estimation of hull skin friction taken from equivalent flat plate data. The formulation derived from these data, applicable as it must be to both model and ship Reynolds number, is vital and the quest for the best skin friction line or extrapolator led to much work over the years. When, in 1957, the ITTC sat down to recommend a formulation a vast array of data assembled by the Froudes, Baker, Hughes, Prandtl, Schlicting, Schoenherr and others were available for consideration. It is a tribute to Hughes' work that the formulation finally recommended was to all intents Hughes' own.

— *The calculation of wave-making resistance*

Building on Wigley's work Gadd has brought this subject to an advanced stage. Thanks to the computer a truly diagnostic analysis can be carried out on any hull shape, or alternative to it, in advance of a model test thus strengthening the arm of the designer.

— *Sea state data*

As model experiments in waves progressed in method and interpretation, wave data from the oceans of the world were needed and Hogben's efforts reached a successful conclusion in the definitive *Global Wave Statistics*. The important computer programs NMIMET and the later PC-Global Wave Statistics are outstanding achievements by BMT workers and will serve the needs of designers of both ships and offshore structures for years to come.

— *Ship manoeuvring*

Although the original manoeuvring basin had its limitations many problems with existing ships were cured by model experiments on modified steering arrangements and the techniques of free-running models were advanced in the 1960s. The modern approach to manoeuvring has led to the collection of manoeuvring derivatives for a variety of ship types using a combination of measurement and theory. The arrival of the ship simulator owes much to the derivatives collected by Ship Division workers and ship manoeuvring equations are further applied today to ship operational safety as well as to the design of new ports and harbours.

— *Improvements in ship hull shape*

The important hull series produced by others in earlier years have been added to by Ship Division. A series for coasters was produced and much of the BSRA series derives from model data obtained in Number One tank. The relatively neglected area of high speed craft was strengthened by the arrival in 1976 of the NPL series. Quite apart from systematic data of this kind is the vast array of resistance and propulsion data for all types of ships that Ship Division accumulated over many years which have recently been added to by data inherited from St. Albans after the tank there closed. These data in total are a legacy to the nation and a resource of immense value. They embody the experience of the past where numerous ship hull designs were submitted for test and often improved.

— *Safety of ship operation*

Work at NMI in the 1970s continued and developed the capability to investigate and enhance the safety of ships. Model test results led directly or indirectly to improvements in fishing vessel design and regulation, determination of the risk of collision in dense flows of marine traffic as well as the measurement of the traffic flows themselves. Improvements in marine safety also stemmed from the development of ship simulation models (aided by extensive research on the topic) for use in ship simulators to train mariners in safe practice at sea. Many present day marine operations are safer as a result of fundamental work carried out in the towing tanks.

— *Offshore developments*

The tanks played a full and vital part in the burgeoning developments offshore as the North Sea oil and gas fields were developed. Many of the North Sea structures, fixed or floating, were tested in the Number Three tank and this, combined with the development of a powerful computer model in NMIWAVE, provided important information for both designers and operators.

— *Ship-model comparisons and correlation data*

Full-scale measurements at sea confirm the experimental procedures used in model tests and improve the prediction process by deriving correction or correlation factors that must be applied to the model result to account for the uncertainties in the scaling process. It is a curious fact that ship owners and builders were more interested in achieving a specified speed than any other aspect of ship performance. The over-riding importance of speed was no doubt linked to the economics of ship operation and it is no surprise to find that the majority of correlation data relates to ship speed, power and propeller RPM. BSRA's systematic and comprehensive programme of ship trials was meticulous and called for a rigorous procedure including measurements of ship hull roughness and retrospective model tests in which the exact loading condition of the ship on trial was reproduced in the tank. The information collected and the subsequent analyses are unparalleled and possibly adequate for the foreseeable future.

It is very unlikely that it will ever be possible to predict exactly the resistance of a ship to forward motion. Today it can be estimated from model experiments, for calm water conditions, with good accuracy and with fair accuracy by calculation. At the time of the closure of the Feltham tank there were some who, because of the growing power of the computer and the expected advances in theoretical methods, thought that the days of model testing were numbered. A phrase "numerical towing tank" was coined to mean the use of programs such as NMISEA and Wallsend's recently developed SEHAM (Semi-Empirical Hydrodynamics Assessment Methods) that were claimed as sufficient for the prediction of ship performance. That this was not true was repeatedly shown in validation exercises where theoretical methods, although invaluable for estimating purposes, failed to predict measurement with sufficient accuracy. In truth the strength of any theoretical method could only be as good as the physical measurements upon which it often depended, a fact recognised long ago by one of the first model experimenters, Beaufoy, who wrote:

Experiments derive their value from the care and skill with which they are conducted. When accurately made and honestly recorded they present a basis for calculation founded upon facts; and fundamental truths once satisfactorily established by actual experiment, the mathematician can proceed with confidence to fix the elements of the theory.

Those words remain as apposite today as when they were written 150 years ago and it will be a long time before physical measurement can be superseded with confidence by calculation. Neither is perfect but the two should be complementary tools in the quest for a complete understanding of physical problems.

Traumatic as the loss of its test facilities was it by no means signalled the end for BMT. On the contrary, the money from the sale of Feltham created a substantial base on which the Board could develop BMT activities elsewhere in the maritime area. A new-found corporate strategy led the Board to set up or acquire subsidiary companies. One of the first, after CEEMAID, was BMT Defence Services Ltd. which under Hannah attracted work from the Ministry of Defence such as design support for Royal Fleet Auxiliary vessels and Royal Navy frigates. A company, BMT International, was set up near Washington in the USA to capitalise on major contracts already under way with the US Navy.

Also in America, Designers and Planners Inc. were bought and a joint venture with the Peter Fraenkel Company (renamed Peter Fraenkel BMT Ltd.) allowed a fuller exploitation of work in the field of ports and harbour design. Activities centred at Wallsend were embraced under the name BMT CORTEC Ltd. and later BMT ICONS, the latter giving access to industries in the north to powerful computing ability. Designers and Planners Inc. succeeded in winning a three-year project worth $15 million with the US Navy's David Taylor Research Centre for support in the development of shipbuilding technology.

The effect of these additional companies (11 in 1990) has given BMT a much wider operating base than had ever been possible in the days when model testing formed such a large proportion of the total activity. The company, now one of Europe's leading maritime technology centres, is thus able to respond to a wider spectrum of requirements even though, overall, there may be reductions in marine technology activity.

But to return to the main substance of this history—ship model testing. As we move towards the next millennium Britain is in danger of possessing few if any research and test facilities in its marine industry. Yet the value of model tests continues to be demonstrated in the more complex maritime areas, a prime example being the recent study into the tragic loss of the *Herald of Free Enterprise*. Surely we do not need to be reminded that we are an island surrounded by oil with a continental shelf rich in sea food and that moving goods at sea remains by far the most cost-effective form of transport? As BMT's managing director has said in a Thomas Lowe Gray lecture,[7] "nobody expects we should try to recreate a major shipbuilding industry in this country" but for strategic reasons alone one must be retained with the ability to design and build ships. If so, then BMT's expertise and use of towing tanks will through the new opportunities at HHTC continue to be a national resource which was, after all, the *raison d'être* of BMT's first tank when it was built over 80 years ago.

REFERENCES

1. *Global Wave Statistics*, published by Richard Joseph, 1986.
2. Meek M., "Taking stock—marine technology and UK maritime performance", trans. RINA, 1985.
3. Holt A., "Review of the progress of steam shipping during the last quarter of a century", Proceedings ICE, 1877–78.
4. Dand I.W., "Hydrodynamic aspects of the sinking of the ferry HERALD OF FREE ENTERPRISE", trans. RINA, 1988.
5. Fuller G.H., "Practical design of ships and mobile units—objectives for research, development and evaluation", 5th symposium PRADS, Newcastle, 1992.
6. Report of Select Committee on Science and Technology—Marine Science and Technology, published by HMSO, December 1985.
7. Goodrich D., "Maritime research and high technology development", Proceedings IME, 1988.

APPENDIX I

TECHNICAL MATTERS

This appendix is in two halves. The first adds to the description already given of the construction methods used in the building of the main test facilities at Teddington and Feltham. The second defines simply the mathematical symbols associated with model tests and describes the scaling methods used when extrapolating model measurements to equivalent full-scale values.

A.   CONSTRUCTIONAL DETAILS OF THE MAIN TEST FACILITIES

Number One Tank at Teddington

A survey of the available land at Teddington showed the ground to be secure, sample diggings revealing sound Thames ballast with a normal water level just below the lowest depth required. The tank, to be built in concrete without reinforcement, 174 metres long, 9 metres wide and 4 metres deep, posed difficulties for such a large structure. Glazebrook had specified that it should be reasonably watertight; evaporation and leakage to be within 1,000 gallons in 24 hours. Since water temperature in the tank was to be about 59°F evaporation problems would be minimal but leakage due to the development of cracks in the walls might be troublesome. Experience at the time indicated that long continuous concrete walls cracked after setting and that such cracks appeared at regular intervals. It was therefore decided to build the tank in sections leaving expansion gaps between each section. But how long should these sections be? Luckily similar work was being carried out at nearby Walton on Thames where the Metropolitan Water Board were having a new reservoir built. The Board needed a long open culvert and were using the same concrete and aggregate that had been chosen for the tank (concrete 6:1 using fine Thames ballast). Cracks appeared at Walton at about 16 metre intervals and from this experience it was decided to build the tank in 18 metre long sections. In accommodating space for an observation window in each wall expansion gaps were positioned 14 metres either side of the centre of each window the remainder of the tank being divided into sections 18 metres long. Apart from the continuous waterway required, two docks were added at one end for use in the preparation of models waiting to be tested. These docks were built on arches so the water depth in them was only $1\frac{3}{4}$ metres. Thinner walls would do and they were made of reinforced concrete.

The site was partially excavated and the unwanted earth dumped at the south end of the tank where it can still be seen today as a verdant mound in the NPL Director's garden. From the end of 1909 until the following July records were kept of the behaviour of the gaps once concreting of the sections had been completed. In the first month the gaps widened by $\frac{3}{4}$ mm, that is the concrete shrank by that amount in 18 metres. Thereafter the gaps widened or contracted with temperature, the greatest expansion of $1\frac{1}{2}$ mm being noted during some hot weeks in June 1910. Finally the gaps were filled and the whole tank rendered with 2:1 cement. Almost $1\frac{1}{4}$ million gallons (5,500 tonnes) of water were drawn from a main in Bushy Park and in September 1910 the tank was full. A certain amount of settlement was expected with some horizontal movement of the tops of the walls. Careful measurements showed this to be very small, no more than 2 mm. The tank has never been emptied but a valve at the north end of the tank will drain the water into a stream which flows in a culvert under the tank. The stream emerges outside the main entrance to the tank building and is still today a source of fascination to passers-by who frequently stop to watch and feed the fish and ducks that make it their home.

Six months after completion no single crack of importance was seen in the tank walls and the loss due to evaporation, leakage and soakage was less than 50 gallons in a 24 hour period, well within Glazebrook's specification. In later years a serious leak did appear at a point on the east wall. This was due to erosion of gravel under the foundations but the ensuing crack has since calcified.

In fitting the carriage rails to the top of the tank walls the contractors proposed supports at 2 metre intervals but feared that the 15 tonnes carriage would deflect as it passed over the rails and affect observations and experiments. Continuous rail bearings were therefore designed. These were made 3 metres long and bolted to the tank walls. Their surfaces were planed throughout so that the rails, which were to be in 6 metre lengths and similarly planed, rested on the planed surface of the bearers. Levelling the bearers and laying the rails proved extremely tedious and took $4\frac{1}{2}$ months but at the end bearers and rails were certified as "being practically level and to have the same curvature as the earth's surface with a maximum error of a little less than $\frac{1}{2}$ millimetre over a 100 metres length". A water level technique was used whereby two jars placed 12 metres apart and connected by a rubber pipe were filled with water and placed opposite tripods set up on the bearers. From the centre of each tripod a needle point dipped into the water jar the point being raised or lowered by a calibrated screw thread. When each tripod gave the same reading the water levels were identical. Once the bearers were laid and bolted to the centres of the walls the rails were placed on them and brought into alignment by means of side wedges. The rail joints were close butted.

To ensure a uniform drive to the carriage on the two sides, the carriage wheels were coupled together as pairs by axles extending across the carriage at each end. Guidance of the carriage was arranged on one carriage rail only, four roller guides 180 mm in diameter being arranged in two pairs at each end of the carriage. To stop the carriage at the end of a run down the tank or on its return, frictional brakes were fitted on each driving wheel. They consisted of fast and loose plates running in an oil bath. At one end of the shaft to which the plates were mounted was a magnetic coil which with current flowing through it held the plates apart. To break the circuit, thus bringing the plates into rubbing contact, a trip catch was positioned at a convenient point towards the end of the waterway so that braking became automatic. The brakes could, alternatively, be operated from the shore by pulling out the clutch switch on the driver's control panel and in addition an emergency brake was installed which was a copy of that seen at the Washington tank. This emergency brake was fitted to the after girder on either side of the carriage and was intended to operate only if the carriage reached a point within 10 metres from the end of the tank. Its arrangement was simple and consisted of fixed plates secured to the tank wall and two loosely hinged plates on the carriage girder pressed together by powerful springs. The carriage in passing the fixed plates sandwiched them between the hinged plates such that when travelling at top speed the carriage was expected to stop in a distance of 7½ metres. On the occasions that it was called into use due to failure in the cut-outs the brake brought the carriage to rest with about a metre to spare. To meet the demand of a large range of speed variation and also a maximum carriage speed of 7 metres per second variable resistance circuitry was designed which changed the strength of the field and consequently the voltage supply to the carriage. The four motors were worked in series, series parallel or parallel. The whole design proved very successful and in exhaustive tests carriage speed was found to vary by not more than ¼ per cent for the majority of speeds set. Long steady runs were possible, 60 metres at a speed of 4½ metres per second and even 35 metres at the top carriage speed. The electrical current was delivered to the carriage by six conductors fixed to the west wall of the tank building. Two of these were for the motor fields, two for the armatures and two for the brakes. Two trolley poles fixed to the west side of the carriage picked up the current through a trolley truck running on guide rails fixed to the wall. The whole arrangement of carriage and control remained essentially the same for many years until in 1955 modern additions, principally an on-carriage speed control unit, replaced the ageing remote drive arrangement.

Number Two Tank at Teddington

Excavation for the tank began in the summer of 1931 and the ferroconcrete containing walls were built and completed by Christmas. The suitability of reinforced cement construction removed the problems that caused so much anxiety and thought when the solid walls of the main tank were built 20 years earlier. It was still necessary to build the tank in sections to avoid undue stresses or cracks during setting and 6 metre lengths were selected with a gap of 1 metre between sections. Once adjacent sections had hardened the gaps were filled in and the tank finally rendered with cement.

The rails for the travelling carriage were cleated to cast-iron sleepers laid parallel to the water surface in the tank and the sleepers embodied a brake rail on which two slipper brakes, actuated by compressed air, could operate. Trip stops were arranged on the sleepers to bring the brakes into operation automatically at pre-arranged positions.

The carriage, constructed as a light mild steel frame weighed 4½ tonnes inclusive of its electrical and mechanical equipment. It consisted of two main transverse structural frames 1½ metres wide supported on ½ metre diameter running wheels spaced 4¾ metres apart. The two frames were connected by six longitudinal girders one over each wheel, the other four carrying the working platforms and instrument supports. The central portion of the carriage was arranged as an open well 3 metres by 1 metre within which the model test apparatus could be set up. With high test speeds a priority, carriage acceleration was important and to increase it pneumatic wheels were considered. Baker had heard that the high speed NACA tank carriage at Langley Field in Virginia was fitted with large rubber wheels about the size used in London buses. After further inquiries into the Michelin Company's train, which also ran on pneumatic wheels over a steel rail between Paris and Versailles, the idea was eventually dropped largely because the requirements at Teddington were on a smaller scale.

Two 56 h.p. electric motors drove the carriage and were placed on the centre of each transverse frame, one at each end of the carriage. The power to the motors was generated from a Ward Leonard set, its power coming from 480 volts main and 110 volts exciter batteries. The generator was placed on the south side of the tank about 30 metres from one end together with a hand operated carriage speed control gear. The control gear was put in that position to relieve the carriage of unnecessary weight but in 1947 it was replaced by an automatic unit fitted to the carriage for greater convenience and the additional weight then restricted the carriage speed to 8 metres per second. A driver now travelled with the carriage starting and stopping it, the latter being achieved either by rheostatic means for low speeds or, for high speeds, using the motors as a regenerative braking system. The air brakes were intended only for emergency use and operated on a fail-safe principle.

The current to the carriage motors was supplied from overhead lines attached to the roof girders, the collecting gear being carried on a light steel tower at the forward end of the carriage. Changes and modernisation of electrical components were made in later years as well as the addition of improved speed measuring devices[1] and the Ward Leonard set superseded, power supply coming direct from NPL's main generating station.

The design and operation of the carriage proved less than entirely successful. Weight distribution was poor and the electrical drive system and circuitry eccentric to say the least. In 1965 when the carriage ran out of control and hit the end wall of the tank with near disastrous consequences, the electrical experts were baffled at the cause and could only emphasise the need for improved safety arrangements, which were in any case largely available at the time. However, the modernisation completed in recent years improved matters considerably but little could be done to improve carriage vibration that occurred at certain speeds and was severe at 6 metres per second (horizontal amplitude of 5 mm). The reasons for such a poor design are difficult to fathom, particularly since the overall arrangement of the carriage in the main tank had proved so successful and could easily have been copied. Nevertheless, at the time of its completion all that had been asked had been achieved. Initial speed tests, conducted by Wigley, produced satisfactory steady carriage speeds up to a maximum of just over 10 metres per second. In later years, following the various changes made, the top speed was reduced to 7 metres per second.

Number One Cavitation Tunnel at Teddington

The tunnel was made up of a pipe circuit fabricated from 1 cm steel plate through which water was circulated by an impeller driven by an 80 h.p. DC motor. The measuring section in which the propeller under test was to be mounted formed part of the top horizontal leg and a contraction in the cross section area ahead of it removed irregularities of flow. The top leg included an air space with a free water surface and the water passed through a 6 to 1 contraction into the measuring length of square section with radiused corners. Passing through this the water then followed a bend in which a central vane encouraged steady flow. At the bottom of the right hand column, three further guide vanes were fitted to lead the water into an impeller section. The combination of the pressure field set up by a rotating propeller and the atmospheric and hydrostatic pressures which naturally occur can produce cavitating conditions where water adjacent to the propeller vaporises to form bubbles of air over its surface causing erosion. For correct conditions in a model test the so-called cavitation number at the model (a function of pressure and speed) must equal that at the ship and in practice this demands pressure lower than atmospheric at the model. Reduced pressure in the tunnel was arranged by use of a vacuum pump.

The selected impeller proved useless and had to be redesigned; its efficiency was only 25 per cent and during operation continuous vibration caused unsteady conditions so that the resulting flow was impossible. Following Collar's work with wind tunnels[2] a new impeller was designed and, as a temporary measure, made in wood. It was much better (efficiency 75 per cent) and after 18 months of use a permanent version was needed and following the generosity of the Manganese Bronze and Brass Company, who manufactured two free of charge, a new impeller was installed. A survey of the velocity variation in the measuring section revealed that although satisfactory periods of steady flow were experienced these were interrupted by moments of fluctuations when water speed varied by 2 per cent from the set value. To discover why this should be static pressure tappings were taken at the inner and outer walls of the tunnel at different sections. At the bend after the measuring section pressure was found to vary considerably and when running at high vacuum the static pressure in the measuring section was small and with the additional drop at the bend reduced the pressure to below vapour pressure. This meant that water vapour and air collected at the top of the bend and caused choking, a problem that could be overcome only by changing the ratios of tunnel width/depth and radius/depth at the cross section of the bend.

It is not surprising in a complicated facility of this kind that many problems arose. Quite apart from choking, difficulties were experienced with the oiling of impeller bearings and cavitation of the impeller itself when rotating at high r.p.m.

Number Three Tank at Feltham

12 borings, some 30 metres deep, revealed satisfactory soil conditions in the area where the tank was to be erected. Ordinary top soil topped a clay bound ballast 2 metres thick and below this was a 5 metres layer of graded ballast with pockets of sand. Further down was blue London clay. Sand and ballast were so plentiful and of such good quality that quantities of each were taken from unwanted parts of the site and used in the mixing of the necessary concrete. A screening and mixing plant was set up in the grounds and concrete carried to the work in skips on railway lines. Cranes then transferred the skip to the actual working position.

The construction of such a huge tank to a standard that demanded precision in the stability of the tank structure, its carriage, the rails on which the carriage would run as well as the need for constancy of carriage speed in a given run was a forbidding task. That it was accomplished so successfully is a tribute to all concerned from the MoW and Ship Division. Beginning with the tank itself its base was founded 2¼ metres below ground level. A concrete slab 1 metre thick and 25 metres wide was set into the ballast bed and the concrete tank waterway made up of 22 separate sections laid on it. Each section was 17 metres long and aligned accurately to its neighbour with a metre gap between. The tank walls were buttressed on their outsides at 4½ metres centres and the buttresses carried a continuous 2 metre wide walkway which ran along each side of the tank. Beneath each walkway at ground level corridors ran the full length of the tank. Gloomy and eerie they were later used for storing models and equipment and were soon dubbed "Monks' Walk" by the staff. All the tank sections were complete and in place by the summer of 1956 and this allowed the subsoil to settle under their weight before joining them together in the cold weather of the following winter. This was done in temperatures that never exceeded 42°F and when the tank was filled with water in the summer of 1957 the higher water temperature (60°F) was maintained by the heating equipment installed in the tank building a few months later, thus keeping the concrete tank in a constant state of compression. 10 million gallons of water were required to fill the tank and the extra load of 40,000 tons on the foundations allowed a further settling period before the carriage running track was laid on the tank walls. Between September 1957 and March 1958 when 7 metres of water were in the tank measurements were taken of the settlement. It was found to be virtually constant along the length of the tank and amounted to a mere 2 mm. Twelve years later a second survey showed the tank had sunk 5 m.m. relative to its ends, a very slight settlement that bore witness to the excellent choice of site.

The building which enclosed the tank included the 18 metres high assembly area, manoeuvring and storage tanks, workshops, offices and a dining room. To avoid the frequency of interior painting in an environment which would experience high humidity—the total water area was 2 acres—aluminium was chosen for the roof frameworks and the inside of walls. To minimise marine growth in the tank water the only direct light came from windows placed high up on the north wall and the large east window. Over the manoeuvring and storage tanks however, direct sunlight could enter through the glazed part of the saw tooth roof trusses and algae and insect growth soon appeared necessitating the fitting of a chlorination plant.

The workshops comprised a large wax model manufacturing and fitting out area, a machine shop which included a small foundry and welding bay and a separate wood working shop. The machines available listed in the "Workshop Prospectus"[3] were amongst the best available and could handle a wide range of work. In addition, specialist machinery included a large model-cutting machine capable of profiling 13 metre models. J.L. Jameson Limited, an engineering company at nearby Ewell, made the cutting machine, its principle being the same as the one at Teddington except that, in view of the larger heavier models to be handled these were anchored in a bin and the vertical columns carrying the cutting knives moved longitudinally as well as transversely at the bidding of the operator. Next to the machine shop a small laboratory contained a small tank of water 6 metres $\times$ 4¼ metres $\times$ 1¾ metres deep intended for vibration work. Built into the roof structure above this tank was a suspension grillage of very high natural frequency. From the overhead beams a model could be suspended and excited into vibration by a rotary exciter.

Number Two Cavitation Tunnel at Feltham

The impeller required to circulate water around the whole tunnel circuit was placed at the top left hand corner and water was pumped down the left hand limb of the U tube, round and into a settling length before entering the test section. The water as it travelled through the large diameter limbs of the circuit slowed down and at the bottom leg it was subjected to high hydrostatic pressure due to the extreme depth (55 metres) in the ground. Any cavitation bubbles were thus successfully reabsorbed before the water entered the test section. Other parts of the tunnel were considered carefully such as details of contraction sections and cascade bends and decisions on these were reached from experience with the Lithgow tunnel which to some extent was used as a guinea pig. The impeller was chosen to provide a maximum water speed of 15 metres per second. A long 7 metres shaft supported on three bearings carried the model propeller which could be driven by a 300 h.p. motor incorporating a dynamometer capable of measuring 5,000 pounds of thrust. There was no free water surface in the tunnel and pressure within was arranged hydraulically, a variation between near zero to 6 atmospheres absolute being possible. The excavation into the soil for the very long vertical legs of the U section was demanding. Sheet piling was driven through the gravel top layer of the soil and as excavation proceeded reinforced concrete rings were put into position. A team of Irish navvies was brought in to dig into and remove the earth in advance of placing the bottom horizontal leg in position.

Circulating Water Channel at Feltham

An axial flow pump of 2,300 h.p. was installed to provide a water flow in excess of 2½ metres per second, its pumping rate of 21 million gallons per hour giving a maximum speed of water through the working section of 3 metres per second. The water was delivered from the sump to a 120 metres long return limb (outside the building). A diffuser connected the return limb to a 27 metres long stilling section which in turn led to a 16 metres long 9 to 1 contraction upstream of the working section and weir. The sump, 11½ metres deep, was fitted with two screens which helped to remove entrained air from the weir and reduce swirl. In the stilling section an array of screens was installed to smooth the flow into the contraction. Provision was made for nine screens rolled on drums but only four were used in the final design. The working section was the heart of the facility. It had to be equipped with an instrument carriage to carry the model, instrumentation and experimental staff. Although stationary in any particular test its position could be moved horizontally if necessary by a hand winch and to set the carriage to its desired height above the water a motor drove shafting and four jacks. Stairs on both sides of the channel gave access to observation windows and, higher up, to walkways surrounding the instrument carriage. The floor of the working section was important. When shallow water was required it was found more economic to raise the floor on jacks rather than drain water from the whole channel. Furthermore to establish a level running water surface the floor had to be tilted. Experience at the Berlin channel had shown that the water slope formed by moving water could be restored to a level line by tilting the channel floor by ±1 degree and a similar ability was arranged in the NPL channel. Finally, so far as the water was concerned, clarity was important. This was achieved by fitting north facing windows to the channel building, by filtration and the use of a horsehair filter which helped to remove air bubbles. Some algae growth did appear but was eliminated by a small degree of chlorination. For experimenters the channel was potentially dangerous. A fall into moving water would almost certainly be fatal in view of the closeness of the weir to the working section. Marwood who was the Safety Officer for the whole Feltham site decreed that at all times workers on the instrument carriage should wear harnesses.

REFERENCES

1. Harris D.J., "Number 2 Tank, Teddington", NPL, Ship Division Tech. Mem. 318, August 1971.
2. Collar A.R., "The design of wind tunnel fans", ARC, R and M 1889, 1940.
3. "Workshop Prospectus", NMI Tech. Mem. 66, 1981.

B.   SYMBOLS IN TEXT AND CURRENT METHODS OF EXTRAPOLATION

Several terms commonly used by naval architects appear in the text.

Block coefficient, C_B:

A coefficient of fineness that describes the fullness or fineness of a ship's hull. Block coefficient is the ratio of the immersed volume of the hull to its circumscribing block made up of the product of the ship's length, breadth and draught.

LCB:

Is the position, longitudinally, of the centre of buoyancy of a hull.

Prismatic coefficient, C_P:

The longitudinal prismatic, the one used in the text, is the ratio of the immersed volume of the hull to the volume of a prism having a length equal to the ship and a cross-sectional area equal to the ship's midship sectional area.

Resistance and speed constants:

Modern methodology uses non-dimensional parameters.

Total resistance, R_T is expressed by the coefficient, C_T and speed through Reynolds number, R_N.

$$C_T = R_T / \tfrac{1}{2}\rho A V^2 \qquad \text{-------- (1)}$$

$$\text{and } R_N = VL/v$$

where V is speed, A is surface area of immersed hull, ρ is density of fluid, L is length and v is kinematic viscosity of fluid.

R.E. Froude used a peculiar constant "circular" notation that was also non-dimensional. Circular C, etc. were represented by symbols Ⓒ, Ⓜ, etc. and based on a unit length U defined as the cube root of the ship's displacement, Δ. Thus,

length constant, Ⓜ = hull wetted length/U

speed constant, Ⓚ = ship speed/speed of wave of length U/2

(Note that speed constant connects the speed of a ship with its wave-making length).

resistance constant, Ⓒ = $1000 \times$ ship resistance / ΔⓀ^{2}

and so on; there were several other circular symbols introduced by R.E. Froude. Later Baker and Kent suggested Ⓟ as an alternative speed constant in which wave length was defined as C_pL, C_p being the prismatic coefficient.

$$Ⓟ = \text{ship speed} / (gCpL / 2\pi)^{1/2}$$

Extrapolating Model Resistance Measurements to give an Estimate of Ship Resistance

Early methods of extrapolation were described by R.E. Froude and Taylor and when a correlation line was agreed in 1957 by the ITTC a third, more popular, procedure became available. All three apply Froude's law of comparison that states that the residuary constant or coefficient is the same for both model and ship.

ITTC method: The measured total resistance at the model is split into two components, frictional and residuary. The frictional part is then calculated and the residuary obtained by subtraction. The ITTC's correlation line defines the variation of skin friction resistance of plane surfaces with Reynolds number.

$$C_F = 0 \cdot 075 / (\log R_N - 2)^2$$

C_F is calculated for the model at its test speed and also for the ship at its corresponding speed. Then, residuary coefficient, $C_R = (C_T - C_F$ for model), C_T being the total resistance coefficient from the model measurement. Since, from Froude, C_R model = C_R ship then:

$$C_T \text{ for ship} = C_R + C_F \text{ for ship}$$

Total ship resistance is then obtained through C_T using equation (1). Note that C_F derives from data from two-dimensional surfaces and takes no account of a ship's form. Modern analyses make allowance for this and increase C_F by a form factor.

Froude method: R.E. Froude avoided splitting the total resistance into two parts by using a circular O method together with the skin friction constant, circular F. The total resistance for the ship at a given speed was found by calculating a skin friction correction, arising from the different lengths of model and ship, and subtracting this from the model measurement.

$$\text{Frictional resistance} = fSV^{1.825}$$

$$\text{and } \textcircled{C}_F = 1000 \times \text{frictional resistance} / \Delta\textcircled{K}^2$$

which reduces to:

$$\textcircled{C}_F = O\textcircled{S}\textcircled{L}^{-0.175}$$

with O (or circular O) = 1000 f / $4\pi\rho(gL/4\pi)^{0.0875}$ -------- (2)

and $\textcircled{S}$ is skin friction constant.

For both model and ship, $\textcircled{C}_T = \textcircled{C}_F + \textcircled{C}_R$

and   ship $\textcircled{C}_T$ = model $\textcircled{C}_T$ – skin friction correction

$$= \text{model } \textcircled{C}_T - (O_m - O_s)\textcircled{S}\textcircled{L}^{-0.175}$$ -------- (3)

with subscripts m and s denoting model and ship.

W. Froude found from his classical experiments with planks that f varied with length and surface roughness. Values of f against L were later modified by R.E. Froude and in 1935 the ITTC reviewed both f and O constants and published recommended values for use in equations (2) and (3).

TOWING TANKS IN EXISTENCE IN 1910 AT THE TIME OF CONSTRUCTION OF NUMBER ONE TANK, TEDDINGTON

Place	Year
Dumbarton, Scotland	1883
Haslar, England	1886
St Petersburg, Russia	1891
La Spezia, Italy	1898
Washington, USA	1899
Berlin, Germany	1903
Ubigau, Germany	1904
Ann Arbor, USA	1904
Clydebank, Scotland	1904
Paris, France	1906
St. Albans, England	1910
Teddington, England	1910

Note: Only tanks more than 30 metres long are listed.

TOWING TANKS IN EXISTENCE IN 1932 AT THE TIME OF CONSTRUCTION OF NUMBER TWO TANK, TEDDINGTON IN ADDITION TO THOSE LISTED IN APPENDIX II

Place	Year
Hamburg, Germany	1913
Vienna, Austria	1916
Hamburg, Germany	1924
Tokyo, Japan	1927 (two)
Tokyo, Japan	1930
Madrid, Spain	1930
Langley Field, USA	1930
Rome, Italy	1931
Haslar, England	1931
Tokyo, Japan	1932
Wageningen, Holland	1932
Teddington, England	1932

Note: Only tanks more than 30 metres long are listed.

APPENDIX IV

TOWING TANKS IN EXISTENCE IN 1959 AT THE TIME OF CONSTRUCTION OF NUMBER THREE TANK, FELTHAM IN ADDITION TO THOSE LISTED IN APPENDICES II AND III

	Place	Year
In Americas:	Carderock, Washington	1941 (three)
	Ottawa, Canada	1942
	Hoboken	1943
	Carderock, Washington	1947 (two)
	Cambridge, Massachusetts	1951
In Asia:	Kharagpur, India	1951
In Europe:	Cowes, England	1946
	Genoa, Italy	1947
	Paris, France	1950
	St Petersburg, Russia	1950
	Newcastle, England	1951
	Hamburg, Germany	1953
	Delft, Holland	1954 (two)
	Duisberg, Germany	1954
	Hamburg, Germany	1955
	Cowes, England	1956
	Berlin, Germany	1957
	Paris, France	1958
	Potsdam, Germany	1958
	Feltham, England	1959
Far East:	Yokohama, Japan	1934
	Tokyo, Japan	1937
	Tokyo, Japan	1941
	Nagasaki, Japan	1943
	Osaka, Japan	1949
	Kyushu, Japan	1956

	Tokyo, Japan	1956
	Shanghai, China	1958
	Tokyo, Japan	1958
In Scandinavia:	Trondheim, Norway	1939
	Gothenburg, Sweden	1940
	Lyngby, Denmark	1958

Note: • Only tanks more than 30 metres long are listed.
       • Information taken from the ITTC Catalogue of Facilities prepared for the 16th ITTC.
       • In 1959 there were about 60 major towing tanks in use in the world. After 1960 the increase in model test facilities including cavitation tunnels, manoeuvring tanks, etc. was so great that by 1990 there were almost 200 establishments worldwide where model tests of one kind or another could be carried out.

TEST FACILITIES AT TIME OF FORMATION OF BMT, 1985 WITH DATES OF SUBSEQUENT CLOSURES
(Dimensions in Metres)

	Dimensions	Built	Closed
at Teddington:			
Towing tank, Number One	152 × 9·1 × 3·7 deep	1910	1994
Towing tank, Number Two	195 × 6·1 × 2·7 (0·6)	1932	1994
Wind/Wave tunnel	deep	1977	1989
Seven wind tunnels			
at Feltham:			
Towing tank, Number Three	400 × 14·6 × 7·6 deep	1959	1987
Calibration tank, Number Five	15 × 1·2 × 1·2 deep	1968	1987
Manoeuvring tank, Number Seven	60 × 60 × 1 deep	1966	1987
Model Ocean Facility	46 × 30 × 2·3 (6) deep	1984	1987
Circulating Water Channels			
Number One		1960	re-erected at Haslar
Number Two		1967	1987
Cavitation tunnels			
Number One		1934	1987
Number Two		1959	1987
at Hythe:			
Towing tank	85 × 9 × 0·8 deep	1964	
Christchurch Bay tower		1974	1988

GROUPING OF SENIOR SCIENTIFIC STAFF AT FORMATION OF BMT 1ST APRIL, 1985

Under G. Ward:

Ship Operations and Engineering Division	D. Byrne
Marine Construction Division	J.L. Hannah
Computing and Information Technology	I.M. Tolmie
Computer Applications	E.A. Williams
Software	J.R. Vardon
Quality Assurance	R.E. Holliday
Hull Geometry	D. Catley
New Projects	D. Boothroyd

Under M.E. Davies:

Fluid Mechanics	vacant
Wind Engineering	R.E. Whitbread
Environmental Fluid Mechanics	J.A.B. Wills
Fundamental Research	M. Gaster
Facilities	J.F.M. Maybrey
Hydrodynamics	A.Y. Odabasi
Vibration and Noise	G.T. Willshare
Computational Hydrodynamics	P.A. Fitzsimmons
Dynamics and Control	D. Clarke
Control and Stability	F. Caldeira-Saraiva
Experimental Ship Hydrodynamics	A. Morrall
Ship Performance	D. Bailey
Numerical Hydrodynamics	G.E. Gadd
Ship Dynamics	J.R. Spouge
Instrumentation	F.J.M. Kirby
Ocean Engineering	S.J. Rowe
Marine Dynamics	I.W. Dand
Instrumentation	M.H. Steele
Offshore Engineering	R.G. Standing
Consultant	N. Hogben
Measurement	H.B. Boyle

AWARDS TO STAFF FROM LEARNED SOCIETIES ETC.

To:

Allan J.F. (with Cutland R.S.)	NECIES, M.C. James Medal, 1956
Baker G.S.	INA Gold Medal, 1913
	IESS Premium, 1915, 1920
	NECIES Gold Medal, 1915
	LES Derby Gold Medal, 1931
Bottomley G.H.	IESS Premium, 1930
Browne R.P.	RINA Bronze Medal, 1975
Conn J.F.C.	IMARE Silver Medal, 1938
	IESS Gold Medal, 1939
Dand I.W.	RINA Silver Medal, 1977, 1983
Emerson A.	NECIES Gold Medal, 1939
English J.W. (with Rowe S.J.)	NECIES M.C. James Medal, 1971
Everest J.T.	NECIES Ayre Prize, 1968
Gadd G.E.	RINA Premium, 1970, 1971
Hogben N. (with Osborne J. and Standing R.G.)	RINA Silver Medal, 1974
	ICE George Stephenson Medal, 1977
	RINA Bronze Medal, 1984
Hughes G.	IESS Premium, 1932
	INA Premium, 1934
	INA Gold Medal, 1954
Kent J.L.	INA Gold Medal, 1922
	IESS Premium, 1933
Lewison G.R.G.	RINA Bronze Medal, 1982
Meek M.	RINA Silver Medal, 1985
Morrall A.	RINA Gold Medal, 1981
	RINA Bronze Medal, 1980

Shearer J.R. (with Steele B.N.)	RINA Premium, 1971
Ship Division, NPL (staff of)	RINA Gold Medal, 1960
Standing R.G.	ICE Manby Premium, 1982
Todd F.H. (with Weedon J.)	NECIES Gold Medal, 1932 INA Premium, 1938 IESS Premium, 1939
Wigley W.C.S.	INA Premium, 1927 INA Gold Medal, 1930, 1941 NECIES M.C. James Medal, 1936
WFL	ICME Bronze medal and Hors Concours certificate, 1930.

ABBREVIATIONS

INA or RINA	Institution of Naval Architects (Royal from 1960)
IESS	Institution of Engineers and Shipbuilders in Scotland
NECIES	North East Coast Institution of Engineers and Shipbuilders
IMARE	Institute of Marine Engineers
ICE	Institution of Civil Engineers
ICME	International Colonial and Maritime Exhibition
LES	Liverpool Engineering Society

INDEX OF SHIP NAMES

Page references in **bold** *type refer to plates*

343

Narica, 261
Northwestern Miller, 75

Ocean Rambler, 113
Ocean Reward, 113, 114
Ocean Vim, 113
Olympic, 30, 31, 43, 57, 173
Orama, 261
Oroya, 69
Oremina, 181
Oriana, 166
Orissa, 261
Oropesa, HMS, 123
Ottawa, 261

Pacific Reliance, 71
Pacific Trader, 72, 104, 181
Partnership, 81
Persephone, HMS, 143
Polyphemus, 70
Priam, 255–256
Princess of Vancouver, 217

Queen Elizabeth, 226–227
Queen Elizabeth II, **66**, 201, 226, 227
Queen Elizabeth, HMS, 144
Queen Mary, 91, 173

Ravahine, 166
Renown, HMS, 44
Roslin Castle, 99
Royal Oak, 301
Royal Oak, HMS, 122
Royston Grange, 248, 249

San Gerardo, 68, 76
Sanguenay, HMCS, 80, 81
San Tirso, 68
Scorpion, HMS, 258, 279, 308

Seatrain, **20**
Simon Bolivar, 221
Sir Claude Inglis, **78**, 262
Sir William Hardy, 181
Skeena, HMCS, 80, 81
Snaefell, 71, 72, 104
Star Hercules, 270
Stirling Castle, 99
Sverige, 301

Tenacity, **66**, 226
Tien Chee, 248
Tiger, HMS, 44
Tina Onassis, 161, 221
Tirpitz, 143, 144
Titanic, 30
Torrey Canyon, 241
Trident, 275, 276, 277
Trojan Star, 99
Twickenham Ferry, **21**, 100

Valiant, HMS, 144
Vic 62, **74**, 247, 263
Viceroy of India, 71
Victory, 221

Warwick Castle, 99
Weather Reporter, 203, 212
White Crusader, 301

Yudachi, 63, 176
Yeoman, 186

Hovercraft:
D1, 210
D2, 210
SRN4, 210
HD2, 234

INDEX OF OFFSHORE STRUCTURES ETC.

GENERAL INDEX

*Page references in **bold** type refer to plates, roman numerals to appendices*

hull appendages. *See* appendages
hulls, surface roughness, ships, 47, 115, 176,
　177; effect on wake, 104–105; ship
　measurements, 176, 182; models, 231
HRS, 100, 262, 272, 273, 292, 293
hydrofoils, depresser type, 128, 229; ships,
　224; tests on foils, 186, 225–226

Idle, G., 29
IMCO, 241, 276, 277
Imperial Trust, 51
Inbucon, 283, 284
Inchcape, Lord, 82
Institution of Civil Engineers, 260
Institution of Mechanical Engineers, 70
interdependence study, 180, 220–221
interaction, between propulsion units and hull,
　258–259. *See also propellers; between ship
　and bank,* 274; *between ships, HAWKE/
　OLYMPIC,* 30–31, 173; *ROYSTON
　GRANGE/TIEN CHEE,* 248–249;
　QUEEN MARY/CURACOA, 173–175
ITTC, 7, 96, 162, 165, 203; ship correlation
　line, 180, 223, 315, 328
invasion beaches, 131
invasion of Normandy, 141

Jackson, G.E., 270
Jacob, R.J., 208, 245, 250
Jameson Co., 325
Jeffrey, D., 304; secretary, BMT, 304
Jenkin, C.P.F., 286, 289
Jenkins, A., 98, 156, 160; open water
　dynamometer, 168; remotely controlled
　models, 166, 196; torsionmeter, 161
Johnson, A.J., 235, 242, 258, 282; chairman
　of OSFLAG, 259
Johnson, D.R., 274; gas ignition tests, 282
Jordan, Dorothy, 12
Joseph, Sir K., 282

Karman von, Prof. T., 72
Keary, Miss E.M., **16**, 49, 52, 79, 81;
　appointment to NPL, 38; seaplane tests, 48
Keble, J., 5
Keelavite Co., 292
keels, 256; wing, 300
Kelvin, Lord, 64, 254
Kempf, G., 63, 95, 96, 102, 181, 185
Kempf & Remmer Co., 229, 291
Kent, J.L., 22, **28**, 50, 52, 56, 62, 75, 76, 78,
　94, 101, 144, 149, 151, 156, 187, 297, 328,
　385, VII; appointment to NPL, 19; book,
　157; buoys, 130; case for third tank, 158;
　CBE, 157; *MULBERRY* harbour, 134, 135,
　136, 138, 139, 141; personality, 157;
　PLUTO, 142; Ⓟ theory, 33; relations with
　NPL, 157; retirement, 155; seakeeping
　research, 52, 57, 66–69, 97, 108–110,

Kent, J.L.—*cont.*
　151–152, 157, 203; ship interaction, 30;
　Supt., 119
Kirby, F.J.M., 240, 243, 308, 309, VI
kites, 40; tests on, 40–41, 123
Korvin-Kroukovsky, B.V., 203

Lackenby, H.C., 101, 179, 220, 221, 222;
　skin friction research, 114–115
lakers (ships for Great Lakes), 300
Lambourne, N.C., 93
laminar flow. *See* flow
Lammeren van, W.P., 96
Lamont, N.S.H., 305
Lanarkshire Steel Co., 194
LANCER tests, 150
launching. *See* trawlers, *MULBERRY* harbour
　and *HIPPOPOTAMUS*
Laws, E., 97; power estimates, 261
Leathard, J.F., 186
lee boards, 133, 136, 140
Lenahan, J., 93
Leonardo da Vinci, 1
Lerbs, H., 92
Lewison, G.R.G., **68**, 230, 235, 242, 246,
　248, 269, 274, 289, VII; catamarans, 252;
　MIRANDA trials, 250; ship safety, 274–
　275; slamming, 256–257; visiting Fellow,
　256
Lexcon, B., 300
Liddell, H., 70
lifeboats, RNLI, 56, 270, 308
lifeboats (ships), 249–250
life-saving appliances, 53
lighters, 147
lightships, 29
Lips, M.M.H., 182
Lithgow, Sir J., 93; background and career,
　92; design of cavitation tunnel, 92–93
Liverpool Engineering Society, 66
Liverpool Steam Ship Owners Association, 37,
　85
Livingstone, C., 37
Lloyd, A.J.R.M., 297
Lloyd's Register, 52, 80, 96, 241, 278, 299
Lobnitz pontoons, 139
Loe, H.G., **68**, 188, 242; remotely-controlled
　models, 196, 198, 230
London Hospital, 14
lubrication (by air), 209
LUCY ASHTON. See BSRA
Luke, W.J., 14, 25, 108
Lumb, F.E., 212, 280, 295

Macdonald, E., 97, 159, 184, 226
Mackenzie, A.J.D., 156, 226, 231; power
　estimates, 242
Mackenzie, Rear Admiral, 123
Maddock, Sir I., 267

GENERAL INDEX

355

vibration, 209, 219–220, 257–258, 278–280; Voith Schneider, 165
propulsion devices. *See* propellers
Ⓟ theory, 33, 119
Pyke, G., 124
pykrete, 124

Quebec Conference, 135

racing shells, 228
radio controlled models, 166, 198, 230, 249
Raff, A.I., 297
Ramsden, J., 191
Ramsey, A.G., 89
Rankine, Prof. W.J.M., 7
Rapson, J.E., 234
Rayleigh, Lord, 12, 14, 23, 47, 53, 55; ideas on bow shape, 27, 32, 33, 105
Rayment, F.J., 28, 79, 80, 98, 159, 165
Reed, E.J., 6, 107
Relf, E.F., 179
ROV, 294, 296
reparations, 169
reports, Ship Division, 209
Requirements Boards, 241, 294
research, cost of, 51–52, 80, 101, 236, 268, 284, 294
resistance, air and wind, 75–77; components of, 180; model, see model resistance; pressure, 180; ship, see ship resistance; skin friction, 4, 47, 62–63, 114–115, 178–180, 251, 315; distribution of, 251–252; measurement of, 176, 221; viscous, 251, 252, 277–278; wave-making, 72–74, 221, 251, 252, 253–254, 315
resorber, 193
Reynolds, O., 47, 162
riblets, 301
Richardson, H.C., 35
Riddle, A.W., 28, 57, 96, 102, 123, 209; appointment to NPL, 52; personality, 57, 145; propeller geometry, 58, 100
Ritter, H., 68, 282; Head of group, 240
Rixon, A.C., 28, 79, 159, 208
Robb, Prof. A.M., 109, 124, 173, 175
Roll, Messrs., 89
ro-ros. *See* ferries
Romme, A., 2, 3
Rosenhain, W.F., 13
rotating arm, 269
Rowe, S.J., 68, 240, 243, 246, 247, 259, 291, VI, VII; offshore engineering, 242, 270, 280, 302
Roy, W., 191
Royal Aircraft Establishment, 48, 72, 85, 239
RINA (formerly INA), 7, 11, 13, 63, 70, 153, 260; centenary, 199
Royal Naval College, 156

Royal Society, 12, 13, 51, 191, 234, 311
Royal Technical College, Glasgow, 111
Royal Thames Yacht Club, 300
rudders, area of, 82; balanced/semi balanced, 64–66; Becker, 248; jet flap, 72, 246–247; large model tests, 63–64; position of, 75; rotating cylinder, 247–248; rudder head torque, 64–65; Schilling, 248
Rudge, A.W., 285, 304
run, angle of, 33
Runciman, Lord, 199

safety, of staff, 98, 327
Sargeant, F.H., 28, 59, 116
Schertel von, Baron, 225
Schlick, O., 184
Schlicting, H., 47, 115, 315
Schneider Trophy, 80
Schoenherr, K.E., 47, 178, 221, 315; friction line, 177, 179, 180
Science and Engineering Research Council, 311
Science Museum, 172, 247
Science Research Council, 233
Scott, J.R., 222, 223
Scottish Maritime Museum, 8
Scott-Paine, H., 79, 148
Scott Russell, J., 6, 7, 107; model experiments, 6
seadromes, 124–125
seakeeping, model expts., 67–68, 69, 114, 125, 126, 137, 203, 225, 226, 245, 256, 275, 276–277; research, 108–110, 151–152, 203, 212–213, 297; test fees, 261
seaplanes, 34, 47–48, 80; America design, 48; Felixstowe Fury, 80; floats for, 28, 34, 48; flying boats, 34, 49; full-scale trials, 48; impact tests, 49
Selman, G.S., 79, 148, 155
shallow water, model expts., in, 30–31, 81–82, 245–246, 249, 307
Shannon, J.F., 111, 112
Sharp, H., 159
Shearer, J.R., 60, 120, 170, 188, 194, 228, 240, 260, VII; design of new test facilities, 158; flow studies, 251–252; Head of group, 187, 208; resistance dynamometer, 168; interdependence study, 180, 220–221
Shell Research Ltd., 282
Ship Division, NPL, 153, 165, 168, 176, 181, 200, 203, 211, 214, 233, 240, 241, 250, 255, 259; merger with DMS, 263; name, 153; research effort, 155, 157, 188
shipbuilders, Austin Pickersgill, 261; Barclay Curle, 165; Bartram, 165; Blyth, 30; Bombay Port, 165; Brown, 14, 174, 227; BHC, 211; British Power Boat, 99, 148, 155; Brooke Marine, 226, 308; Caledon, 165; Cammell Laird, 99, 165; Camper &